Benedictine
Maledictions

Also by Lester K. Little

Liberty, Charity, Fraternity: Lay Religious Confraternities at Bergamo in the Age of the Commune

Religious Poverty and the Profit Economy in Medieval Europe

Benedictine Maledictions

Liturgical Cursing
in Romanesque France

BY LESTER K. LITTLE

Cornell University Press / Ithaca and London

First published 1993 by Cornell University Press.

International Standard Book Number 0-8014-2876-9
Library of Congress Catalog Card Number 93-25079
Printed in the United States of America
Librarians: Library of Congress cataloging information appears on the last page of the book.

⊗ The paper in this book meets the minimum requirements of the American National Standard for Information Sciences—Permanence of Paper for Printed Library Materials, ANSI Z39.48–1984.

Contents

Illustrations

Figures

Maps

Preface

AMONG THE casualties of challenges to Enlightenment
views of the past, along with the image of a stagnant, priest-ridden
Middle Ages was a moth-eaten monasticism of ignorance, superstition,
and social uselessness. In its place the romantic imagination constructed a monasticism of mystery, haunting beauty, and profound
faith, expressed visually as a contemplative and solitary cowled figure
in a cloister or a row of robed and hooded shapes in a Gothic choir.
This newer image of mystery and refinement has been sustained ever
since by literature, in more recent decades by cinema as well, and not
least by sublime recordings of Gregorian chant. Neither image, though,
adequately prepares us to understand the reality of unprotected monastic communities having to confront contentious and sometimes rapacious enemies and, by way of counterattack, resorting to a religious
ritual of cursing. That monks and nuns sometimes faced enemies has
been well known for over a century from the narrative sources that
historians long made it their prime task to edit and explicate. Some of
these texts even mention the monastic resort to curses at the culminating point of an occasional account of a dispute. But liturgical sources,
hitherto considered useful only for the history of organized worship
and impervious to all other study, have recently been coaxed into supplying evidence of thought and behavior that can be related to particular historical contexts. In the present instance they have yielded up a
church service of cursing, complete with stage directions, prayers, and
biblical references, that monastic communities used in times of trouble.
This service, sometimes free-standing and sometimes part of the mass,
called in some manuscripts "malediction" (Latin *maledictio*) and in others "clamor" (*clamor*), is the principal subject of this book. And since
the book's title fully embraces the subject, the simplest way to begin is
by commenting on each of its elements.

Benedictine. Christian monasticism originated in Egypt, Palestine, and Syria in the late third century and began to take root in the western provinces of the Roman Empire a century later. Various monastic ideals from the East, some more individualistic, others more collegial, were transplanted in North Africa, Italy, Spain, and Gaul, whence also to the British Isles. Some of the writings of Eastern ascetics were translated into Latin, but soon there were indigenous Western ascetic writings, including rules by which to govern the monastic life. A shadowy figure in this history, Benedict of Nursia, active in central Italy in the second quarter of the sixth century, edited, shortened, tightened, and in general improved one of these monastic rules, making it his own. But in his time and through the two and one-half centuries following, many kinds of monastic communities and many different monastic rules coexisted in western Europe. During that period Benedict's fame was established and his memory kept vivid because Pope Gregory the Great (590–604) gathered the oral tradition concerning Benedict into a biography, basically a collection of miracle stories, that subsequently gained wide circulation. Then, once the Franks had brought about the political unification of much of the Continent in the years around 800, they set out to institute uniformity of practice in many different spheres, one of which was the monastic life. In 817 Benedict's rule for monks became the standard by which all monasteries were governed. Memory of the competing rules faded, and monks and nuns created the myth of Benedict as founding father of Western monasticism and of his rule as the Holy Rule (see Fig. 1). The Benedictine monopoly then held firm for three centuries.[1]

Criticism by the reformers who first challenged this monopoly fell heavily upon the accumulated wealth of monasteries, including such details as the use of dyed cloth for monastic habits. Monks and nuns symbolized their renunciation of this world, their "death to the world," by wearing black cloth. To reformers attacking monastic wealth in the name of apostolic simplicity and poverty, wearing dyed cloth, for whatever reason, was a costly affectation. Several of the new religious groups of the twelfth century (the Cistercians, Carthusians, and Premonstratensians, among others) adopted natu-

---

1. Clifford H. Lawrence, *Medieval Monasticism: Forms of Religious Life in Western Europe in the Middle Ages,* 2d ed. (London, 1989), pp. 1–104.

Figure 1. Saint Benedict enthroned, instructs monks in the precepts of his rule. In this psalter produced in the early eleventh century at Christ Church, Canterbury, the saint is identified in the nimbus about his head as the "father and leader of monks" (*Sanctus Benedictus pater monachorum et dux*). The headband, inscribed "fear of God" (*timor Dei*) is perhaps the artist's graphic translation of this sentence from the rule: "The first step of humility, then, is that a man keep the fear of God always before his eyes and never forget it." The figure crouched at the saint's feet is labeled "zone of humility" (*zona humilitatis*). The book held before him is the rule, for the beginning of its prologue can be seen on the open page: "Listen, O son, to the instructions" (*Ausculta o fili precepta*). The hand extending from the sky holds a stole whose biblical inscription confirms Benedict's (and because of the plural form perhaps also the monks') divine commission: "Whoever listens to you listens to me" (*Qui vos audit me audit* [Luke 10:16]). MS, London, BL, Arundel 155, f. 133r; by permission of the British Library.

ral, undyed cloth for their habits on grounds of principle, leaving the old-fashioned kind of religious to be known as "black monks." The sting of criticism and the existence of various new groups of "white monks" spurred black monks to reflect upon their own identity and come to their own defense, like the abbot of Cluny Peter the Venerable, who argued in letters of the second quarter of the twelfth century that black was the color chosen by the heroic men and women of early monastic history to signify humility, penance, and mourning. Peter's contemporary, the monastic historian Ordericus Vitalis, drew on the Song of Songs (1:4)[2] to suggest that black, in addition to being humble, penitent, and mournful, was beautiful.[3]

Each monastery, whether of men or women, was an independent institution. The individual newcomer joined a particular monastery or religious house, and did so for life. The modern notion of a monastic order—with a table of organization, a headquarters, meetings, and mobility between one house and another within the order—did not yet exist. The term *ordo* referred to a group of persons sharing a common status, an abstraction in the same way that a mathematical set is an abstraction. Thus the order of bishops was the collectivity of all bishops; the order of married people, all married people; and the *ordo monachorum*, all monks and nuns. Only with the proliferation of different forms of the religious life in the twelfth and thirteenth centuries did there come into existence the modern notion of a religious order, as in the Order of Friars Minor (the Franciscan order), with its hierarchy of officers starting with the minister general at the top, its headquarters at Assisi, its hundreds of convents organized into provinces, and the considerable mobility of its members, who were members of the whole order, among those convents. But the black monks had no such organization, at least not until the first attempt to form one in the fifteenth century, and the adjective "Benedictine" came into use later still; its

2. All biblical citations follow the numbering in *Biblia Sacra iuxta Vulgatam versionem*, ed. Bonifatius Fischer et al., 3d ed., 2 vols. (Stuttgart, 1985); for English translations I have consulted various modern versions and made occasional modifications of my own.

3. *The Letters of Peter the Venerable*, ed. Giles Constable, 2 vols. (Cambridge, Mass., 1967), 1:57, 285–291, 368–371, 2:116. The letters, with respective dates, are no. 28 (1127?), 111 (1144), and 150 (1149). *Historia ecclesiastica*, 5:19 and 8:26, in *EHOV* 3:196–197, 4:310–313. The name of Noirmoutier (Black Monastery), on an island at the mouth of the Loire, is a corruption of the original seventh-century name, but from the post-Viking restoration on it was thought to derive from the color of the monks' habits.

use here in reference to the ninth through the twelfth century is a deliberate anachronism, both conventional and convenient.[4]

Maledictions. Benedict's traditional Latin name derives from a phrase that means to speak or say well (*bene dire*) and that also gives us the noun "benediction," meaning "blessing." The opposite phrase, meaning to speak or say ill (*male dire*), gives us "malediction," or "curse."[5] Understandably the word *maledictus* was not used as a personal name, but the pairing of the opposites *benedictus* and *maledictus* was a frequently used rhetorical device. Even Gregory the Great made a pun on the two words in his life of Benedict, where he recounts a scene in which the devil calls out Benedict's name a few times (*Benedicte, Benedicte*) in trying to tempt him. The "man of God" refuses to acknowledge these tauntings of the "enemy," and eventually the devil shouts in exasperation: "Maledict, not Benedict" (*Maledicte, non Benedicte*).[6] It is in the spirit of this ancient conceit that monastic curses are here referred to as "Benedictine maledictions."

But the curses involved were more than just monastic. Many came from churches presided over by bishops, and these episcopal churches frequently supported communities of canons. At various moments in ecclesiastical history the relations between monks and bishops, and those between monks and canons as well, were marked by competition and even hostility. But in the age of the black monks' monopoly, which was not entirely lacking in such competition and hostility, the monastic model was so dominant as to produce many bishops with monastic backgrounds or sympathies and to render many critical aspects of canons' lives imitative of those of monks. All religious life bore the imprint of monastic spirituality, and so bishops and canons, like monks, engaged both in cursing and in blessing. A basic function of bishops was (and of course still is) to impart blessings; one special type of liturgical book, the benedictional, attests to the hundreds of blessing formulas at

---

4. David Knowles, *From Pachomius to Ignatius: A Study in the Constitutional History of the Religious Orders* (Oxford, 1966), pp. 47–48, 59–61. *Dictionary of Medieval Latin from British Sources* (Oxford, 1975), 1:191, where the earliest use of *benedictinus* is dated 1526.

5. On *benedicere* as a delocutive verb (meaning derived from a locution), see Emile Benveniste, *Problems in General Linguistics*, tr. Mary E. Meek (Coral Gables, Fla., 1971), pp. 239–246.

6. Gregory the Great, *Vita Sancti Benedicti* (*Liber dialogorum*, 2), ch. 8 (PL 66:152).

the disposition of bishops.[7] And canons shared in the monastic practice of frequent, if not incessant, praying for divine blessings.[8] Moreover, as we shall see, there existed a close correspondence between the power to bless and the power to curse. Thus it is with these additional factors in mind that the intended meaning of "Benedictine maledictions" extends beyond the strictly monastic sphere to embrace the canonical and episcopal as well; the meaning becomes curses on the part of those whose usual function was to bless (see Fig. 2).

Liturgical cursing. Here we will deal only with liturgy—communal worship according to prescribed forms—and thus with neither expletives nor scatological language.[9] Such worship took place in churches and followed well-established directions and formulas. It expressed corporate, never individual, indignation, no matter how much any individuals involved might have identified with their institutions or been personally invested in seeing an enemy humbled. Not least significant, these ceremonies of worship were entirely legitimate; however deep and eclectic their roots, they were neither flotsam from the ancient Mediterranean past nor seepage from Celtic or Germanic sources. They were Christian church services.

Romanesque France. Liturgical cursing was legitimate and in use within certain boundaries of space and time. "France" is a modern geopolitical term that is convenient for getting oriented but not adequately precise for delimiting the area to be discussed here. The contemporary term "Francia" is more accurate, although the boundaries it described changed over time. The territory in question, in any case, stretches from the valley of the Charente, which lies about 120 miles south of the Loire, north and east to the valley of the Rhine. Perhaps the most apt name for it would be "Land of the Franks," since it corresponds so well to the area settled by that most powerful of the Germanic peoples.

7. *Corpus benedictionum pontificalium,* ed. Edmond Moeller, 4 vols., Corpus Christianorum, series Latina 162 (Turnhout, 1971–1979).

8. Caroline Bynum, "The Spirituality of Regular Canons in the Twelfth Century," in her *Jesus as Mother: Studies in the Spirituality of the High Middle Ages* (Berkeley, Calif., 1982), pp. 22–58; although the author's purpose was to define the distinctiveness of the spirituality of the canons, she also called attention, for example on p. 35, to the similarities between the monastic and canonical spiritualities.

9. Enthusiasts of *Maledicta: The International Journal of Verbal Aggression* may be excused. Book curses and the hue and cry are also not dealt with here.

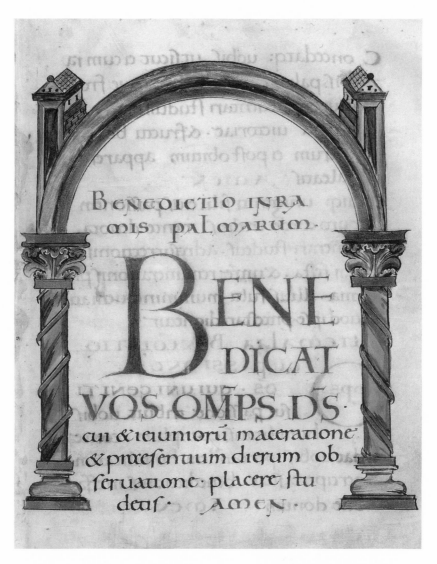

Figure 2. A Palm Sunday benediction in a benedictional made at Winchester in the eleventh century. The arch and columns frame a blessing whose principal words are written in capital letters: "May almighty God bless you" (*Benedicat vos omnipotens Deus*). MS, Paris, BN, lat. 987, f. 26r; by permission of the Bibliothèque Nationale.

The period under discussion stretches from the ninth century to the twelfth. "Religion" in that time was equated with the monastic life, which in turn was devoted to the performance of the liturgy; "good religion" was the faithful, or regular, carrying out of prescribed rituals, and the setting for this activity was the Romanesque church building. The term "Romanesque" is reserved by art historians for monuments of the eleventh century and the first half of the twelfth, although the styles of the immediately preceding centuries, usually known by dynastic or ethnic names such as "Carolingian" or "Lombard," have at various times been regarded as "pre-Romanesque," "proto-Romanesque," or "first Romanesque." The term "Romanesque" dates from the early nineteenth century and was initially pejorative. Changes in taste have completely inverted that connotation, but the term still has value. The culture of the age was an amalgam of Germanic and Roman elements, with occasionally striking and original Celtic contributions. But overall, cultural legitimacy came from Rome or, more accurately, was sought by invoking some connection with Rome, and in particular a remote, earlier Rome. To cite the liturgical amalgamations that took place north of the Alps as an example, we can consider works like the Gelasian and Gregorian sacramentaries: not only were they given papal names, but these were the names of popes from earlier centuries. The same principle was at work in the extensive use of forged papal privileges and in spurious claims of Roman origins or of travels to and from Rome. A vigorous and in important ways new culture, the Romanesque was traditional especially in the way it denied its newness. Yet the period of the Gothic, which began in the later twelfth century—with its cities and commerce and universities and crusades and friars and heresies and lay piety—learned even to value innovation.[10] The contexts that had once fostered the composition and use of liturgical curses then gave way to others that either ignored or rejected them.

This study of Benedictine maledictions in Romanesque France has taken several years. It all began, naturally, with a manuscript—and a Benedictine monk. The first time I met Dom Jean Becquet he told me about a manuscript containing maledictions he had seen that day in

10. For specific references and more discussion on all these matters, see Lester K. Little, "Romanesque Christianity in Germanic Europe," *Journal of Interdisciplinary History* 23 (1992–1993): 453–474.

the Bibliothèque Nationale. These were inscribed on a blank folio at the end of a Bible produced at the Abbey of Saint-Martial of Limoges in the late tenth century.[11] He was interested in what he had found for a very precise, and limited, reason.[12] For the rest, he generously put the material at my disposal, along with his extensive knowledge of Saint-Martial, Limoges, and monastic history in general. I remain deeply grateful to him for his spontaneous generosity and assistance.

Two accomplished historians of monasticism, Barbara H. Rosenwein and Lisa M. Bitel, read a draft of this work and helped me improve it considerably. Their good influence is thus not confined to those pages where I lean heavily upon their writings. I have also learned much from the works of Patrick Geary and express appreciation for insights to him and the other participants in a workshop on dispute settlement in me- dieval society that he organized at the University of Florida in the spring of 1990. I thank Adelaide Bennett of the Index of Christian Art for advice on iconography. My examination of manuscripts in preparation for this book has made me think often and with gratitude of the introduction to Latin paleography I was given years ago by James J. John.

My gratitude goes to Smith College, where I enjoy fine company and an excellent library, to the John Simon Guggenheim Foundation for a fellowship in 1983, and to the National Endowment for the Humanities for a summer stipend in 1982 and a fellowship in 1991–1992.

I have lectured on various aspects of this subject in several univer- sities, beginning with the seminar of Jacques Le Goff at the Ecole des hautes études en sciences sociales. Always I have gained from the ques- tions posed and suggestions offered by colleagues and students on those occasions. I am especially grateful for the opportunities I have had to work through the sources and the problems they raise in sem- inars at Smith College over the past few years, at the University of California, Berkeley, in the spring semester of 1988, and at the Univer- sity of Venice in the spring of 1992.

LESTER K. LITTLE

Northampton, Massachusetts

11. MS, Paris, BN, lat. 5[II], f. 220r–v.

12. It made clear what Stephen of Muret was referring to in criticizing the contem- porary monastic practice of cursing enemies. See *Liber de doctrina*, ch. 59, in *Scriptores ordinis Grandimontensis*, ed. Jean Becquet, Corpus Christianorum, continuatio medievalis 8 (Turnhout, 1968), p. 35 and below, the Conclusion of this book.

Abbreviations

AASS   *Acta sanctorum* (Antwerp and Brussels, 1643–).

AASSOSB   *Acta sanctorum ordinis Sancti Benedicti*, ed. Luc d'Achery and Jean Mabillon, 9 vols. (Venice, 1733–1738).

Annales ESC   *Annales: Economies, Sociétés, Civilisations*

Annales OSB   *Annales ordinis Sancti Benedicti*, ed. Jean Mabillon, 6 vols. (Lucca, 1739–1745).

BL   British Library, London

BM   Bibliothèque Municipale

BN   Bibliothèque Nationale, Paris

CIC   *Corpus iuris canonici*, ed. Emil Friedberg, 2 vols. (Leipzig, 1879–1881).

DACL   *Dictionnaire d'archéologie chrétienne et de liturgie*, ed. Fernand Cabrol and Henri Leclercq, 6 vols. (Paris, 1907–1927).

DHGE   *Dictionnaire d'histoire et de géographie ecclésiastique* (Paris, 1912–).

DMA   *Dictionary of the Middle Ages*, ed. Joseph R. Strayer, 13 vols. (New York, 1982–1989).

DS   *Dictionnaire de spiritualité*, ed. Marcel Viller et al. (Paris, 1937–).

DTC   *Dictionnaire de théologie catholique*, ed. A. Vacant et al., 15 vols. (Paris, 1909–1950).

Du Cange   Charles Du Cange, *Glossarium mediae et infimae latinitatis*, new ed., 10 vols. (Niort, 1883–1887; repr. Graz, 1954).

EHOV   *The Ecclesiastical History of Ordericus Vitalis*, ed. and tr. Marjorie Chibnall, 6 vols. (Oxford, 1969–1980).

ER   *The Encyclopedia of Religion*, ed. Mircea Eliade, 16 vols. (New York, 1987).

FS   *Frühmittelalterliche Studien*

IB   *The Interpreter's Bible*, ed. George A. Buttrick et al., 12 vols. (New York, 1952–1957).

Mansi   *Sacrorum conciliorum nova et amplissima collectio*, ed. G. D. Mansi, 31 vols. (Florence, 1759–1798).

MGH	*Monumenta Germaniae historica*
AA	*Auctores antiquissimi*
Capit.	*Capitularia regum Francorum*
Conc.	*Concilia*
Const.	*Constitutiones et acta publica imperatorum et regum*
Epist.	*Epistolae*
Form.	*Formulae*
Leg.	*Legum*
LNG	*Legum nationum Germanicarum*
SRG	*Scriptores rerum Germanicarum*
SRM	*Scriptores rerum Merovingicarum*
SS	*Scriptores*
NCE	*New Catholic Encyclopedia*, 15 vols. (New York, 1967).
ODCC	*Oxford Dictionary of the Christian Church*, 2d ed., ed. Frank L. Cross and E. A. Livingston (New York, 1974).
PG	*Patrologiae cursus completus, series Graeca*, ed. Jacques Paul Migne, 161 vols. (Paris, 1857–1866).
PL	*Patrologiae cursus completus, series Latina*, ed. Jacques Paul Migne, 222 vols. (Paris, 1844–1864).
PRG	*Le pontifical romano-germanique*, ed. Cyrille Vogel and Reinhard Elze, 3 vols. Studi e testi 226, 227, and 269 (Vatican City, 1963–1972).
RB	*RB 1980: The Rule of Saint Benedict in Latin and English with Notes*, ed. Timothy Fry et al. (Collegeville, Minn., 1981).
RS	Rolls Series, 99 vols. (London, 1858–1896).
Vat.	Biblioteca Apostolica Vaticana, Vatican City

Introduction:
Of *Tristram Shandy*
and French Monastic Curses

''SMALL CURSES, Dr. Slop, upon great occasions are but so much waste of our strength and soul's health to no manner of purpose.'' Tristram Shandy's father was the first to speak after Dr. Slop had cut his thumb and cursed Obadiah for tying the strings on his instruments bag with knots so hard he had to take his penknife to them. The others agreed. '' 'I own it,' replied Dr. Slop. 'They are like sparrow shot,' quoth my uncle Toby (suspending his whistling), 'fired against a bastion.' '''[1]

Mr. Walter Shandy had not finished. ''For my own part, I seldom swear or curse at all,'' he continued, ''but if I fall into it . . . I swear on, till I find myself easy.'' Next he expounded upon the wisdom of maintaining a just proportion between the vent given to humors stirring within oneself and the size and ill intent of the offense that stirred them up. Then he mentioned a written curse he kept right there by the fireplace, although, he added, '' 'tis too violent for a cut of the thumb.'' Dr. Slop, an excellent midwife but a Catholic and hence the object of Mr. Shandy's derision, snapped at the bait: ''Not at all . . . the devil take the fellow,'' and in a moment he had promised to read aloud ''a form of excommunication of the church of Rome, a copy of which, my father (who was curious in his collections) had procured out of the leger-book of the church of Rochester, writ by Ernulphus the bishop.'' With his

---

1. Laurence Sterne, *The Life and Opinions of Tristram Shandy, Gentleman*, ed. Ian Campbell Ross (Oxford, 1983), 3:10 (p. 134). The passages from this work cited in the following paragraphs are all found in volume 3, chapters 10 and 11 (pp. 132–143); they appear by permission of Oxford University Press. Paul Pickrel, professor emeritus of English literature at Smith College, kindly brought this text to my attention, and my guide in studying it has been Frank H. Ellis, also professor emeritus of English literature at Smith College.

thumb wrapped in his handkerchief, Dr. Slop read aloud as follows, "my uncle Toby whistling *Lillabullero,* as loud as he could, all the time":

> By the authority of God Almighty, the Father, Son, and Holy Ghost, and of the holy canons, and of the undefiled Virgin Mary, mother and patroness of our Saviour,

Dr. Slop paused to protest. "I think there is no necessity," he began, but Mr. Shandy would not release him from their agreement. And when Uncle Toby offered to read it in his stead, Dr. Slop decided he would do better to continue reading it himself under cover of the latter's whistling. So he started again, holding the paper in front of his face to hide his chagrin, with Uncle Toby whistling not quite so loud this time as before:

> By the authority of God Almighty . . . and of all the celestial virtues, angels, archangels, thrones, dominions, powers, cherubins and seraphins, and of all the holy patriarchs, prophets, and of all the apostles and evangelists, and of the holy innocents, who in the sight of the holy Lamb, are found worthy to sing the new song of the holy martyrs and holy confessors, and of the holy virgins, and of all the saints together with the holy and elect of God. May he (Obadiah) be damn'd (for tying these knots).

The tale of strings, knots, penknife, and injured thumb was an elaborate contrivance Laurence Sterne employed to introduce the text of an excommunication formula into his novel, *The Life and Opinions of Tristram Shandy, Gentleman.* He placed it in the third volume, which appeared early in 1761, following the simultaneous publication of the first two volumes by just over a year. In the first volume he had included a theological discussion, in French, concerning fetal baptism, and since some critics had expressed doubts about its authenticity, he sought to head off any such doubts about the excommunication formula. This he did by having the original Latin text printed on the left-hand pages with the English translation on the right. On the Latin side blank spaces corresponded to Sterne's interpolations about Dr. Slop's chagrin, Uncle Toby's whistling, and the like. Sterne also inserted a footnote expressing Mr. Shandy's gratitude to the dean and clerk of the chapter of Rochester.

The excommunication formula was far from finished, for only now did Dr. Slop arrive at the operative phrase:

We excommunicate, and anathematize him, and from the thresholds of the holy church of God Almighty we sequester him, that he may be tormented, disposed and delivered over with Dathan and Abiram and with those who say unto the Lord God, Depart from us, we desire none of thy ways. And as fire is quenched with water, so let the light of him be put out for evermore, unless it shall repent him (Obadiah, of the knots which he has tied) and make satisfaction (for them). Amen.

At this point begins a great litany of curses, which the fame of Sterne's novel has made one of the more famous of that genre in the English language:

May the Father who created him, curse him. May the Son who suffered for us, curse him. May the Holy Ghost who was given to us in baptism, curse him (Obadiah). May the holy cross which Christ for our salvation triumphing over his enemies, ascended, curse him.

   May the holy and eternal Virgin Mary, mother of God, curse him. May St. Michael the advocate of holy souls, curse him. May all the angels and archangels, principalities and powers, and all the heavenly armies, curse him. [Our armies swore terribly in Flanders, cried my uncle Toby, but nothing to this. For my own part, I could not have a heart to curse my dog so.]

Uncle Toby made frequent reference to the war in Flanders, not least because of a wound in the groin he suffered at the siege of Namur in 1695; it was the occasion of his lengthy convalescence in the home of his brother Walter. Dr. Slop went right on after the interruption.

May St. John the precursor, and St. John the Baptist,[2] and St. Peter and St. Paul, and St. Andrew, and all other Christ's apostles, together curse him. And may the rest of his disciples and four evangelists, who by their preaching converted the universal world, and may the holy and wonderful company of martyrs and confessors, who by their holy works are found pleasing to God Almighty, curse him (Obadiah).

The holy choir of virgins and all the saints are next called upon to do their part. Then the subject is cursed in different places ("in the home or the stables"), in performing different functions ("in eating and drinking"), and in different parts of his body (from head to toe, with stops at all points in between and an interjection by Uncle Toby at the predictable point). The Son of God is called on for one final curse

2. This is a faulty translation, for the original says *Sanctus Joannes praecursor et baptista Christi* (ibid., p. 138), and hence the translation should read "Saint John the precursor and baptizer of Christ."

against this now thoroughly cursed malefactor, "unless he repent and make satisfaction. Amen. So be it, so be it. Amen."

Any inquisitive reader would want to know where Sterne got this text. His answer, we recall, was that he had procured it (if we are now permitted to drop the pretense that Tristram Shandy's father was the one responsible) "out of the leger-book of the church of Rochester, writ by Ernulphus the bishop." In addition, he inserted that footnote thanking the dean and the clerk of the chapter of Rochester for a copy of the original. There is, however, more than a touch of obfuscation in this view of the matter presented by the author.

The first step toward clarification is to separate the search for the origins of the Latin text from the search for those of the English version. The Latin original was indeed kept, and has continued to be until recently, in the library of the cathedral church of Rochester. The "leger-book" referred to by Sterne is the *Textus Roffensis*, a compendium of documents of particular importance to, or at least in some way related to, the church of Rochester; these include charters, Anglo-Saxon as well as Anglo-Norman laws, papal decrees, papal and royal privileges, and so on.[3] Such compendiums or collections, which brought coherence and convenience of consultation to hitherto helter-skelter archives, were not unusual in the twelfth century; this one was assembled during the reign of Bishop Ernulf, 1114–1124.[4] But Sterne did not have to go or even send to Rochester, for a nearly complete edition of the *Textus Roffensis* had been published by Thomas Hearne at Oxford in 1720. Various copies of Hearne's book were undoubtedly accessible to Sterne; one he surely could have consulted was the copy in the minster library at York.[5]

On the other hand, Sterne was silent about his source for the English version, leaving any reader to whom the question might have occurred to surmise that he had simply made the translation himself. But in fact he used an English translation of the formula that was published more than once in 1745, appearing, for example, in *The Harleian Miscellany*

3. The manuscript is now found at Maidstone, Kent County Archives, DRc/R1; the curse formula is on ff. 98r–99v. For a facsimile, see *Textus Roffensis: Rochester Cathedral Library Manuscript A.3.5*, ed. Peter Sawyer, 2 vols., Early English Manuscripts in Facsimile 7, 11 (Copenhagen, 1957–1962).

4. A contemporary example, from Llandaff in Wales in the time of Bishop Urban (1107–34), is the *Liber Landavensis*, ed. John G. Evans and John Rhys (Oxford, 1893; repr. Aberystwyth, 1979).

5. William A. Jackson, "The Curse of Ernulphus," *Harvard Library Bulletin* 14 (1960): 394, n. 2. *Textus Roffensis*, ed. Thomas Hearne (Oxford, 1720).

and in *Gentleman's Magazine.*[6] Even then it was not a new translation, for these publications were reprinting a text that had appeared for urgent polemical reasons in the succession crisis of 1681. At that time Protestants afraid that the crown would pass into Catholic hands produced a broadside that featured, in English translation, the Rochester excommunication formula. The heading placed over it said: "The Popes Dreadfull Curse. Being the Form of an Excommunication of the Church of Rome. Taken out of the Leger-Book of the Church of Rochester now in the custody of the Dean and Chapter there. Writ by Ernulfus the Bishop." And the postscript added at the end said: "The Publication of this is to shew what is to be expected from the Pope, if he come to be Supream Head of the Church in this Nation."[7] The source of Sterne's phrase: "out of the leger-book of the church of Rochester, writ by Ernulphus the Bishop," which any reader would assume referred to the Latin original, we now see came from the heading on a 1681 broadside in English that was reprinted in 1745 (see Fig. 3).

The reprintings of 1745 were no mere matter of antiquarian curiosity. In July of that year the young Catholic pretender Charles Edward Stuart landed in the Hebrides; by mid-September he was at Edinburgh with a small army, and on the twenty-first of that month they demolished an English army sent to halt his advance. The archbishop of York preached in his church on 22 September to rally the defense of Yorkshire and resistance to "Popery and Absolute Power." It was then, in the September issues of some magazines, that the text of the 1681 broadside was reprinted; furthermore, the broadside itself was then reissued. According to an advertisement in the *Daily Post* of 26 September 1745, "The Pope's Dreadful Curse" was available at a cost of threepence and declared "fit to be framed and hung up in all Protestant

6. Jackson, "Curse of Ernulphus," pp. 392–394.

7. The imprint is "London, Printed and are to be sold by L. C. on Ludgate-Hill, 1681." The publisher was one Langly Curtis of Ludgate Hill, who had a reputation for issuing inflammatory publications and who had more than once been reprimanded on that account and even punished by the law. See Jackson, "Curse of Ernulphus," p. 392. Eight copies of this broadside have been located: Balliol College, Beinecke Library of Yale University (Broadsides 4°/By 6/1681), Bodleian Library, British Library, Huntington Library, John Rylands University Library, Newberry Library, and the University of Pennsylvania. Copies of the same broadside but with the imprint "Reprinted for Joseph Howes Bookseller in Castle-street, Dublin. 1681" are found at Trinity College, Dublin, and in the Houghton Library of Harvard University (*57-1632F); the latter copy is reproduced in Jackson, "Curse of Ernulphus," pl. 1. See *Short-Title Catalogue of Books Printed in England 1641–1700,* ed. Donald Wing, 2d ed. rev. (New York, 1982), 2:12 (E3241 and E3241A).

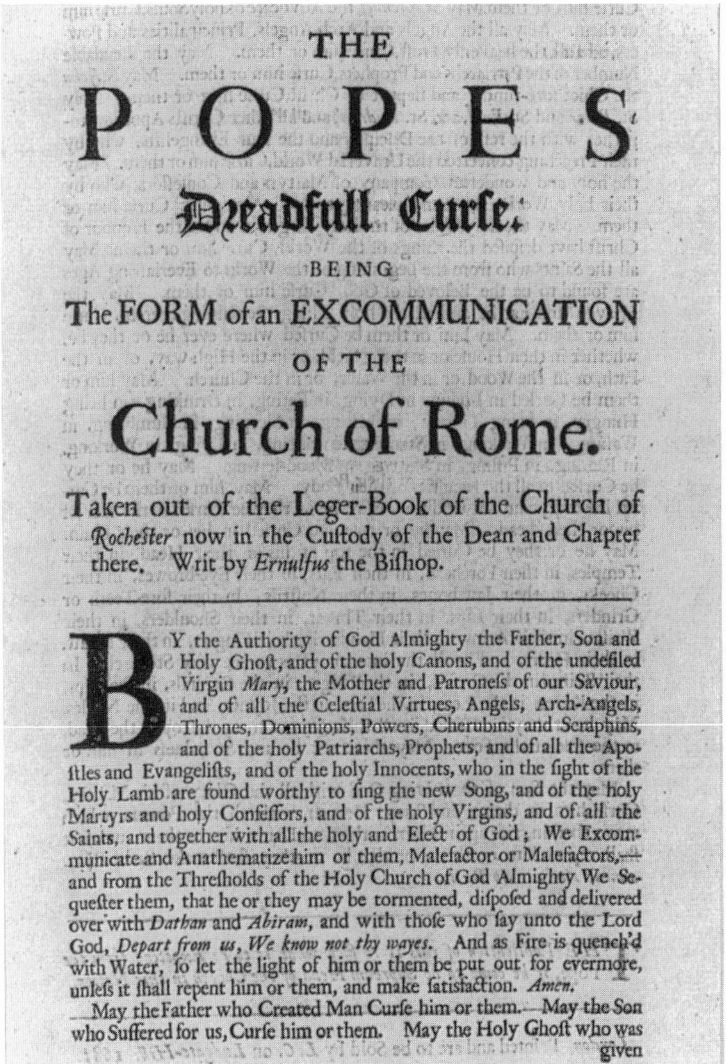

THE
POPES
Dreadfull Curse,
BEING
The FORM of an EXCOMMUNICATION
OF THE
Church of Rome.

Taken out of the Leger-Book of the Church of *Rochester* now in the Cuſtody of the Dean and Chapter there. Writ by *Ernulfus* the Biſhop.

BY the Authority of God Almighty the Father, Son and Holy Ghoſt, and of the holy Canons, and of the undefiled Virgin *Mary*, the Mother and Patroneſs of our Saviour, and of all the Celeſtial Virtues, Angels, Arch-Angels, Thrones, Dominions, Powers, Cherubins and Seraphins, and of the holy Patriarchs, Prophets, and of all the Apoſtles and Evangeliſts, and of the holy Innocents, who in the ſight of the Holy Lamb are found worthy to ſing the new Song, and of the holy Martyrs and holy Confeſſors, and of the holy Virgins, and of all the Saints, and together with all the holy and Elect of God ; We Excommunicate and Anathematize him or them, Malefactor or Malefactors, and from the Threſholds of the Holy Church of God Almighty We Sequeſter them, that he or they may be tormented, diſpoſed and delivered over with *Dathan* and *Abiram*, and with thoſe who ſay unto the Lord God, *Depart from us, We know not thy wayes.* And as Fire is quench'd with Water, ſo let the light of him or them be put out for evermore, unleſs it ſhall repent him or them, and make ſatisfaction. *Amen.*

May the Father who Created Man Curſe him or them.—May the Son who Suffered for us, Curſe him or them. May the Holy Ghoſt who was
given

Figure 3. "The Popes Dreadfull Curse," a broadside (of which just the front is reproduced here) published in London in 1681. The main text is a translation of the Rochester curse formula of about 1120, whose origins go still farther back by two centuries. Reproduced by permission of the Beinecke Rare Book and Manuscript Library, Yale University.

Families.'"[8] The burning issues of 1681 were thus rekindled in 1745, when they engaged the energies of so many people, including Laurence Sterne. The curate of a rural parish in Yorkshire, Sterne benefited from the patronage and protection of an uncle who held an influential position in the curia of the archbishop. He shared his uncle's fiercely partisan Whiggism and bitter anti-Catholicism; their sermons and writings against the Pretender, the Jacobites, and Catholics in general were relentless, just as their pursuit and persecution of persons suspected of Jacobite sympathies were pitiless. Their obsessive hounding of the noted Catholic obstetrician and antiquarian Dr. John Burton of York went on for about a decade, some of it in courts and prisons; Sterne's own hounding of Dr. Burton has lasted longer still in the character he invented and named Dr. Slop.[9]

But the question of sources need not be limited to eighteenth-century publications that Sterne might have seen. What do we know about the curse "writ by Ernulphus" and its origins? One might begin by looking at the *Textus Roffensis* itself, where besides the curse of Ernulphus there are curses in a confirmation of privileges dated 1103. In the first of its three parts, King Henry I confirms all the possessions, rights, customs, and privileges of the Church of Saint-Andrew of Rochester; no sanctions are mentioned. In the second part Archbishop Anselm of Canterbury confirms the royal confirmation and excommunicates and promises the fate of Judas the traitor to all who attempt to take away or otherwise diminish anything belonging to this church. And in the third part, Gundulf the bishop of Rochester confirms both the royal confirmation of rights and the archiepiscopal excommunication of violators and adds that the names of such violators shall be struck from the book of the living, that they shall not be listed among the just, and that on the day of just and eternal retribution they shall be placed upon the left-hand side and receive a sentence of severe punishment (*sententiam districtae ultionis. Amen. Amen. Amen*). At the end come the signatures of the king, the prelates, and several witnesses.[10]

Such was the standard language for an ecclesiastical sanction in the

<hr />

8. *The Florida Edition of the Works of Laurence Sterne*, ed. Melvyn New and Joan New, 3 vols. (Gainesville, Fla., 1978–1984), 2:953, n. 4.

9. Wilbur L. Cross, *The Life and Times of Laurence Sterne*, 3d ed. (New Haven, Conn., 1929), pp. 70–87.

10. *Textus Roffensis*, ed. Hearne, pp. 224–227.

circles frequented by the person responsible for the Rochester compilation, Bishop Ernulf. Born in Normandy in 1040, he was brought up at the monastery of Le Bec, where he developed close ties with two future archbishops of Canterbury—his teacher Lanfranc and his slightly older school companion Anselm. He became a monk at the Abbey of Saint-Symphorien at Beauvais for a few years, until Lanfranc summoned him to a post at Canterbury in the 1070s. After the latter's death in 1089 he stayed on in the service of Anselm until he was named abbot of Peterborough in 1107. His final career move was in 1114, when he went to the see of Rochester, where he remained until his death in 1124.[11]

There are no known English sources for the excommunication formula in the Rochester compilation, yet clearly the place to look for such texts is northern and central France, where the future prelates of the Anglo-Norman church received their training and started their careers. Although no French manuscript containing the immediate (or even a distant) relative of the Rochester formula is currently known, a seventeenth-century scholar, Etienne Baluze, did find and publish a formula that turns out to be its exact prototype. Baluze gave no indication of where the manuscript was from and only an indirect indication of its date, roughly about 900, but many other texts corroborate the choice of this general area and time period for situating it.[12]

A formula with many similarities to that of Rochester comes from the Abbey of Fécamp, founded by Duke Richard I of Normandy in 990 on lands close by the English Channel.[13] One could consider it an ex-

11. Reginald Lane Poole, "Ernulf, Bishop of Rochester (1040–1124)," in *Dictionary of National Biography*, 17:396–397. Poole and others place Ernulf at Saint-Lucien of Beauvais, but for the more recent judgment in favor of Saint-Symphorien, see Peter Cramer, "Ernulf of Rochester and Early Anglo-Norman Canon Law," *Journal of Ecclesiastical History* 40 (1989): 483–510, especially p. 484.

12. *Capitularia regum Francorum ab anno 742 ad annum 922*, ed. Etienne Baluze, 2 vols. (Venice, 1772–1773), 2:469–470. Reprinted in Mansi 18B:679–680 and PL 87:952–954. For the text, see appendix C, text 2. That the text edited by Baluze is the same as the Rochester formula was pointed out by Henry Charles Lea, *Studies in Church History* (Philadelphia, 1869), p. 337, n. 1.

13. Dom Edmond Martène transcribed and published this text in the early eighteenth century: *De antiquis ecclesiae ritibus*, 4 vols. (Antwerp, 1736–1738), 2:911–912. The manuscript is now lost, however, according to Aimé-Georges Martimort, *La documentation liturgique de Dom Edmond Martène*, Studi e testi 279 (Vatican City, 1978), pp. 422–423. Since this formula, of whose date Martène gave no indication, has marked similarities to the sanction clause in the foundation charter of 990 for Fécamp, it can be assigned to the late tenth or early eleventh century. For the charter, see *Recueil des actes des ducs de Normandie de 911 à 1066*, ed. Marie Fauroux, Mémoires de la Société des antiquaires de Normandie 36 (Caen, 1961), pp. 72–74.

communication formula, although "we curse" and "we separate" are the principal verbs used, and "we excommunicate" does not appear at all. The authorities invoked at the start are God the Father, the Son, and the Holy Spirit, the Holy Catholic Church of God, Saint Mary the Mother of God, Saint Michael with nine orders of angels, Saint Peter prince of the apostles with twelve apostles, four evangelists, Saint Stephen with all the martyrs, Saint Roman and Saint Ouen with all the confessors and all the virgins, and 144,000 innocents. With such authority,

> we curse them and we separate them from the company of the holy mother church and of all faithful Christians, unless they change their ways and give back what they unjustly took away. But if they will not do that, may there come over them those curses by which Almighty God cursed those [the wicked, in Job 21:14] who said to the Lord God: "Stay away from us, we do not wish to know of your ways," and those [referred to in Ps. 82:13] who said "Let us take possession for ourselves of the sanctuary of God."

More than one form of death is then called down upon the objects of this formula, as well as the company in eternal flames of Korah, Dathan, Abiron, Judas, Pilate, Ananias, Sapphira, Nero, Decio, Herod, Julian, Valerian, Simon Magus, and the devil. Then comes a litany of curses:

> May their bodies be cursed. May they be cursed in the head and the brain. May they be cursed in their eyes and their foreheads. May they be cursed in their ears and their noses. May they be cursed in fields and in pastures. May they be cursed in the mouth and the throat, cursed in the chest and the heart, cursed in the stomach, cursed in the blood, cursed in the hands and feet and in each of their members. May they be cursed going in and coming out. May they be cursed in towns and in castles. May they be cursed in streets and in squares. May they be cursed when sleeping and when awake, when going out and returning, when eating and drinking, when speaking and being silent. May they be cursed in all places and at all times.

One last ingenious curse asks that the sky over them be made of brass and the earth underfoot of iron so that heaven will be unable to receive their souls and earth unable to receive their bodies. The extinguishing of candles concludes the ceremony and puts a symbolic end to the persons damned.

From the English Channel in the north, the zone that produced curse formulas extended southward slightly more than halfway to the Mediterranean. There, along its southern edge, at the Abbey of Saint-Martial of Limoges, a Bible produced in the tenth century contains a notice, itself inserted in the late tenth century, that contains elements not seen in the Rochester and Fécamp formulas.[14] It has no title, but its key verbs are "curse," "excommunicate," "anathematize," and "separate." Furthermore, the opening reference to men who are preying upon the monastery's lands gives an indication of the underlying problem. "We hereby inform you, brothers," it says, "that certain evil men are devastating the land of our lord Martial."

> They are invading, preying upon, and destroying it; they are hurting our poor tenants, taking from them the little they have and with which they are supposed to serve Saint Martial, the lord abbot, and the monks. They behave like those who said, "Let us take possession for ourselves of the sanctuary of God."[15]

According to legend, Martial was a Christian who came from Rome to Gaul in the middle of the third century. Like his contemporary Denis, who preached Christianity in Paris and was martyred there, Martial formed a Christian community at Limoges, became its first bishop, and suffered martyrdom at the hands of Roman authorities.[16] His tomb just outside the city walls became the focal point of a cult sustained by several generations of believers. In 848 the canons in charge of the site and the relics became monks and adopted the Rule of Saint Benedict.[17]

The Abbey of Saint-Martial became one of the most prosperous and influential religious communities in western France. Pilgrims flocked there to see and be near the golden, nearly life-size statue of the saint, its right hand raised in a gesture of benediction over the faithful.[18] The

14. MS, Paris, BN, lat. 5[II], f. 220r–v. Cf. *Bibliothèque Nationale: Catalogue général des manuscrits latins*, vol. 1, ed. P. Lauer (Paris, 1939), pp. 4–5.

15. Lester K. Little, "Formules monastiques de malédiction aux IXe et Xe siècles," *Revue Mabillon* 58 (1975): 377–399; an edition of this text from Saint-Martial quoted here and in the following paragraphs is found on pp. 386–387 and also below in appendix C, text 7.

16. Gregory of Tours, *Historia Francorum*, 1:30 (*MGH, SRM* 1:48).

17. Monique Langlois and Michel Duchein, "Notice historique sur l'abbaye de Saint-Martial de Limoges," in *L'art roman à Saint-Martial de Limoges* (Limoges, 1950), pp. 11–24; Henri Leclercq, in *DACL* 9, pt. 1:1063–1167, s.v. "Limoges," especially cols. 1109 and 1127. Michel Aubrun, *L'ancien diocèse de Limoges: Des origines au milieu du XIe siècle* (Clermont-Ferrand, 1981), pp. 73–80, 130.

18. The statue-reliquary (or *maiestas*) was made after the fire that destroyed so much of the monastery and its belongings in 952. See Jean Hubert and Marie-Clotilde Hubert,

figure was enthroned in majesty upon the main altar. In 1018 the press of the crowd was so great there that fifty-two people were trampled and suffocated.[19]

The monks accumulated one of the largest libraries of the time (450 volumes by the early twelfth century), and one of their number, Adémar of Chabannes, wrote several works of history;[20] their precocious experimentation with liturgy is attested to by the numerous musical manuscripts they produced.[21] Their scriptorium also turned out massive, elaborately decorated Bibles. In one of these, now in the Bibliothèque Nationale in Paris, the monks inserted writings in the blank spaces between the various biblical books. Like the families of more recent centuries who recorded vital statistics in their Bibles, the monastic *familia* placed some of its most highly prized documents amid the sacred books.[22] One such addition records an agreement concluded in 942 for the exchange of prayers among the monks of Fleury, Solignac, and Saint-Martial. Another is a copy of a letter from Pope Alexander II confirming the abbey's privileges.[23] Yet another such doc-

---

"Piété chrétienne ou paganisme? Les statues-reliquaires de l'Europe carolingienne," in *Cristianizzazione ed organizzazione ecclesiastica delle campagne nell'Alto Medioevo: Espansione e resistenze*, 2 vols., Settimane di studio del Centro italiano di studi sull'Alto Medioevo 28 (Spoleto, 1982), pp. 235–275; also Ilene H. Forsyth, *The Throne of Wisdom: Wood Sculptures of the Madonna in Romanesque France* (Princeton, N.J., 1972), pp. 39, 79; and Amy G. Remensnyder, "Un problème de cultures ou de culture? La statue-reliquaire et les *joca* de Sainte Foy de Conques dans le *Liber miraculorum* de Bernard d'Angers," *Cahiers de civilisation médiévale* 33 (1990): 351–379, especially p. 365.

19. Adémar of Chabannes, *Commemoratio abbatum* (PL 141:83). See Elie Lambert, "L'ancienne église abbatiale de Saint-Martial de Limoges," in *L'art roman à Saint-Martial de Limoges* (Limoges, 1950), pp. 27–42; and on this incident, Richard A. Landes, "Between Aristocracy and Heresy: Popular Participation in the Limousin Peace of God, 994–1033," in *The Peace of God: Social Violence and Religious Response in France around the Year 1000*, ed. Thomas Head and Richard A. Landes (Ithaca, N.Y., 1992), pp. 202–203.

20. Richard A. Landes, *The Making of a Medieval Historian: Adémar of Chabannes and Aquitaine at the Turn of the Millennium* (Ann Arbor, Mich.: University Microfilms International, 1985).

21. Léopold Delisle, "Les manuscrits de Saint-Martial de Limoges," *Bulletin de la Société archéologique et historique du Limousin* 43 (1895): 1–60; Richard Crocker, "The Repertory of Proses at Saint Martial of Limoges in the Tenth Century," *Journal of the American Musicological Society* 11 (1958): 149–164; Jacques Chailley, *L'école musicale de Saint-Martial de Limoges* (Paris, 1960); Paul Evans, *The Early Trope Repertory of Saint Martial of Limoges* (Princeton, N.J., 1970).

22. For an English example, dated between 1069 and 1072, there is the record of a donation by Bishop Leofric to Saint Peter's Abbey at Exeter written into a Gospel book. See *Anglo-Saxon Charters*, ed. Agnes S. Robertson (Cambridge, 1939), pp. 226–227.

23. Danielle Gaborit-Chopin, *La décoration des manuscrits à Saint-Martial de Limoges et*

ument, added in the late tenth century, is our notice concerning troubles on the abbey lands. The notice continues.

> So those who overrun and hold the land of Saint Martial do not serve the lord abbot and the monks. May they be cursed and excommunicated and anathematized [and separated][24] from the consortium of all the faithful Christians of God. May the curse of all the saints of God come upon them. May the angels and archangels of God curse them. May the patriarchs and the prophets curse them. May all the apostles and all the martyrs and all the confessors and all the virgins and especially Saint Martial, whom they are treating so badly, curse them. May he confound and destroy them, and disperse them from the face of the earth. May all these curses come upon them and seize them.

The curses now go on to specify place and activity rather than agent.

> May they be cursed in town. May they be cursed in the fields. May they be cursed inside their houses and outside their houses. May they be cursed standing and sitting. May they be cursed lying down and walking. May they be cursed when asleep and when awake. May they be cursed while eating and while drinking. May they be cursed in castles and in villages. May they be cursed in forests and in waters.

The curses spread.

> May their wives and their children and all who associate with them be cursed. May their cellars be cursed, as well as their casks and all the vessels from which they drink and eat. May their vineyards and their crops and their forests be cursed. May their servants, if these remain loyal to them, be cursed. May all their cattle and their work animals, both inside and outside the stables, be cursed.

The curses become specific.

> May the Lord send over them hunger and thirst, pestilence and death, until they are wiped off the earth. May the Lord strike them with heat and cold.

---

en Limousin du IXe au XIIe siècle (Paris, 1969). She devotes a chapter (pp. 42–52) to this Bible and mentions (p. 177) each of the insertions on blank folios except the curse.

24. With no addition of words to the original, the phrase could be translated "and anathematized by the consortium," but that seems unlikely for two reasons. First, authority to curse or excommunicate is nowhere else given to the whole Christian community. Second, the verbs *excludere* and *separare* occur routinely in sanction clauses and excommunication formulas. Examples: "et ab omnium coetu Christianorum tamdium separetur," Mansi 19:832; "a liminibus sanctae matris ecclesiae excludimus et ab omni societate et communione christiana separamus," *PL* 140:89.

May the sky above them be brass and the earth they walk on iron. May the Lord toss their bodies as bait to the birds of the sky and the beasts of the land. May the Lord strike them from the bottoms of their feet to the tops of their heads. May their homes be deserted and may no one inhabit them. May they lose what they have, and may they not acquire what they do not have. May the sword devastate them on the outside and fear on the inside. If they sow seeds in the earth may they reap little, and if they plant vines may they not drink wine from them.

A curse follows that looks like just one more to be piled on, but it suddenly reveals an escape hatch: "May the Lord send great plagues upon them, and the worst, most relentless illnesses, unless they change their ways." Just as suddenly, the escape hatch snaps shut again.

But if they are not willing to change, then let them accept from God and Saint Martial damnation with the devil and his angels in hell, and may they burn in eternal fires with Dathan and Abiron. Amen, amen. Thus may all memory of them be extinguished for ever and ever.

These two late tenth-century texts, from Fécamp and Saint-Martial, neither of which names particular malefactors, appear to be formulas for use in times of trouble. The escape clause of the former says "unless they return the things mentioned above," and the latter makes a specific charge against certain men who prey upon the monastery's lands. There is no mention of any doctrinal dispute, nor is there reference to Rome or to papal authority; the same things could be said of the Rochester formula and its French forebear.

All these formulas have escape clauses close to the end. The Rochester text finishes simply with "Amen" and "So be it"; that of Saint-Martial, as we have just seen, with "Amen, amen. Thus may all memory of them be extinguished for ever and ever." It is the Fécamp text that makes clear what is taking place as the reading of these texts concludes, for it says: "And just as these lights are extinguished, so may their souls and bodies lie extinct in dark shadows," suggesting that candles were extinguished at this climactic moment of the ceremony.

Building out from these examples, I will present a survey of different types of maledictory formulas, followed by a search for their sources and an inquiry into their legitimacy. Then it will be a matter of observing them in action, noting when and where they were used, and of course with what results. The specific contexts will be examined closely in order to give as full a historical explanation of this practice as possible, as well as to allow one to judge whether the curse in any given situation measured up, as Walter Shandy would have put it, to the greatness of the occasion.

part one Curses in Texts

Again I lifted my eyes and saw, and behold, a flying scroll!
And [the angel] said to me, "What do you see?" I answered,
"I see a flying scroll; its length is twenty cubits and its
breadth ten cubits." Then he said to me, "This is the curse
that goes out over the face of the whole land; for every one
who steals shall be cut off henceforth according to it, and
every one who swears falsely shall be cut off henceforth according to it. I will send it forth, says the Lord of hosts, and
it shall enter the house of the thief, and the house of him
who swears falsely by my name; and it shall abide in his
house and consume it, both timber and stones."

Zacharias 5:1-4

I
Formulas

MALEDICTORY FORMULAS have never constituted
a category or even subcategory of liturgical organization. A few bear
the title "malediction," and they are similar in many particulars to a
recognized liturgical form, the clamor. The clamor itself has several
variants, and not all of them contain curses. Thus the subject matter at
hand does not lend itself to division into sharply defined categories. A
minimal organization is necessary if we are to engage in any discourse,
but an attempt to make all formulas of, say, the tenth and eleventh
centuries fit neatly into a fixed pattern would violate the liturgical history of that period, when spontaneous, localized inventiveness was still
possible and neither centralized institutions nor hubs of learning bent
on imposing conformity yet existed. It was not at all the case, though,
that radically new liturgical forms simply sprouted at random points
on the landscape. Liturgy by its nature must be conservative; even as
it maintains an aura of timelessness, at certain moments it needs up-
dating to remain effective, but its effectiveness can be harmed by
changes seen as radical departures from the familiar. A middle way of
adaptation and barely perceptible modification is best suited to
changes in liturgy. In keeping with these general principles, the liturgical clamor was not invented at a precise moment; it had deep roots,
and these were not grounded in liturgy or even in an area having to
do with religion.

In late antiquity and in the time of the Germanic successor kingdoms,
"clamor" was a juridical term meaning claim or appeal. To make a
clamor (*facere clamorem*) meant to go before a magistrate to bring a suit,
present a petition, request a favor, or appeal a decision.[1] But there is

---

1. *Vocabularium codicis Iustiniani*, ed. R. von Mayr, 2 vols. (Prague, 1923), 1:620, 667;
Mediae Latinitatis lexicon minus, ed. Jan F. Niermeyer (Leiden, 1976), pp. 184–185.

more to this term than just its legal aspect, for it also connotes commotion and shouting. When a common person in late Roman imperial times made a clamor before a magistrate, who was of course seated upon a throne elevated on a platform, he stood in a boisterous crowd and raised his hand and his voice to get the attention of this local representative of Roman sovereignty.[2] The wealthy presumably had more efficacious as well as quieter and less physically demanding ways of gaining access to authority.

The court of the Visigothic king Theodoric II at Clermont resembled those of Roman officials even in these details of how petitioners came forward and the noise they made. As we learn from a letter of Sidonius dated about 455, after a busy morning in the court the king retired for his lunch and siesta (and a board game), then back came the ushers and the importunates, and the king resumed his post: "On all sides the rivalry of the petitioners makes an uproar, a sound that lasts until evening and does not diminish until interrupted by the royal dinner."[3] In Italy the Lombard king Ratchis issued a law about 745 directing all judges to hold court every day and to ensure justice for all; his candidly stated reason was "because we cannot go anywhere or attend any celebration or ride anywhere without being besieged by the appeals of many men" (propter reclamationes multorum hominum).[4]

In Frankish Gaul, Gregory of Tours spoke of a magnus clamor addressed by a group of poor people (pauperes) to King Guntram about 585. Their clamor concerned powerful individuals (potentes) from the entourage of his predecessor Chilperic who had devastated their lands. The clamantes got some satisfaction, but though the particular terms of the settlement need not detain us, it is important to note that Guntram, whom Bishop Gregory characterized as a rex bonus, gave a full hearing to these people.[5] Over the next three centuries a continuing preoccupation of Frankish legislation was precisely this protection of the poor's right of access to justice.

---

2. Peter Brown, *The World of Late Antiquity, A.D. 150–750* (London, 1971), p. 43, fig. 32. Christian leaders assembled at the Council of Nicea in 325 ruled that all persons addressing prayers to God should do so standing up. See *Decrees of the Ecumenical Councils*, ed. Norman P. Tanner, 2 vols. (London, 1990), 1:16.

3. Sidonius Apollinaris, *Epistolae*, 1:2 (*MGH, AA* 8:4).

4. *MGH, Leg.* 4:183; Katherine F. Drew, *The Lombard Laws* (Philadelphia, 1973), p. 216.

5. *Historia Francorum*, 7:7, 19 (*MGH, SRM* 1:295, 301); for the "good king," 4:25 (ibid., p. 160).

A capitulary, or administrative decree, issued by Charlemagne at Mantua in 781 opened with an order to bishops, abbots, and counts to hear out and to judge fairly all cases concerning the churches of God, widows, orphans, and the "less powerful."[6] In a capitulary of 789, the king's government directed counts to hear the cases of minors and orphans first; this recommendation reappeared several times in the following decades, with only minor variations in the listing of categories of the poor.[7] The capitulary of Thionville, in 805, reminds royal officials that "representatives of churches, widows, orphans, and minors bringing cases before public tribunals should not be treated with contempt, but on the contrary listened to attentively." During the 820s the imperial court reiterated most of these points in the following article of a capitulary:

> Concerning the affairs of widows, minors, orphans, and other poor people, let their disputes and complaints be heard and resolved during the first session, in the morning. Then in the afternoon let cases concerning the Crown, churches, or the powerful be taken up, for the poor lack the means to protect themselves if they are denied justice, which is the reason they bring so many complaints to our ears [*tantos clamores faciunt ad aures nostras*].[8]

The reiteration of these directives may attest to the difficulty the poor had in airing their grievances. The point remains that in late antiquity and in Carolingian Europe, "clamor" was a juridical term for presenting a petition before a duly constituted tribunal. It was an institutionalized means of access to those in power, specifically to ask for justice. Later on, in the years around 1000, religious communities found themselves in a continuous, often elusive quest for justice, and out of this trying experience they developed a novel reorientation of the clamor.[9] This reorientation—reincarnation even—is properly seen along with the development of a ritual of humiliation and of formulas for excommunication and anathema.

---

6. *MGH, Capit.* 1:190. On capitularies see Rosamond McKitterick, *The Carolingians and the Written Word* (Cambridge, 1989), pp. 27–37.

7. *MGH, Capit.* 1:63, 209, 281.

8. Ibid., pp. 122, 333.

9. Just because I am here concentrating on the new, religious manifestation of the clamor does not mean that the term then lost its juridical meaning and value. For the continuation of the legal clamor, see L. L. Hammerich, *Clamor: Eine rechtsgeschichtliche Studie* (Copenhagen, 1941).

Clamors

In the book of customs of the Abbey of Cluny compiled by the monk Bernard about 1075, there appears a chapter titled "How to Make a Clamor, in Case of Trouble, to the People or to God" (*Quomodo fiat clamor pro tribulatione ad populum sive ad deum*).[10] The presence of "the people" in such a prominent and responsible role is immediately noteworthy. Indeed, the first action to be taken when some predator is attacking church property, according to this chapter, is for the monks to assemble the people—meaning the laypeople who live near the monastery—in the main church, where the morning mass is to be said in front of the crucifix. After the reading from the Gospel, followed by the Creed and the Offertory, one of the brothers is to get up in the pulpit, talk about divine precepts (presumably those contained in the passages from Scripture read out minutes earlier), and then reveal the trouble the community faces. He is to suggest that they offer alms and that they ask God to turn evil into good and make the malefactor be at peace with them. Then the brother is to add some humble, persuasive words, saying: "You know that if our property is taken away from us we shall not be able to live; and so pray to God, brothers, and we shall make our clamor [*proclamationem*] to him." The significance of the title is perhaps clearer now, for it is apparent that the monks' clamor is to be addressed to God, but in the presence of the people.

The choir sings a scriptural response, either "Look upon me, Lord" (*Aspice, Domine*) or "Our enemies are gathered" (*Congregati sunt inimici nostri*), while all the bells are sounded slowly. Then the monks join in reciting three psalms, all suited to the occasion: Psalm 3, "Why, O Lord, have those who afflict me multiplied"; Psalm 45, "God is our shelter and our refuge, a timely help in trouble"; and Psalm 122, "I lift up my eyes to thee." Bernard's chapter next prescribes several *capitula*, which are short lessons consisting of one or two verses of Scripture such as "You have been my hope, a tower of strength against the face of the enemy" (Ps. 60:4), while at the end this list of devotions closes with the phrase "and others relating to troubles."[11]

10. MS, Paris, BN, lat. 13875, ff. 83r–84r; *Ritus et consuetudines Cluniacenses*, ch. 40, in *Vetus disciplina monastica*, ed. Marquard Herrgott (Paris, 1726), pp. 230–231. See appendix C, text 12.

11. *ODCC*, pp. 1177, 1433. Josef A. Jungmann, *The Mass of the Roman Rite: Its Origins and Development*, tr. Francis A. Brunner, 2 vols. (New York, 1950), 1:64, 427.

The power and influence of Cluny led to the general diffusion of various sets of customs drawn up during the eleventh and twelfth centuries. The set of customs attributed to Bernard, however, is found in only a few surviving manuscripts. One of these is a twelfth-century copy made for the Abbey of Corbie, near Amiens, which faithfully reproduces the entire book of customs (customal).[12] The title on the clamor chapter differs from the one we have seen, though, for the puzzling phrase *ad populum* is absent. Perhaps the inclusion of that phrase in the Cluniac manuscript, which is also a twelfth-century copy, was in error. In any case, the simpler chapter title in the Corbie customal reads: *Quomodo clamor fiat pro tribulatione ad deum.*

The Abbey of Saint-Amand near Valenciennes produced a missal that includes a formula for making a clamor.[13] The title is *Quomodo fit clamor pro tribulatione,* and the structure of the formula is decidedly Cluniac.[14] After the Offertory at the main mass the monks sang four responses, including the two listed in Bernard's customs, and after the fourth the text says, "or others appropriate for this matter." While these were sung all the bells were rung slowly three times. Then the monks lay prostrate and sang three psalms, the same three as at Cluny. The capitula are also nearly identical. The end differs from the Cluny formula because four short prayers of the type called "collect" are to be recited. A collect consists of an invocation to God, a petition stating the object of the prayer, and a conclusion. One of the four used at Saint-Amand is *Hostium nostrorum* ("Of our enemies"): "Break down, we beseech you, O Lord, the pride of all our enemies, and lay it low by the might of your right hand."[15]

The final example of this type of clamor, identified by that term, comes from the basilica of Saint-Martin of Tours. It occurs in a book of customs of that church and is unique in making a distinction be-

12. MS, Paris, BN, lat. 13874, f. 83r–v.

13. On missals and other types of liturgical books developed between the seventh and twelfth centuries, see Oscar Hardman, *A History of Christian Worship,* 2d ed. (London, 1948), pp. 85–91, 118–121.

14. MS, Valenciennes, BM, 121, f. 89r–v.

15. Fernand Cabrol, *Liturgical Prayer, Its History and Spirit* (London, 1925), pp. 37–40; Albert Blaise, *Le vocabulaire latin des principaux thèmes liturgiques* (Turnhout, 1966), p. 36; also Jungmann, *Mass of the Roman Rite,* 1:372–390, and ODCC, p. 313. The Latin original of the quoted collect is *Hostium nostrorum omnium quaesumus domine elide superbiam, et dextere tue virtute prosterne.* The other three collects at Saint-Amand are "Grant us" (*Concede nobis*), "We entreat you to render favorable" (*Propitiare quaesumus*), and "Almighty everlasting God" (*Omnipotens sempiterne Deus*).

tween a long and a short clamor.[16] For the moment we will look only
at the short version and come back to the long one further on. The
formula for this short clamor says: "When the church is not able to get
any change of behavior from some malefactor, then during the mass
after the Lord's Prayer but before the Pax Domini is said, a deacon says
the short [or little] clamor [*clamorem parvum*]." This short clamor is in
turn defined as "Almighty everlasting God, who alone looks after the
afflictions of men, and so forth" (*Omnipotens sempiterne Deus qui solus
respicis afflictiones hominum, et cetera*). While that is said the canons lie
on the floor, and the priest, kneeling before the altar, holds the consecrated wafer in his hands. They then say Psalm 122, the bells sound,
the priest says the capitula and the collect *Hostium nostrorum*, and all
join in saying "amen."

The centerpiece of this formula, the part identified as a "short
clamor," is the prayer of which only the first line is given. Fortunately,
the full text appears in a missal from another church at Tours, the
cathedral church then dedicated to Saints Maurice, Gatien, and Lidor.[17]
In this book it is identified not as a clamor but as a "Prayer when there
is persecution." It says:

> Almighty everlasting God [*Omnipotens sempiterne Deus*], who alone looks af-
> ter the afflictions of men calling out [*clamantes*] to you, who mercifully allows
> the tearful crying of minors and widows to reach your ears, take care of us,
> the servants of Saints Maurice, Gatien, and Lidor. Grant us justice in the
> matter of those who are disturbing and disrupting your sanctuary, unless
> they reconsider their behavior and make up for it.

This prayer, called a *parvus clamor* at Saint-Martin of Tours, appears
in several other manuscripts without the clamor label. A notably early
instance is found in a pontifical of the late ninth century from Sens,
now in Saint Petersburg. (A pontifical contains the forms for rites performed by a bishop.) The saints invoked in this version are Mary, Stephen, and Peter. Following the prayer, a charge is made against
malefactors who are devastating (*devastando*) and preying upon (*depre-*

16. See appendix C, text 13. *Rituel de Saint-Martin de Tours (XIIIe siècle)*, ed. A. Fleuret
(Paris, 1899–1901), p. 147. The date on this work is 1227, but it would be a mistake to
assume that the practices it describes were new at that time. The purpose of such a book
was not to report anything new but rather to record the customs of that church. We have
every reason to believe that these particular customs date from about two centuries earlier
than the book in which they were set down (and that has happened to survive).

17. MS, Paris, BN, lat. 10504, ff. 261r–263v.

dando) the goods and lands of the church of Sens. The four lines following, which have been scraped from the page, perhaps listed particular malefactors' names. Where the writing resumes, it goes on to say:

> May there come over them all the maledictions by which almighty God cursed those who said to the Lord God, "Stay away from us, we do not wish to know of your ways" (Job 21:14) and who said, "Let us take possession for ourselves of the sanctuary of God" (Ps. 82:13). May their lot and inheritance be perpetual flames with Dathan and Abiron, Judas and Pilate, Simon and Nero.

A wish that the transgressors have the company not of Christ and the saints but rather of the devil and his companions follows, and then: "May they be cursed in cities, may they be cursed in fields," and so on for eleven lines. Then comes a full page of specific curses, strongly reminiscent of those from Saint-Martial. Thus, by late in the ninth century the short clamor existed in fact but not yet in name, and it was inextricably linked with curses.[18]

This lengthy text from Sens continues with seven psalms, including Psalm 3, which Bernard of Cluny also used, and finishing with 108, perhaps the most maledictory of all psalms and for that reason frequently employed in texts of this sort (it will retain our attention later on). Then come the Kyrie, the Pater Noster, the capitula, and five collects: "Of our enemies" (*Hostium nostrorum*), which we have encountered already, plus "Of your church" (*Ecclesiae tuae*), "Almighty God" (*Omnipotens Deus*), "O God who" (*Deus qui*), and "Protect O Lord your servants" (*Protege Domine famulos tuos*).[19]

The Sens text is remarkable in many ways. First of all, there is its string of curses. Second, these curses are combined with a prayer, which is the same as one identified as a clamor at Tours. Third, the combination is a lengthy service of the sort called a clamor at Cluny, Corbie, and Saint-Amand. And fourth, we gain insight from it into the genre and purpose of the puzzling text written into a Bible at Saint-Martial.

18. See appendix C, text 1. MS, Saint Petersburg, Public Library, lat. 4° v.I. 35, ff. 101v–103v. Further on in the same manuscript, ff. 105v–107r, in an excommunication formula (discussed below), the names of the persons excommunicated are written in and still legible; the same is true of the Pontifical of Winchester, dated late tenth or early eleventh century; see MS, Rouen, BM, Y 7, f. 191v.

19. MS, Saint Petersburg, Public Library, lat. 4° v.I.35, ff. 103v–104r.

Most of these elements present in the Sens text can be found together in another document, extant only in a sixteenth-century copy, originally composed in the ninth or tenth century at the Abbey of Saint-Wandrille. This monastery is on the right bank of the Seine close to where the river enters the English Channel.[20] The text begins with a long historical introduction, going back to the foundation of the monastery in the seventh century. It recounts a trip by the saintly founder to Rome, where he received from Pope Martin I (649–655) some saints' relics, indulgences for pilgrims who came to the monastery, and a solemn malediction for use where and when needed against *molestatores, perturbatores, raptores, latrones et predones* of the monastery's possessions. Following this introduction, the text refers three times to itself as a malediction: "the tone of the malediction" (*tenor maledictionis*), "the way to carry out this malediction" (*modus exequendi hujusmodi maledictionem*), and "once the malediction is finished" (*finita maledictione*). The prayer *Omnipotens Deus qui solus respicis afflictionem omnium ad te clamantium* is headed "Invocation to God" (*Invocatio ad Deum*). The repertory of maledictions is the largest we have encountered so far. The seven psalms include Psalm 108. The five collects include *Hostium nostrorum* and another that recurs often in maledictory texts: "Almighty God, do not disdain your people who cry out to you in their affliction, but for the glory of your name be pleased to help us who are so sorely troubled" (*Ne despicias omnipotens Deus nos famulos tuos in afflictione clamantes, sed propter gloriam nominis tui tribulationibus succurre placatus*).[21]

To complete this survey of the textual elements of the clamor, we turn to a prayer that was probably regarded most widely as the defin-

20. MS, Rouen, BM, Y 208, ff. 148r–151v; it is edited in Lester K. Little, "Formules monastiques de malédiction aux IXe et Xe siècles," *Revue Mabillon* 58 (1975): 390–399. The text includes much information on the history of the abbey from its foundation in the seventh century until the year 837. Then began the period of Viking raids; Saint-Wandrille escaped destruction in 845, 851, 852, and 856–857 but was destroyed and abandoned in 858. It was occupied again in the middle of the tenth century, although continuous historical documentation dates from no earlier than 1025. See Ferdinand Lot, *Etudes critiques sur l'abbaye de Saint-Wandrille*, Bibliothèque de l'Ecole des hautes études 204 (Paris, 1913), pp. xxxv–lxv. Since the only surviving manuscript with the malediction dates from the early sixteenth century and is thus of little help in establishing the date of composition, the likely periods in which such a date could fall are the middle of the ninth century and the middle or later part of the tenth.

21. *Les oraisons du missel romain: Texte et histoire*, ed. Pierre Bruylants, 2 vols. (Louvain, 1952), 2:202.

ing element of a clamor, judging by the number of surviving manuscripts. It is the prayer identified in the Tours customal as the long
clamor (*magnus clamor*).[22] The oldest known manuscript in which it
appeared came from Chartres cathedral and was dated about 1020.[23]
The heading is similar to others already seen: "This is the order for
how a clamor is made" (*Hic est ordo qualiter fit clamor*). After the Lord's
Prayer and the Pax Domini, the Agnus Dei is omitted, the bread and
wine are prepared, the canons lie prostrate in the choir, and the priest,
flanked by the deacon and subdeacon, kneels before the altar. This
prayer, identified by its opening words, "In the spirit of humility" (*In
spiritu humilitatis*), is then recited:

> In the spirit of humility and with contrite soul we come before your sa-
> cred altar and your most holy body and blood, Lord Jesus, redeemer of
> the world, and we acknowledge ourselves guilty against you on account
> of our sins, for which we are justly afflicted. To you, Lord Jesus, we
> come; to you, prostrate, we clamor, because iniquitous and proud men,
> emboldened by their own followers, invade, plunder, and lay waste the
> lands of this your sanctuary and of other churches subject to it. They
> compel your poor ones who till these lands to live in pain and hunger
> and nakedness; they kill both by the sword and by torment. And our be-
> longings as well, by which we are supposed to live and which blessed
> souls bequeathed to this place for their own salvation, they seize and vi-
> olently take away from us. This your church, Lord, which in ancient
> times you founded and raised up in honor of the blessed and glorious
> ever-virgin Mary, sits in sadness. There is no one who can console it or
> liberate it except you, our God. So rise up, Lord Jesus, in support of us.
> Comfort us and help us. Attack those who are attacking us, and break
> the pride of those who afflict your place and us. You know, Lord, who
> they are and what their names are; their bodies and their hearts have
> been known to you alone from before they were born. Wherefore, Lord,
> judge them as you know how in your strength. Make them aware, to the
> extent that it pleases you, of their misdeeds, and free us by your mercy.
> Do not despise us, Lord, who call out [*clamantes*] to you in affliction, but
> because of the glory of your name and the mercy with which you
> founded this place and dedicated it in honor of your mother, visit us in
> peace and bring us out of our present distress.

There follow the now familiar psalms, capitula, and collects. Whether
accompanied by such other forms of devotion or standing alone, the

---

22. See appendix C, text 13. Fleuret, *Rituel de Saint-Martin*, pp. 147–148.

23. MS, Chartres, BM, nouv. acq. 4; René Merlet and J.-A. Clerval, *Un manuscrit chartrain du XIe siècle* (Chartres, 1893), pp. 237–238.

prayer *In spiritu humilitatis* has survived, with only slight variations, in texts emanating from over thirty different churches.[24] Three Norman monasteries, Jumièges, Saint-Etienne of Caen, and Sainte-Barbe-en-Auge, had a slightly different, and longer, version of this prayer; the longer version also appears in two relatively late copies from Cambrai cathedral.[25]

Thus the term "clamor," even in its restricted liturgical context, held different meanings. It was applied to two different prayers, *Omnipotens sempiterne Deus* and *In spiritu humilitatis*. The shorter prayer goes back at least to the ninth century; the longer one and the use of the term "clamor" to designate these liturgical forms date from the early eleventh century. During the eleventh century, monastic customals also used the term to designate a service consisting of one or both of these prayers plus psalms and other prayers, all based on the theme of tribulation. However the combination of texts was arranged, the whole was recited before the altar in an attitude of extreme humility. There the patron saint, materially present even if only in a miniscule fragment, and Jesus Christ, likewise fully present in the consecrated bread and wine, with both of them symbolically present in images, usually presided in places of honor. Even so, in yet another variant of the clamor, gesture and text were so combined as to withhold if not actually reverse such veneration.

Humiliation of Relics

Since the word "humble" and related words derive from *humus*, meaning ground or earth, the humble petition of the monks or canons for assistance was properly made with them stretched *per terram*, on the floor of the church. It was in the same posture that they had sought entry into the community as novices and later sought reintegration into

---

24. See appendix C, text 8, for the variant from Besançon. For texts that include this prayer, see appendix F under the following locations: Admont, Arras, Autun, Besançon, Caen, Cambrai, Chartres (Abbey of Saint-Père and cathedral), Cluny (not extant, but Farfa's is a copy), Compiègne, Constance, Dijon, Farfa, Fleury, Jumièges, Marcigny-sur-Loire, Poitiers, Reims, Remiremont, Rome (Trinity of the Irish and San Paolo), Saint-Denis, Sainte-Barbe, Senlis, Sens, Toul, Tours (cathedral and Saint-Martin), Trier, Verdun (Saint-Airy, Saint-Maur, and cathedral), and Vienna.

25. Jumièges: MS, Rouen, BM, A 293, ff. 149v–150v; Caen: MS, Montpellier, Bibl. de la Faculté de Médecine, 314, ff. 93r–94v; Sainte-Barbe: MS, Paris, Bibl. Sainte-Geneviève, 96, ff. 220r–221v; Cambrai: MSS, Cambrai, BM, 29, f. 286r–v, and 55, ff. 175v–176v.

the community after being punished for a misdeed.[26] Outside religious communities as well as within, the predominant political model was lordship, itself a projection of the imagined divine order. The fundamental transactions of power involved humble petitions from below and generous grants from above.[27] We are reminded that "below" and "above" are relative terms by the startling scenes in which the mighty made supplication: Emperor Henry IV standing barefoot in the snow before the castle in which the pope was staying at Canossa, or King Henry II of England, also barefoot, lying flat before the tomb of the assassinated archbishop of Canterbury.[28] Prostration was also the proper posture for a young warrior on the eve of his passage to knighthood.[29] The language of the prayer *In spiritu humilitatis*, although traditional and based upon earlier sources,[30] was thus vigorously contemporary as well as relevant to the theories and realities of power around the year 1000. But there is more in the way of clamor gestures than the monks' prostrating themselves, for they were also able to ground their patron saints. Two liturgical formulas for the clamor, one from Cluny via Italy and the other from Tours, include directions for the deposition of the saints' relics and the cross from the altar and for their subsequent "humiliation" on the floor in front of it. Directions for

26. *Rule for Monks*, 58:23 (entry), 44 (reintegration) in *RB*, pp. 268–269, 244–247. On the postures of prayer, see Richard C. Trexler, *The Christian at Prayer: An Illustrated Prayer Manual Attributed to Peter the Chanter (d. 1197)* (Binghamton, N.Y., 1987), especially pp. 35–43 on "body prayer."

27. On petitionary formulas, see Alain de Boüard, *Manuel de diplomatique française et pontificale*, 2 vols. (Paris, 1929–1948), 1:66–69; cf. Harry Bresslau and Hans W. Klewitz, *Handbuch der Urkundenlehre für Deutschland und Italien*, 2d ed., 2 vols. (Leipzig, 1912–1931; photo reprint, Berlin, 1968–1969), 2:25–27, 193–201.

28. Henry IV: *The Epistolae Vagantes of Pope Gregory VII*, ed. Herbert E. J. Cowdrey (Oxford, 1972), pp. 52–53, letter of February–March 1077 referring to the events at Canossa on 28 January and to Henry IV: "We were overcome by his humility and the manifold tokens of his repentance." Harald Zimmermann, *Der Canossagang von 1077, Wirkungen und Wirklichkeit* (Wiesbaden, 1975), pp. 163–175; Rudolf Schieffer, "Von Mailand nach Canossa: Ein Beitrag zur Geschichte der christlichen Herrscherbusse von Theodosius der Grosse bis zu Heinrich IV.," *Deutsches Archiv* 28 (1972): 333–370. Henry II: Gervase of Canterbury, *Chronica*, RS 73 (London, 1879), pt. 1:248–249; also William of Newburgh, *Historia rerum Anglicarum*, 2:35, "De memorabili humilitate regis Anglorum," RS 82 (London, 1884), pt. 1:187–188.

29. Maurice Keen, *Chivalry* (New Haven, Conn., 1984), p. 65. For the social ties involved in lordship, along with related symbols and gestures, see Geoffrey Koziol, *Begging Pardon and Favor: Ritual and Political Order in Early Medieval France* (Ithaca, N.Y., 1992), pp. 25–103; also Heinrich Fichtenau, *Living in the Tenth Century: Mentalities and Social Orders*, tr. Patrick J. Geary (Chicago, 1991), pp. 36–37.

30. See chapter 2, under "The Liturgy."

a related humiliation ceremony are extant from the cathedral of Rouen.[31]

The first of these formulas containing the humiliation comes from the Abbey of Farfa, situated in Sabina, north of Rome; it is in a customal copied probably during the 1020s from a customal of Cluny that is no longer extant.[32] The Farfa customal indeed contains two chapters that are relevant to the history of the clamor. The first of these is titled "How Prayers on Account of Calamities Are to Be Done," and it reads thus:

> An ecclesiastical clamor to God should be made in this way. At the principal mass, after the Lord's Prayer, the ministers of the church cover the pavement before the altar with a coarse cloth, and on this they place the crucifix, the text of the Gospels, and the bodies of the saints. And each cleric lies prostrate on the floor silently singing Psalm 73. Meanwhile two bells are rung by the church's custodians. The priest stands alone before the newly consecrated body and blood of the Lord and in front of the aforementioned relics of the saints, and in a loud voice he begins to say this clamor: "In the spirit of humility . . . [here follows the full text of the familiar prayer] . . . and deliver us from our present distress. Amen." The clamor being thus finished, let the relics be put back in their proper places and let the priest say silently the collect "Deliver us we beseech you, O Lord" [*Libera nos quaesumus domine*].[33]

The following chapter is titled "Again, concerning the Same Matter, in Another Version." This title may indicate that the Cluniac model

31. On the humiliation of saints' relics, see the brief treatment by Nicole Herrmann-Mascard, *Les reliques des saints: Formation coutumière d'un droit* (Paris, 1975), pp. 226–228, and the much fuller analysis by Patrick J. Geary, "Humiliation of Saints," in *Saints and Their Cults: Studies in Religious Sociology, Folklore and History*, ed. Stephen Wilson (Cambridge, 1983), pp. 123–140.

32. *Liber tramitis aevi Odilonis abbatis*, ed. Peter Dinter, Corpus consuetudinum monasticarum 10 (Siegburg, 1980). During the abbacy of Odilo at Cluny (994–1049), Abbot Joseph of Montepuli in Sabina sent a monk named John to Cluny to make a copy of the customs of Cluny, either by copying one book of customs or by making a composite copy from different books. John's mission took place during the second or third decade of the eleventh century. The whereabouts of the copy he made, as well as of the original book(s) he copied, are not known. But a copy of John's copy was made for the Abbey of Farfa, and it in turn underwent at least two revisions, one after the abbot of Farfa visited Cluny himself in the 1030s and the other as the result of a visit to Farfa in the 1050s by a monk from Cluny named Martin. The earliest surviving manuscript of this much revised copy of a copy dates from the third quarter of the eleventh century. The resulting text, long regarded as a customal of Farfa, remains essentially, in spite of the many hands involved in its production, yet another customal of Cluny.

33. Ibid., pp. 244–247. See appendix C, text 9. The Farfa MS is Vat. lat. 6808. An abbreviated copy of this text was made for Saint Paul's outside the Walls in Rome: MS, Rome, San Paolo f.l.m., Archivio, 92, p. 167.

contained two versions, or that the monk-copyist read two different sets of customs at Cluny. In any case, this chapter specifies:

> On a Sunday, after the chapter meeting, there is a signal and prayers; then the priest goes with the young boys to prepare for mass, and then other bells are rung. During the mass, after the reading of the Gospel, the Credo is said. When that is done, let the librarian [in Latin, *armarius*] get up in the pulpit and announce to the people the wickedness of the persecutors.

Thus far this chapter resembles very closely the parallel and later one in Bernard's customs; but then it changes:

> Now another brother comes forward and reads the anathemas and maledictions from the New as well as the Old Testament according to their utility and to the instructions received from the apostolic see and the approval given by neighboring bishops, malediction for those unwilling to change their ways and benediction for those who prepare to make amends. When this reading is finished, let the candles be extinguished and all the bells be rung.

The monks lie on the floor and recite psalms, capitula, and collects.

Specifications for humiliating saints' relics appear in the same text as the *magnus clamor* in the Tours customal, under the heading "Concerning the Long Clamor and the Placing of Relics on the Floor."[34] Except for the unique qualification of *magnus*, little about this clamor differs from what we have seen. After the Pater Noster and before the Pax Domini, the deacon says the great or long clamor, here defined as the prayer *In spiritu humilitatis*; all in the choir are lying on the floor, and the priest stands before the altar holding in his hands the consecrated bread. When the deacon finishes, the canons say Psalm 51, "Why do you glory in wickedness?" (*Quid gloriaris*), bells ring, and the capitula and the collects conclude the ceremony.

The actual humiliation in the Tours version does not take place during these proceedings, or indeed during any of the regular services, but instead occurs early in the morning after prime. Once everyone is gathered in the choir, they begin with seven psalms and a litany. Then the leading personages in the community and the ministers of the church place the silver crucifix and all the reliquaries of the saints on the floor in front of the subdeacon's seat. Next they place thorns on top of and all around the tomb of Saint Martin. A wooden crucifix,

---

34. See appendix C, text 13. Fleuret, *Rituel de Saint-Martin*, pp. 147–148.

also circled by thorns, is placed in the middle of the nave. All the doors of the church except one minor entry are closed and barricaded with thorns. The text makes no mention of the restoration of the reliquaries, crucifixes, or doorways to their usual disposition. The separation of the humiliation in this version from any particular office suggests that this condition of humiliation could last through the full daily cycle of services, or indefinitely. The blocking of the doors suggests a liturgical strike.

In the 1230s, a further variant on humiliation occurred in directions given by Archbishop Maurice of Rouen for a humiliation to be carried on throughout his archdiocese on account of spoliations of churches. In this variant, images of Mary were to be placed on a chair (not on the floor) next to the altar in the nave. Except for the cautious reserve expressed in this use of a chair, the cult of Mary, which over the preceding century had made a spectacular entry upon the liturgical scene, was therefore now clearly coming of age.[35]

Excommunication and Anathema

Excommunication has a much longer history than does the clamor; it came into use well before the earliest form of clamor and has by now far outlived the last. Between the tenth and thirteenth centuries, however, their roughly parallel histories converged. A hint of the resulting confusion can be seen in the very first curse of the Saint-Martial clamor, which says: "May they be cursed, excommunicated, and anathematized."[36]

By the third century at the latest, the church had sufficient sense of itself as a community to assume the power to exclude certain persons from its company and privileges. Separation from the community, like any other form of penance, was a grave, public matter, prescribed only by competent (meaning usually episcopal) authority. Yet no matter how terrible excommunication could seem, it always left open the possibility of repentance, forgiveness, and reintegration. The figures of speech commonly used to explain the purpose of excommunication

35. *Sanctae Rotomagensis ecclesiae concilia ac synodalia decreta*, ed. François Pommeraye (Rouen, 1677), p. 219.
36. See appendix C, text 7. On excommunication and related concepts, see Roger E. Reynolds, "Rites of Separation and Reconciliation in the Early Middle Ages," in *Segni e riti nella chiesa altomedievale occidentale*, Settimane di studio del Centro italiano di studi sull'Alto Medioevo 32 (Spoleto, 1987), pp. 405–437; also Elisabeth Vodola, *Excommunication in the Middle Ages* (Berkeley, Calif., 1986), pp. 1–20.

evoked discipline and medicine rather than punishment and vindictiveness. To be sure, there were degrees of excommunication, ranging from exclusion from participation in the Eucharist to a more general social exclusion. The proper attitudes of other members of the community varied according to these degrees; at the more moderate end of the spectrum they were to comfort excommunicants and encourage their return to full status; at the further end they were to avoid all contact with such persons under penalty of sharing their fate.[37]

The term "anathema" came to be associated with the more advanced degrees of excommunication. From its original meaning of offerings or of things devoted to the deity, and thus not for common use, it had in New Testament times come to refer to things and persons to be rejected and damned. Saint Paul used it to denounce those who did not love the Lord (1 Cor. 16:22) and those who preached a gospel different from the one he preached (Gal. 1:8). This anger and intolerance are only the reverse image of the severity of some of his more zealous Jewish compatriots, who swore to kill him for preaching a message other than the Mosaic law (Acts 21:27–28, 23:12–15).[38]

The earliest use of anathema as a form of ecclesiastical discipline was at the Council of Elmira in about 305. Subsequently it was regularly used against those defined as heretics. Anathemas against the Arians were appended to the Nicene Creed. The councils of the patristic era regularly dealt with definitions of orthodoxy and anathematized those who did not qualify. The same continued to be the case in the councils held at Toledo in the Visigothic kingdom and also in the Frankish councils. Anticipatory anathemas against future heretics were added to those that went directly into use.[39]

In the seventh and eighth centuries, when Celtic ideas on penance started to gain currency in Frankish Gaul, penance began simultaneously to become repeatable and relatively private; for the same reason, excommunication became correspondingly less permanent and less

---

37. F. Donald Logan, "Excommunication," in *DMA* 4:536–538; Walter Doskocil, *Der Bann in der Urkirche: Eine rechtsgeschichtliche Untersuchung*, Münchener theologische Studien 3, Kanonistische Abt., 11 (Munich, 1958); Kenneth Hein, *Eucharist and Excommunication: A Study in Early Christian Doctrine and Discipline* (Frankfurt, 1973).

38. Heim, *Eucharist and Excommunication*, p. 105.

39. *Decrees of the Ecumenical Councils*, ed. Tanner, 1:5; *Concilios visigóticos e hispanoromanos*, ed. José Vives (Barcelona, 1963), for thirty-seven councils from Elvira (c. 300–306) to Toledo XVII (694), examples on pp. 10, 27, 446. *Concilia antiqua Galliae*, ed. Jacques Sirmond, 3 vols. (Paris, 1629; photo reprint Darmstadt, 1970), 1:43–44, 341–342.

public. Bishops in the Frankish kingdom made excommunication something less grave than it had been in the early church; it consisted of a temporary exclusion from the sacraments until amends were made.

At the same time anathema, once largely reserved for heretics, became a kind of first-class excommunication that kept up the old standards, including the public ceremony and separation both from the sacraments and from the community of Christians. A council held at Tours in the 560s warned that an unrepentent usurper of ecclesiastical goods would die "not only excommunicate but also anathematized."[40] This phrase acknowledging the greater force of anathema became common, although it did not have a universally accepted meaning. The lesser exclusion usually referred to religious contacts and the greater to all social contacts. In 1027 the Council of Toulouges set excommunication as the sanction for a certain infraction, adding, though, that if it produced no result within three months, anathema would be joined to it.[41] Excommunication and anathema retained this relationship in Gratian's *Decretum* (c. 1140), with anathema still seen as both a more elaborate and a more terrible form of sanction than "mere" excommunication.[42] To some extent this division was perpetuated in the distinction made by canon lawyers early in the thirteenth century between major and minor excommunication, "major" corresponding roughly to what had previously been called anathema.[43]

In about 850 a collector and falsifier of church law known as Benedict the Levite defined anathema as "nothing other than separation from God"; it was the appropriate punishment for the truly obdurate plunderer of church property.[44] This punishment was spelled out at the Council of Saint-Laurent-lès-Mâcon in 855; it involved not only exclusion from contact with Christian society and the church's rejection of any offerings from the offender, but also withholding of the proper burial with psalms and prayers that was usual for the faithful, and no mention afterward of the offender's name at the altar in the prayers

---

40. Mansi 9:804.

41. Mansi 19:484.

42. Gratian, *Decretum*, Causa 3, quest. 4, can. 12 (*CIC* 1:514).

43. *Decretales Gregorii IX*, lib. 5, tit. 39, cap. 59 (*CIC* 1:912). For excommunication as understood by trained canon lawyers during and after the twelfth century, see Vodola, *Excommunication in the Middle Ages*, pp. 28–43.

44. *MGH, Capit.* 2:97. On the False Decretals, to which Benedict was one of the contributors, see chapter 2, under "Canon Law."

said for the faithful dead.[45] In councils held at Meaux in 845 and both at Paris and at Epernay the year following, anathema was defined as "condemnation to eternal death."[46] Thus defined, anathema was too terrible for a bishop to decide upon alone. Only with the consent of his archbishop or his fellow bishops could he impose anathema, and then only for a mortal crime and upon someone who would respond to no other form of correction. This unrelenting definition of anathema from the 840s entered into the principal canon law collections: the *Decretum* compiled by Burchard of Worms at the start of the eleventh century, the *Panormia* and the *Decretum* assembled later in the century by Ivo of Chartres, and the *Decretum* of Gratian in about 1140.[47]

Anathema had the further peculiarity of often being followed by the word *maranatha*, an Aramaic expression long generally understood as related to the Second Coming and the end of time, and now specifically thought to be a prayer for the Parousia, meaning "O Lord, come."[48] A few texts acknowledge a need to explain the meaning of this term, such as the one used against the murderers of the archbishop of Reims in the year 900: "Let them be anathema maranatha and let them perish in the Second Coming of the Lord."[49] The connection with the Parousia is there made, even if not explained. A similar connection, presented as a definition, occurs at the end of an excommunication formula in an eleventh-century pontifical from Cologne: "May they be anathema maranatha, that is, may they perish at the Second Coming of the Lord" (*Sintque anathema maranatha idest pereant in secundo adventu domini*).[50] Yet

45. *Die Konzilien der karolingischen Teilreiche, 843–859*, ed. Wilfried Hartmann (*MGH, Conc.* 3:376).

46. Ibid., p. 111 (for Meaux and Paris); *MGH, Leg.* 1:392 (for Epernay).

47. Burchard of Worms, *Decretum*, 11:10 (*PL* 140:861–862); Ivo of Chartres, *Decretum*, 14:80, and idem, *Panormia*, 5:93 (*PL* 161:848, 1232); Gratian, *Decretum*, Causa. 11, quest. 3, can. 41 (*CIC* 1:655). After citing the definition of anathema given at Meaux, Reynolds observes, in "Rites of Separation and Reconciliation," p. 407, n. 5, "Hartmann notes that the designation of anathema as eternal death appears nowhere else." Indeed Hartmann, in *Konzilien*, p. 111, n. 166, says that that definition appears nowhere else but adds that Hinschius "names at least only this text." The reference is to Paul Hinschius, *Das Kirchenrecht der Katholiken und Protestanten in Deutschland*, 6 vols. (Berlin, 1869–1897), 5:7, n. 10, where there are references to Meaux, Epernay, and Gratian. Vodola says in *Excommunication in the Middle Ages*, p. 14, "Several ninth-century councils proclaimed that anathema meant eternal death," and the accompanying note says: "E.g., the 846 Council of Epernay."

48. *ODCC*, s.v. "Maranatha."

49. Mansi 18B:670.

50. MS, Vat. Ottob. lat. 167, f. 103v; cf. MS, Valenciennes, BM, 107, f. 83v.

such textual elaborations and definitions were exceptional, and it is likely that phonetics can shed more light here than philology, because the word was more often exploited for its sound than for its meaning. Saint Paul did not translate it into Greek when he wrote, "If any man love not our Lord Jesus Christ, let him be anathema, maranatha" (1 Cor. 16:22). Nor was it subsequently translated into Latin or into the modern vernacular languages. It became instead a mysterious term, without precise meaning, repeating most of the sound of "anathema," which it normally followed. *Anathema maranatha* thus shares some of the magical qualities of such incantations as *abracadabra* and *hocus-pocus dominocus, maranatha* serving to intensify the terror exuded by the word *anathema*. The compiler of a modern dictionary of medieval Latin, interested not in the original Aramaic meaning but in what the term signified during the European Middle Ages, defines *maranatha* simply as a malediction formula.[51]

The appropriate moment for pronouncing an excommunication came during the mass right after the reading of the Gospel, when the sermon, if there was to be one, was delivered. That point also marked the conclusion of the Mass of the Catechumens (Initiates), and one might surmise that this was the moment of optimum public presence and attention at the mass. Archbishop Hincmar of Reims (845–882) noted, however, that in his experience malefactors (who came to church only out of habit) rushed away as soon as the Gospel had been read; therefore he notified his clergy that when they had to read a formal warning or else a declaration of excommunication against some malefactor, they do it not in the customary way, after the Gospel, but earlier—right after the reading of the Epistle.[52]

The critical period for the formation of excommunication formulas was in the decades immediately before and after the year 900, roughly a century before the coalescing of the clamor. In the Sens pontifical in Saint Petersburg, right after the short form of the clamor and the

51. *Mediae Latinitatis lexicon*, ed. Niermeyer, p. 651. Cf. Du Cange 5:258, s.v. "Maranatha," where he first gives the "Syriac" meaning: "Dominus venit," followed by this definition: "Imprecationis genus quod in chartarum infractores intentari solitum erat." See also Wade T. Wheelock, "Sacred Language," in *ER* 8:441. A quite common linking of the verbs "excommunicate" and "anathematize" is found in a short formula that begins by invoking the authority of the Trinity, the Virgin, Saint Peter, and the patron saint of the church. An example from the Abbey of Saint-Thierry is found in MS, Reims, BM, 349, f. 138v.
52. *PL* 126:101.

lengthy string of curses, there is an excommunication formula that begins with a lament about the enemies the church faces and then a series
of charges against a specific group of malefactors—names included.
The text comes quickly to the point: "We excommunicate them and
strike them with the sword of anathema . . . we anathematize them by
the Father and the Son and the Holy Ghost." Restrictions then follow
against their entering churches, having masses said, having contact
with other Christians, receiving priestly assistance if they are dying, or
getting a Christian burial if they do die. Then comes the familiar litany
beginning, "May they be cursed in town, may they cursed in the fields,
amen." The curse extends to their homes and granaries; it closes by
urging the Lord to strike them with poverty, fever, extreme cold and
heat, and unrelieved anxiety as well as to persecute them until they
perish. "And as this light is put out in the eyes of men," it concludes,
"so may their light be extinguished in perpetuity. Amen."[53]

A nearly identical version of this formula is found in a sacramentary
of the earlier half of the tenth century from Sens, this one in the Vatican.
The formula lacks the opening paragraph about enemies of the church,
but it continues and becomes a much longer text, combining the
prayers, collects, and capitula that constituted parts of various clamors.
The whole is gathered under the title "Malediction against Persecutors of the Church of God" (*Maledictio adversus ecclesiae dei persequtores*)
and is written in the margins of two facing pages, running over by a
few lines onto the margin of the following page. On the two facing
pages it occupies all the blank space at the top, down the sides, and
at the bottom. This marginal writing is small and difficult to read,
but the first two words of the title, *Maledictio adversus*, stand out clearly.
The original writing of the main liturgical text, however, is consistently
clear; the most prominent word on this particular double-page spread,
at the top of the right-hand page, is *Credo* ("I believe"), indicating the
beginning of the Creed. Since the saying of the Creed, when it is said,
follows the reading of the Gospel, this excommunication formula, titled
"Malediction," was placed in the margins of the service book at precisely the point where a sentence of excommunication was to be pronounced. Also, as we observed earlier, the Farfa formula for a clamor

---

53. MS, Saint Petersburg, Public Library, lat. 4° v.I. 35, ff. 105v–107r. The formula was
transcribed and published by Luc d'Achery in his *Spicilegium sive collectio veterum aliquot
scriptorum*, 13 vols. (Paris, 1655–1677), 10:635–636.

had the *armarius* begin the proceedings right after the Creed was said. Liturgical books tend, as historical sources, to be timeless and impersonal, unspecific and repetitious. But here is an exception to be treasured, where a glimpse at the Credo page tells of a tenth-century canonical scribe who sought out that specific page on which to record this text, so important for the defense of Sens cathedral (see Fig. 4).[54]

Meanwhile the cathedral church of Reims had available in 900 a particularly well composed and also harsh formula; it has a lucid statement of authority at the beginning and a noteworthy reference to biblical maledictions at the closing:

> In the name of the Lord and by the power of the Holy Spirit and the authority divinely granted bishops by blessed Peter, prince of the apostles, we separate them from the bosom of holy mother church and we condemn them with an anathema of perpetual malediction, that they might not have help from any man or contact with any Christian. May they be cursed in town and cursed in the fields. May their barns be cursed and may their bones be cursed. May the fruit of their loins be cursed as well as the fruit of their lands, their herds of cattle and their flocks of sheep. May they be cursed going in and coming out. May they be cursed at home and may they be fugitives outside their homes. May they drain out through their bowels, like the faithless and unhappy Arius. May there come upon them all those maledictions by which the Lord through Moses threatened transgressors of the divine law.

Then comes the anathema we have already seen: "Let them be anathema maranatha, and let them perish in the Second Coming of the Lord. May they endure whatever curses are provided in the sacred canons and the apostolic decrees for homicide and sacrilege." The text then warns the faithful against having anything to do with the malefactors and thus concludes: "And so as these lights thrown from our hands are extinguished today, so may their lights be extinguished in eternity."[55]

The first known collection of such formulas dates from about 906 and was the work of a German abbot named Regino of Prüm (c. 845–915). Regino was a compiler: he had to his credit a historical chronicle, a catalog of liturgical chants, and a collection of canon law. For the last of these he assembled a dossier of four excommunication formulas and two appropriate episcopal allocutions for use with them. One formula

54. MS, Vat., Reg. lat. 567, ff. 48v–49v, where there is a lenten baptismal mass.
55. Mansi 18B:669–670.

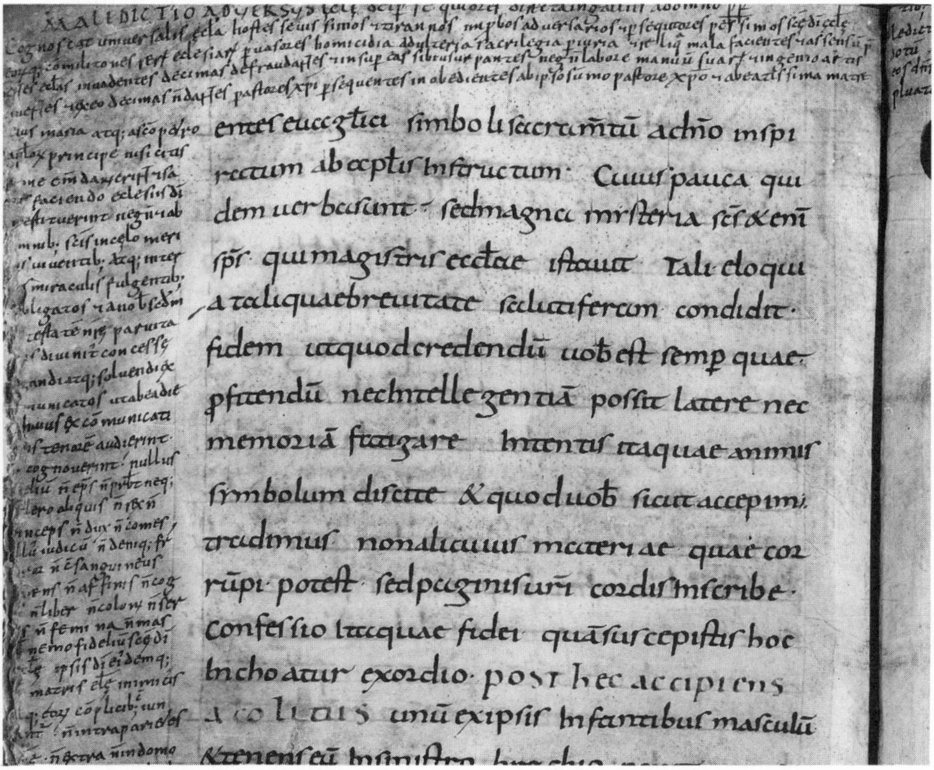

Figure 4. A marginal curse in a sacramentary written in the tenth century for the cathedral church of Sens, open at the point where, in the top margin of the left-hand page (shown above) there begins a cursing formula with the words: "Malediction against the persecutors of the church of God" (*Maledictio adversus ecclesiae Dei persequutores*). At the top of the right-hand page (not shown), the formula continues in the margin, while the central text on the page consists of the Creed. MS, Vat., Reg. lat. 567, ff. 48v–49r; by permission of the Biblioteca Apostolica Vaticana.

is for an *excommunicatio brevis* that consists of just one sentence; the key phrase is "we eliminate from the bosom of holy mother church." Two others, both called simply *excommunicatio*, stress the justification for the excommunication and the specific prohibitions it entails. The fourth formula, a *terribilior excommunicatio*, is addressed to murderers and to violators of the churches of God and invaders of and predators upon their possessions. Its terms are a combination of the maledictions noted in the Sens and Reims formulas. Regino's compilation was decisive, for most of his section on excommunication was absorbed into the *Romano-Germanic Pontifical*, which was assembled at Mainz between 950 and 969 and was thereafter frequently copied. His compilation also passed into the major law collections of Burchard of Worms and Ivo of Chartres in the following century.[56]

Along with the formulas and speeches, Regino includes a set of directions for what happens after the reading of a sentence. The first of these directions states that all present should say three times *Amen* or *Fiat, fiat* or *Anathema sit*. The next makes explicit what is implied by the several concluding phrases about extinguishing lights mentioned thus far: "Twelve priests should gather about the bishop holding burning candles in their hands, which upon the conclusion of the anathema or excommunication they should throw to the floor and stamp on with their feet." Then "the bishop is to explain this excommunication to the people in common language" (*episcopus plebi ipsam excommunicationem communibus verbis debet explanare*) and to warn them against having any contact with the excommunicated person—henceforth regarded as not a Christian but a pagan—under penalty of suffering the same fate. Finally, the bishop is to send letters to the priests of neighboring parishes telling of this excommunication, which they in turn are to announce publicly on Sundays after the reading of the Gospel.[57]

Not long after the time of Regino there came into circulation a letter containing an excommunication formula dense with curses that purported to be sent by a pope named Leo, presumably Leo VII (936–939). The first of the two main variants of this letter is addressed by name to five archbishops (of Bourges, Lyons, Reims, Sens, and Tours), who

---

56. See appendix C, text 3. Regino of Prüm, *Libri duo de synodalibus causis et disciplinis ecclesiasticis*, ed. F. G. A. Wasserschleben (Leipzig, 1840), pp. 369–375; *PRG* 1:308–314; Burchard of Worms, *Decretum*, 11:2–7 (*PL* 140: 856–860); Ivo of Chartres, *Decretum*, 3:126, 14: 75–79 (*PL* 161:226, 844–848).

57. Regino, *Libri duo de synodalibus*, pp. 371–372.

together with Leo VII all coincided in office for about a year, from mid-938 to mid-939. It calls upon these prelates and the bishops subordinate to them to assist Abbot Odo and his monks in defending the possessions of Saint-Benôit-sur-Loire at Fleury, in particular that they bind with the chain of anathema anyone who disturbs those possessions. Moreover, lest excommunication by a few bishops not suffice, the same authority is extended to the abbots of the region. Just over a decade later, this letter was refashioned for a monastery in the Pyrenees much influenced by Fleury, the Abbey of Ripoll. The name of Pope Leo was on that letter too, and the addressees were the same five prelates, but with the addition of the names of the bishops of Barcelona, Elne, Gerona, Narbonne, Urgel, and Vich, who were in office simultaneously between 949 and 952. The second variant of the Pope Leo letter was addressed to the archbishops and their suffragans and to the abbots and congregations of monks *in Francia*; one surviving copy was sent to Saint-Martin of Trier, and another to Saint-Maximin of Trier. In the Saint-Maximin manuscript, the Pope Leo anathema immediately follows a brief version of the clamor beginning *In spiritu humilitatis*. The second variant of this spurious papal document gained wide diffusion through its absorption into the *Romano-Germanic Pontifical*.[58]

At the Council of Reims in 990 Archbishop Arnulf issued a warning to despoilers of the church of Reims and a special anathema for use against them. The tone of both is decidedly angry: "Like it or not, your Lord himself, whose judgment you cannot escape, will in your case be witness, judge, and avenger." The charge is of the most reckless looting—of desiring everything they set eyes on and stealing anything they can lay their hands on. Still, the most vigorous denunciation is reserved for the malefactors' cruel indifference to the fate of their victims: to the tears of the widows and orphans and the pleas of those they have made hungry and homeless.[59]

Not only was there variety in liturgical formulas, but we should

---

58. See appendix C, text 4. *Papsturkunden, 896–1046,* ed. Harald Zimmermann, 3 vols. (Vienna, 1984–1989), 1:154–162; *PRG* 1:315–317, where the patron of the possessions to be protected is given as Saint Peter, but with no indication of which particular monastery, if any, is intended. For Saint-Maximin the manuscript is now lost, but a description of part of it by Hampe includes this pairing of the clamor with the Pope Leo text; see Karl Hampe, "Reise nach England vom Juli 1895 bis Februar 1896," *Neues Archiv* 22 (1897): 410–415.

59. See appendix C, text 6. Mansi 19:95–96.

notice that variety was attained in good measure through extensive, sometimes mutual, borrowing. The result is disorder in the classifying of liturgical texts. The neat categories of the modern discipline of canon law are frustrated by the shifting definitions and usages found in texts from before the time of the Scholastic organizers of law and theology.

A ceremony of excommunication, however simple or elaborate, is a sentencing; the presiding cleric sentences a person, who is subject to his jurisdiction, to this particular ecclesiastical punishment. To repeat the ceremony would add nothing, at least of a juridical nature, to the original sentence. But the drama of cursing and clamoring was eminently repeatable, and for purposes other than juridical. Such repetition was present in one of the excommunication formulas collected by Regino and later included in the *Romano-Germanic Pontifical*. It says at the end, just after the escape clause: "If he is not frightened by this excommunication and he fails to leave alone the flock entrusted to our care, we shall not fail to carry out such incantations daily."[60]

Malediction, excommunication, and anathema are joined under the heading "clamor" in a Spanish manuscript dated 1116. It is the rule for a confraternity drawn up at the Abbey of Oña, in Castile north of Burgos. The members of this religious association, which included monks, clerics, and laypeople, women as well as men, engaged in corporate worship, shared meals, gave mutual support in times of difficulty, and above all, if the length of this provision in the rule is an accurate indicator, participated fully in all the rites surrounding the death and burial of a confrere. The rule provides for the expulsion of a member for serious cause, after which the members in good standing are to look upon the one expelled as an enemy. But in the case of someone who, because of pride, no longer wishes to be under the discipline of the confraternity and wants to leave it, the reaction is far more grave. The abbot must try three times to dissuade the individual who desires to leave. If all three of these attempts should fail, then the members must assemble in the church and "together make a great clamor before God. While on their knees, let them raise their hands toward heaven and curse him. And let the abbot excommunicate him. And may he be cursed, excommunicated, and anathematized." In this case no rite called a "clamor" is joined to a rite of excommunication,

60. *PRG* 1:313.

but a group cursing and excommunicating of someone is identified as "making a great clamor."[61]

There are texts from Compiègne, Jumièges, and Toul that tie excommunication formulas closely to the clamor. Two of these from Compiègne each bear the title "Prayers on Account of the Suffering of the Church" (*Pro tribulatione ecclesiae preces*).[62] They begin with four short prayers for use in times of trouble, continue with the clamor starting *In spiritu humilitatis*, and conclude with a brief excommunication:

> By the authority of the Father and of the Son and of the Holy Spirit and of the Blessed Mary ever virgin and of the blessed apostles Peter and Paul and of the holy martyrs Cornelius and Cyprianus, we excommunicate [them] from the company of all Christians, and we bar them from the thresholds of the holy church of God so that they undergo eternal punishments with Dathan and Abiron and with those who said to the Lord God: "Stay away from us, we do not wish to know of your ways." And so may their lights be extinguished forever and ever unless they come forward and make amends.

The text from the Abbey of Jumièges, which is preceded by a handsome double-page of maledictions (see Fig. 5), joins together a clamor beginning *In spiritu humilitatis* with an excommunication formula.[63] The text from Toul has the added interest of being partly in French. It is found in a pontifical that is dated 1420, and it bears the title "Malediction in French against Those Who Cause Trouble for the Church" (*Malediction en fransois contre les malefactours de laglise*). Certain troubles are spelled out, and then the troublemakers are "cursed from the mouth of God with the curse by which God, through the mouths of the holy prophets, cursed those who went against his commandments." These curses include the litany beginning *Maldis soient ils en villes et en citey*. The text switches to Latin and announces "another malediction against malefactors of the church," and this "malediction" happens to be the text beginning *In spiritu humilitatis*. It in turn leads into a formula, which includes the litany of curses whose operative phrase is "we excommunicate, we anathematize, and we exclude from the holy church of God."[64]

---

61. MS, London, BL, Add. 30044, ff. 66v–72r. Gerald Bonner of the School of Religious Studies at the Catholic University of America very kindly brought this text to my attention and provided a copy of his transcription for me to compare with my own.

62. MSS, Paris, BN, lat. 17319, f. 216r–v, and nouv. acq. lat. 2358, ff. 36v–37v.

63. MS, Rouen, BM, A 293, ff. 149v–150v.

64. See appendix C, text 14. MS, Paris, BN, lat. 12079, ff. 265v–272r.

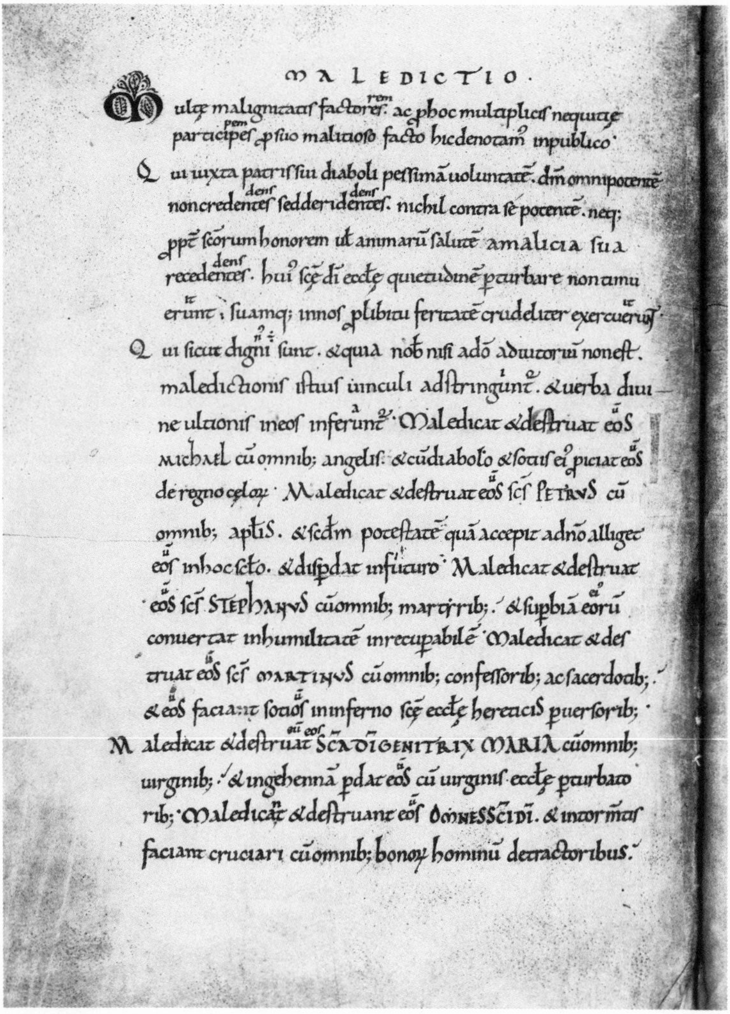

Figure 5. A monastic malediction clearly identified in an eleventh-century gospel book from the Norman monastery of Jumièges. A litany of curses begins halfway through line ten: "May Michael with all the angels curse and destroy them" (*Maledicat et destruat eos Michael cum omnibus angelis*); it goes on to invoke Saint Peter with all the apostles (*sanctus Petrus cum omnibus apostolis*); Saint Stephen with all the martyrs (*sanctus Stephanus cum omnibus martiribus*); Saint Martin with all the confessors (*sanctus Martinus cum omnibus confessoribus*); the holy mother of God Mary with all the virgins (*sancta Dei genitrix Maria cum omnibus virginibus*); and all the saints of God (*omnes sancti Dei*). MS, Rouen, BM, A 293, f. 148v; Collection Bibliothèque Municipale de Rouen.

The combination of humiliation and malediction with excommunication appears in a notice drawn up in 1210 by the canons of Chartres describing the rites observed in dealing with lay troublemakers. According to this notice, parish priests could continue to celebrate masses, but with humble, submissive voices and no singing. At the cathedral—where, as in monasteries, the usual services were suspended—the altar was cleared off and the most holy relic of the Virgin (a shift) was placed on the floor before the altar, along with other saints' relics and the crucifix. Every day a priest of that church would get up in the pulpit and pronounce against the perpetrators of sacrilege the sentence of excommunication with its horrendous malediction, which is called a "great excommunication" (*excommunicationis sententiam et ejusdem horrende maledictionis que excommunicatio magna dicitur*). This is done with candles lighted and the bells ringing in churches throughout the city.[65]

The mixing of curse and excommunication is even indulged in for rhetorical effect in a formula used by Pope Benedict VIII against vassals of the count of Provence in 1014; these vassals were seeking from the count control of lands that happened also to be claimed by the Abbey of Saint-Gilles:

May they be cursed in the four corners of the earth. May they be cursed in the East, disinherited in the West, interdicted in the North, and excommunicated in the South. May they be cursed in the day and excommunicated at night. May they be cursed at home and excommunicated while away, cursed in standing and excommunicated in sitting, cursed in eating, drinking and sleeping, excommunicated in waking, cursed when they work and excommunicated when they rest. May they be cursed in the spring and excommunicated in the summer, cursed in the autumn and excommunicated in the winter.[66]

65. *Cartulaire de Notre-Dame de Chartres*, ed. Eugène de Lépinois and Lucien Merlet, 3 vols. (Chartres, 1862–1865), 2:56–58.

66. Benedict VIII, ep. 32 (*PL* 139:1630–1632). For more examples of maledictions included in excommunication formulas, see liturgical books from the following places: Amiens (MS, Paris, BN, lat. 13221, f. 105v); Bobbio (MS, Turin, Biblioteca Nazionale Universitaria, F.III.15, f. 47r–v); Capua (MS, Vat., Barberini lat. 697, f. 44r–v); Reims (MS, Reims, BM, 349, f. 138v); Saint-Quentin (MS, Saint-Omer, BM, 794, ff. 41v–42r); and Tours (MS, Tours, BM, 196, ff. 289v–290r). Two vivid formulas belonging to the canons of Saint-Julien of Brioude are found in Augustin Chassaing, ed., *Spicilegium Brivatense: Recueil de documents historiques relatifs au Brivadois et à l'Auvergne* (Paris, 1886), pp. 22–25.

In Chaucer's time "to cursen," in Middle English, still meant "to excommunicate."[67]

Geography of Maledictory Formulas

To establish the chronological and geographical coordinates of liturgical clamors and related maledictory formulas, we need review what is known of their approximate dates of composition and then inquire into the kinds of churches for which these formulas were written and the locations of those churches.

The earliest example of the clamor whose main prayer is *Omnipotens sempiterne Deus qui solus* is found in a manuscript of Sens dating from the late ninth century. The earliest example of the *In spiritu humilitatis*, as mentioned earlier, is from Chartres cathedral and dated about 1020; the same manuscript also includes the earliest extant use of "clamor" as the name for a liturgy. The formula for a clamor with humiliation of relics that an Italian monk copied at Cluny was available to him at the latest in the 1030s.[68] The earliest documented use of a humiliation, however, is dated 996 and thereby antedates any known extant formula for that practice.[69] The formative period for the liturgical clamor was thus in the years around 1000. The excommunication formulas charged with maledictions can be traced back to the end of the ninth century.[70]

Looking at the latest examples of liturgical texts helps little in establishing chronological limits because they are, most likely, copies. The malediction of Saint-Wandrille, for example, is known only through a manuscript of the early sixteenth century, yet it was probably composed in the tenth century, or possibly early as the middle of the ninth.[71] Even so, the sharp decline in the number of surviving maledictory texts in manuscript in the early thirteenth century does suggest a lack of interest in and use of ecclesiastical curses starting about 1200.

Can any of these texts be attributed to a historically identifiable au-

---

67. See, for example, the General Prologue to *The Canterbury Tales*, line 486. *The Riverside Chaucer*, 3d ed., ed. Larry D. Benson (Boston, 1987), p. 31, note on p. 819. Cf. *A Chaucer Glossary*, ed. Norman Davis et al. (Oxford, 1979), p. 30. I am grateful to my colleague Craig R. Davis of the English Department at Smith College for making this observation and for supplying me with the references.

68. Sens: MS, Saint Petersburg, Public Library, lat. 4° v.I.35, f. 101v; Chartres: *Un manuscrit chartrain*, ed. Merlet and Clerval, pp. 237–238; Cluny: *Liber tramitis*, ed. Dinter, pp. 244–247.

69. *Annales OSB* 4:100.

70. Mansi 18B:669–670.

71. Little, "Formules monastiques," pp. 378–381.

thor? The excommunication formulas associated with the name of Pope Leo, whatever their origins and whoever their composer, were probably put together in the 930s, in the time of that pope. These formulas thus supply a fairly certain date, even if not an author.

A reasonable although not conclusive attribution of the clamor *In spiritu humilitatis* can be made to Fulbert, bishop of Chartres from 1006 to 1028. A manuscript probably written in the final decade of the eleventh century includes a copy of that version of the clamor under this title: "Clamor in Front of the Altar to Be Said before the Pax Domini, Composed by Lord Fulbert concerning Enemies of the Church" (*Proclamatio ante altare antequam dicatur pax domini composita a domno fulberto pro adversariis ecclesiae*). The manuscript is Italian, but the formula for the clamor probably came from the Swiss city of Constance, and that formula in turn very likely came from Besançon, whose cathedral church had a formula identical to one belonging to the Abbey of Cluny, whose abbot was in frequent contact with Fulbert.[72]

The attribution to Fulbert of Chartres is entirely plausible. He wrote several devotional works, and he was deeply involved in the problem of defending ecclesiastical property.[73] In a letter to King Robert II dated 1021–1022 he reported on two local knights, Herbert and Geoffrey, who were causing havoc in the region. What harm they were not actually doing, said Fulbert, they were threatening to do; then he added, "May the power of the Most High trample them down and destroy them in their pride." About three years later, Fulbert again complained to Robert, this time about the depredations of Viscount Geoffrey of Châteaudun and the failure of Odo, the count of Chartres, to do anything about them. Because of the injury and sorrow this had caused him, Fulbert says,

> we have ordered that the bells, which usually signify our joy and gladness, are to give some evidence of our sadness by their silence, and that divine worship, which in the past by God's grace has usually been celebrated in our church with great joy of heart and voice, is now to be performed mournfully, with low voices and almost in silence.

He begs the king to intervene to protect the church, adding: "On you alone after God totally depends our consolation and recovery from the

---

72. MS, Vat., lat. 3832, f. 195r. For a discussion of this attribution, see appendix D.

73. *The Letters and Poems of Fulbert of Chartres*, ed. and tr. Frederick Behrends (Oxford, 1976), pp. xvi–xxi.

troubles with which we are afflicted." And if the king were not willing to order Odo to do his job, he, Fulbert, would have no choice but to suspend divine worship throughout his diocese. This clear sense of God as the last resort is an essential element of the clamor, while the details about celebrants using low, mournful voices find an echo in that directive of the canons of Chartres in 1210 for dealing with lay malefactors, where priests were instructed to use humble, submissive voices and to allow no singing.[74] Fulbert in this way qualifies as a plausible candidate for composer of the clamor. Moreover, whereas in most churches that had a clamor only one copy of the clamor text has survived, from Chartres there are no fewer than seven.[75] The earliest of these, as I have already pointed out more than once, is dated about 1020, thus squarely in the reign of Bishop Fulbert.

As for provenance, with two exceptions all these texts came from communities of religious men, either monks or canons. The exceptions are clamor formulas from the Cluniac priory for women at Marcigny-sur-Loire and from the Abbey of Remiremont, a community of nuns in the Vosges Mountains. All the monastic groups adhered to the Rule of Saint Benedict; they were all of the classic type epitomized by Cluny, with a spirituality built of liturgical celebration and conspicuous consumption.[76] No extant manuscript with maledictory formulas comes from any of the reformed monastic groups of the twelfth century or later. The communities of canons, meanwhile, were those found in cathedral or collegiate churches. Monks and canons had much in common. Although monks were originally all laymen, in the post-

74. Ibid., pp. 102–103, 180–183. The key verbs in the maledictory passage of the earlier letter, *conterat* and *disperdat*, are also used together in Deut. 9:3. For the directive of the canons in 1210, see *Cartulaire de Notre-Dame de Chartres*, ed. Lépinois and Merlet, 2:57–58; for a similar suspension of music, see Du Cange 6:64. For insight into Fulbert's mode of reasoning, see Charles M. Radding, *A World Made by Men: Cognition and Society, 400–1200* (Chapel Hill, N.C., 1985), pp. 159–166.

75. (1) MS, Chartres, BM, 577, f. 1r, destroyed by fire in 1944; see Victor Leroquais, *Les sacramentaires et les missels manuscrits des bibliothèques publiques de France*, 4 vols. (Paris, 1924), 1:75–76. (2) MS, Chartres, BM, nouv. acq. 4, ff. 134v–135v; Merlet and Clerval, *Un manuscrit chartrain*, pp. 237–238. (3) MS, Chartres, BM, 1058, destroyed by fire in 1944; Yves Delaporte, *L'ordinaire chartrain du XIIIe siècle, publié d'après le manuscrit original* (Chartres, 1953), pp. 196–197. (4) MS, Chartres, BM, 502, f. 430r–v, destroyed by fire in 1944; see Leroquais, *Sacramentaires*, 2:197. (5) MS, Paris, BN, lat. 17310, f. 309r–v. (6) MS, Chartres, BM, 509, f. 77r–v, destroyed by fire in 1944; see Leroquais, *Sacramentaires*, 2:347. (7) *Cartulaire de Notre-Dame de Chartres*, ed. Lépinois and Merlet, 2:57–58.

76. See chapter 6, on contexts, under "Religion," on the religious life. In the middle of the eleventh century the nuns of Remiremont became canonesses.

Carolingian period they tended to become priests. And though canons were by definition priests, who mostly served on the staffs of large, usually cathedral churches, they tended in post-Carolingian times to become more and more like monks, devoting their principal efforts and their material resources to the liturgy.[77]

Neither monks nor canons dominated, let alone monopolized, any of the types of liturgical text under examination. Both the canons of Sens and the monks of Saint-Wandrille had the clamor beginning *Omnipotens sempiterne Deus*.[78] Both the canons of Chartres and the monks of Saint-Bénigne of Dijon had the clamor beginning *In spiritu humilitatis*.[79] Both the canons of the Basilica of Saint-Martin at Tours and the monks of Cluny had the formula for the humiliation of relics.[80] Only the maledictory excommunication might one expect to find particularly tied to cathedral churches, because of the special authority of bishops to excommunicate. But versions of the excommunication formula supposedly granted by Pope Leo VII were provided for monasteries; and no excommunication formula is more bristling with curses (e.g., "May they be buried with dogs and asses; may rapacious wolves devour their cadavers") than the one from the Norman monastery of Lyre.[81]

The churches for which the extant copies of clamors were made are concentrated in the land between the Charente and Rhine valleys, or those areas that correspond to the northern half of modern France (except for Brittany), the Rhineland, and modern Belgium. The geopolitical organization of this territory changed so much over the centuries when these manuscripts were produced as to disqualify any one name or even any set of names from being consistently valid. For the earlier part of the period these areas were Neustria and the western half of Austrasia, the western and central lands of the Carolingian empire. One of the meanings attributed to "Francia" comes close to describing the

77. See Lester K. Little, *Religious Poverty and the Profit Economy in Medieval Europe* (Ithaca, N.Y., 1978), pp. 99–101, and notes.

78. Sens: MS, Saint Petersburg, Public Library, lat. 4° v.I.35, f. 101v; Saint-Wandrille: Little, "Formules monastiques," pp. 394–395.

79. Chartres: MS, Chartres, BM, nouv. acq. 4, ff. 134v–135v; *Un manuscrit chartrain*, ed. Merlet and Clerval, pp. 237–238. Saint-Bénigne: MS, Dijon, BM, 122, f. 3v.

80. See above under "Humiliation of Relics."

81. Lyre: MS, Rouen, BM, A 425, f. 2v; Edmond Martène, *De antiquis ecclesiae ritibus*, 4 vols. (Antwerp, 1736–1738), 2:910–911; Aimé-Georges Martimort, *La documentation liturgique de Dom Edmond Martène*, Studi e testi 279 (Vatican City, 1978), p. 422.

region in question. But in the twelfth century the area included the northern part of Aquitaine plus Poitou, Anjou, Maine, Blois, Normandy, Ile-de-France, Berry, Champagne, Artois, Picardy, Flanders, Burgundy, Liège, and Lotharingia (see Map 1).[82]

Just a few places with formulas fall outside the area I have described. The spread of Cluniac customs is clearly responsible for the texts associated with Farfa in central Italy and Saint Paul's outside the Walls in Rome.[83] The use of the term "clamor" to describe a rite of cursing at Oña may show Cluniac influence, because Oña was reformed by Cluniac monks in 1033 and remained a Cluniac stronghold in Spain for a century thereafter. No clamor formulas as such have come to light from the Iberian Peninsula, but the customs of Bernard were taken over by the Abbey of Sahagún, even though the chapter on the clamor has not survived, and from Sahagún these are thought to have passed to Pombeiro in Portugal.[84] There is no such clear explanation for the presence of clamors at Admont in Austria, at Saint Mary's of the Irish in Vienna, or at Holy Trinity of the Irish in Rome, although the last two suggest an Irish connection.[85] Other than these bits of evidence from Italy, Iberia, and Austria, there is nothing from Languedoc or Provence, nothing from Germany, and nothing from the British Isles, except for the formulas from Rochester, Saint Germans, and Winchester, which

82. Edward James, *The Origins of France: From Clovis to the Capetians, 500–1000* (London, 1982), pp. 5, 31; Rosamond McKitterick, *The Frankish Kingdoms under the Carolingians, 751–987* (London, 1983), pp. 18–19; Jean Dunbabin, *France in the Making, 843–1180* (Oxford, 1985), pp. 4–5, 23, 100, 220–221, 374–379.

83. Farfa: *Liber tramitis*, ed. Dinter, pp. 244–247; Saint Paul's: MS, Rome, San Paolo f.l.m., Archivio, 92, p. 167.

84. Oña: MS, London, BL, Add. 30044, f. 72r. Sahagún: *Corónica general de la Orden de San Benito, patriarca de religiosos*, ed. Antonio Yepes, 7 vols. (Yrache and Valladolid, 1609–1621), vol. 3, ff. 190r–199v. Pombeiro: José Mattoso, *Le monachisme ibérique et Cluny: Les monastères du diocèse de Porto de l'an mille à 1200*, Université de Louvain, Recueil de travaux d'histoire et de philologie, ser. 4, fasc. 39 (Louvain, 1969), pp. 126, 160–165, 271–281.

85. Admont: MS, Admont, Stiftsbibliothek, 86, ff. 72v–74r; Adolf Franz, *Die Messe im deutschen Mittelalter* (Freiburg im Breisgau, 1902), pp. 206–207. Saint Mary's of the Irish, Vienna: MS, Vienna, Schottenkloster, 189, f. 77v; reference in Albert Huebl, *Catalogus codicum manu scriptum qui in Bibliotheca Monasterii B. V. M. ad Scotos Vindobonae servantur* (Vienna, 1899), pp. 203–204; the heading on the prayer in this version, *Oracio Volperti episcopi pro tribulacione*, suggests a possible connection with the Besançon and Constance formulas. Holy Trinity of the Irish, Rome: MS, Vat., Chigi. C.VI.173, f. 27r–v; José-Maria Canal, *Salve Regina Misericordia: Historia y leyendas en torno a esta antifona* (Rome, 1963), pp. 301–302. As for a possible Irish connection, see chapter 5, under "The Irish Sphere of Influence."

Map 1. Churches with clamors. Location of churches that had available a liturgical formula for some type of clamor. These churches are almost all found between the valleys of the Charente and Rhine rivers.

are all northern French imports.[86] Our evidence thus points to the western and central parts of the old Carolingian empire, that part of the Continent hardest hit by the Viking invasions and most characterized by the devolution of political authority to the level of local strongmen.

To sum up, the overlapping and interlocking nature of the various maledictory formulas renders problematic an orderly classification of these texts. Still, we can define the usual clamor as a portion of the mass, appropriate for a time for offering special prayers, consisting of prayers, psalms, and other scriptural passages all on the theme of tribulation, which acknowledge mankind's moral inadequacy and utter reliance upon the omnipotence of God. About A.D. 1000 the characteristic elements of the clamor, including that name, came together. The prayer *In spiritu humilitatis* was widely considered to be its essential element. Closely associated with it in one version of the influential Cluniac customs were the directions for acting out the community's suffering by ritually deposing and humiliating the most sacred objects in its possession. The ancient practice of excommunication was not unaffected by the growth of the clamor. Indeed, each so influenced the other that at times they were inextricably commingled.

The clamor of late antiquity and early Carolingian times, I noted previously, was directed to a magistrate, and special attention was given to guaranteeing poor people a fair hearing for their grievances. The poor specified in Carolingian documents included widows, orphans (or sometimes minors), and clerics. No mention was made of these people as being poor in material resources, although that point is not necessarily excluded. What these categories of people did have in common was a condition of powerlessness.[87] To be poor meant principally to be without power. Meanwhile, power was in the hands of

---

86. For Rochester, see the introduction to this book. For Saint Germans: MS, Rouen, BM, A 27, ff. 183r–184r; *Pontificale Lanaletense: A Pontifical Formerly in Use at St. Germans, Cornwall (Bibliothèque de la Ville de Rouen A.27. CAT. 368)*, ed. Gilbert H. Doble, Henry Bradshaw Society 74 (London, 1937), pp. 130–131. Winchester: MS, London, BL, Royal 2.B.V, f. 1r–v.

87. Karl Bosl, "Potens und Pauper: Begriffsgeschichtliche Studien zur gesellschaftlichen Differenzierung im frühen Mittelalter und zum 'Pauperismus' des Hochmittelalters," in *Alteuropa und die moderne Gesellschaft: Festschrift für O. Brunner*, ed. Alexander Bergengruen and Ludwig Deike (Göttingen, 1963), pp. 60–87.

military lords.[88] Monks and nuns and canons then and still in the eleventh century considered themselves poor. At this time most people lived at subsistence level, and among the few who were relatively well-off were some of those same monks and nuns and canons. Certain of their churches were monumental in size and elaborate in decoration. Their claims to be poor should not be cast aside as hypocritical, however, for they were consistent in their renunciation of horses and weapons, the means and symbols of contemporary social power.[89]

As people who were poor in this sense of powerlessness and thus in need of protection, the religious made their clamors in times of trouble to the duly constituted authorities of their time—God and the local patron saint. The monks of Saint-Cybard of Angoulême pronounced maledictions and excommunications against an oppressor, confident that God would not turn a deaf ear "to the clamors of the poor," which they then defined as the "prayers of his servants."[90] This transference of the clamor from the sphere of law to that of liturgy exemplifies the development of a liturgical culture in late Carolingian Europe and supplies at least one answer to the question of the origins of the liturgical clamor. But the search for its origins reaches both wider and deeper.

88. See the observation on this point by Georges Duby, *The Early Growth of the European Economy: Warriors and Peasants from the Seventh to the Twelfth Century*, tr. Howard B. Clarke (Ithaca, N.Y., 1974), p. 13, in speaking of the low population in the seventh and eighth centuries: "In this human void, space was plentiful. What constituted the real basis of wealth at that time was not ownership of land but power over men, however wretched their condition, and over their rudimentary equipment."

89. Lester K. Little, "Pride Goes before Avarice: Social Change and the Vices in Latin Christendom," *American Historical Review* 76 (1971): 34.

90. MS, Angoulême, Archives de la Charente, H' 1, f. 117r.

2
Sources

MANY OF the curses clamors abound with also appear in the sanction clauses of contemporary charters. This is no casual coincidence, for sanction clauses and clamors were integral parts of a single system for maintaining social order. Their histories are intertwined, and searches for their sources often lead in the same direction. For the clamor the single most important source, in the literal sense of supplying words and phrases, was the Bible. Other aspects of its origins, however, can be traced within the liturgical tradition itself and, to a lesser extent, in canon law.

Sanction Clauses

No alleged malefactor who became the object of ecclesiastical curses should have been surprised; there was ample warning. Virtually every ecclesiastical, especially monastic, possession and privilege was attested by a written instrument—a charter—and virtually every charter contained a sanction clause warning of dire consequences for anyone who contravened its terms.

Charters are written records of actions or facts of a legal nature; they include such documents as deeds, privileges, contracts, and constitutions. They usually were drawn up according to prescribed forms. Each gave the name of the actor or author, what he or she did, and the name of the recipient in whose favor the charter was issued and to whom it was given as a legal record. Public charters were issued by individuals or institutions invested with public authority and trust, private charters by those who lacked such authority or trust. The legal force of charters varied greatly according to place, time, local custom, institutional continuity, and a host of other circumstances; at the very least, a charter should have provided the basis for a judicial inquiry and aided the memory of witnesses, whose testimony as to what happened or what was agreed constituted the actual proof. This memory function is explicit in a charter from the Abbey of Redon that begins, "This charter recalls to memory how the bishop, together with the abbot and the monks" did such and such.[1]

Charters of donation constitute the most numerous single type of written act from the medieval centuries, and almost all of these record gifts by laypeople to religious institutions. The cartulary, or collection of charters, of the Abbey of Cluny, for example, contains over 5,500 individual charters.[2] Farfa in central Italy had over 1,300;[3] Ramsey Abbey in England nearly 700;[4] and Sant-Cugat del Vallés in Catalonia had just short of 1,400 charters.[5] The cartulary was usually one of the most jealously guarded possessions of a monastery, along with the relics of the patron saint and the sacred books.[6] It was all the more important given that a monastery did not directly command the physical or military means to defend its own properties.

The standard structure of a charter consists of the protocol, the text, and the eschatol. The first includes the names of the principals and a greeting, and the last includes the date and the signs or signatures. The central part of the text is the disposition, the act or decision that the charter is meant to record. It is sometimes preceded by a notification and sometimes by a *narratio*, which provides background to the forthcoming disposition, whereas it is sometimes followed by qualifying clauses, one type being the sanction clause, nearly always introduced by the words "if anyone" (*si quis*).[7]

The sanction clause comes straight out of Roman law, an example being the clause in a contract establishing a fine for violating the terms of the contract itself. In the Benedictine centuries there were always

1. Leonard Boyle, "Diplomatics," in *Medieval Studies: An Introduction*, ed. James M. Powell (Syracuse, N.Y., 1976), pp. 69–101. For the charter of Redon, see *Cartulaire de l'abbaye de Redon en Bretagne*, ed. A. de Courson (Paris, 1863), p. 313.

2. *Recueil des chartes de l'abbaye de Cluny*, ed. Auguste Bernard and Alexandre Bruel, 6 vols. (Paris, 1876–1903).

3. *Il regesto di Farfa compilato da Gregorio di Catino*, ed. I. Giorgi and Ugo Balzani, 5 vols. (Rome, 1879–1914).

4. *Cartularium monasterii de Rameseia*, ed. William H. Hart and Ponsonby A. Lyons, 3 vols., RS 79 (London, 1884–1893).

5. *Cartulario de "Sant Cugat" del Vallés*, ed. J. Rius Serra, 3 vols., Textos y estudios de la corona de Aragón 3–5 (Barcelona, 1945–1947).

6. Note also that particularly precious documents were sometimes copied into sacred books, as in the example from Saint-Martial mentioned in the introduction, where a confirmation of papal privileges was copied into a Bible.

7. Boyle, "Diplomatics," p. 84.

some sanction clauses that stipulated fines. In charters of the monastery at Cava, near Salerno, where the circulation of money never slowed to the moribund state it reached in most of western Europe, money fines never disappeared from sanction clauses.[8] Where fines did remain in use north of the Alps, they expressed generically large quantities, symbolic more than realistic. This can be seen in a charter attesting a grant from Charlemagne to Saint-Aubin of Angers in 808; it calls for a fine of six-hundred silver shillings to be paid by anyone who violates it, two parts to the monastery and one part to the imperial fisc.[9] For the most part, though, fines simply dropped from use.

The earliest systematic study of charters, the *De re diplomatica* of Jean Mabillon, which first appeared in 1681, isolated the punishments and distinguished between material or physical sanctions and spiritual sanctions. The latter were mostly imprecations, petitions that misfortune, itself in turn either material or spiritual, would befall any who violated the terms of the document.[10] Arthur Giry, in the influential handbook he published in 1894, identified the age in which imprecations and maledictions dominated sanction clauses as lasting from the eighth through the eleventh century, with a marked decline in the course of the twelfth.[11] In Giry's time, known for its devotion to the scientific elucidation of documentary sources, and with charters so abundant and constituting such a rich source of information, editing cartularies was a standard task of historical scholarship. Charters have thus long been extensively and deeply studied. The focus of interest in the heyday of such studies understandably fell upon their operative clauses, the dispositions with their unique bits of information, along with the names of persons and places and the witness lists. Only in more recent times, with historians more interested in the ordinary, the regular, or the often-repeated, have scholars focused on some of the more formulaic elements of charters. Studied in great numbers and over long periods, these show little in the way of immediate or abrupt change but are especially well suited to reveal sea changes in conven-

---

8. *Codex diplomaticus Cavensis*, ed. M. Morcaldi, M. Schiani, and S. de Stephano, 8 vols. (Naples, 1873–1893), passim.

9. *Cartulaire de l'abbaye de Saint-Aubin d'Angers*, ed. Arthur Bertrand de Rouissillon, 3 vols. (Angers, 1903), 1:23–24.

10. Jean Mabillon, *De re diplomatica*, 2:8 (Paris, 1709), pp. 96–104.

11. Arthur Giry, *Manuel de diplomatique* (Paris, 1894), pp. 562–567, 855–858.

tions—in ways of thinking about things that people usually do not think about.[12]

An exhaustive study of Catalonian charter formulas showed that the oldest surviving charters include only temporal or material sanctions. In the course of the tenth century spiritual sanctions came increasingly into use until they were the dominant and, later still, the unique type of sanction. The anger of God (*ira Dei*) took the place of fines, a transformation that can be attributed to the rapid disappearance in the tenth century of Carolingian public justice in Catalonian territory. When the reverse transformation occurred in the second quarter of the twelfth century, the newly constituted authority of the count was being presented as the guarantor of charters. It was no longer the *ira Dei* that awaited transgressors but, as the count had explicitly stated in documents emanating from his court, *ira mea*, or *indignatio mea*.[13]

A similar pattern has been discerned in Portuguese charters. The period for which one can find charters there that used spiritual sanctions exclusively lasted from 883 to 1086.[14] And in Italian charters, too, the most frequent use of spiritual sanctions took place in the tenth and eleventh centuries, with a decline to the point of being exceptional in the twelfth and disappearing by the mid-thirteenth.[15] The Italian charters revealed some regional variations in this timing, just as a study of Norman charters highlighted differences of usage between older, well-established monastic houses and more recent foundations.[16] Thus various elements were introduced that refined but did not basically change the overall pattern.

The particular menaces found in spiritual sanctions are rich in variety but not notably associated with particular regions. Indeed, one risk

12. For discussion of the value of including formulaic as opposed to only operative elements of charters in publications of cartularies, see *Informatique et histoire médiévale*, ed. Lucie Fossier, André Vauchez, and Cinzio Violante, Collection de l'Ecole française de Rome 31 (Rome, 1977), pp. 182–184, 187–190, 249–262, and 426.

13. Michel Zimmermann, "Protocoles et préambules dans les documents catalans du Xe au XIIe siècle: Evolution diplomatique et signification spirituelle," *Mélanges de la Casa de Velazquez* 10 (1974): 41–76, especially 51–54.

14. José Mattoso, "Sanctio (875–1100)," *Revista Portuguesa de Historia* 13 (1971): 299–338; reprinted in his *Religião e cultura no Idade Media Portuguese* (Lisbon, 1982), pp. 394–440.

15. Luciana Mosiici, *Le formule di sanzione spirituale nei documenti privati italiani dei secoli VIII–XII* (Florence, 1979). The author generously sent me a copy of this privately printed volume through the kind offices of Giancarlo Savino and Claudio Rosati.

16. Emily Z. Tabuteau, *Transfers of Property in Eleventh-Century Norman Law* (Chapel Hill, N.C., 1988), p. 205.

in citing specific examples lies in suggesting an association of a given text with some one place, whereas variants of that text are likely to turn up practically anywhere else in Christendom. With that caution in mind we can look at a few examples, such as a charter of 910 from Conques that says, "If anyone presume to contradict this charter, let him be excommunicated and cursed as well as damned forever with Judas the traitor and with the devil."[17] From Sauxillanges in about 1000 comes this sanction clause: "May he incur the anger of God almighty and of the holy apostles and of all the saints, and may he remain damned in hell with Dathan and Abiron and with Judas the traitor of the Lord."[18] Others in the company of the damned frequently invoked in sanction clauses included Ananias, Sapphira, Annas, Caiaphas, Herod, Pilate, Nero, Simon Magus, and the people of Sodom and Gomorrah.[19]

A charter dated 1113 from Sardinia shows a wondrous fascination with numbers in its imagined punishments; the sanction clause says:

> And if any wish to destroy this charter, may God strike their names from the book of life and toss their flesh to the birds of the air and the beasts of the earth. May the Lord send them to an abominable death and banish them quickly from this world. May they have the curses of the three patriarchs, Abraham, Isaac, and Jacob; and of the four evangelists, Mark and Matthew, Luke and John; and of the twelve apostles and of the sixteen prophets and of the twenty-four elders and of the 318 holy fathers who deliberated on the canons at Nicea; and may they have the curse of the 144,000 martyrs who died for the Lord; and may they have the curse of the cherubim and the seraphim, who hold the throne of God, and of all the saints of God. Amen, amen. So be it, so be it.[20]

The summoning of members of the celestial court to join in the cursing is altogether usual, whereas it is rare that living persons are called upon, as in this Anglo-Saxon charter: "And if anyone is puffed up and so greatly covetous of earthly things that he desires to alienate this our gift, he shall have the curse of God and Saint Mary and Saint Oswald

17. *Cartulaire de l'abbaye de Conques en Rouergue,* ed. Gustave Desjardins (Paris, 1879), p. 11.

18. *Cartulaire de Sauxillanges,* ed. Henry Doniol (Clermont, 1864), pp. 292–293.

19. Zimmermann, "Protocoles et préambules," pp. 68–72. For a papal *si quis* clause that uses Annas, Caiaphas, and Judas (from the reign of John XIX and dated 1032/1033), see *Cartulaire de l'abbaye royale de Saint-Jean d'Angély,* ed. Georges Musset, 2 vols. (Paris, 1901–1904), 1:32–33.

20. *Codex diplomaticus Sardiniae,* Historiae Patriae monumenta 10 (Turin, 1861), p. 186.

and all men in holy orders here in this life." The conclusion reverts to being utterly common: "And he shall be excommunicated on the Judgment Day in the presence of the Lord by God and by all his saints and tormented for all time in everlasting punishment along with Judas and his companions, unless he desist and turn to a proper mode of conduct."[21]

Since a charter is the formal record of an act, the appearance in the conclusions of some charters of such words as *amen* or *fiat*, as in the Sardinian example cited above, appears to be a vestige of a ceremony surrounding the act. An Anglo-Saxon charter of about 930 makes explicit this connection between act and document. It describes the scene in which Earl Aethelstan granted an estate to Saint Mary's of Abingdon. At the end:

> Archbishop Wulfhelm and all the bishops and abbots there assembled excommunicated from Christ and from all the fellowship of Christ and from the whole of Christendom anyone who should ever undo this grant or reduce this estate in meadow or in boundary. He shall be cut off and hurled into the abyss of hell for ever without end. And all the people who stood by said, "So be it, amen, amen."[22]

Here the sanction clause goes beyond the menace of some future punishment; it records that those present at the earl's granting an estate to the church actually carried out a provisional excommunication. The more dramatic the acting out, the less likely it was that a witness would forget the scene.

The near universality of particular spiritual sanctions within Latin Christendom suggests common models, and indeed there were models available; they are found in formularies, or books of formulas for the redaction of documents such as contracts, letters, mandates, bills of sale, or charters. These books were produced in the scriptoria of monasteries and cathedral churches beginning in the seventh century.[23] The *Liber diurnus* of the papal court was one of these, developed in various redactions in the course of the seventh and eighth centuries. In the model grants or confirmations of privileges it contains, one can find sanction clauses that talk of eternal fires, the chains of anathema, and

---

21. *Anglo-Saxon Charters*, ed. Agnes J. Robertson (Cambridge, 1939), pp. 210–211.
22. Ibid., pp. 44–45.
23. Harry Bresslau and Hans W. Klewitz, *Handbuch der Urkundenlehre für Deutschland und Italien*, 2d ed., 2 vols. (Leipzig, 1912–1931; photo reprint, Berlin, 1968–1969), 2:225–247.

the curse of Judas the traitor.[24] Other formularies were assembled in Visigothic Spain and in several centers spread throughout the Carolingian empire. Of the forty extant manuscripts of formularies, the earliest is from the eighth century, over half (twenty-four) date from the ninth century, and the latest was made in the twelfth century.[25] The only one of these books that bears a compiler's name is that written by Marculf, a monk who lived in the Paris region in the middle of the seventh century.[26]

The *si quis* clause was present in these formularies with both material and spiritual sanctions. The latter include anathemas: "may he be anathema, and not only he who did it but also he who consented to it, and may he descend alive into hell in the same way that Dathan and Abiron were swallowed by the earth";[27] "may he share to the fullest the company of Judas, the traitor of our lord Jesus Christ";[28] "may he incur the anger of the triune majesty, and may he be summoned before the court of Christ";[29] and "may no religious or laypersons dare to protect them."[30] The compilers of formularies were of course not making up these texts; they had models for the books they produced in such works as the letter collection of Cassiodorus called the *Variae*, and models for the particular texts were found in contemporary and recent documents they happened to have at hand.[31]

Spiritual sanctions were thus very much a part of the same culture as clamors. In the western part of the Carolingian empire, the same bishops and abbots whose charters included curses against potential transgressors had formal, liturgical curses ready for actual transgressors. Spiritual sanctions were not eccentric or rare but common and widespread, attesting to a standard attitude of mind that was not the preserve of any region or class or order. Even within one monastic community it did not seem inappropriate to menace someone who in the future might alter the terms of a bequest establishing an anniver-

24. *Liber diurnis Romanorum pontificum*, ed. Hans Foerster (Bern, 1958), pp. 166, 176, 178, 267, and 381; *Liber diurnus: Studien und Forschungen von Leo Santifaller*, ed. Harald Zimmermann, Päpste und Papsttum 10 (Stuttgart, 1976).

25. *Formulae Merovingici et Karolini aevi*, ed. Karl Zeumer (*MGH, Form.*).

26. Marculf, *Formulae* (ibid., pp. 32–106).

27. Marculf, *Formulae*, bk. 2, ch. 1 (ibid., p. 73).

28. Marculf, *Formulae*, bk. 2, ch. 3 (ibid., p. 76).

29. Marculf, *Formulae*, bk. 2, ch. 6 (ibid., p. 79).

30. *Formulae Visigothicae*, ch. 7 (ibid., p. 578).

31. Bresslau and Klewitz, *Handbuch*, 2:227–229; Edward James, *The Origins of France: From Clovis to the Capetians, 500–1000* (London, 1982), p. 60.

sary dinner. Walter de Luci, for thirty-three years (1139–1171) abbot of Battle Abbey (established by William the Conqueror at the site of the Battle of Hastings), reallocated the income from a manor and used a portion of the remaining surplus to endow a late summer banquet. He provided that each year on the day of the decollation of Saint John the Baptist (29 August) or, after he himself died, on the anniversary of his death, there was to be a dinner for all the monks consisting of "two cooked dishes of the best quality," of which one, if circumstances permitted, was to be fresh salmon, along with the usual bread but a special pepper cake; moreover, "the measure of [white] wine for each brother should be not less than a gallon." Walter de Luci did not regard this specificity lightly, for

> lest any of his successors should dare in the future to lessen his decree, or to oppose him by any change in it, before the brothers in chapter he put on his stole and took a lighted candle, and commanded each of the brothers who were priests or deacons to take up stoles and lighted candles. The subdeacons had their maniples and lighted candles, while those who were of inferior grade, and the lay brothers, had lighted candles only.

The stage was set. "Then, in the presence and with the consent of all, he pronounced a perpetual and irrevocable anathema on all violators of his decree." A modern reader would make a terrible blunder in thinking that manipulative monks sought to frighten—to control—laypeople with threats of spiritual punishment they themselves did not believe in, for the monks and their lay contemporaries shared the same culture and the same system of beliefs. When the time came to menace potential transgressors of an endowment set up within the precincts of Battle Abbey, the abbot threatened monastic wrongdoers with the same kinds of sanctions that were then being routinely promised to their lay counterparts.[32]

The Bible

The principal source of the clamor, in the sense of a literary quarry that supplied most of its distinctive phrases, was the Hebrew Bible, especially Deuteronomy and the Psalms. Considerably less important although not insignificant as a source was the Christian Bible. To make graphic the importance of the Bible (in both its parts, "old" and "new")

---

32. *The Chronicle of Battle Abbey*, ed. and tr. Eleanor Searle (Oxford, 1980), pp. 252–255; Walter de Luci died on 21 June 1171 (ibid., pp. 266–267).

as a source, here once again is the Saint-Martial clamor, this time with all its biblical passages italicized and identified.

We hereby inform you, brothers, that certain evil men are devastating the land of our lord Martial. They are invading, preying upon, and destroying it; they are hurting our poor tenants, taking from them what little they have and with which they are supposed to serve Saint Martial, the lord abbot, and the monks. They behave like *those who said, "Let us take possession for ourselves of the sanctuary of God"* [Ps. 82:13]. So those who overrun and hold the land of Saint Martial do not serve the lord abbot and the monks. May they be cursed and excommunicated and anathematized [and separated] from the consortium of all the faithful Christians of God. *May the curse* of all the saints of God *come upon them* [Deut. 28:15, 45]. May the angels and archangels of God curse them. May the patriarchs and the prophets curse them. May all the apostles and all the martyrs and all the confessors and all the virgins and especially Saint Martial, whom they are treating so badly, curse them. May he confound and destroy them, and disperse them from the face of the earth [cf. Jer. 1:10; Ps. 1:4; Josh. 23:13, 15]. *May all these curses come upon them and seize them* [Deut. 28:15, 45]. *May they be cursed in town. May they be cursed in the fields* [Deut. 28:16]. May they be cursed inside their houses and outside their houses. May they be cursed standing and sitting. May they be cursed lying down and walking. May they be cursed when asleep and when awake. May they be cursed while eating and while drinking. May they be cursed *in castles and in villages* [cf. Gen. 25:16; 2 Macc. 8:6; Matt. 9:35; Luke 8:1, 9:12, 13:22]. May they be cursed in forests and in waters. *May their wives and their children* [cf. Deut. 28:4, 18; Ps. 108:9] *and all who associate with them be cursed* [Esther 14:13; Acts 5:36, 37]. *May their cellars be cursed* [cf. Deut. 28: 8], as well as their casks and all the vessels from which they drink and eat. May their vineyards and their crops and their forests be cursed. May their servants, *if these remain loyal to them* [Esther 14:13; Acts 5:36, 37], be cursed. *May all their cattle* and their work animals, both inside and outside the stables, *be cursed* [cf. Deut. 28:4, 11, 51, 30:9]. *May the Lord send over them hunger* [Deut. 28:20] and thirst, *pestilence* and death, *until they are wiped off the earth* [Deut. 28:21]. *May the Lord strike them with heat and cold* [Deut. 28:22]. *May the sky above them be brass and the earth they walk on iron* [Deut. 28:23]. *May the Lord toss their bodies as bait to the birds of the sky and the beasts of the land* [Deut. 28:26]. *May the Lord strike them from the bottoms of their feet to the tops of their heads* [Deut. 28:35]. *May their homes be deserted and may no one inhabit them* [Ps. 68:25]. May they lose what they have, and may they not acquire what they do not have. *May the sword devastate them on the outside and fear on the inside* [Deut. 32:25]. *If they sow seeds in the earth may they reap little* [Deut. 28:38], *and if they plant vines may they not drink wine from them* [Deut. 28:30, 39]. *May the Lord send great plagues upon them, and the worst, most relentless illnesses* [cf. Deut. 28:59], *unless they change their ways* [cf. Deut. 28:58]. *But if they are not willing* to change [Deut. 28:15], then let them accept from God and Saint Martial damnation *with the devil and his angels in hell, and may they burn in eternal fires* [Matt. 25:41] with *Dathan and Abiron* [Num. 16:1–33]. *Amen, amen* [Deut. 27:15–26]. *Thus may all memory of them be extinguished for ever and ever* [Deut. 32:26; Job 18:17; Ps. 9:7, 33:17, 108:15; Eccles. 10:17, 44:9].

The first great supplier of phrases for this text is clearly Deuteronomy, which is almost entirely an exposition of the faith of Israel composed in the form of speeches by Moses to his people.[33] He teaches about the covenant between God and Israel and the resulting need for a definite act of decision (chs. 5–11). Moses calls for a commitment whose consequences are those of life and death, expressed as a blessing or a curse (Deut. 11:26–28):

Behold, I set before you this day a blessing and a curse: the blessing, if you obey the commandments of the Lord your God, which I command you this day, and the curse, if you do not obey the commandments of the Lord your God, but turn aside from the way which I command you this day, to go after other gods which you have not known.

The blessings and curses become associated with particular places in the promised land: "And when the Lord your God brings you into the land which you are entering to take possession of it, you shall set the blessing on Mount Gerizim and the curse on Mount Ebal" (Deut. 11: 29).

These places figure importantly in the instructions given by Moses in chapter 27, which experts regard as an intrusion into the orderly flow of the text, for the chapters immediately before and after it are neatly balanced between blessings and curses, whereas this one only mentions blessings but gives the full texts of curses.[34] Moses gives instructions for what the people should do when they enter the land flowing with milk and honey.

When you have passed over the Jordan, these shall stand upon Mount Gerizim to bless the people [here he names six tribes]. And these shall stand upon Mount Ebal for the curse [he names the other six tribes]. And the Levites shall declare to all the men of Israel with a loud voice: "Cursed be the man who makes a graven or molten image, an abomination to the Lord, a thing made by the hands of a craftsman, and sets it up in secret." And all the people shall answer and say, "Amen." "Cursed be he who dishonors his

33. Gerhad von Rad, *Studies in Deuteronomy, Studies in Biblical Theology*, tr. David Stalker (Chicago, 1953), pp. 11, 14, 70, 72; cf. *IB* 2:311–330. I am grateful for much help in dealing with the Bible and biblical scholarship from my colleague at Smith College Bruce Dahlberg of the Department of Religion and Biblical Literature.

34. *IB* 2:315, 488–492.

father or his mother." And all the people shall say, "Amen." "Cursed be he who removes his neighbor's landmark." And all the people shall say, "Amen." (Deut. 27:11–17)

And so it continues for nine more curses.

Chapter 28 resumes the balanced offering of blessings and curses, starting with a series of blessings upon those who obey the commandments of the Lord: "May you be blessed in the city and blessed in the field. Blessed be the fruit of your body and the fruit of your ground" (28:3–4). The change comes at verse 15: "But if you will not obey the voice of the Lord your God or be careful to do all his commandments and his statutes which I command you this day, then may all these curses come upon you and overtake you. May you be cursed in the city and cursed in the field." And so on.

In addition to the many individual curses of which the originals are found here, the precedent for the litany of curses is found in Deuteronomy. The rhetorical power of some of the maledictory clamors comes from insistent, tirelessly detailed repetition, and indeed in the biblical model there was surely no intention to be concise or efficient. Instead, Moses' purpose appears to have been to formulate a ceremony of reaffirmation of the covenant that was to be carried out regularly in the future.[35] And so each of the commandments was to be stated in full, once in a positive version and once in a negative, and punctuated by all the people joining in to say "amen." Deuteronomy concludes with Moses' lengthy, detailed blessing upon all the people of Israel, and then his death (chs. 33–34).

The Book of Psalms is the other great contributor of phrases to the clamor. It consists of 150 religious poems, mostly songs of praise, that express the voice of the Jews directed to God. These poems appear in no discernible order; there are worshipful hymns and hymns that give thanks, as well as soulful laments. The laments are notable for their relentless denunciation of enemies, their defiant attitude toward enemies, their appeals for divine assistance, and their curses.[36]

Among the psalms recited in their entirety in some clamors are numbers 3, 12, 45, 51, 58, and 93. Psalm 3 is of the type that presents the laments of one person: "Why, O Lord, have those who afflict me mul-

---

35. See 4 Kings 22:11–13, 19, where the curses of Deuteronomy were subsequently read, with immediate, dramatic effect.
36. *IB* 4:3–7.

tiplied!" (3:1). Those enemies taunt the speaker by saying that God will not help him, but he maintains his faith in God's protection: "I cried out to the Lord [*clamavi ad dominum*] and he answered me from his holy hill" (3:4). There follows a candid reminder of how God deals with enemies, and then at the end comes a benediction: "You strike all my enemies across the face and you break the teeth of the wicked. The victory is yours, and may your blessing be upon your people" (3:7–8). Whereas Psalm 12 reasserts faith in God's love and help in the face of despair and seeming abandonment by God, Psalm 45 is a hymn of confident faith in God as the ever-present refuge of his people. Psalm 51 dispenses with any appeal to God for help and launches into a denunciation of an evil person: "Why do you glory in wickedness, O mighty man?" (51:1). Other charges follow, and then a curse: "So may God pull you down to the ground, sweep you away, leave you ruined and homeless, uprooted from the land of the living" (51:5). Psalm 58, "Rescue me from my enemies" (58:1), combines a communal with an individual lament; its curse against the enemies says: "Let them be cut off for their cursing and falsehood; bring them to an end in your wrath, that they may not be any more" (58:12–13). And Psalm 93, called "O Lord, God of vengeance," concludes in this way: "He will turn back on them their iniquity and wipe them out for their wickedness; the Lord our God will wipe them out" (93:23).

Psalm 68, "Save me, O God," is one of those frequently cited. It is an individual's plaintive cry for deliverance that, after listing grievances, turns into a petition that terrible things should happen to his persecutors:

> May their own table be a snare to them and their sacred feasts lure them to their ruin; may their eyes be darkened so that they do not see, let a continual ague shake their loins. Pour out your indignation upon them and let your burning anger overtake them. May their settlements be desolate and may no one live in their tents; for they pursue him whom you have struck down and multiply the torments of those whom you have wounded. Give them the punishment their sin deserves; exclude them from your righteous mercy; let them be blotted out from the book of life and not be enrolled among the righteous. (Ps. 68: 22–28)

The psalm most renowned for its curses, cited frequently both in full and in part, is number 108: "Be not silent, O God, in my praise." The heart of this psalm is a string of imprecations against some unnamed enemy.

May his days be few; may another seize his goods. May his children be fatherless, and his wife a widow. May his children wander about and beg; may they be driven out of the ruins they inhabit. May the creditor seize all that he has; may strangers plunder the fruits of his toil. Let there be none to extend kindness to him, nor any to pity his fatherless children. May his posterity be cut off; may his name be blotted out within a generation. May the iniquity of his fathers be remembered before the Lord, and let not the sin of his mother be blotted out. Let them be before the Lord continually; and may his memory be cut off from the earth. (Ps. 108: 8–15)

Here as in Psalm 58 a wicked person is denounced for cursing: "He loved to curse; let curses come on him. He did not like blessing; may it be far from him. He clothed himself with cursing as his coat; may it soak into his body like water, and into his bones like oil" (108: 17–18).

Just like Deuteronomy, which in addition to supplying many particular phrases provided the clamor with a major formal element—the litany of curses—so also the Psalms made an important contribution to form. This was the use of repetitive parallelism, itself one of the defining stylistic features of Hebrew poetry. In it can also be seen the inspiration for antiphonal singing, in which the two sides of a choir alternate in singing lines from the Psalms. The key to this poetic style rests in parallelism of thought and line, in which the thought or construction of the first line is echoed in the second; for example, "May his children be fatherless, and his wife a widow" (Ps. 108:9). The symmetry may come from juxtaposing opposites, as we have just seen: "He loved to curse; let curses come on him" (Ps. 108:17). Sometimes fixed pairs of words are used, one word in each of these paired lines, to signal the repetition. For example, the words "strange" and "foreign" (to use modern English equivalents, to be sure) as used in Psalm 80:10 are such a pair: "There shall not be with you a strange God, neither shall you bow down to a foreign God." "King" and "ruler" in Ps. 104: 20 offer another example: "The king sent and released him; the ruler of the peoples set him free." An action described abstractly in one line and concretely in the next represents still another variant on the parallel form; this one comes at the end of Psalm 136, verses 8–9: "Happy shall be the man who repays you for all that you did to us; happy shall he be who takes your little ones and dashes them against the rock."[37]

37. Stanley Gevirtz, *Patterns in the Early Poetry of Israel*, 2d ed. (Chicago, 1973), pp. 6–14, 44–46. Roman Jakobson, "Grammatical Parallelism and Its Russian Facet," in his *Poetry of Grammar and Grammar of Poetry*, Selected Writings 3 (The Hague, 1981), pp. 98–135; IB 4:11.

In the malediction of Saint-Wandrille, the brothers are directed to sing seven psalms, the last of which is number 108. Then come the following phrases, called "prayers," with their biblical passages here italicized and identified:

May their eyes be darkened so they cannot see. And may their backs always be bent [Ps. 68:24].
Pour out your indignation upon them. And let your burning anger overtake them [Ps. 68:25].
May their homes be deserted. And may no one live in their tents [Ps. 68:26].
Let death come upon them. And may they descend alive into hell [Ps. 54:16].
You will make them as a blazing oven when you appear. The Lord will swallow them up in his wrath, and fire will consume them [Ps. 20:9].
You will destroy their offspring from the earth. And their children from among the sons of men [Ps. 20:10].
May their way be dark and slippery. And let the angel of the Lord persecute them [Ps. 34:6].
Let ruin come upon them unawares. And let the net that they hid ensnare them [Ps. 34:8].
May God destroy them in the end. He will snatch them and tear them away from their tents, and uproot them from the land of the living [Ps. 51:5].
As fire consumes the forest and as the flame sets the mountain ablaze, so shall you pursue them with your tempest and confound them with your anger [Ps. 82:14–15, 17].
With God we shall do valiantly. And it is he who will tread down our foes [Ps. 107:13].[38]

The composer of this text, as the italics show, hardly contributed an "original" word, and yet the whole text taken together is highly original. It is an artful composition, conceived of and worked out entirely in Latin during the ninth or tenth century. With or without the composer's awareness, it was firmly rooted in the demands and patterns of ancient Hebrew poetry, as expressed in the Psalms.

Including single biblical verses or pairs of verses—capitula—in the clamor was standard practice. Nearly all the known versions of the clamor contain on the average three capitula. Certain of these recur often, so that in all the known clamors there are just sixteen different capitula, and all sixteen come from the Psalms.

The names that occur most frequently in curses, after Judas, are Dathan and Abiron; these two names never appear separately, al-

38. Lester K. Little, "Formules monastiques de malédiction aux IXe et Xe siècles," *Revue Mabillon* 58 (1975): 397–398. A similar formation but with a different selection of verses is found in MS, Cambrai, BM, 29, f. 286r–v.

though occasionally the name Korah is linked to them. Their stories are told in the Book of Numbers, which relates what took place while the Israelites were in the desert between Sinai and the Land of Promise; the very title of the book in Hebrew means "In the Desert."

Korah was the leader of a group of 250 Levites who challenged the religious authority of Moses and Aaron. The rebels claimed that every member of the community was holy and thus able to present offerings to the Lord, whereas these two were wrongly trying to set themselves above everyone else. Moses accepted the challenge, calling on Korah and his followers to prepare to burn incense in their censers before the Lord, and claiming that the Lord would show them who was holy. As the opposing groups faced each other at the appointed time,

> the glory of the Lord appeared to the whole community. And the Lord spoke to Moses and Aaron and said, "Stand apart from this company, so that I may make an end of them in a single instant." Fire came out from the Lord and consumed the 250 men who were presenting the incense. Then the Lord commanded Moses and Aaron to have the censers beaten into plate to be used to cover the altar. (Num. 16:1–11, 16–24, 35–50)

This Levitical challenge concerning priestly authority has a "lay" counterpart in the rebellion of the Reubenites, Dathan and Abiron. These two complained bitterly of conditions in the desert and of the powers Moses assumed: "Must you also set yourself up as prince over us?" Here too there took place a dramatic confrontation, with Moses calling on the Lord to give a sign that would confirm his authority and warning the whole community to stand well away from the tents of the rebels.

> If these men die a natural death and share the common fate of man, then the Lord has not sent me; but if the Lord makes a great chasm, and the ground opens its mouth and swallows them and all that is theirs, and they go down alive to Sheol, then you will know that these men have held the Lord in contempt.

The climax came without delay. "Hardly had Moses spoken when the ground beneath them split; the earth opened its mouth and swallowed them." The rebels went to the underworld alive, and the earth closed over them (Num. 16:12–15, 25–34) (see Fig. 6).

These two incidents are easily confused, and indeed they are already intertwined in a manner difficult to unravel in chapter 16 of Numbers. Thus it is not surprising that some later references to this biblical text

Figure 6. The punishment of Dathan and Abiron, leaders of a rebellion against Moses (Num. 16:12–15, 25–34), depicted at the beginning of the book of Numbers in a Bible made in western England around 1180. The text says: "Here begins the book of Numbers. And the Lord spoke to Moses in the Sinai Desert" (*Incipit liber Numeri. Loqutusque est Dominus ad Moysen in deserto sinai*). The tall figure of Moses calls out to those not in sympathy with the rebels: "Stand back from the tents of the impious" (*Recedite a tabernaculis impiorum*). Dathan and Abiron are shown twice: first as they sink into a hole in the ground (they are identified by name and they are portrayed in the hostile caricature newly devised for depicting Jews), and second as they slide head-first into a monstrous hell-mouth. MS, Oxford, Bodleian Library, Laud misc. 752, f. 49v; by permission of the Bodleian Library, Oxford.

repeat the confusion between the two stories, especially between the two punishments, and that the name of Korah was sometimes linked to that of Dathan and Abiron.[39]

Along with the evocation of Dathan and Abiron, another standard component of maledictions was the striking out or eradication of the name or memory of the person being cursed. At the conclusion of a ceremony of excommunication, as I noted earlier, text and gesture combined to dramatize this point: "And now, just as this flame is extinguished, so may all memory of him vanish forever."[40] Several biblical passages stand behind this component of the obliteration of names. In Deuteronomy, for example, the Lord revealed to Moses how enemies would be treated: "I will make the memory of them cease from among men" (Deut. 32:26); and more specifically for those who made a molten image: "Let me alone that I may destroy them and blot out their name from under heaven" (Deut. 9:14). Following the curses laid out in chapters 27 and 28 of Deuteronomy, the punishment for the Israelite who still worshiped the gods of other nations was summarized thus: "The Lord will not pardon him, but rather the anger of the Lord and his jealousy will smoke against that man and the curses written in this book will settle upon him, and the Lord will blot out his name forever" (Deut. 29:20). And recall that awesome Psalm 108: "May his posterity be cut off; may his name be blotted out within a generation (108:13); may his memory be cut off from the earth" (108:15).

The devastating impact of these curses cannot be felt fully if the meaning of "name" is limited to a mere label that identifies its bearer. Existence itself was bound up in a name. The concepts of memory, memorial, and reputation were also clearly mingled with that of name. After all, "a good name," the Book of Proverbs reminds us, "is rather to be chosen than great riches" (Prov. 22:1). For the ancient Hebrews, a name expressed the essential nature or character of its bearer—to know someone's name was to know that person, and to know the name of God was to know God. Nothing existed unless it had a name. A change of name meant a change of character. One's existence continued posthumously in one's name,[41] and thus to blot out or erase or eradicate

39. Num. 26:9–10.

40. See chapter 1, under "Excommunication and Anathema."

41. *The Interpreter's Dictionary of the Bible*, ed. George A. Buttrick et al., 4 vols. (New York, 1962), 3:500–508.

or cut off a name meant nothing less than to destroy its bearer.[42] The point is made explicit in Ecclesiasticus 44, "Let us now praise famous men" (44:1). The good fate of these men of renown and of their heirs is celebrated in verse after verse, "those who have left a name behind them to be commemorated in story" (44:8). But the flow is interrupted by a contrasting line about the terrible fate of certain others "who are unremembered; they are dead, and it is as though they had never existed, as though they had never been born or left children to succeed them" (44:9).

There are many other curses in the Hebrew Bible that one could cite in this context. Although it seems foolish to count them, there is an invitation to do so in the sanction clause of a tenth-century charter from the church of Apt. For any transgressor of the terms it sets down, this wish is expressed: "May there come upon him the thirty-two maledictions that are contained in the Old Testament."[43]

There are sources, too, in the Hebrew Bible for more than the actual words contained in a clamor. In particular, there is a model for the attitude one assumes—attitude of body as well as of mind—in reciting a clamor and lying down before humiliated relics; it can be seen in this psalm lamenting utter defeat: "Arise, why do you sleep, O Lord? Rise up, do not abandon us for good. Why do you turn away your face, ignoring our worries and difficulties? For our souls are humbled in the dust, our bellies are pressed to the earth. Arise, O Lord, help us, and redeem us for your name's sake" (Ps. 43:23–26).

The search need not stop at the Hebrew Bible. Indeed, one of the clamors calls down upon a malefactor the curses of both the Old and New Testaments.[44] There are curses in the New Testament, many fewer than in the Old but nonetheless potent. The Book of Acts tells of the couple Ananias and Sapphira, who sold some property and gave the proceeds to the apostles, but secretly held back a portion of the sale money for themselves. Peter learned of this, became enraged, and accused Ananias of lying to God. "When Ananias heard these words he

---

42. For other examples, see Deut. 7:24; Josh. 7:9; 1 Sam. 24:22; 4 Kings 14:27; Job 18: 17; Ps. 9:6–7, 33:17, 82:5; Prov. 10:17; Eccles. 6:10; Wisd. of Sol. 4:19; Sir. 10:21, 45:1, 46: 14–15; Isa. 14:22; Zeph. 1:4; and 1 Macc. 3:7.

43. *Cartulaire de l'église d'Apt (835–1130?)*, ed. Noël Didier, Henri Dubled, and Jean Barruol, Essais et travaux de l'Université de Grenoble 20 (Paris, 1967), p. 129: "Veniant super eum triginta duae maledicciones quae in veteri testamento continentur."

44. See the second text from Farfa (*Liber tramitis aevi Odilonis abbatis*, ed. Peter Dinter, Corpus consuetudinum monasticarum 10 [Siegburg, 1980], p. 247).

dropped dead." Three hours later Peter asked Sapphira, who as yet knew nothing of her husband's fate, why they had conspired to put the spirit of the Lord to a test. " 'Listen, there at the door are the footsteps of those who buried your husband, and they will carry you away, too.' And suddenly she dropped dead at his feet" (Acts 5:1–12).

Paul declared anathema anyone who did not love the Lord and also anyone who preached a gospel at variance with the gospel he was preaching (1 Cor. 16:22; Gal. 1:8–9). The Book of Revelation—and hence the New Testament—concludes with (in Latin versions) a double *si quis* clause (Rev. 22:18–19). The first says that if anyone adds to what is written in that book God will add to him the plagues that are described in it. The second says that if anyone takes away from what is written there, God will take away his share in the tree of life and in the holy city, which are also described in the book.

Even Jesus cursed. He did so abruptly one morning as he came from where he had slept in the village of Bethany into the city of Jerusalem. He was hungry and spotted a fig tree. When he got close to it he saw that it was barren, so he said: " 'May no fruit ever come from you again.' And the fig tree withered at once." In reply to his disciples' astonishment, he said that this showed what faith could do. If they had faith they could just by speaking uproot a mountain and cast it into the sea (Matt. 21:18–21; Mark 11:12–14). Jesus cursed the cities of Chorazin, Bethsaida, and Capernaum, whose inhabitants remained impenitent even after he had performed miracles in those places (Matt. 11: 20–24; Luke 10:13–15).

The last of Jesus' teaching before the events that culminated in his death was a foretelling of the Day of Judgment. He described that most grandiose scene, centered upon the throne of the Son of man, come in all his glory with a retinue of angels. Before him are gathered all the nations, and he begins to separate the sheep from the goats, the saved from the damned. The saved gather on his right hand; he praises them and invites them to receive as their inheritance the kingdom that has been prepared for them. With a symmetry that recalls Moses facing Mounts Gerizim and Ebal, he then turns to those on the left side and says: "Depart from me, you that are cursed, into the eternal fire prepared for the devil and his angels" (Matt. 25:31–46) (see Fig. 7).

Thus it was the Bible—from the curse upon the serpent in the Genesis creation story through the parting, provisional curses of Revelation—that provided the principal source of material to the composers

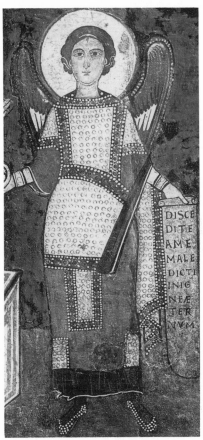

Figure 7. Benediction and malediction at the Last Judgment in details from a painting executed by two Romans named Nicholas and John for a monastery of Benedictine nuns in Rome around 1100. In the center of the painting stands Jesus flanked by these two angels. The angel on the left (at the right hand of Jesus, the side of the saved) holds a scroll that says: "Come, O blessed of my father, inherit the kingdom prepared for you" (*Venite benedicti patris mei percipite paratum vobis regnum*); the scroll held by the angel on the right says: "Depart from me, you that are cursed, into the eternal fire" (*Discedite a me maledicti in ignem aeternum*). The texts are from Matthew 25:34,41. Pinacoteca Vaticana, "Il Giudizio universale," inven. 526. Photo Vatican Museums.

of liturgical clamors. Besides the dazzling variety in the content of its curses, the Bible also supplied such formal elements as the repetitive parallelism of the Psalms and the Deuteronomic litanies of accursed persons, places, things, and activities.

The Liturgy

Religious specialists of the era when the clamors were composed had considerable knowledge of the Bible. This knowledge was based far more upon the Old Testament than the New. The religious culture that fostered their spirituality was markedly formal; its chief form of expression was liturgy. In fact, the biblical knowledge of these religious people was basically mediated through their liturgical experience, and thus important sources for the liturgy of the clamor, in addition to sanction clauses and scriptural passages, are found within the liturgy itself.[45]

The period starting with the accession of the Carolingian dynasty in the middle of the eighth century was marked by great vitality in liturgical history. The Roman Missal with its claim to authenticity and universal applicability was more than four centuries in the future.[46] Instead, local variations (some based on indigenous cultural influences), formulas considered not as set pieces but as models for improvisation, and peculiar practices legitimized by generations of usage characterized the liturgies of the several Germanic kingdoms that had settled in the western provinces of the old Roman Empire. Meanwhile, the liturgies of the eastern Roman Empire were far advanced toward assuming their final form. The earliest attempts at gathering authoritative texts in the West and at imposing conformity in following them came at the instigation not of the Roman popes but of the Carolingian monarchs, and that process went on during the century and a half between 750 and 900.[47]

For the mass, the main kinds of liturgical books produced and used were ordinals and sacramentaries. The former gave procedural direc-

45. Jean Leclercq, *The Love of Learning and the Desire for God: A Study of Monastic Culture,* tr. Catherine Misrahi (New York, 1961), p. 87: "The liturgy is the medium through which the Bible and the patristic tradition are received."

46. Cyrille Vogel, *Medieval Liturgy: An Introduction to the Sources,* tr. William Storey and Neils Rasmussen (Washington, D.C., 1986), p. 4. "We must make a real effort at imagining the kind of ritual chaos that existed in the Latin Church before the XIII century" (ibid., p. 105).

47. Gregory Dix, *The Shape of the Liturgy* (New York, 1982), pp. 546–584.

tions for the actual performance of the mass; the latter, lacking ceremonial indications, contained all the texts, principally prayers with
their many variants, that the celebrant needed.[48] Neither by itself provided enough information for the proper celebration of a mass. Although the prototypes for both kinds were Roman, the oldest surviving
copies of both were of Frankish manufacture.[49] The names of the most
influential sacramentaries recalled papal names and thus suggested at
least papal sponsorship, if not authorship: the Gelasian, the Gregorian,
and the Hadrianum. Yet all these contained elements considerably later
than the popes alluded to, and all were in fact amalgams of Frankish
with Roman texts and practices.[50] The liturgy of the eighth and ninth
centuries is a Romano-Frankish hybrid, rather like the architecture of
Charlemagne's "New Rome" at Aachen, with its columns and marbles
brought from Ravenna and Rome, or like a piece of Frankish jewelry,
its traditional Germanic band of beaten gold set with a Roman cameo
among other precious gems.[51]

The variant prayers in sacramentaries correspond to the variety of
occasions on which or for which masses are celebrated. Prayers varied according to the calendar of the liturgical year; they were also
made into special variants for the feast days of certain saints and
martyrs. The latest category of variants to emerge, about the sixth
century, was the votive mass, a mass dedicated to expressing a particular wish (*votum*). While one might expect that a mass on behalf
of a good harvest would be offered at about the same time every
year, most votive masses could not be regularly scheduled but were
offered only when given occasions arose, such as the coronation of
a ruler or the departure of an abbot on a perilous journey. And
while prayers, and hence masses, could be said for someone or
something, they could equally well be said against someone or
something, such as an impending catastrophe. In the middle of the

48. Vogel, *Medieval Liturgy*, p. 64. For ordinals, see *DS* 9:903, and *Les "Ordines romani"
du Haut Moyen Age*, ed. Michel Andrieu, 5 vols., Spicilegium sacrum lovaniense 11, 23–
24, 28–29 (Louvain, 1931, 1948–1951, 1956–1961; repr. 1960–1965). For sacramentaries, see
Jean Deshusses, ed., *Le sacramentaire grégorien*, Spicilegium Friburgense 16 (Fribourg,
1971), and Henri Leclercq, in *DACL* 15, pt. 1:242–285, s.v. "Sacramentaires."

49. Vogel, *Medieval Liturgy*, pp. 135–137.

50. See the works of Deshusses, *Le sacramentaire grégorien*, and Leclercq, "Sacramentaires," cited above.

51. Einhard, *Vita Caroli Magni*, ch. 26 (*MGH, SS* 2:457). On jewelry, see Peter Lasko,
Ars Sacra, 800–1200 (Harmondsworth, Eng., 1972), for example, the Lothar Cross, pl. 95
and pp. 99–101.

eighth century there were about 60 votive formulas; by 900, following the period of their most rampant proliferation, they numbered 278.[52] The earliest sacramentaries already included formulas for masses in time of war (*in tempore belli*) and on account of trouble (*pro tribulatione*).[53]

Under a title like the two just mentioned, one would ordinarily expect to find in a sacramentary three prayers: the collect, the secret, and the postcommunion. The collect is that principal prayer of the first part of the mass that comes right before the readings from Scripture. It is usually related in theme to the lessons that follow. The secret comes at the offertory and is an offertory prayer, and the postcommunion obviously follows communion and in theme refers to the reception of that sacrament. All three are of the structural type that also goes by the name "collect."[54]

Certain of the titles that appear on clamors show a connection with votive masses. Examples include one from Cluny already noted, "How to Perform a Clamor in Case of Trouble" (*Quomodo fiat clamor pro tribulatione*), also one from the Abbey of Remiremont, "Invocation on Account of Trouble" (*Invocatio pro tribulatione*), and one from Compiègne, "Prayers in Times of the Church's Suffering" (*Pro tribulatione ecclesiae preces*).[55] The use of a clamor had the effect of making a mass into a *missa pro tribulatione*. The central element in a clamor, the text beginning *In spiritu humilitatis*, not only is called a prayer but is frequently preceded by the phrase "let us pray" (*oremus*). Although this central element sometimes stands alone in formulas, more often it is part of a larger whole, the rest being made up mostly of psalms, capitula, and collects. Whereas psalms and capitula come directly from the Bible, the collects instead come from liturgical sources.

Some clamors have just one collect; the maximum number of collects

52. *DMA* 8:200–201.

53. *Liber sacramentorum Romanae ecclesiae ordinis anni circuli*, ed. Leo C. Mohlberg (Rome, 1960), pp. 194, 214; *The Gregorian Sacramentary under Charles the Great*, ed. Henry A. Wilson, Henry Bradshaw Society 49 (London, 1915), pp. 197–199, 201. Cf. *Liber sacramentorum Gellonensis*, ed. A. Dumas and Jean Deshusses, 2 vols., Corpus Christianorum, series Latina 159, 159A (Turnhout, 1981), 1:298.

54. Geoffrey G. Willis, "The Variable Prayers of the Roman Mass," in his *Further Essays in Early Roman Liturgy*, Alcuin Club Collections 50 (London, 1968), pp. 89–131.

55. Cluny: *Vetus disciplina monastica*, ed. Marquard Herrgott (Paris, 1726), pp. 230–232. Remiremont: MS, Paris, BN, lat. 823, f. 344v. Compiègne: MS, Paris, BN, lat. 17319, f. 216r.

in a clamor is five.[56] In all the known clamors just ten different collects are used. Next to *Hostium nostrorum*, the collect that recurs most frequently is *Ecclesiae tuae*:

> We beseech you, O Lord, to hear the peaceful prayers of your church, so that, with her enemies and all their errors destroyed, she may serve you secure in her freedom [*Ecclesiae tuae quaesumus domine preces placatus admitte ut, destructis adversitatibus et erroribus universis, secura tibi serviat libertate*].[57]

These and the other collects found in clamors are all present in the earliest surviving sacramentaries, within the votive masses for times of war or times of trouble.[58] They are almost certainly older still than these sacramentaries, but their appearance in these books in any case precedes the earliest appearance of an identifiable liturgical clamor.

Another one of these collects is nestled within and toward the end of the text *In spiritu humilitatis*. It says:

> Almighty God, do not disdain your people who cry out to you in their affliction, but for the glory of your name be pleased to help us who are so sorely troubled [*Ne despicias, omnipotens deus, nos famulos tuos in afflictione clamantes, sed propter gloriam nominis tui tribulationibus succurre placatus*].[59]

This too is a collect found in the earliest sacramentaries. Within some of the clamors it is transformed and lengthened to say:

> Do not despise us, Lord, who call out to you in affliction, but because of the glory of your name and the mercy with which you founded this place and dedicated it in honor of the most blessed Mother of God, visit us in peace and bring us out of our present distress [*Ne despicias nos, domine, clamantes ad te in afflictione, sed propter gloriam nominis tui et misericordiam, qua locum istum fundasti et in honore beatissimae dei genetricis sublimasti, visita nos in pace et erue nos a presenti angustia*].[60]

The search for collects affords a glimpse into the work of the compiler(s) of the clamor, and into the work of liturgical compilers more generally. Just as with the composition made up of verses from many

---

56. Two clamors with five collects each are Sainte-Barbe: MS, Paris, Bibl. Sainte-Geneviève, 96, ff. 220r–221v, and Sens: MS, Saint Petersburg, Public Library, lat. 4° v.I.35, ff. 102r–104r.

57. *Liber sacramentorum*, ed. Mohlberg, p. 218; *Liber sacramentorum Gellonensis*, 1:427.

58. These can be traced via the work of Pierre Bruylants, ed., *Les oraisons du missel romain: Texte et histoire*, 2 vols. (Louvain, 1952); for *Ecclesiae tuae*, 2:140–141, and for *Hostium nostrorum*, 2:174.

59. Ibid., 2:202.

60. *Liber tramitis*, ed. Dinter, pp. 246–247.

of the psalms, a compiler has here reached into the familiar liturgical repertory, taken out whole pieces, and inserted them into a new framework. In tracing such a process it does little good to search for "authors" or "original versions." Instead, there seems to be at work here a process of appropriation and reutilization.[61] Even the now familiar opening phrase of the clamor, *In spiritu humilitatis et cum animo contrito*, itself of biblical origin (Dan. 3:39), comes from one of the oblation prayers of the mass; it is found already in a sacramentary from Amiens of the second half of the ninth century.[62]

The placing of the clamor shortly after the Lord's Prayer gives further indication of terrain well prepared. Traditionally a prayer called the "embolism" (from a term meaning insertion or wedge) was inserted immediately after the Lord's Prayer. Its Western form was set at the latest by the time of its appearance in the so-called Bobbio Missal of the eighth century;[63] its opening words take up again the final petition of the Lord's Prayer: "but deliver us from evil" (*sed libera nos a malo*). The embolism reads:

> Deliver us we beseech you, O Lord, from all evil, past, present, and future, and at the intercession of the blessed, glorious, and ever-virgin Mary, Mother of God, and with your blessed apostles Peter and Paul, and Andrew, and all the saints, grant graciously peace in our times so that, aided by your mercy, we may be both ever free from sin and secure from all disturbance [*Libera nos, quaesumus domine, ab omnibus malis praeteritis presentibus et futuris, et intercedente beata et gloriosa semperque vergine dei genetrice maria, cum beatis tuis apostolis petro et paulo, atque Andrea, et omnibus sanctis, da propitius pacem in diebus nostris ut, ope misericordiae tuae adiuti, et a peccato simus semper liberi et ab omni perturbatione securi*].[64]

In one of the Cluniac formulas for a clamor that includes a humiliation, this prayer is called a collect and is recited silently by the priest while the relics are being returned to their usual place.[65]

Within the prayer *In spiritu humilitatis*, there is a specific reference to that part of the mass into which the clamor is inserted. Following the

61. Vogel, *Medieval Liturgy*, pp. 62–64.
62. Victor Leroquais, "L'ordo missae du sacramentaire d'Amiens," *Ephemerides liturgicae* 41 (1927): 435–445. The prayer in question is on p. 441.
63. *The Bobbio Missal: A Gallican Mass-Book*, ed. Elias A. Lowe, Henry Bradshaw Society 58 (London, 1920), p. 13.
64. Edmund Bishop, *Liturgica Historica: Papers on the Liturgy and Religious Life of the Western Church* (Oxford, 1918), pp. 88–91.
65. *Liber tramitis*, ed. Dinter, p. 247.

opening phrase about the humble spirit and contrite heart, it says: "We come before your sacred altar and your most holy body and blood, Lord Jesus, redeemer of the world" (*Ante sanctum altare tuum et sacratissimum corpus et sanguinem tuum, domine Iesu, redemptor mundi, accedimus*). This is indeed a time when the consecrated bread and wine are on the altar.

Carolingian enthusiasm for votive masses, as I noted earlier, was expressed in the nearly fivefold increase in their number between A.D. 750 and 900. This can also be seen in the several ways the Carolingian monarchs fostered spiritual preparation for military conflict, the cult of military relics, prayers for victory, and liturgical commemorations of victory. Indeed, prayer was one of the political mainstays of the dynasty. Religious communities were expected to offer regular prayers on behalf of the prince and of his government; noncompliance was taken to indicate infidelity.[66]

By the early ninth century the celebration of special propitiary services, especially in times of military danger, had become an established tradition, and it continued to be so through the century. Monarchs issued edicts ordering that religious observances be conducted for the supplication of divine assistance in particular, troubled circumstances. Loyal subjects were urged not to wait to be told when such circumstances arose. By the capitulary of Thionville in 805, Charlemagne advised against awaiting a royal edict "when famine occurs, or plague or pestilence, or unseasonable weather, or any such tribulations," in favor of starting to pray right away for God's mercy. Regular and repeated litanies of supplication called "rogations" entered the springtime calendar at 25 April and in preparation for Ascension Day. Three days of fasting and processions set the stage for reciting invocations to saints and petitions, along with psalms, which together make up a rough but recognizable reverse image of liturgical maledictions.[67]

The appeal of a troubled community for divine assistance, whether orchestrated or spontaneous, was no Carolingian invention. In the sixth century (to deal only with more recent precedents), the devastating

---

66. Michael McCormick, "The Liturgy of War in the Early Middle Ages: Crisis, Liturgies, and the Carolingian Monarchy," *Viator* 15 (1984): 1–23.

67. *MGH, Capit.* 1:122–123. André Vauchez, *Les laïcs au Moyen Age: Pratiques et expériences religieuses* (Paris, 1987), pp. 145–155; *The Golden Legend of Jacobus de Voragine*, tr. Granger Ryan and Helmut Ripperger, 2 vols. (New York, 1941), 1:278–280.

visits of the plague elicited elaborate liturgical responses. At Marseilles in 588,

> King Guntram ordered the entire people to assemble in church and rogations to be celebrated there with great devotion. He then commanded that they should eat and drink nothing but barley bread and pure water, and that all should be regular in keeping the vigils. His orders were obeyed. For three days his own alms were greater than usual, and he seemed so anxious about all his people that he might well have been taken for one of our Lord's bishops rather than a king. He put his hope in the compassion of our Lord, directing all his prayers toward him, for through his agency he believed with perfect faith that his wishes would be realized.[68]

At Rome in 590 the newly installed pope Gregory I preached on the plague as God's punishment for sin; he ordered the people to repent and to pray and sing psalms for three days. Then he had simultaneous processions organized, starting off from seven peripheral churches and all converging upon the basilica of Santa Maria Maggiore. These united to form one tremendous penitential demonstration, with the continuous praying punctuated by the collapsing of the dead and dying.[69] A century and a half later on the eve of the Carolingian take-over, when Boniface, the leader of the mission to the Germans, complained to Pope Zacharias about the dangers and setbacks he faced, the pope gave him this advice: "To the peoples entrusted to you, most reverend brother, preach fasting and the supplications of litanies before God, and his supreme clemency will aid you."[70] Thus the resort to liturgy in difficult times represents no major departure in the post-Carolingian or even the Carolingian period, and the constituent components of the "new" liturgies of clamor in the tenth and eleventh centuries were evidently standard parts of the liturgical repertory by the time of Charlemagne's father.

In connection with the Avar campaign of 791, Charlemagne called for three days of litanies and of abstention from wine and meat. Every priest was to perform a votive mass, and every cleric who knew the psalms was to sing fifty of them.[71] This last detail calls attention to the preponderant role of the psalms in Carolingian spirituality, a role

---

68. Gregory of Tours, *Historia Francorum*, 9:21–22 (*MGH, SRM* 1:379–380).

69. Jeffrey Richards, *Consul of God: The Life and Times of Gregory the Great* (London, 1980), pp. 41–42. Cf. McCormick, "Liturgy of War," pp. 19–20.

70. *MGH, Epist.* 3:323; tr. Ephraim Emerton, *The Letters of Saint Boniface* (New York, 1970), p. 108.

71. McCormick, "Liturgy of War," pp. 8–9.

found, though, not in the mass—where heretofore we have been seeking liturgical sources of the clamor—but in the daily office of the
monks.

"Seven times a day have I praised you" is a line from the Psalms
(118:164) quoted by Saint Benedict in his monastic rule to justify the
holding of seven services each day: lauds, prime, terce, sext, none, ves-
pers, and compline. He asserted, moreover, that the psalmist had been
referring to these seven "hours." To this he added that the psalmist
had also indicated a night office (vigils or matins) in saying, "At mid-
night I arose to give you praise" (Ps. 118:62).[72]

Upon this scriptural authority Benedict based the daily cycle of eight
services that make up the Divine Office; the main component of these
services was the singing of psalms. His rule sets out in detail that
certain psalms are to be sung at certain hours, but it also includes
discretionary guidelines. For example, not every psalm is assigned to
a particular hour, and thus "The remaining psalms not accounted for
in this arrangement for the day hours are distributed evenly at vigils
over the seven nights of the week."[73] The limits of discretion are clearly
set, for anyone finding the distribution of psalms as suggested to be
unsatisfactory is given latitude to arrange them differently, "provided
that the full complement of 150 psalms is by all means carefully maintained every week." There follows a challenging reminder that the Desert Fathers recited all 150 psalms each day. "Let us hope that we,
lukewarm as we are, can achieve it in a whole week."[74] Indeed, those
monks who in the course of a week say less than the full psalter "betray
extreme indolence and lack of devotion in their service."[75] On the recitation of the psalms, then, as on several matters, Benedict's rule is not
an exact prescription that a monk or nun must follow to the letter, but
a minimal program with a built-in challenge, to those who are able, to
go beyond its requirements.

Benedict's program of psalmody was indeed minimal by comparison
with monastic usage in Carolingian and later times. In the reform of

72. Ch. 16 in *RB*, pp. 210–211; cf. the corresponding passages in the Rule of the Master,
33, 34, *La règle du maître*, ed. Adalbert de Vogüé, 3 vols., Sources chrétiennes 105–107
(Paris, 1964–1965), 2:176–177, 188–189. Pierre-Marie Gy, "La Bible dans la liturgie au
Moyen Age," in *Le Moyen Age et la Bible*, ed. Pierre Riché and Guy Lobrichon (Paris, 1984),
pp. 537–552.
73. Ch. 18 in *RB*, pp. 214–215.
74. Ibid. Cf. Gy, "La Bible dans la liturgie," pp. 548–549.
75. Ch. 18 in *RB*, pp. 214–215.

Benedict of Aniane, monastic adviser to both Charlemagne and Louis the Pious, each monk was to recite fifteen psalms privately each night immediately before the start of vigils. Of this second Benedict it was said that even outside the liturgical hours, when he worked with his hands, he kept his tongue busy with psalms.[76] At the monastery of Baume in the late ninth century, the number of psalms sung in the full daily cycle of offices reached 138, while two centuries later, according to the Cluniac customs compiled by the monk Ulrich, it stood at 170. The Desert Fathers had met their match.[77]

The plainchant that modern people associate with monastic psalmody came into being at the same time as this expansion of the number of psalms sung in monastic usage. As with the sacramentaries, which were in fact recent mixtures of Roman and Frankish elements but were paraded as Roman, indeed papal, and ancient in origin, the chant was credited to Pope Gregory I; and when notation was introduced in the tenth century, this sixth-century pope was depicted as dictating neums as well as words to a scribe.[78] The chant did not render the precise wording of the psalms less clear or less important or less memorable; on the contrary, chant enhances speech. Building on the demonstrated superiority of singing over speech in projection and carrying power, the chant slows down and regulates speech; it reduces the chances of rushing speech or of slurring words. It may be useful to recall that in the directions for liturgical texts of the period under study, distinction is rarely made between speaking and singing; although *cantare*, "to sing," does appear, the verb more commonly used to cover both meanings is *dicere*, "to speak."[79]

To say that a prayer or other liturgical passage composed in the tenth

76. Bishop, *Liturgica Historica*, p. 214. Ardo, *Vita Benedicti Anianensis*, chs. 21, 38 (*MGH, SS* 16, pt. 1:209, 216).

77. Barbara H. Rosenwein, "Feudal War and Monastic Peace: Cluniac Liturgy as Ritual Aggression," *Viator* 2 (1971): 129–157.

78. Leo Treitler, "Homer and Gregory: The Transmission of Epic Poetry and Plainchant," *Musical Quarterly* 60 (1974): 333–372; idem, "Reading and Singing: On the Genesis of Occidental Music-Writing," *Early Music History* 4 (1984): 135–208. Already in the ninth century Gregory was depicted with a dove, representing the Holy Spirit, hovering over or perched upon his right shoulder, whispering to him the text that he in turn dictated to a scribe.

79. Richard H. Hoppin, *Medieval Music* (New York, 1978), pp. 78–80. My forays into reading about medieval music have been undertaken with the generous and learned guidance of two experts: Paul Evans of the Music Department at Smith College and Thomas F. Kelly of the Oberlin College Conservatory of Music.

century includes a quotation from a psalm or else paraphrases or at least echoes one, and then to indicate the precise reference in a note, could imply that the composer had done the reverse—looked up the psalm and then quoted or paraphrased or echoed it. Such an interpretation would in this case be incorrect. Even though the practice of silent reading had been introduced as far back as the fourth century, the principal way to read continued to be out loud. The religious recited texts and heard them. And what texts? Sacred texts, the Scriptures that they considered holy and that they venerated, were what they said and listened to. It was not their task to examine these texts critically or to break them down into explicable units by means of searching questions. Instead they were to coax out the truth they believed was contained in them. Through repetition and prolonged rumination they absorbed these texts, which in turn supplied them with a rich biblical vocabulary and idiom. They spoke a language based on the Bible, much as, in the United States some Southerners—white and black both, and not only preachers—do. They did not search the Bible in order to quote from it, because they had it in their minds already.[80]

One result of this spoken culture was that their biblical quotations were not always exact. Four or five centuries later, when university scholars quoted texts with greater precision, the reason was that they knew those texts much less well and had to look them up in order to quote them at all. During the 1230s Dominican scholars at Paris invented the concordance, a word index of the Bible, so as to retrieve any passage quickly and accurately; but monks and nuns of earlier times kept countless biblical passages stored, more or less accurately, in their minds.[81]

They knew some of these texts better than others, and surely knew the psalms best of all. Even at the minimum rate of 150 per week, the psalms could soon permeate the mind of a regular participant in the Divine Office.[82] Each of the day hours, moreover, began in the same

---

80. Gy, "La Bible dans la liturgie," p. 552. Cf. Paul Saenger, "Silent Reading: Its Impact on Late Medieval Script and Society," *Viator* 13 (1982): 367–414. Jean Leclercq refers to "acoustical reading" and points out that *legere*, "to read," included in its meaning *audire*, "to hear"; see his *Love of Learning*, p. 19.

81. Richard H. Rouse and Mary A. Rouse, "The Verbal Concordance to the Scriptures," *Archivum fratrum praedicatorum* 44 (1974): 5–30.

82. And there were punishments for those who made mistakes. According to the rule, mature persons are to humble themselves and make satisfaction before their peers; "children, however, are to be whipped for such a fault." Ch. 45 in *RB*, pp. 246–247.

way, with verse 2 from Psalm 69, which as it happens sets a tone appropriate for a clamor: "God, come to my assistance; Lord, make haste to help me" (*Deus in adiutorium meum intende, Domine ad adiuvandum me festina*).[83] The texts of the liturgical clamors of the tenth and eleventh centuries thus did not come out of the void.

The liturgy also supplies background to aspects of the clamors other than the strictly textual. The order for baptism provided a liturgical precedent for the use of ritualized hostility, if not, technically speaking, curses. Because the unbaptized person was believed to be possessed by the devil, the rite of baptism included an exorcism, and within that exorcism the presiding priest addressed the devil directly, calling him "accursed devil" (*maledicte diabole*) and heaping abuse on him as he angrily sent him away.[84] The Desert Fathers had often had to contend with demons, and their way of showing contempt had been by hissing or spitting at them.[85] Along this line there is a fourth-century baptism ritual that specified, at the moment of the renunciation of Satan, a *sputatio*.[86] In what became standard practice, vestiges of these earlier gestures lingered in the exsufflation, the priest's blowing into the candidate's face, and also in the priest's touching one ear of the candidate with spittle to symbolize both the healing power of baptism and contempt for the devil.[87]

The exorcism of the devil logically enough precedes baptism. Burchard of Worms (c. 965–1025) insisted on this point in writing that no one could be baptized until first exorcised.[88] Baptism usually took place at Easter, and so the exorcisms were done in the course of preparatory services called scrutinies held during Lent.[89] At Rome in the late fifth century there were three scrutinies in Lent; a century later the number had become fixed at seven.[90] In the Gelasian Sacramentary the devil is repeatedly addressed as *maledicte diabole* or *maledicte Satanas*.[91] One elaborate formula insults the devil as a "most unclean, damned spirit,

83. Ch. 18 in *RB*, pp. 212–213.
84. Several examples in Edward C. Whitaker, *Documents of the Baptismal Liturgy*, Alcuin Club Collections 42 (London, 1960).
85. Jeffrey B. Russell, *Lucifer: The Devil in the Middle Ages* (Ithaca, N.Y., 1984), p. 126.
86. Louis Gougaud, *Ascetic and Devotional Practices in the Middle Ages*, tr. G. C. Bateman (London, 1927), pp. 45–46.
87. Russell, *Lucifer*, p. 126.
88. Burchard, *Decretum*, 4:10 (*PL* 140:730); cited by Russell, *Lucifer*, p. 127.
89. Oscar Hardman, *A History of Christian Worship*, 2d ed. (London, 1948), p. 24.
90. Henry A. Kelly, *The Devil at Baptism* (Ithaca, N.Y., 1985), pp. 201–203.
91. *Liber sacramentorum*, ed. Mohlberg, pp. 44–46, 67, 249.

grown old in evil, the substance of crimes, the origin of sin, you who revel in deceit, sacrilege, defilement and slaughter." The call to go away is equally hostile: "Through the power of all the saints you are tormented, crushed, and sent down to eternal flames. . . . Depart, depart, from wherever you may be, and never again seek to enter bodies dedicated to God. May they be forbidden to you forever."[92] This physical presence of the devil in the body is emphasized in one exorcism in the Stowe Missal (produced in late eighth-century Ireland), where the devil is expelled from each part of the body individually.[93]

The manner and gestures proper to the clamor had their own liturgical precedents. The offertory prayer, *In spiritu humilitatis*, was to be said in a way that acted out the words themselves, with the priest bowing deeply before the altar.[94] In some churches the saying of the embolism called for a full *prostratio*.[95] Similarly, for saying psalms prostration often was indicated as the proper attitude. This was the case with the so-called penitential psalms, a grouping of seven psalms, coalesced by the sixth century, thought particularly suitable for use in performing penance.[96] During Lent, these plus the first seven gradual psalms, known all together as the "prostrate psalms," were to be sung, as the name suggests, with the religious flat on the floor.[97] Moreover, all the liturgies concerning preparation for war and celebrations of victory included forms of humility, especially fasting and reciting psalms and litanies while barefoot.[98]

Script, gestures, action: some bishops of the sixth and seventh centuries employed liturgical threats or actions in ways that anticipate the clamor. The first case involves a series of incidents at Agde in the sixth century. The bishop, named Leo, and an Arian count named Gomarcharius became locked in a dispute over land. The story includes heresy, threats, miraculous illnesses and recoveries, and at the end, when the penitent wrongdoer comes to the church, his death on the spot. At the height of the action that concerns us, the bishop went one evening

92. Kelly, *Devil at Baptism*, pp. 238–239.

93. *The Stowe Missal*, ed. George F. Warner, 2 vols., Henry Bradshaw Society 31–32 (London, 1906, 1915), 2:24.

94. Josef A. Jungmann, *The Mass of the Roman Rite: Its Origins and Development*, tr. Francis A. Brunner, 2 vols. (New York, 1950), 2:292.

95. *ODCC*, s.v. "Embolism."

96. The penitential psalms are nos. 6, 31, 37, 50, 101, 129, and 142.

97. The first seven gradual psalms are nos. 119–125.

98. McCormick, "Liturgy of War," pp. 8–11.

into his church, prostrated himself in prayer, celebrated vigils, and so passed the entire night in tears, singing psalms. In the morning he reached up to the lamps overhead with a stick and smashed them, saying: "No lamp will be lighted here again until God has vengeance on his enemies and regains the goods belonging to this house." Negotiations followed, and these culminated in the return of the land to the bishop, the count's embrace of orthodoxy, and, at the church door, the latter's dramatic death.[99]

An equally vivid tale is told of the strained relations between Bishop Franco of Aix-en-Provence and King Childericus in the 560s. The king laid claim to a villa he believed was wrongly held by the bishop. The bishop went before the king right away, stating his claim and protesting (clamans et obsecrans), and warning the king that he would be condemned by heavenly judgment, "for I know the force of Saint Mitrias (the patron of his church), who is quick to inflict vengeance on those who do him wrong." The king heard the case and decided to fine the bishop three hundred gold pence. The condemned and despoiled priest returned to his church and prostrated himself in prayer before the tomb of the saint. Having recited a lesson from the Psalms, he said: "No light will be kindled here nor measure [modulatio] of the Psalms sung [canetur], O glorious saint, unless first you avenge your servants of their enemies and you restore to the holy church those things that were violently carried off from it." This he did with a great effusion of tears, as also when he then placed sharp thorns upon the saint's tomb, closed the doors of the church, and blocked the entrance with more thorns. Without delay the king was struck by a fever, which confined him to his bed for over a year. As soon as he recovered, he gave back the disputed land, paid back double the amount of the fine he had collected, and died. "As for the bishop, he obtained, as he had promised, by the power of God's champion, vengeance against the enemy of the church."[100]

A third precedent to the clamor involves Eloi, bishop of Noyon (c. 590–660), who was approached early one morning by the custodian of the Basilica of Saint Columba the Virgin. Trembling all over and throwing himself at the bishop's feet, the man announced that during the past night all the church's precious furnishings had been stolen. Eloi

99. Gregory of Tours, Liber de gloria confessorum (MGH, SRM 1:540–541).
100. Ibid., p. 789.

was greatly saddened, but he gently reassured the custodian and then went to pray before the saint. These are the words he spoke to her:

> Listen, Saint Columba, to what I have to say. May my redeemer know that if you do not get the goods stolen from this church back in here right away, I will assuredly block this doorway with thorns in such a way that never again from this day on will any veneration be offered to you in this place.

He then left and went about his duties. The saint apparently intervened, for the following morning the custodian came early to the church and found everything back just as before, down to the last scrap of cloth.[101]

These early examples of threats to suspend worship, drawn from the lives of three bishops, demonstrate precedents not within any particular liturgy but in the actual manipulation of liturgy. Rather than liturgical clamors, these were out-and-out humiliations of saints, without a hint that their purpose was to make malefactors feel sorrowful for the sufferings of the saints. The exclusive, and rather simplistic, goal was to goad the saint into action under the threat of no further veneration.

A closely related form of liturgy stoppage was the interdict, by which ecclesiastical officials could declare closed, for cause, a church or the churches of a given geopolitical area and thus halt the dispensing of the sacraments therein. In the account of such a suspension of liturgy at Saint Peter's in Rome in 878, we learn that all the liturgical paraphernalia was moved from Saint Peter's to Saint John's-in-the-Lateran and that the altar of Saint Peter's was covered with a coarse cloth. This account affords us a glimpse of another possible precedent for a detail of the humiliation ceremony. Extant historical remains probably record a miniscule percentage of such incidents, yet they attest in still another way how the seeds of the clamor lay embedded within the liturgical culture itself.[102]

Canon Law

Disputes within Frankish society and the Frankish church in the middle years of the ninth century stimulated the production of four col-

---

101. Audoenus, *Vita Eligii episcopi noviomagensis*, 1:30 (*MGH, SRM* 4:686–687).

102. *Annales Fuldenses*, for 878 (*MGH, SS* 1:392). For a collection of texts on interdict, see Wilhelm Richter, *De origine et evolutione interdicti usque ad aetatem Ivonis Carnotensis et Paschalis II* (Rome, 1934).

lections of canon law. These purport to bring together conciliar and papal decrees dating as far back as A.D. 90, to a time when neither church councils nor the papacy yet existed. They constituted a massive exercise in the fabrication of false documents. One of these came much later to be called the Pseudo-Isidorian Decretals, while later still that name and its simpler variant False Decretals were applied to all the collections together. These collections have common sources of inspiration and common political goals. They represent the points of view of Frankish bishops both against their ecclesiastical superiors, the archbishops, and against the leading secular powers of their time. Besides their exaltation of the episcopal office, one of the major themes they share is fierce opposition to infringement upon church property.[103]

One of the forgers, introduced earlier, was Benedict the Levite, whose assumed identity was that of a deacon in the church of Mainz. His work—"his" if indeed it was the work of an individual—was probably executed in the area of Reims between 847 and 857. It was addressed to the sons of Louis the Pious as a compendium of the capitularies issued by their father, their grandfather Charlemagne, and their great-grandfather Pepin. Roughly three-quarters of the material in the collection is apocryphal.[104]

The first entry of the False Decretals into the public arena was at the Council of Quierzy in 857, where three passages from them were cited in a special section of the council's deliberations headed "Collection concerning Plunderers" (*Collectio de raptoribus*). The first passage argues that whoever steals anything from his father or mother commits homicide. "Our father is obviously God, who created us; our mother is just as surely the church, which regenerated us spiritually in baptism. Therefore whoever steals money from Christ or takes anything away from or defrauds churches is a murderer and will be prosecuted as such in the eyes of the just judge." The second passage defines ecclesiastical possessions as "oblations," since they were offerings to the Lord. They represent vows of the faithful and fines for their sins; they constitute the patrimony of the poor. Whoever steals these is guilty of

103. Horst Fuhrmann, *Einfluss und Verbreitung der pseudoisidorischen Fälschungen von ihrem Auftauchen bis in die neuere Zeit*, 3 vols., Schriften der MGH 24 (Stuttgart, 1972–1974), 1:137–194. See also Roger E. Reynolds, "Rites of Separation and Reconciliation in the Early Middle Ages," in *Segni e riti nella chiesa altomedievale occidentale*, Settimane di studio del Centro italiano di studi sull'Alto Medioevo 32 (Spoleto, 1987), pp. 409–410, 413.

104. *MGH, Leg.* 2, pt. 2:17–158; Fuhrmann, *Einfluss und Verbreitung*, 1:163–167.

the crime of Ananias and Sapphira. The third passage says that plunderers of ecclesiastical properties commit sacrilege and thus merit damnation and anathema. They and their accomplices and all who support them should be driven from the threshold of the holy church. These same passages were cited about six more times each in surviving documents of the quarter-century following Quierzy.[105]

Over the next two centuries and more, numerous maledictory formulas quoted or in some way alluded to these passages, as well as many others that originated in the False Decretals but happened not to be cited at the Council of Quierzy. By raising the stakes in the plundering of church property from theft to murder, by calling attention to the crime and the instant, fatal punishment of Ananias and Sapphira (by Peter, from whom all bishops derive their authority), and by escalating the rhetoric of clerical condemnation of lay antagonists, canon law too, even if in a relatively modest way—along with spiritual sanction clauses, the Old Testament spirituality of the time, and the propitiatory character of the liturgy—made its contribution to the form and practice of religious cursing.

---

105. *MGH, Conc.* 3:392–394; Fuhrman, *Einfluss und Verbreitung*, 1:211–218, especially the chart on p. 213. An additional example comes from the Council of Ravenna in 877, which decreed that those who stole from churches should, besides being struck with perpetual anathema, suffer the punishment of Ananias and Sapphira (Mansi 17:340).

3
Justifications

IN THE Sermon on the Mount, Jesus said, "Love your enemies; do good to those who hate you; bless those who curse you" (Luke 6:27–28). Paul commented on this teaching with the terse formula, "Bless them who persecute you; bless and curse not" (Rom. 12:14). The Epistle of James (3:1–11), as we shall see, stresses the corrosive influence of cursing upon the capacity to bless. The combination of these New Testament rejections of cursing with the huge repertory of biblical—mostly Old Testament—curses, some of which we looked at earlier, created what Saint Augustine called "a problem that surely cannot be ignored."

> Many passages in Scripture, if read superficially and without much reflection, seem to go counter to this precept of the Lord wherein he admonishes us to love our enemies, do good to them that hate us, and pray for those that persecute us; for in the prophets we find many imprecations against enemies that are held to be curses.[1]

For a book on Christian liturgical cursing, here indeed is a problem that cannot be ignored. To deal with it in manageable parts, I shall consider first the question of how cursing in general was regarded, then how curses in the Bible were interpreted and explained, and finally how formal, liturgical curses were justified. The leading medieval theological reflections on cursing will be shown to be in basic harmony with the approaches of some modern philosophers of language.

---

1. Augustine, *De sermone Domini in monte*, 1:71 (*PL* 34:1265); tr. John J. Jepson in Augustine, *The Lord's Sermon on the Mount*, Ancient Christian Writers 5 (Westminster, 1948), p. 82. In preparing this chapter, I learned much from the work of Alison Beach, a Smith College senior in 1985, and of Joanne Watson, a master's candidate in 1989.

Occasional Curses

Monks and nuns were not supposed to curse. The "tools for good works" listed in Benedict's rule include the biblical instructions to love one's enemies and to return blessings for curses.[2] Gregory the Great tells of the terrible effects of the curse uttered by a holy man, a hermit named Florentius, who had a pet bear that kept him company and served him. This arrangement appeared so attractive to four monks of a nearby monastery that they grew envious of Florentius and killed his bear. Florentius, "distracted with grief, pronounced a curse on the monks," who soon contracted leprosy and died horrible deaths. Florentius wept for the rest of his life, and it is this sad fate that Gregory presses upon his readers, not that of the four monks. "It may be," muses Gregory, "that almighty God brought this about in order to prevent Florentius from ever again presuming to hurl the weapons of malediction in a state of anger."[3]

Laypeople as well as religious were not supposed to curse. Church councils of the period when the Christianization of the Germanic peoples took place made the point by repeatedly prohibiting the full range of practices that clerics considered pagan. A council held in 551 at Eauze, a former Roman provincial capital north of the Pyrenees, included those who make incantations among the people whom the faithful should avoid.[4] The Council of Auxerre in 578 forbade discharging vows at bramble bushes or springs or sacred trees, the proper place being instead a church; it also forbade turning to soothsayers or fortune-tellers.[5] The decrees of councils held in Frankish lands from 742 onward had the backing of the Carolingian rulers, who reissued the decrees in the capitularies they sent to administrators throughout their territories. Conciliar canons and royal capitularies denounced over and over as execrable and offensive to God such pagan "superstitions" as sorcery, spells, charms, placing lighted candles (*luminaria*) by trees or

2. Benedict, *Rule for Monks*, 4:31–33, 7:43, in *RB*, pp. 182–183, 198–199. *Rule of the Master*, 3:34–38, 10:60, in *La règle du maître*, ed. Adalbert de Vogüé, 3 vols., Sources chrétiennes 105–107 (Paris, 1964–1965), 1:366–369, 432–433.

3. Gregory the Great, *Dialogues*, 3:15 (*PL* 77:249–253); tr. Odo J. Zimmerman (New York, 1959), pp. 135–137. This is just one of many passages cited by Francis Clark in questioning Gregory's authorship of the *Dialogues* in his *The Pseudo-Gregorian Dialogues*, 2 vols., Studies in the History of Christian Thought 37, 38 (Leiden, 1987); see, though, the review by Carole Straw in *Speculum* 65 (1989): 397–399.

4. Mansi 9:912.

5. *MGH, Conc.* 1:114.

rocks or springs, burying precious objects with the dead, perjury, and magical formulas.[6]

Cursing was understood to be something pagans did. In 666 Wilfrid of York and his companions were thrown off course while crossing the Channel and soon found themselves stranded amid hostile pagans. "The chief priest of their idolatry set himself up on a high mound like Balaam and started to curse God's people, trying to bind their hands by his magic art." The response of God's people was to bless a stone, which one of them then fired with a sling right into the brain of the pagan priest.[7] And later when the missionary-saint Boniface cut down the oak of Thor at Geismar, a great throng of pagans gathered around to curse him bitterly because, in the view of Boniface's companions, he was considered an enemy of their gods. But then the tree fell down gently in four equal parts, "and the pagans who had cursed him stopped cursing and, believing, blessed God."[8]

A major preoccupation of clerics was that many people who accepted baptism held on to their old beliefs and practices, or at times reverted to them. Martin, bishop of the western Iberian town of Braga (near Porto), composed a tract in the 570s for the instruction of peasants who in just such a way had taken on Christianity without shedding much of what they had believed before. "Don't you understand that the demons are lying to you in these superstitious practices that you vainly observe?" He warns that those who squander their faith in frivolous ways will rush to their own destruction. In particular they seek in vain to gain knowledge of the future, which God alone can know. Their task is to live in fear of God and pray to God for guidance. In a series of rhetorical questions, Martin asks whether their practices are not really devil worship. "To light candles beside rocks and trees and fountains and at crossroads, what else is this but worship of the devil?" He asks the same about invoking the names of pagan gods and goddesses when

6. Ibid., vol. 2, pt. 1:3–4, 209, 292; *MGH, Capit.* 1:25, 45, 59, 96, 104, 110, 202, 223, 228, 399, 402. See Carlo de Clercq, *La législation religieuse franque de Clovis à Charlemagne: Etude sur les actes de conciles et les capitulaires, les statuts diocésains et les règles monastiques (507–814)* (Louvain, 1936), pp. 16, 31, 42–43, 65, 78, 169, 176, 257, 311; also Pierre Riché, *Daily Life in the World of Charlemagne,* tr. Jo Ann McNamara (Philadelphia, 1978), pp. 181–186, 319–320.

7. *The Life of Bishop Wilfrid by Eddius Stephanus,* ch. 13, ed. and tr. B. Colgrave (Cambridge, 1927), pp. 26–29.

8. *Vita Bonifatii auctore Willibaldo,* ch. 6, in *Vitae Sancti Bonifatii archiepiscopi Moguntini,* ed. W. Levison (Hannover, 1905), p. 31.

particular needs arise and about calculating whether one day is more favorable than another for commencing a journey. "To chant over herbs in order to make poisons and to invoke the names of demons in incantations, what else is this but worship of the devil?"[9]

Backsliding occurred at the higher end of the social scale too. A letter sent by a group of Anglo-Saxon bishops to King Aethelbald of Mercia (716–757) warns the king against following the ways of his predecessor, who was notorious for his greed and violence in dealing with ecclesiastical lands and personnel: "While he sat feasting amid his companions he was suddenly stricken in his sins with madness by an evil spirit, who had seduced him into rash defiance of the law of God. So without repentance or confession, raving mad, talking with devils and cursing [abominans] the priests of God, he passed on from this life to the torments of hell."[10]

The question why curses and incantations are so clearly associated with pagans and are so unacceptable and dangerous for Christians does not arise in most of the sources thus far examined here. In Gregory's *Dialogues*, though, immediately after the story of Florentius and the bear, the disciple asks: "Do we really need to consider it a serious matter if in a fit of anger we happen to curse someone?" Gregory's reply is swift and authoritative: "How can you ask me about the gravity of this sin, when Saint Paul himself says that 'those who curse [maledicentes] shall not inherit the kingdom of heaven'? (1 Cor. 6:10)."[11]

There were many such biblical attacks available for constructing a theological prohibition of cursing. One in particular that attracted comment was the Epistle of James, which teaches about the dangers of that "intractable evil," the tongue: "We use it to sing the praises of our Lord and Father, and we use it to invoke curses upon our fellowmen, who are made in God's likeness. Out of the same mouth come blessings and curses. My brothers, this should not be so. Does a fountain gush with both fresh and brackish water from the same opening?" (James

9. Martin of Braga, "Reforming the Rustics," chs. 12, 16, in *Martini episcopi Bracarensis opera omnia*, ed. Claude W. Barrow (New Haven, Conn., 1950), pp. 191, 197–200, and in *Iberian Fathers*, vol. 1, ed. and tr. Claude W. Barrow (Washington, D.C., 1969), pp. 77, 81–82. See also the references to pagan customs and superstitions in the sermons of Caesarius of Arles, *Sermons au peuple*, ed. Marie-José Delage, 2 vols., Sources chrétiennes 175, 243 (Paris, 1971, 1978), 1:138–142, and sermons 129, 130, 265, 277, 278, and 279.

10. *MGH, Epist.* 3:152–153; tr. Ephraim Emerton, *The Letters of Saint Boniface* (New York, 1940), pp. 129–130.

11. Gregory, *Dialogues*, 3:15 (*PL* 77:253); tr. Zimmerman, pp. 137–138.

3:8–11). Bede (672–735) explains that by adding salt water (*aqua amara*, sour water) to fresh (*dulcis*, sweet) the fresh will be made salty, whereas adding fresh water to salt water will not make the salt water fresh. "In the same way, blessing and cursing cannot be mixed in one mouth; whoever is used to bless God when praying to him or preaching his word but does not refrain from cursing men demonstrates that the bitterness of malediction will overpower the sweetness of benediction."[12]

The famous Carolingian abbot Smaragdus of Saint-Mihiel (c. 760 to c. 830), used this and other biblical passages in his commentary on the Rule of Saint Benedict to explicate the rule's prohibition of cursing by monks and nuns. He grants that it may seem impossible to comply with the rule on this point, but he shows that both Paul (1 Cor. 4:12, 6:9–10) and Peter (1 Pet. 3:9) were categorically opposed to cursing and that cursing has far deadlier consequences than most people realize. Whoever wishes to possess eternal benediction had better bless, not curse, his enemy. Cursing is a sin that can take away the possession of the (heavenly) kingdom and plunge a man into the depths of hell; it can turn sons of God into sons of wrath. Smaragdus shortens Ecclus. 22:30 to say, "Just as vapor and smoke come before fire, so cursing and reproaches before blood" (*Ante ignem vapor et fumus, et ante sanguinem maledicta et contumeliae*). Also, he cites James 3:9–10 on the dangers of the tongue and on the two kinds of speech issuing from the same mouth; then he quotes extensively from Bede's commentary upon that passage.[13]

Although Smaragdus refers to *maledictio* as both a sin and a vice, he does not assign the corresponding opposites to *benedictio*. Cursing was something anyone could do, and of course the argument was that no Christian should do it.[14] But "blessing" was not a corresponding form of virtuous behavior available to everyone; instead, it was a very special function reserved to individuals with religious authority. The distinction appears at the close of Smaragdus's paragraph: "But however terrible is the vice of malediction [*vitium maledictionis*], so much better

12. Bede, *Super divi Jacobi epistolam*, ch. 3 (PL 93:28).
13. *Smaragdi abbatis expositio in regulam S. Benedicti*, ed. A. Spannagel and P. Englebert, Corpus consuetudinum monasticarum 8 (Siegburg, 1974), p. 113.
14. Two paragraphs earlier, in his exhortation to love and cultivate the virtue of patience, Smaragdus concludes by saying that this point should be understood as applying to all people, "not only monks but all Catholic Christians." Ibid., p. 112.

is the office of blessing [*officium benedictionis*]." The former, he says, gets one only punishment, whereas the latter brings grace and glory; "through the one, opprobrium in hell, through the other, the eternal prize in heaven."

Another of the leading ecclesiastics of the early ninth century to write about cursing, Jonas of Orléans (c. 780–843), composed a tract on the moral duties of laypeople, the *De institutione laicali*. His approach was to deal with the prevailing vices of his lay contemporaries. Among the vices he identified were lukewarm observation of religious duties, such as receiving communion only on major religious holidays, and over-zealous attention to worldly pastimes like hunting, dogs, and gambling. One of Jonas's chapters was devoted to the problems of "contentious and thoughtless speech, and cursing."[15]

Jonas's section on cursing begins with an unusual selection of texts. The first is Lev. 19:14, "Do not curse the deaf, or place obstacles in the way of the blind." The second, Ecclus. 3:11, reads: "The father's blessing establishes the houses of the children, but the mother's curse pulls out their foundations." Jonas apparently chose this latter passage in order to lead into a story told by Augustine in the *City of God*.[16] The story is about the curse pronounced by a widow in Asia Minor upon her ten children. All of them suffered terrible physical afflictions as a result of the curse and all left home, dispersed to various parts of the Mediterranean basin. One son and a daughter showed up together at Hippo while Augustine presided there as bishop. Augustine is matter-of-fact in telling about the curse and about the ailments of those cursed; these details served him only as background to what really interested him, namely the great display of devotion by the brother and sister at the tomb of Saint Stephen the Martyr, the great display of charismatic power by the saint in curing the two, and the tremendous display of awe and emotion by the crowds who witnessed the whole scene. "They shouted God's praises with such noise," says Augustine, "that our ears could scarcely bear it." Jonas, however, restricts his retelling to the curse and the suffering it caused, drawing the lesson that no one should use such curses, and that all should keep in mind what the apostle Paul said. From there to the end Jonas goes over familiar ground: 1 Cor. 6:10 on those who, because they curse, will not inherit

15. Jonas of Orléans, *De institutione laicali* 3:8 (PL 106:248–250).
16. Augustine, *De civitate Dei*, 22:8 (PL 41:769–771).

the kingdom of God, James 3:8–11 on the tongue and the mouth, and Bede's fresh water/salt water commentary.

Another tract by Jonas addressed the question of royal power, the *De institutione regia*.[17] And one measure of Jonas's influence is that the entire text was included in a report drawn up by him and his fellow bishops at the Council of Paris in 829 and addressed to Emperor Louis the Pious. Elsewhere in that report the bishops undertook to list many forms of behavior to be avoided in order to keep from alienating one-self from God. In this vein they counsel avoidance of careless speech, including lies, obscenities, foolish chatter, and curses, at which point they cite Paul on the *maledicentes* who will not inherit the kingdom of God.[18]

There are of course numerous other commentaries on biblical de-nunciations of cursing that contributed to a theological prohibition. But it is perhaps enough to see that the writings of a few of the most influential theologians and ecclesiastics, joined with conciliar legisla-tion and a saintly tradition, culminated in the early ninth century in statements accorded something approaching official status by the lead-ing authorities of the time.[19] These several invocations of biblical au-thority lead inevitably, however, to the question of how the numerous curses and instances of cursing in the Bible itself were regarded before and during the Carolingian era.

Biblical Curses

The unavoidable problem raised by Saint Augustine had to do spe-cifically with developing a Christian understanding of the "many im-precations against enemies that are held to be curses" found in the Bible. The key to solving this problem, according to Augustine, lay right within the New Testament, in the Gospel of John and in the ac-count of the election of a replacement for Judas in the opening chapter

17. Text and commentary in Jean Reviron, *Les idées politico-religieuses d'un évêque du IXe siècle: Jonas d'Orléans et son "De institutione regia"* (Paris, 1930); tr. in R. W. Dyson, *A Ninth-Century Political Tract: The "De Institutione Regia" of Jonas of Orléans* (Smithtown, N.Y., 1983).

18. *MGH, Capit.* 2:45.

19. These became standard arguments against casual cursing by individuals and re-mained so centuries later in sermons on the sins. For examples in two fifteenth-century sermons: MSS, Vat. lat. 1239, ff. 19v–21r (for this reference I thank Nancy Caciola of the University of Michigan), and Vat. lat. 1257, ff. 141v–145v (thanks to Kate Jansen of Prince-ton University).

of the Acts of the Apostles. In the former, Jesus said of his followers in a prayer shortly before his arrest in the garden: "Not one of them is lost except the one who must be lost for Scripture to be fulfilled" (John 17:12). In the latter, Peter announced to the assembled apostles that the prophecy in Scripture was bound to come true by which the Holy Spirit, speaking through David, foretold the fate of Judas (Acts 1:15–21). Peter related that Judas had used the betrayal money to buy some property and that now no one would go near it. This combination of facts fulfilled, according to Peter, the text of Ps. 68:25, which said, "May his habitation become desolate and may there be no one to live in it." And since it was also written in Ps. 108:8, "May his position [*episcopatum*] be taken over by another," Peter argued that they should choose a successor to Judas. Thus certain New Testament passages carefully juxtaposed suggest that some of the maledictory psalms were prophetic. The first two examples given by Augustine in his analysis of the problem of curses were none other than Psalms 68 and 108.

The standard interpretation that emerged of Psalm 108, with its relentless curses, treated it as a prophecy, a foretelling of what would happen to Judas. "Prophecy in the guise of imprecation," Chrysostom called it.[20] And this was not so unusual, he maintained. When Jacob called in his sons to tell them of their futures, many of his predictions were curses (Gen. 49:1–27). So it was with Noah and Canaan (Gen. 9: 25), with Moses and those who rejected the law (Deut. 28:16), and with Jesus and the towns that rejected him (Luke 10:13–15). Now Jacob, Noah, Moses, and Jesus obviously predicted good things as well, a point that leads Chrysostom to the thoughtful observation that benedictions as well as maledictions are really prophecies.[21]

For Jerome, Psalm 108 is a work of prophecy in which the voice is that of Jesus. His comment on the opening line, "Be not silent, O God of my praise," begins: "Judas betrayed me, the Jews persecuted and crucified me, and they thought in the end to have done away with me, but you, God of my praise, are not silent."[22] Jerome's polemic with the Jews was further served by verse 28, "They curse but you bless," on

<hr />

20. John Chrysostom, *Expositiones in Psalmos*, no. 108 (*PG* 29:260). This line follows closely after his quoting of Peter from Acts 1:20.

21. Ibid., cols. 260–261. In this connection see the discussion of performative utterances at the close of this chapter, especially the matter of precisely when a curse becomes operative.

22. Jerome, *Breviarium in Psalmos*, no. 108 (*PL* 26:1224).

which he commented: "They curse in the synagogue and the Lord blesses in the church."[23] For Augustine also, Psalm 108 is directed by the prophet against the person of Judas, but the voice, again, is that of Jesus.

> Whoever reads carefully the Acts of the Apostles will recognize that this psalm contains a prophecy of Christ, for it is abundantly clear that what is written here, "May his days be few and may his position be taken over by another," is a prophecy concerning Judas, the betrayer of Christ, when Matthew is chosen to take Judas's place, bringing the number of apostles back up to twelve.[24]

As the first-person voice of this psalm, Jesus assumes a host of terrible hurts and insults ("They have lied to my face," "They have attacked me without cause," "They have repaid me evil for good"). The blame for these falls upon Judas, but then by extension upon all the Jews, who, says Augustine, hated Jesus when he walked the earth and continue to hate him even now.[25] The appalling curses with which Jesus retaliates are to be understood, again, not as curses, but as predictions concerning Judas.

In Psalm 78, what starts as a lament over Israel's sufferings turns into a cry for vengeance (78:10): "Why should the other nations ask, 'Where is their God?' Let your vengeance for the bloody slaughter of your servants fall on those nations before our very eyes." Augustine asserts that this text also is a prophecy, not a wish. Under the guise of a request for vengeance upon enemies, it is in truth a prophecy of the punishment of the ungodly. The holy men of God responsible for such prophecies love their enemies and wish no one anything but good. When wicked men are punished, these holy men derive no pleasure from the suffering of those who are punished, but only from the goodness of God's judgment; in Augustine's view, we should follow this example.[26]

Augustine's fullest exposition of these and related ideas is found in his commentary upon the Sermon on the Mount, at the point where Jesus teaches his followers to turn the other cheek and to love their enemies (Matt. 5:38–48). There Augustine argues that punishment

23. Ibid., col. 1231: *Illi maledicunt in synagoga, et Dominus benedicit in ecclesia.* Cf. Ambrose, *De obitu Valentiniani consolatio* (PL 16:1430).
24. Augustine, *Enarrationes in Psalmos*, no. 108 (PL 37:1431).
25. Ibid., col. 1432.
26. Augustine, *Enarrationes in Psalmos*, no. 78 (PL 37:1017–1018).

based upon a desire for correction and not for vengeance is legitimate. Only a person in whom love is stronger than any hatred that would feed a desire for vengeance is qualified to inflict punishment (as parents are qualified to punish their own children). As for capital punishment, great and holy men, who understand that death liberates the soul from the body and is nothing to be feared, sometimes have to impose the death penalty; they thereby instill a salutary fear in the living and save the executed from further sin.[27]

Augustine does not claim that the Bible is entirely free of vindictive punishment; indeed, he says there are many instances of it in the Old Testament, because people in those times were kept down by servile fear. Yet even in the Acts of the Apostles there is vindictiveness, he acknowledges, in the case of Ananias and Sapphira, who fell dead at the words of the apostle Peter.[28] Apart from such exceptions, though, biblical imprecations were to be understood as predictions. Subsequent commentary on cursing in the Psalms continued to emphasize the main lines of this interpretation, and such a later refinement as relating the thirty maledictions of Psalm 108 to the thirty pieces of silver paid to Judas did little to alter its foundations.[29]

The locus of discussion on these points by Gregory the Great is in his book on Job where, under the burden of the multiple trials he is made to face, Job curses the day he was born. Gregory goes over the text line by line to demonstrate the inadequacy of a literal reading. He shows internal contradictions in the text and passages at variance, in his view, with reason. To get a reading that makes sense, he turns first to other biblical passages that contain curses. "But as we know for certain that Scripture forbids cursing, how can we say that that is something done correctly, which we yet know to be forbidden by the same holy writings?"[30]

27. Augustine, *De sermone Domini in monte,* 1:63–64 (*PL* 34:1261–1262); tr. Jepson, pp. 75–76.
28. Ibid., col.1262; tr. Jepson, p. 77. In the chapter immediately following, Augustine gives an example of a curse by the apostle Thomas in the Gospel of Thomas. He does so in order to argue against certain "heretics" who do not accept the authority of the Old Testament but who hold that Gospel in high esteem. Ibid., ch. 65 (*PL* 34:1263); tr. Jepson, pp. 77–78. For the Thomas story, see *The Apocryphal New Testament,* tr. Montague R. James (Oxford, 1924), pp. 367–368.
29. Haymo of Auxerre, *Explanatio in Psalmos* (*PL* 116:573). On the question of authorship, see Beryl Smalley, *The Study of the Bible in the Middle Ages* (Oxford, 1952), p. 39.
30. Gregory the Great, *Moralia in Job,* 4:1–5 (*PL* 75:633–637); tr. *Morals on the Book of Job* (Oxford, 1844), pp. 177–184.

Gregory distinguishes two sorts of curses that occur in the Bible, one that it approves and one that it condemns. "For a curse is uttered one way when based upon the judgment of justice and in quite another way when based on the malice of vengeance." He then demonstrates that Scripture shows on the one hand God and holy men cursing, and on the other hand the apostle teaching men not to curse. "Thus," continues Gregory, "God is said to curse and yet man is forbidden to curse, because what man does from the malice of revenge, God does only in the exactness and perfection of justice." When holy men deliver a sentence of cursing, they do so not out of a desire for revenge, notwithstanding that in some cases they employ the optative mood (e.g., "May he suffer deprivation and loss"). The governing factor is their understanding of the needs of divine justice. Gregory's analysis allows him to conclude that Job's cursing came not out of the malice of one guilty of sin but out of the integrity of a judge; not from a man agitated by passion, but from one sober in instruction.[31]

Gregory's distinction does not tie the prohibition against cursing strictly to laymen, nor does it limit acceptable cursing strictly to clerics. After all, in the story he told of one who cursed in anger, Florentius was a holy recluse. But Gregory's position nonetheless comes close to making such a discrimination. Except in the story about Florentius, no agent is specified in his denunciations of curses uttered in anger. When he writes of legitimate curses, those founded upon an understanding and love of justice, he always makes the agents of these either God or holy men (*sancti viri*). Agents of both kinds of curses are mentioned in the passage above about Job, where Gregory contrasts a judge, who made a legitimate curse, with a (plain) man, who was malicious or angry and who thereby made an illegitimate one.

Thus there are different kinds of curses; moreover, prophecies or judgments that appear to be curses can be misleading, as can failure to understand the intention of the speaker. We might note in passing that Scholastic vocabulary later on provided a way to resolve this confusion concisely. For Thomas Aquinas in the thirteenth century, scriptural curses were of the sort that are not really curses in substance, but

31. Ibid., ch. 6 (*PL* 75:638–639); tr. *Morals*, pp. 185–186. Cf. Cassiodorus on Psalm 82 (*PL* 70:596) where, when the psalmist curses enemies by asking the Lord to treat them as he has treated certain malefactors in the past, he is seeking vindication out of a desire for correction and not out of an instinct for cursing (*vindicari, correctionis voto, non maledictionis instinctu*).

only accidentally so, because the chief intentions of the speakers are directed not to evil but to good.[32]

Gregory's thoughts on casual or occasional cursing by individuals became dominant in Western formulations on the question of the legitimacy of curses. His distinction between a curse that is prohibited, because it proceeds from hatred and a desire for revenge, and a legitimate curse, which is pronounced out of a love of justice, was the principal text cited in the major collections of canon law. Ivo of Chartres quoted it in the 1090s in both of his compilations, the *Decretum* and the *Panormia*. Likewise Gratian cited it in his *Decretum* in the 1140s, effectively ensuring its lasting authority and influence.[33]

Whereas in the first instance above we saw that commentaries on biblical passages that attack curses brought forth a theology opposed to cursing, those commentaries on passages that do contain curses (and that appear to condone them as well) yielded more complex results. Although both types were exploited in the formation of an anticursing ethic, the latter were also used to justify certain kinds of curses. The resulting distinction can be stated simply in this way: Ordinary cursing by ordinary people was decidedly not legitimate. But cursing by holy people, which is really not cursing and indeed only has the appearance of cursing, is not only legitimate but a social and spiritual necessity.

The linking of such "official" cursing with a particular sociopolitical problem came about in the second quarter of the ninth century. The problem—not new—was the violation of the independence and integrity of ecclesiastical wealth. It was the same problem that was in part responsible for bringing forth, at this very time and by many of the same people, the False Decretals. Churchmen had kept alive horror stories of massive spoliation of church lands that took place toward the close of the Merovingian era. What followed was seen as the relative stability of the reigns of Pepin, Charlemagne, and, until the 820s, Louis the Pious. Then the problem reemerged owing to conflicts involving Louis the Pious and his sons. Although spoliation was not new, the clerical reaction to it was. One reason for the change was that the

---

32. Thomas Aquinas, *Summa theologica*, 2a 2ae, q. 76, in *Opera omnia*, vol. 9 (Rome, 1897): 143–146; "Of Cursing," tr. Fathers of the English Dominican Province, 10 (London, 1929), pp. 309–316.

33. This key passage was included in Odo of Cluny's shortened version of the *Moralia*; see Odo of Cluny, *Epitome moralium S. Gregorii in Job*, ch. 4 (*PL* 133:135). Ivo of Chartres, *Decretum*, 14:4 (*PL* 161:827); idem, *Panormia*, 5:82 (*PL* 161:1229). Gratian, *Decretum*, Causa 24, quest. 3, can. 12 (*CIC* 1:994).

leading clerics were far better schooled and trained than their predecessors of a century and more before, and they exercised far greater
influence in shaping ideology, in directing policy, and in curbing some
of the excesses of the powerful. After all, no seventh-century Merovingian was nicknamed "the Pious." Indeed, many prelates were themselves powerful lords who felt little inhibition in dealing on an equal
footing with the Frankish lay aristocracy.

In the course of this strife within the imperial family, the sons of
Louis the Pious were briefly united at one point in opposition to their
father the emperor, whom they captured and put in prison. Abandoned
by his soldiers, a prisoner forced to beg his own sons for mercy, Louis
was made to face a hostile assembly of clerics at Compiègne in October
833. He was charged with angering God, scandalizing the church, and
driving the people subject to him to kill one other. The bishops warned
him about his sins and of the dangers they posed for his eventual
salvation. Later they forced the emperor to appear in the basilica of
Saint-Médard at Soissons to read a public confession they had drawn
up for him. He admitted to being a murderer and perjuror, a disturber
of the peace. He took personal responsibility for "all the killings, rapine, conflagrations, and all the usurpations of church property under
which the Christian people were languishing." With utmost humility,
the emperor begged for absolution from those "to whom God has
given the power to bind and to loose."[34] With the memory of this scene
of a humiliated emperor in mind, how could anyone have been
shocked or surprised by the humiliation of a relic?

These new clerical attitudes toward rulers are also apparent in the
changing reputation of Charles Martel, the key figure in establishing
the power base of the Carolingian dynasty at the start of the eighth
century. By the middle of the ninth century, what had been many stories of earlier, disconnected spoliations by various Frankish warriors
became conflated into a tale of systematic, purposive depredation by
Charles Martel himself. This tale is epitomized in a report made in 858
by Archbishop Hincmar of Reims to the Council of Quierzy, concerning
a vision that Bishop Eucherius of Orléans had supposedly seen over a
century before. While in an ecstatic trance, Eucherius was taken by an

---

34. Astronomus, *Vita Hludowici imperatoris*, chs. 35, 49 (*MGH, SS* 2:626, 636); cf. Rudolf
Schieffer, "Von Mailand nach Canossa: Ein Beitrag zur Geschichte der christlichen
Herrscherbusse von Theodosius der Grosse bis zu Heinrich IV.," *Deutsches Archiv* 28
(1972): 333–370, especially pp. 352–359.

angel to see those who suffer in hell, and among them was Charles Martel. To the inquiries of Eucherius the angel explained that Charles was there, condemned body and soul to eternal punishment, for his seizures of church property. To verify this vision, Eucherius asked two monks to check the tomb of Charles Martel at the Abbey of Saint-Denis. When they had the tomb opened, a dragon slithered out of it, and they found the walls of the empty tomb blackened as if by fire. The vision was thereby confirmed. Such was the new manner, in the middle of the ninth century, in which prelates spoke publicly before the Frankish monarchs about their ancestor.[35] They called Charles Martel "abominable king," "not king but tyrant," and "thief of the belongings of the poor."[36] One does not imagine the Frankish bishops humiliating Charlemagne in such a way, or Einhard insulting the memory of Charles Martel in Charlemagne's presence.

The linkage of spoliation with curses came about via biblical commentaries, in particular those of Rhabanus Maurus (c. 780–856). After his schooling at the monastery of Fulda and a brief period under the tutelage of Alcuin at Tours, Rhabanus served first as director of the school and then for twenty years, 822 to 842, as abbot of Fulda. In the final decade of his life he was archbishop of Mainz. Over the course of this career, which frequently intersected with the most powerful as well as the most learned figures of his time, Rhabanus produced hundreds of letters and sermons in addition to commentaries on twelve books of the Bible.[37]

Rhabanus completed a commentary on Deuteronomy in the year 834.[38] Much of the substance of his text (and of Carolingian commentaries in general) consists of quotations from the biblical passages he was commenting on, and much of the connecting material was taken, more or less precisely and usually without acknowledgment, from ear-

---

35. *MGH, Conc.* 3:414–416. The vision is not mentioned in an earlier life of Eucherius, or indeed in any surviving text from earlier than this council. In the view of Jean Devisse, the "damnation of Charles Martel" began in 858; see his *Hincmar, archevêque de Reims, 845–882,* 3 vols. (Geneva, 1975), 1:322–325, especially p. 323. Ulrich Nonn, "Das Bild Karl Martells in den lateinischen Quellen vornehmlich des 8. und 9. Jahrhunderts," *FS* 4 (1970): 70–137; on the vision of Eucherius, pp. 106–114.

36. In addition to Nonn, "Das Bild Karl Martells," see Michel Rouche, "La Matricule des Pauvres: Evolution d'une institution de charité du Bas Empire jusqu'à la fin du Haut Moyen Age," in *Etudes sur l'histoire de la pauvreté,* ed. Michel Mollat, 2 vols. (Paris, 1974), 1:103.

37. *DTC* 13, pt. 2:1601–1620.

38. Rhabanus Maurus, *Enarratio super Deuteronomium* (*PL* 108:837–998).

lier commentators.[39] Rhabanus, however, gives more attention to chapters 27 and 28 of Deuteronomy than any previous commentator.[40] In his retelling of the scene with the two opposed groups on Mounts Gerizim and Ebal, he explains the role of the Levites, who by longstanding tradition were regarded as forerunners of the Christian clergy; this role was "to show the priests of Christ that they must proclaim the word of God to the people earnestly, not halfheartedly, so that [the people] may know that danger threatens them should they disregard the Lord's commandments.[41] He presents each of the commandments in the form of a curse—for example, "Cursed be the one who does not honor his father and mother"—and gives a Christian interpretation of each, in this case asserting that the father is understood to be God the father and the mother to be the church. In the mandate concerning incest, "clearly an abomination," incest is taken to mean defilement of the bride of Christ, the church.[42]

Rhabanus's explanation of who the people standing on the two hills were supposed to be and to represent came from Isidore of Seville.[43] Although those on Mount Gerizim, the side of the blessings, are referred to in the biblical text as "more noble" than those on Mount Ebal, the latter were not after all standing upon Mount Ebal in order to be cursed. The Levites were to stand in the middle and recite the curses taught them by Moses, and the people on Mount Ebal were to repeat "Amen" after each one of them. In the view of Isidore, repeated by Rhabanus, the distinction between the two groups is that the people on Mount Gerizim represent those who observe the law out of a love of fulfilling the heavenly promise. Those on Mount Ebal, meanwhile, stand for those who do what is prescribed by law; they do so not out of any love of blessings or promises but out of fear of future punishment. The curses are threats, and they are needed for use with people who respond only to threats.[44]

39. Smalley, *Study of the Bible*, p. 38; Max L. W. Laistner, *Thought and Letters in Western Europe, A.D. 500–900*, 2d ed. (Ithaca, N.Y., 1957), p. 301; and Rosamond McKitterick, *The Frankish Kingdoms under the Carolingians, 751–987* (New York, 1983), pp. 201–202.

40. Rhabanus, *Enarratio super Deuteronomium*, 3:24–25 (PL 108:947–961).

41. Ibid., col. 949.

42. Ibid., col. 950.

43. Ibid., cols. 948–949. This passage exactly repeats the following: Isidore of Seville, *In Josue*, 10 (PL 83:376); and Pseudo-Bede, *Questiones super Jesu Nave librum*, 10 (PL 93: 420). The same passage appears, attributed to Jerome, in Gratian, *Decretum*, Causa 24, quest. 3, can. 11 (CIC 1:993).

44. *PL* 108:949.

Rhabanus repeats in full the terrible curses listed in Deuteronomy, and he makes no attempt to soften them. Referring to Moses, he says, "Just as he promised to those who abide by the commandments of God benedictions and perpetual blessedness, so on the other hand, using the same forms that he used before with the benedictions, he announced to those who did not wish to observe the divine precepts maledictions and perpetual fire."[45] Such suffering was never without purpose or divine approval, especially since God wishes, according to Rhabanus, that everyone be saved and come to recognize the truth.[46] He completes the argument with a quotation from Saint Augustine to the effect that God can alter the wills of men in any way he likes. If God does this, he does it out of mercy, and if he does it not, it is out of justice that he does it not.[47]

Within three years of the composition of this commentary, the prelates of the realm gathered in a council at Aachen. Once again the major problem they had to confront was lay spoliation of ecclesiastical property. In addition to the conciliar decrees, which essentially repeated those of Paris in 829, the participants issued a long admonitory letter to one of Louis the Pious's sons, Pepin of Aquitaine.[48] The principal author of this letter is believed to have been Jonas of Orléans. The principal subject throughout is the history of ancient Hebrew sanctuaries, especially the Temple of Solomon. The history of the temple and of various altars is interlaced with that of various foundations and donations. The underlying premise of the letter is the traditional view by which the ancient temple was regarded as prefiguring the Christian church.[49]

The argument of the admonitory letter focuses on the need for material support of the priestly caste entrusted with running these sanctuaries. To this effect the author cites the instructions the Lord gave to Moses (Num. 35:1–3): "Tell the Israelites to set aside towns in their patrimony as homes for the Levites, and give them also the common lands surrounding the towns. They shall live in the towns, and keep their beasts, their herds, and all their livestock on the common land."

45. Ibid., col. 955.
46. Ibid.
47. Augustine, *Enchiridion*, ch. 98 (*PL* 40:277).
48. *Concilium Aquisgranensis* (*MGH, Conc.* 2). The decrees of the council are on pp. 702–724; the *Epistola concilii Aquisgranensis ad Pippinum regem directa* is on pp. 724–767.
49. Ibid., pp. 733–734, 759.

Moreover, they were instructed to give to the Levites in proportion to their respective patrimonies (Num. 35:8).[50] The text then says that the Book of Joshua demonstrates that this is what the Israelites in fact did. Then the letter continues:

> It is sufficiently clear and open to all who wish to know that God taught his people to give out of their inheritance houses and fields and properties, and beyond that, which is greater still, cities and surrounding lands to the servants at his sanctuary, so that the ministers of his sanctuary might perform his holy rite earnestly, honorably, and regularly and freely fulfill their service. From these words it can be clearly gathered that anyone who carries off or plans to carry off what other faithful people had given to God out of their patrimony in order to save their souls for the honor and adornment of this church and for the use of his ministers assuredly turns the gifts of others into dangers for their souls.[51]

The notion that a gift to the Lord could turn into a danger for one's soul was not novel. Taking back a gift that was the Lord's led to the precipitous deaths of Ananias and Sapphira; and we recall that in the time of Rhabanus the formulators of the False Decretals were urging the fate of Ananias and Sapphira as an appropriate punishment for usurpers of church property.

The letter to Pepin sums up what it had extracted from Numbers, saying that what the Lord taught there was backed by both promises of reward and threats of punishment. Then it moves on to Deuteronomy to say that among many other commandments that Moses addressed to the sons of Israel in that book is one that offers a choice between a blessing and a curse. The letter quotes Deut. 11:26–28, "Understand that this day I offer you a choice . . . the blessing if you listen to the commandments . . . and the curse if you do not." Then it comments:

> It should be noted carefully that those who obey the divine precepts deserve a benediction, while those who disobey them merit a malediction. It is clearer than day that those who steal ecclesiastical belongings inflict insult upon and disobedience to God and thus become transgressors of his precepts. Whence they should look out carefully lest they undergo malediction of the sort the lawgiver proposed instead of benediction. Whoever wishes to know what that malediction is really like should read the earlier and later decla-

50. Ibid., p. 744.
51. Ibid.

rations of the divine law and find out for certain how terrible and horrible and frightening that malediction is.[52]

Thus the council held at Aachen in 837, under the immediate influence of recent biblical scholarship, promised to invoke curses, in the manner of Deuteronomy, against lay predators upon ecclesiastical wealth. The curses of Deuteronomy, recall, were arranged in long, repetitive litanies. They were launched by the priestly tribe of Levites, who were organized by a charismatic leader (Moses), who in turn was commissioned in his role and directly instructed by God.

Liturgical Curses

"Every ritual has a divine model, an archetype," wrote Mircea Eliade; "it acquires effectiveness to the extent that it exactly repeats an act performed at the beginning of time by a god, a hero, or an ancestor."[53] Eliade's perspective suggests that carefully reasoned argument may not be the appropriate kind, or at least the only appropriate kind, of justification for any ritual and thus in particular for liturgical curses. A case in point is the new basis of political legitimacy devised for the upstart Carolingian dynasty in 751; descent from the gods was then put aside (along with the last Merovingian ruler) in favor of anointment with holy oil by a bishop.[54] Whereas an immediate precedent can be found in eighth-century formulas for ordination anointing of priests, justification for making sacred kings in a religious unction ceremony relied upon Old Testament models, namely the anointing of Saul and David by Samuel (1 Sam. 10:1, 16: 13).[55]

These models were evocative rather than literal, "typological links" rather than exact parallels.[56] Carolingian ritual was performed against

52. *MGH, Conc.* 2:745.

53. Mircea Eliade, *Myths, Rites, and Symbols: A Mircea Eliade Reader,* ed. W. C. Beane and W. G. Doty, 2 vols. (New York, 1975), 1:134.

54. Fritz Kern, *Kingship and Law in the Middle Ages,* tr. S. B Chrimes (Oxford, 1956), pp. 34–35.

55. Pierre Riché, "La Bible et la vie politique dans le Haut Moyen Age," in *Le Moyen Age et la Bible,* ed. Pierre Riché and Guy Lobrichon (Paris, 1984), pp. 385–400, especially pp. 388–391; and Janet Nelson, "Inauguration Rituals," in her *Politics and Ritual in Early Medieval Europe* (London, 1986), pp. 283–307, especially p. 291.

56. Nelson, "Inauguration Rituals," p. 291: "It was not a precise situational model, but a more general one that the Frankish clergy found in the Old Testament. The typo-

an Old Testament backdrop. The ceaseless quoting and paraphrasing of the Old Testament in maledictory texts, especially phrases from Deuteronomy and the Psalms, took place in a setting that was consciously but only impressionistically, not literally, reminiscent of ancient biblical society. Arnulf, the iron-fisted count of Flanders in the mid-tenth century, called himself Judas Maccabeus after the rebuilder of the Temple of Jerusalem in order to call attention to his own rebuilding of the Abbey of Saint Peter at Ghent.[57] A pervasive theme of Carolingian political propaganda was that of the Frankish people as the new Israel. The enemies of the Franks were associated with the enemies of the ancient Hebrews. The tribulations of the Franks recalled the tests to which God had put his chosen people. And if the Carolingian kings were the heirs of the Old Testament kings, the obvious corollary was that the bishops who counseled them were the successors to the prophets.[58]

The prophets, we recall, issued warnings and prophecies in the form of curses. Rarely, though, do curse formulas—which of course contain many Old Testament curses—make explicit reference to the fact that many curses are found in the Old Testament, as if to point to a model and thus establish justification. One example of such a reference, occurring just before a series of quotations from Deuteronomy 27 and 28, is in an excommunication formula pronounced against assassins in the year 900 at Reims; it specifies that there should fall upon the assassins' heads "all the maledictions by which the Lord through Moses threatened transgressors of the divine law."[59]

Insofar as the curse formulas include any explicit attempts at justification, these consist almost entirely of claims that the formulas and permission to use them had been granted by a higher authority. The Reims formula just mentioned begins thus: "In the name of the Lord

---

logical link existed not only between Carolingian and Davidic kingship and between reformed Frankish and Levitic priesthood, but between the whole Frankish *gens* and the people of Israel. The 'inventors' of Frankish royal anointing belong in the same milieux that produced the Second Prologue to Lex Salica and the also contemporary Frankish *Laudes* with their invocations of divine blessings on the *iudices* and the *exercitus* as well as the king and princes of the Franks."

57. Geoffrey Koziol, *Begging Pardon and Favor: Ritual and Political Order in Early Medieval France* (Ithaca, N.Y., 1991), pp. 141–142.

58. Riché, "La Bible et la vie politique," pp. 391–395.

59. Mansi 18B:670.

and by the power of the Holy Spirit and the authority divinely granted to bishops by blessed Peter, prince of the apostles."[60] Sometimes no mention of such a grant is made, and one finds instead just the names of various authorities invoked. The excommunication formula of Bishop Ernulf of Rochester contains a longer list of authorities than most, invoking God almighty, the Father, the Son, and the Holy Spirit, the holy canons, the holy and undefiled Virgin Mary, Mother of God, all the celestial virtues, angels, archangels, thrones, dominions, powers, cherubim and seraphim, the holy patriarchs, the holy prophets, all the apostles and evangelists, the holy innocents, the holy martyrs, the holy confessors, the holy virgins, and all the elect of God.[61]

By far the most elaborate explanation for a community's possession of a maledictory formula came from the Abbey of Saint-Wandrille. The text containing this formula begins with a historical sketch of Wandrille's search for a site and his successful establishment of the monastery at Fontenelle in Normandy. Once the church had been built, according to this account, Wandrille left for a visit to the court of Pope Martin I (649–655) in Rome. He received from this pope official approbation of his recent foundation with all its appurtenances, including those to be acquired in the future. He received relics of the apostles Peter and Paul as well as of several of the martyrs. And he received a promise of perpetual apostolic benediction and plenary indulgence for pilgrims who came to the abbey church.[62]

In addition, the historical account continues, lest the possessions, rights, and liberties of said monastery be disturbed by troublemakers (*molestatores, perturbatores, raptores, latrones, et predones*), the pope gave Wandrille a malediction that he could use by apostolic authority wherever and whenever he deemed necessary. This malediction dated from the time of the emperor Constantine and of Pope Sylvester I and had been passed on from one pope to another, always for use against those who in any way attack or steal from or persecute the holy church of God. To emphasize the legitimacy of this papal malediction, the names

60. Ibid.

61. *Die Gesetze der Angelsachsen*, ed. Felix Liebermann, 3 vols. (Halle, 1903–1916), 1:439–440.

62. Lester K. Little, "Formules monastiques de malédiction aux IXe et Xe siècles," *Revue Mabillon* 58 (1975): 377–399; an edition of this text from Saint-Wandrille is found on pp. 390–399.

of all the popes from Sylvester I (314–335) to Gregory I (590–604) are listed as having confirmed it. The succession then passes, oddly, via the archbishops of Tours, in order to fill in the half-century between Pope Gregory and Pope Martin. The list of approving prelates then goes on after the time of the grant by Martin to Wandrille. The compiler of the text inserted the names of the prelates who attended a council at Rouen in 689; it happens that at this council the holdings and privileges of the monastery at Fontenelle were confirmed, although the council canons make no mention of any malediction. Finally, this genealogy is brought further along in time by an accurate list of the archbishops of Rouen from the middle of the seventh century on down to the time of one who reigned from 828 to 837. It was a considerable feat of the historical imagination to marshal the names of prelates from a period of over five centuries to lend authority to a curse.[63]

The dates 828–837 provide the earliest period for the composition of this historico-liturgical text. The backward glance to the time of Constantine and Sylvester is quintessentially Carolingian.[64] This was, after all, the age of that famous "forgery" the Donation of Constantine, and the Saint-Wandrille text in its own, relatively modest way can be thought of as a "Donation of Sylvester." The very idea of a seventh-century holy man traveling from northern Gaul to Rome is suspect. It fits all too neatly the pattern of travels *ad limina* by the Anglo-Saxon missionaries of the late seventh century and first half of the eighth, those loyal servants of Saint Peter who went to Rome to get confirmations, privileges, relics, and books.[65] As it happens, there is a nearly contemporary biography (late seventh century) of Saint Wandrille, and it contains no mention of a trip to Rome; but a ninth-century revision, or amplification, of this biography does include such a trip.[66]

The case of Saint Wandrille is not unique in this regard. His contemporary Saint Amand, "apostle to the Belgians," was granted a similar trip to Rome by a late eighth-century biographer.[67] Amand also was alleged to have visited Martin I, from whom he received the text, not

63. Ibid., pp. 391, 393–394.

64. Richard Krautheimer, "The Carolingian Revival of Early Christian Architecture," *Art Bulletin* 24 (1942): 1–38.

65. Wilhelm Levison, *England and the Continent in the Eighth Century* (Oxford, 1946), pp. 15–44.

66. The two lives, A and B, are in *AASS*, Iul. 5: Vita A, pp. 265–271, and Vita B, pp. 272–281. The addition of the trip to Rome is in Vita B, ch. 10 (p. 275).

67. *Vita I Amandi episcopi*, ch. 6, ed. B. Krusch (*MGH, SRM* 5:434).

known to be extant, of an anathema directed against heretics.[68] About the 850s a monk at the monastery between Tournai and Valenciennes founded by Amand and eventually named for him wrote what was claimed to be Amand's testament. It includes specifications for his burial and curses of the type noted in sanction clauses against anyone who disturbs his remains.[69] Still another of these Frankish monastic founders of the late seventh century was said to travel to Rome: Saint Hunegund, who established a monastery for women at Homblières on the Somme River in Picardy. Destined for marriage by her noble parents but determined instead to enter the religious life, she traveled to Rome, according to her tenth-century biographer, in the company of her fiancé. Together they met—it will come as no surprise—Pope Martin I, who supported her resolve to become a nun and even converted the young man to the religious life.[70]

From these cases there emerges a pattern showing that seventh-century Frankish saints did not make trips to Rome in their own times, but went only in retrospect. This retrospect was that of later writers who were steeped in the history of the Anglo-Saxon missionaries and of the Frankish clerics they helped to Romanize in the middle of the eighth century. By then a trip to Rome had become a standard appurtenance if not actually a necessity in the curriculum vitae of a proper saint.

Another essential fiction was that liturgical innovations came from Rome. This was the case with the different kinds of liturgical books, as we have seen, and with the development of "Gregorian" chant and musical notation. None of this is intended to suggest that nothing could or did emanate from Rome. Saint Boniface did seek advice from Pope Zacharias in 745 concerning how to cope with severe problems, and the authentic papal reply, as mentioned earlier, suggested "fasting and the supplications of litanies before God," although no maledictions. But to cite a case from Wales, which for centuries had no contact with Rome: when in the early twelfth century the bishop of Llandaff in southeastern Wales sought to transform his traditional Welsh church into a proper Roman diocese, he found (or provided) for the bishops

---

68. Ibid., pp. 450–452; see below, chapter 4, for evidence that curses were used at his monastery.

69. *Vita Amandi episcopi II* (ibid., pp. 483–484).

70. *AASS*, Aug. 5:227–232; *The Cartulary and Charters of Notre-Dame of Homblières*, ed. Theodore Evergates, with Giles Constable, material prepared by William M. Newman, Medieval Academy Books 97 (Cambridge, Mass., 1990), pp. 1–2.

of his see "a great sentence of excommunication" that one of their sixth-century predecessors, Saint Teilo, had supposedly obtained at the papal court in Rome.[71]

In the Vatican sacramentary from Sens, the curses written in the margins about the Credo page belong unmistakably to the Frankish clerical circles that produced such an outpouring of legal texts, biblical commentaries, tracts, and conciliar canons devoted to maledictions. And yet the full title of the Sens formula includes a statement of authority pointing toward Rome. "Malediction against Persecutors of the Church of God" (*Maledicitio adversus ecclesiae dei persequtores*) is all of the title that I noted earlier, but its continuation says, "sent to Gaul by the lord pope" (*directa in gallis a domno papa*). Given the age of this book (first half of the tenth century) and the central importance in the Frankish church of the ecclesiastical province of Sens (whose subordinate dioceses included Auxerre, Chartres, Meaux, Nevers, Orléans, Paris, and Troyes), this page could well have helped shape the thinking of many clerics.[72]

It is also in the spurious letter of Pope Leo, which as noted above dates from the 930s, that one finds wholesale maledictory formulas, akin to those in so many Frankish documents supposedly supplied by the papacy. That there are several extant versions from a brief period suggests a concerted distribution campaign, but the network utilized appears more monastic than papal. If the formula did come from Rome, the impetus for it very likely came from the French side, for Odo of Cluny was abbot of Fleury and made a journey to Rome in the time of Leo VII. Either way, the value attributed to the document in question came not from the authority or prestige of the papacy, but from the continuing presence and activity in Rome of the body of Saint Peter.[73]

71. *MGH, Epist.* 3:323; tr. Emerton, *Letters of Saint Boniface*, p. 108. *The Text of the Book of Llan Dav,* ed. John G. Evans and John Rhys (Oxford, 1893; repr. Aberystwyth, 1979), pp. 121, 350.

72. MS, Vat., Reg. lat. 567, f. 48v.

73. *Papsturkunden, 896–1046,* ed. Harald Zimmermann, 3 vols. (Vienna, 1984–1989), 1: 154–162. Earlier editors considered the formula "suspect" based on its style and closing: *Recueil des chartes de l'abbaye de Saint-Benoît-sur-Loire,* ed. Maurice Prou and Alexandre Vidier, 2 vols. (Paris, 1900–1907), 1:114–119. On Saint Peter, Richard W. Southern, *Western Society and the Church in the Middle Ages* (Harmondsworth, Eng., 1970), pp. 94–97; on p. 94 Southern writes: "For the western church from the seventh to the eleventh century the existence of the tomb of St Peter was the most significant fact in Christendom. The body within the tomb, which would one day clothe the door-keeper of heaven, was the link between the presence in heaven and the church on earth. It was pre-eminently through his continuing physical presence that St Peter continued to bless and to curse, to cure and to guarantee. Men thought of him as being there, in Rome."

Even though there were pilgrims to the tomb of Peter in the tenth century (and an Orléanais noble carried his father's body to Rome for burial close by that tomb), Rome at the time was more myth than reality. The real Rome was a depopulated and dilapidated shell of its once glorious self. The greater and in a sense more real city was an *arche*, an imagined, faraway place of origins, set in remote times. It was a mental construct whose adherents based upon it critical aspects of their individual and corporate identities and legitimacy. The learned clergy of the Carolingian period and after displayed great command of the Bible, as we have seen, along with great skill in handling legal and theological texts. But when they were faced with the need to justify authority, they showed a marked preference for ancient models, or archetypes, over carefully reasoned argument. This was entirely consistent with the premise of Germanic law that what is old is good, and that constructive changes in the law come about not through innovation but through liberating old, good law from recent, less desirable accretions. Moreover, in this society the transmission of legitimate power came exclusively via liturgy, and liturgy, as we have seen, whatever its origins, was always said to come from Rome. Law and theology undoubtedly prepared the way, but the preferred means of explaining the source of a maledictory formula was to say it was sent by a pope from Rome.[74]

Another system of values began very slowly to assert itself in the course of the twelfth century, with the beginnings of an urban revival, the exertions of an ambitious, increasingly influential papacy, and the formal, academic study of jurisprudence. The thought of any post-Gregorian pope—that is, from after about 1100—issuing or approving a maledictory formula gives one pause. And yet there are several

74. I learned much from discussing the notion of an *arche* and other elements in the history of religions with Marilyn Robinson Waldman of Ohio State University. Cf. Elizabeth A. R. Brown, *"Falsitas Pia sive Reprehensibilis*: Medieval Forgers and Their Intentions," in *Fälschungen im Mittelalter*, Schriften der MGH 33, 6 vols. (Hannover, 1988–1990), 1:101–120, especially pp. 107–109. For a brief summary of insightful views concerning motives for forgery, see Giles Constable, "Forgery and Plagiarism in the Middle Ages," *Archiv für Diplomatik* 29 (1983): 20–21. For the Orléanais noble, see Thomas Head, *Hagiography and the Cult of Saints: The Diocese of Orléans, 800–1200* (New York, 1990), pp. 258–259. On Germanic law, see the essay of Fritz Kern on law in his *Kingship and Law in the Middle Ages*, pp. 149–180, in which the main headings include: "Law Is Old," "Law Is Good," "Good Old Law Is Unenacted and Unwritten," "Old Law Breaks New Law," and "Legal Innovation Is Restoration of the Good Old Law." Richard Krautheimer, *Rome: Profile of a City, 312–1308* (Princeton, N.J., 1980), pp. 109–160.

twelfth-century papal privileges granting monasteries the right to excommunicate their enemies, while the lone sure instance of papal approval of prayers against enemies survives from the reign of Innocent
III (1198–1216). It occurs in a letter addressed to the prior and convent
of La Charité-sur-Loire and dated 14 April 1204.[75] La Charité was a
dependency of Saint-Benôit, which as it seems worthwhile to mention
now, although I will come back to the point later—was equipped with
a *clamor in malefactoribus.*[76] In his letter, Pope Innocent acknowledges
the problem of monastic vulnerability to lay violence and approves the
custom by which the monks of La Charité lie prostrate on the church
floor during a solemn mass and humbly supplicate divine assistance
against those who are persecuting them. He certifies the custom as
pious and urges them to use it with humility and devotion, both so
that they can acquire peace and quiet and so that the iniquitous "may
be called back from evil."[77]

Thus genuine papal approval of clamors came only toward the end
of the period of their viability. Earlier on, though, views concerning
curses congealed around certain aspects of the problem. The New Testament injunctions against cursing were critical in the formation of
broadly held doubts about the moral propriety of curses. Cursing came
to be seen as fundamentally inconsistent with Christian life, whether
religious or lay. As Chrysostom had put it back in the late fourth century, "When you say, 'Curse him, down with his house, away with
everything,' you are no better than a murderer."[78]

At the same time, the examples of curses in both the Old and the
New Testaments came under intense scrutiny only to be declared legitimate because they were understood to be curses in form only; basically they were prophecies, used by God or by God's holy men to
carry out the responsibilities of divine justice. Out of this biblical exegesis there came both a theological and a legal underpinning for re-
jecting casual or occasional cursing, most often spoken by individuals

---

75. *PL* 217:107–108. Examples from the twelfth century include a privilege for Llandaff
by Calixtus II in 1119, for which see Wendy Davies, *The Llandaff Charters* (Aberystwyth,
1979), pp. 18–19, and a privilege for Etival by Eugenius III in 1147, for which see *PL* 180:
1277.

76. See below, chapter 4, note 44.

77. *PL* 217:107–108.

78. John Chrysostom, *Homilia XIX in Matthaeum* (*PG* 31:285); cited by Aquinas in the
passage referred to above in note 32. Although the key verb in the Migne ed. is *discerpere*
(to tear down with words), the Latin translation available to Aquinas used *maledicere.*

inflamed by anger; there also came from it a model and justification for formal, liturgical cursing by duly constituted ecclesiastical authorities. The compilers of liturgical curse formulas, however, took virtually no account of this exegesis; instead they relied almost exclusively upon claims of special permission to invoke curses, especially that granted by the Roman papacy. Such permission seems at first to have been a fiction created in Francia, but later on it became a verifiable reality.

Speech Acts

Modern philosophers of language have elucidated the functioning of a particular class of locution of which one subcategory is the curse. Their aims in doing so and the methods they have used are obviously very different from those of the theologians and biblical commentators of earlier centuries, and yet on essential points their results are compatible.

Building upon foundations prepared by Ludwig Wittgenstein, who directed the attention of philosophers toward the study of language as an activity governed by rules, the English philosopher John Austin identified and defined locutions usually called "speech acts" or, as he preferred to call them, "performative utterances."[79] In particular, Austin showed that there are ordinary and meaningful sentences that are neither true nor false, and that a speaker in uttering one is "*doing* something rather than," as he put it, "merely *saying* something."[80] The classic examples of such sentences that do something when uttered also usually can or do contain the word "hereby," as in "I hereby pronounce you husband and wife," "I hereby christen this ship," or "I hereby declare you persona non grata."[81] Austin argued that it is absurd to regard these sentences as reports of the performance of the actions they mention. Instead, in his view they accomplish these very

---

79. Ludwig Wittgenstein, *Philosophical Investigations*, 3d ed., tr. G. E. M. Anscombe (New York, 1973), pp. 1–40; John L. Austin, *How to Do Things with Words*, 2d ed. (Cambridge, Mass., 1975), and idem, "Performative Utterances," in *The Philosophy of Language*, ed. Aloysius P. Martinich (New York, 1985), pp. 105–114. I hereby thank my mentors in these matters, Murray Kitely of the Philosophy Department at Smith College and Richard Parmentier of the Anthropology Department at Brandeis University. I also learned much from seminar papers on aspects of this topic by two Smith College students, Ann Castle in 1982 and Ellen Heller in 1985.

80. Austin, "Performative Utterances," p. 106.

81. On "hereby" in legal discourse, see Dennis Kurzon, *It Is Hereby Performed: Explorations in Legal Speech Acts* (Amsterdam, 1986), pp. 6–7.

actions through being uttered.[82] In some sense the sentence in being uttered is itself the action named; it is the marrying, it is the christening, it is the excluding. As for the subject at hand, since a curse is simultaneously a verbal utterance and a deed performed, it qualifies as a speech act or performative utterance as understood by Austin.[83]

The simplest form for these utterances, as in the examples given above, is the first-person singular present tense, active voice, indicative mood, but numerous variants are available. Certainly speech acts of cursing, as we know from many examples, can assume various forms. The most straightforward form is the same as that in the examples of speech acts just given, such as, "I hereby anathematize you." But curses are very often expressed in the optative subjunctive mood ("May he die"), and it in turn is frequently put in the passive voice ("May he be killed"), which allows the speaker either to express an agent ("May he be killed by his worst enemy") or not (again, "May he be killed" or "May he be cursed").

Austin's work is helpful in understanding the functioning of curses because it permits us to deal with the question of what really happens when a curse is pronounced. Let us suppose that X curses Y, calling

82. The potential presence of "hereby" and mention of the name of the action undertaken are important, for the notion of speech act has been diluted by a standard criticism of Austin's work that argues that all speech is activity. I shall cite just two examples. First, John T. Kearns, *Using Language: The Structure of Speech Acts* (Albany, N.Y., 1984), p. 8: "People who use language are *doing* something when they speak and write." It would be difficult to deny that point. Indeed, I would add to it that in certain instances not saying something—keeping silent when one could (or perhaps should) say something—is an act. And second, Austin has been stood on his head by François Recanati, who argues in *Meaning and Force: The Pragmatics of Performative Utterances* (New York, 1987), pp. 72–73, that what Austin considered speech acts are not fundamentally speech acts. To utter a phrase like "I baptize you in the name of the Father, etc." in the appropriate circumstances is, according to Recanati, "to *do something*, not simply to say something; it is to perform an act that cannot be reduced to a simple 'speech act.'"

83. Even though Austin stimulated the growth of a substantial branch of the philosophy of language dedicated to speech-act theory, he himself barely mentioned curses (*How to Do Things*, p. 160), and his followers and critics have mostly ignored them. Among later works to consult are David Holdcroft, *Words and Deeds: Problems in the Theory of Speech Acts* (Oxford, 1978); Jerrold J. Katz, *Propositional Structure and Illocutionary Force: A Study of the Contribution of Sentence Meaning to Speech Acts* (New York, 1977); Jerrold M. Sadock, *Toward a Linguistic Theory of Speech Acts* (New York, 1974); and John R. Searle, *Expression and Meaning: Studies in the Theory of Speech Acts* (Cambridge, 1979), *Speech Acts: An Essay in the Philosophy of Language* (New York, 1969), "What Is a Speech Act?" in *Philosophy of Language*, ed. Martinich, pp. 221–239, and with Daniel Vanderveken, *Foundations of Illocutionary Logic* (New York, 1985). There is, however, an entry under "curse" in Anna Wierzbicka, ed., *English Speech Act Verbs: A Semantic Dictionary* (Sydney, 1987), pp. 163–164.

upon various agents to cause several terrible things to happen to Y. The curse is pronounced, and then what? Nothing happens. Y continues to flourish, and though he may eventually fall victim to some misfortune, perhaps even one named in the curse, he most likely will not suffer all the ills named there. What, then, if anything, did happen at the time of the curse? The simple answer is that Y was cursed. Though not wounded or killed or taken ill or abandoned or beaten or robbed or the like, Y nonetheless was placed under a curse. In the view of those present at the pronouncing of the curse, Y's life was changed thereby, and his chances for salvation were diminished. That view would probably then spread to other people as they heard about what had happened. Whether Y knows about the curse or acknowledges it once he does hear about it has no effect upon the fact of his having been cursed. No matter how he reacts, something deeply significant has happened. Furthermore, not only has the curse "happened" by being "said," but in order to undo the terrible circumstances in which Y finds himself as a result of the curse, something else would have to happen, and almost certainly someone else would have to intervene, most likely with another performative utterance.[84]

But if all it took was mere words—a single speech act—to put Y in these circumstances, was it not easy for X to do so, and would it not be equally easy for Y's enemies A, B, and C to do likewise? The answer is no, for in order for any speech act to be valid, according to Austin's scheme, it must meet a set of conditions he called the "conditions of felicity." The first of these is that there be an accepted, conventional procedure for the type of utterance in question. The second is that the persons and circumstances involved in a given case in which this procedure is invoked be appropriate for its invocation. And the third is that the performer of the procedure be in the proper frame of mind for carrying it out. The lack of any of the requisite conditions gives an infelicitous result.[85] In a useful amendment to the second of these con-

---

84. In this connection, the useful scholarship to pursue is not so much the post-Austin philosophy of language (see the previous two notes) as the application of Austin's ideas to ritual language by anthropologists. See, for example, Stanley J. Tambiah, "The Magical Power of Words," *Man*, n.s., 3 (1968): 175–208; R. Finnegan, "How to Do Things with Words: Performative Utterances among the Limba of Sierra Leone," *Man*, n.s., 4 (1969): 537–552; Benjamin Ray, " 'Performative Utterances' in African Rituals," *History of Religions* 13 (1973–1974): 16–35; and Wade T. Wheelock, "The Problem of Ritual Language: From Information to Situation," *Journal of the American Academy of Religion* 50 (1982): 49–71.

85. Austin, *How to Do Things*, pp. 12–38.

ditions, the one about appropriate persons and circumstances, one scholar suggested that what really distinguishes the classic performative utterance is its impact upon conventional social relations, that is, the fact that it alters those relations. This amendment specifies that the central figures involved stand in some formal relation to one another.[86]

Seen in the light of this discussion of requisite conditions, a clamor or a *maledictio* had to be carried out (1) in accordance with a carefully prescribed liturgy, (2) by a duly authorized religious person (2a) against someone subject to the religious authority of the person presiding, and (3) by a person who adopted a humble attitude, free of anger, following upon a prolonged fast. Moreover, this discussion of conditions elucidates the functioning of provisional curses, for those can be understood as curses in which at least one condition is not yet met, although it is more a matter of a basic element that is missing than of a condition of felicity. An example would be the standard type of provisional curse that occurs in most *si quis* sanction clauses ("If anyone should disturb this agreement, may he suffer such and such"), where the speech act is not complete upon utterance because of the lack of one of the necessary conditions, namely the anticipated offense by a malefactor. But the moment some person commits that offense, thus becoming the malefactor, the missing condition is met, the malefactor is cursed, and the speech act is accomplished.[87]

Where the moderns (speech-act theorists) come closest to the ancients (theologians/biblical commentators) on these matters is precisely in the discussion of felicitous conditions, for all agree that the substance and impact of the locution can be affected by such extrinsic factors as the setting, the speaker's qualifications, the speaker's intentions, and the accompanying gestures. Together, and joined by historians of religion, they give meaning to the structure of a curse, whose main parts are a justificatory introduction, an operative clause, an escape clause, and a conclusion. The introduction may include a narrative of events leading up to the grievance that precipitates the curse; a specially long example would qualify as an "epic introduction," and an elaborate one might include a "magical antecedent" that reaches deep into the past to pro-

---

86. Alexander Sesonske, "Performatives," *Journal of Philosophy* 62 (1965): 459–468.

87. One might consider in this connection the development, in the twelfth century and later, of excommunication *latae sententiae*; see Elisabeth Vodola, *Excommunication in the Middle Ages* (Berkeley, Calif., 1986), pp. 28–35.

vide a justification for the act about to be performed.[88] Some appeal to authority must in any case be included here.

In the operative clause, there takes place the "sacred speech act," which alters the status of the person(s) regarded as inimical to the community.[89] This may be brief, although several examples we have seen are rather long and complex. In a social setting where the law is generally acknowledged and the authority of those charged with executing it generally respected, a sentence can be delivered by the appropriate authority in a most simple form; a bishop could, for example, simply say: "I excommunicate you." But where there are attempts to heighten the drama of the encounter, as with liturgical robes and candles, and to pile up multiple curses (in addition to supplying a lengthy inventory of sponsoring authorities), more than likely there is a social setting in which authority is both weak and insecure.[90]

The escape clause may be a generous offer to a relentless offender; it may be quite reasonable in that it still places resolution of the troublesome issue ahead of apocalyptic retaliation; it may, though, also serve the interest of the one who curses, given the widespread belief that a curse unjustly directed at another person will bounce back against the one who pronounced it.[91] And in the closing there is a contractual conclusion by all present who signify their acquiescence in the proceedings by joining in to say "amen" or "so be it."[92]

For philosophers of language, then, the issue is whether a given curse

88. Gerardus van der Leeuw, *Religion in Essence and Manifestation*, tr. J. E. Turner, 2 vols. (New York, 1963), 2:423–424.

89. Wade T. Wheelock, "Sacred Language," in *ER* 6:439–446.

90. F. Donald Logan, "Excommunication," in *DMA* 4:537, points out a disjuncture between the elaborate ceremonial of excommunication and the fact that in over 15,000 excommunication cases in English ecclesiastical courts this solemn rite was not once performed; in most cases the presiding judge simply stated, "I excommunicate you." In his study of these 16,869 cases, *Excommunication and the Secular Arm in Medieval England: A Study in Legal Procedure from the Thirteenth Century to the Sixteenth*, Pontifical Institute of Mediaeval Studies, Studies and Texts 15 (Toronto, 1968), p. 68, Logan gives the inclusive dates as 1250 and 1534. The apparent disjuncture can be explained by noting first that the ceremonial was developed two centuries and more before 1250, when judicial authority was far from stable, and that between the middle of the thirteenth century and the beginning of the English Reformation the authority of English ecclesiastical courts was relatively solid. The mode developed in an essentially liturgical culture was inappropriate in a properly juridical culture.

91. Alfred E. Crawley, *Oath, Curse, and Blessing—and Other Studies in Origins* (London, 1934), pp. 1–39; Keith Thomas, *Religion and the Decline of Magic* (London, 1971), p. 604.

92. Van der Leeuw, *Religion in Essence*, 2:405, 422.

is a proper speech act of cursing, whereas for theologians from Augustine to Aquinas it was more a matter of whether a curse was legitimate. But the ways by which curses gained justification long ago or now get declared genuine speech acts run closely parallel.

part two   Curses in Action

One of the druids was insolent to the saint's face and dispar-
aged the Christian faith in arrogant terms. Saint Patrick
glared fiercely at him as he spoke, and then, *cum magno clamore*, confidently addressed the Lord: "O Lord, who can do
all things and in whose power all things lie, who sent me
here, may this impious man who blasphemes your name be
carried up from here and die without delay." At these words
the druid was carried high into the air and then dropped
from above; he fell headfirst and crushed his skull against a
rock, was smashed to pieces and died before their eyes. The
heathen were frightened.

                              Muirchu, *Life of Saint Patrick*

4
Uses

ACCOUNTS OF the use of maledictory formulas are found almost exclusively in narrative sources. In contrast to the timeless aura that floats about liturgical sources, with their claims of authority that reach into remote, mysterious periods and premises, the narratives found in historical sources such as chronicles, annals, saints' lives, miracle stories, and sometimes even charters tend to be rooted in particular times and places. A charter of the Abbey of Saint-Cybard of Angoulême records how, during a crisis around 1100, the monks used maledictions and excommunications against their adversaries, although the formulas employed have not come to light.[1] Such a lack of both kinds of evidence is the norm, whereas the church of Reims supplies an exceptional instance of the intersection of the two types. Among the formulas available at the cathedral of Reims at the end of the ninth century we found the excommunication text cited earlier, with its litany of appalling curses based upon Deuteronomy 27 and 28, with its petition that "they drain out through their bowels like the faithless and unhappy Arius," and with its concluding anathema. In addition, however, we happen to know that this very text was put to use in the year 900 when assassins struck down no less a personage than the archbishop of Reims. The attempts of the count of Flanders, Baldwin the Bald, to gain the abbacy of the wealthy Flemish monastery of Saint-Bertin had been frustrated by Archbishop Fulk, who managed to hold on to that abbacy himself in addition to his archiepiscopal office. In 900 Baldwin sent one of his knights, named Winemar, to plead with both Fulk and the king, Charles the Simple, for the prize of Saint-Bertin. Fulk refused to budge, and the king, who was much in the archbishop's debt for political support, did nothing to help Baldwin's cause. Eventually Winemar and his companions took matters into their own hands:

1. MS, Angoulême, Archives de la Charente, H' 1, f. 117r.

they set a trap for Fulk and killed him. The bishops who assembled for the consecration of Hervey, the new archbishop, joined in the condemnation of Winemar and his accomplices by reciting the long formula, "May they be cursed in town and cursed in the fields. May their barns be cursed," and so on. We know of these matters, including the recitation of the excommunication formula, from Flodoard's *History of the Church of Reims*, which also informs us of the results:

> For when Winemar the murderer, along with his accomplices, was excommunicated—and more than that, struck with irreparable anathema—by the bishops of the kingdom of the Franks, his flesh began to rot, he exuded pus, and he was devoured alive by worms. The stench was so grotesque that no one could get near him, and so with this miserable death he finished his miserable life.[2]

It would be difficult to measure the circle of readers, or perhaps more significantly auditors, of this text. But historical accounts such as Flodoard's chronicle were typically composed for urgent, polemical motives and thus were not kept modestly out of sight. Moreover, since the metropolitan church of Reims was one of the most powerful corporations in Frankish society, the circle of those who knew the details of Winemar's "miserable death" included, at a minimum, an elite corps of high-powered and influential clerics.[3]

Such a neat pairing of formula and narrative from a particular church as that from the cathedral of Reims in 900 remains, incontestably, an exception. The irregular survival of documents is partly to blame, but certainly there are many more sources, of both the liturgical and narrative types, that have survived but have not yet been brought to light. And as for the narrative materials that are extant and that, even though uncorroborated by liturgical texts, tell us that clamors were performed or maledictions pronounced, they give us every right to think that the churches in question possessed a formula. Such is the obvious deduction from this shred of information divulged in passing by a charter of

2. Flodoard, *Historia Remensis ecclesiae*, 4:10 (*MGH, SS* 13:574–575). For discussion of the text, see Gerhard Schneider, *Erzbischof Fulco von Reims (883–900) und das Frankenreich*, Münchener Beiträge zur Mediävistik und Renaissance-Forschung 14 (Munich, 1973), pp. 178–182. Beryl Smalley, *Historians in the Middle Ages* (London, 1974), pp. 79–82. The excommunication formula, discussed in chapter 1, under "Excommunication and Anathema," is found in Mansi 18B:669–670.

3. Auguste Dumas, "L'église de Reims au temps des luttes entre Carolingiens et Robertiens (888–1027)," *Revue d'histoire de l'église de France* 30 (1944): 5–38; W. T. H. Jackson, "Flodoard of Rheims (c. 893–966)," in *DMA* 5:90–91.

about 1110 from the Abbey of Nouaillé, near Poitiers: three brothers renounce the unjust claims pressed by their late father against the monastery and acknowledge that they were driven by fear of divine vengeance to parley with the abbot because of the daily clamor his monks made before the body and blood of our Lord Jesus Christ. This last phrase is so clearly an echo of if not a quotation from *In spiritu humilitatis* that we can go one step further than surmising that the monks of Nouaillé had a formula and specify which one they most likely used.[4]

Since the two types of sources are so different and usually unrelated, it would be interesting to see whether the narratives produce a geographical pattern in any way similar to that of the formulas. The present inquiry thus turns to what use was made of the liturgical clamors and what results came of their use. It begins in the British Isles and then moves to the Continent. The map of known cases in which clamors were used can then be drawn and subsequently compared with the map showing the provenance of extant formulas.

Ireland and Wales

In 1197 the archbishop of Dublin, John Cumin, suffered "great injuries" at the hands of the deputies of Earl John, brother of King Richard and future king. The account of this affair found in Roger of Hoveden's *Chronicle* reveals almost in passing that the "injuries" consisted in confiscations by these powerful men of lands held by the church of Dublin. John Cumin went into exile, but before leaving he excommunicated his tormentors and placed the archdiocese under interdict. In addition, "he ordered that the crosses and images of the cathedral church be placed on the floor and surrounded by thorns, so that these malefactors would be stricken with fear and restrained from their intention to violate the property of the church."[5] Self-imposed exile was not a common tactic for aggrieved clerics, but just three dec-

---

4. *Chartes de l'abbaye de Nouaillé de 678 à 1200*, ed. Pierre de Monsabert, Archives historiques du Poitou 49 (Poitiers, 1936), pp. 279–282. For two other excommunication formulas that appear to have been used on specific occasions by the canons at Saint-Julien of Brioude, see *Spicilegium Brivatense: Recueil de documents historiques relatifs au Brivadois et à l'Auvergne*, ed. Augustin Chassaing (Paris, 1886), pp. 22–25. For an example that combines the formula for a clamor with its use in a specific instance at Poitiers, see Du Cange 7:113.

5. Roger of Hoveden, *Chronica*, ed. William Stubbs, 4 vols., RS 51 (London, 1868–1871), 4:29.

ades had passed since Thomas Becket stormed off to the Continent, and as in that more famous instance, "exile" provided an opportunity to carry a grievance before the papal court.[6]

Meanwhile, with the prelate absent and the malefactors unperturbed in their "malignant scheme," a miracle "unheard of in our times" took place:

> There was in the cathedral church of Dublin a certain cross on which a rather expressive [*expressius*] figure of Christ was carved; all the Irish, and other people as well, held this cross in the greatest veneration. Now, while this image of the crucified one lay prostrate on the floor and surrounded by thorns, it went into agony on the sixth day. Its face reddened vehemently as if it were close to a roaring fire, and it perspired freely. Drops fell from its eyes as if it were weeping.

Then came the most prodigious feat of all: a mixture of blood and water poured from the right side and breast of the figure; the cathedral priests collected this liquid and sent word of it to the archbishop "so that this matter could be mentioned to our lord the pope." John Cumin went before Pope Innocent III, and in September 1198 the pope intervened with a strongly worded remonstrance addressed to Earl John. The "malefactors" remained unresponsive for several months, but a temporary peace was made by the time of John's coronation in 1199.[7]

This is the only known case of a humiliation in Ireland; the account of it includes no mention of special prayers. The humiliation itself appears to have no roots in the indigenous culture. The humiliation practiced at Dublin in 1197 was an import, like the archbishop himself. John Cumin was the first Englishman to be named to the see of Dublin. When chosen by King Henry II in 1181, he was a proven servant of the Crown, with a career of royal service going back to the time of Henry's struggle with Thomas Becket. In fact John Cumin had undertaken two embassies to Rome concerning the Becket affair and frequently went to France on the king's business. When named to Dublin in 1181 he first went to Rome to get papal confirmation. Thus when trouble erupted in 1197 he followed a familiar path by going to the

6. William Fitz Stephen, *Vita S. Thomae*, chs. 61–62, 66–68, in *Materials for the History of Thomas Becket, Archbishop of Canterbury*, ed. J. C. Robertson, 7 vols., RS 67 (London, 1877), 3:82.

7. Roger of Hoveden, *Chronica*, ed. Stubbs, pp. 29–30. On the continuation of this controversy, see *Selected Letters of Pope Innocent III concerning England (1198–1216)*, ed. Christopher R. Cheney and W. H. Semple (Edinburgh, 1953), p. 51.

papal court.[8] Since no formula for a humiliation, or for any other kind of clamor, remains extant from any English church, monastic or other, in either the Anglo-Norman period or the Anglo-Saxon, we are left with the circumstantial evidence of Cumin's Continental sojourns to suggest where the idea for a humiliation came from.[9]

The absence of formulas in England renders all the more stunning the record of repeated ritual cursings and humiliations at the church of Llandaff, just over the border in southeastern Wales. The bishops of Llandaff had a long history of wielding efficacious spiritual sanctions against powerful lay opponents. Early in the eleventh century, for example, in the course of a furious and bloody feud between King Edwin of Gwent and Bishop Bleddri, the latter intervened to try to make peace but was attacked and wounded by one of Edwin's kinsmen. The wounded prelate retaliated by summoning a synod to anathematize the king and his family and to place the county of Gwent under a curse and leave it without baptism (*sub maledictione et sine baptismo*). King Edwin delivered the offenders for judgment and submitted himself to penance.[10]

No fewer than twenty-four such cases appear in the *Book of Llandaff*, a twelfth-century collection of charters, saints' lives, papal privileges, council records, and episcopal correspondence. Since the documents

8. *Medieval Ireland, 1169–1534*, ed. Art Cosgrove, vol. 2 of *A New History of Ireland* (Oxford, 1987), pp. 120, 122, 149; Thomas F. Tout in the *Dictionary of National Biography*, 4:911–914 (note that the subject's name is given there as Comyn); John A. Watt, *The Church and the Two Nations in Medieval Ireland* (Cambridge, 1970), pp. 45–69.

9. The Winchester prayer, the Saint Germans curse, and the Rochester excommunication formula contain nothing that could be construed as an influence on the events of 1197 in Dublin. To say that no clamor is extant from any English church is a negative argument, to be sure, but one backed by the authoritative opinions of Christopher E. Hohler and Michael Lapidge, whose very helpful letters are acknowledged in appendix A; the responsibility for the argument used here remains mine of course, not theirs.

10. These pages on Wales constitute a shortened version of my essay "Spiritual Sanctions in Wales," in *Images of Sainthood in Medieval Europe*, ed. Renate Blumenfeld-Kosinski and Timea Szell (Ithaca, N.Y., 1991), pp. 67–80. The standard edition of the *Liber Landavensis* is that of John G. Evans and John Rhys, eds., *The Text of the Book of Llan Dav* (Oxford, 1893; photo reprint, Aberystwyth, 1979). The standard study of the charters it contains is Wendy Davies's *The Llandaff Charters* (Aberystwyth, 1979). Davies has assigned consecutive numbers to all the charters in the *Liber Landavensis*; in citing these charters I will follow her practice of first giving the page numbers in the Evans and Rhys edition (occasionally followed by a small letter if more than one charter begins on that page) followed in parentheses by the number she assigned. Thus the references to the dispute between King Edwin and Bishop Bleddri are combined to read Evans and Rhys, *Book of Llan Dav*, p. 249b (141).

range from the sixth century to the twelfth, this collection clearly constitutes one of the treasures of early Welsh history. Five of the cases involve cursing, usually in combination with excommunication, while nine, including some of the earliest ones, contain humiliations.[11] In one of these Bishop Berthwyn called a synod about 700 to excommunicate King Clodri for killing King Idwallon, the two having previously pledged friendship over sacred relics. When the excommunication was pronounced, the altar was completely cleared off and the crosses were placed on the floor (*denudando altaria dei et deponendo cruces ad terram*).[12] A similar case involving a vow to keep the peace followed by a killing led Bishop Euddogwy in about 665 to place the crosses on the floor, but then he cursed the king, saying, "May his days be few and may his sons be orphans and his wife a widow" (*et inclinando cruces ad terram . . . maledixit regem cum progenie confirmante sinodo et dicente: "Fiant dies eius pauci et fiant filii eius orphani et uxor eius vidua"* [Ps. 108:9]).[13] Along with the crosses, sacred relics were also put on the floor (*denudando altaria dei et prosternando cruces ad terram simul et reliquias sanctorum*)[14] and a further variant involved silencing the bells by turning them over (*depositis crucis ad terram simul et cimbalis versis*).[15] Four cases employ the combination of deposed crosses and relics and overturned bells, three of them in conjunction with an excommunication.[16]

The most elaborate combination of sanctions occurs in a case from Christmas Day in about 1070, when King Cadwgon of Morgannwg visited Llandaff to participate in the holiday festivities. These got dangerously out of hand and led to the death of a nephew of Bishop Herewald. The bishop convened a full synod; he had the crosses and relics placed on the floor and the bells turned over; moreover, he had the doors of the church closed and barricaded with thorn bushes. "And so the people remained," continues the account, "without service or pastor, for days and nights, while the anathema and separation from the faith rested on the king's family." The king soon became

11. For the cases involving cursing, see Evans and Rhys, *Book of Llan Dav*, pp. 218 (110), 237b (133), 255 (144), 261 (149), 271 (156).
12. Ibid., p. 176b (59).
13. Ibid., p. 147 (23).
14. Ibid., p. 167 (47).
15. Ibid., p. 180b (65).
16. Ibid., pp. 189 (75), 212 (105), 214 (106), 222 (112).

anxious both to be at peace with his pastor and to have his family rejoin the company of Christians, and so he had the culprit brought to justice.[17]

The obvious importance of this collection has not prevented its being the subject of extended debate by historians. Discussion has arisen because, to cite only the more egregious problems, just one of the 158 charters it contains bears a date, the lives of the patron saints it contains find only the sketchiest corroboration in other sources, and there seems not even to have been a diocese of Llandaff for most of the period supposedly covered by the book. Some have referred to it, and a few have dismissed it, as a forgery.[18]

The *Book of Llandaff* dates from the early twelfth century, when the Anglo-Norman conquerors were consolidating their recent takeover of Wales. Its purpose was to advance the claims put forth by Bishop Urban, formerly a priest at Worcester, who held the see of Llandaff in Glamorgan from 1107 to 1134. Archbishop Anselm consecrated him at Canterbury and extracted from him a profession of canonical obedience and subjection to the church of Canterbury, the first such profession by a bishop in Wales. The tasks confronting post-Conquest bishops were extremely complex. The first of these, a Breton named Hervé who became bishop of Bangor in 1093, was forcibly thrown out of his diocese. The matter went far beyond a struggle between natives and foreigners. Such bishops had to construct territorial dioceses on the Roman model where they had not previously existed. This need drew them into conflict with one another and with the land-hungry Anglo-Norman aristocracy. In seeking independence for their dioceses, they fell into conflict with Canterbury. They quarreled with nearly everyone except the pope, and the reason they did not quarrel with him is that they took their quarrels to his court; thus they quite readily thrust the Welsh

17. Ibid., p. 267 (154).
18. Evan D. Jones, "The Book of Llandaff," *National Library of Wales Journal* 4 (1945–1946): 3–53; Christopher N. L. Brooke, "The Archbishops of St David's, Llandaff, and Caerleon-on-Usk," in *Studies in the Early British Church*, ed. Nora K. Chadwick et al. (Cambridge, 1958), pp. 201–242; and Wendy Davies, "*Liber Landavensis*: Its Construction and Its Credibility," *English Historical Review* 88 (1973): 335–351. Davies has also studied these Welsh charters in the broader Celtic context in "The Latin Charter-Tradition in Western Britain, Brittany and Ireland in the Early Medieval Period," in *Ireland in Early Medieval Europe*, ed. Dorothy Whitelock, Rosamond McKitterick, and David Dumville (New York, 1982), pp. 258–280.

church, which previously had had little to do with Rome, directly into the hands of the papacy.[19]

Urban's first meeting with a pope took place at the council called by Pope Calixtus II in 1119 at Reims. He introduced the church of Llandaff to the pope as having been founded in honor of the apostle Peter. Actually it was only in the following year that he had construction begin on a new cathedral church, and this church he had dedicated to Saint Peter, as well as to Saints Dyfrig (whose relics Urban had translated from Bardsey to Llandaff also in 1120), Teilo, and Euddogwy. Notwithstanding confirmation by Calixtus of all his claims, Urban's conflicts carried on over the next decade and a half, especially those with the bishops of Saint David's and of Hereford. His journeys to Rome yielded papal confirmations, but his competitors got these rescinded so that he was nearly always struggling to get them back. It is a poignant comment on Urban's career that we last hear of him on yet another trip to Rome, where he died in 1134.[20]

For Bishop Urban the *Book of Llandaff* was a combined archive, treasury, and arsenal, accumulated through at least a decade and a half of tense competition on several fronts; without it he was powerless. The original manuscript survives, and most of its contents were executed by one hand only, in the second quarter of the twelfth century. It contains no liturgical formulas, but the charters in it have been shown to contain many archaic terms and names as well as omissions and other scribal errors, thus indicating probable derivation from earlier sources. The result of these studies is a complete inventory of the charters, with approximate dates (which have been used in the present discussion

19. Glanmor Williams, *The Welsh Church from Conquest to Reformation* (Cardiff, 1962), p. 2. On Urban, see Wendy Davies, "Saint Mary's Worcester and the *Liber Landavensis*," *Journal of the Society of Archivists* 4 (1972): 478–483. On the Norman Conquest of Wales, see Lynn Nelson, *The Normans in South Wales, 1070–1171* (Austin, Tex., 1966), pp. 160–165; and David Walker, *The Norman Conquerors* (Swansea, Wales, 1977), pp. 82–95.

20. Wendy Davies, *An Early Welsh Microcosm: Studies in the Llandaff Charters*, Royal Historical Society, Studies in History 9 (London, 1978), p. 5; Evans and Rhys, *Book of Llan Dav*, pp. 30–48, 54–67, 84–96; Davies, "*Liber Landavensis*," pp. 337–338. For a full review of the troubled reign of Bishop Urban, see *Episcopal Acts and Cognate Documents relating to Welsh Dioceses, 1066–1272*, ed. James C. Davies, 2 vols. (Cardiff, 1946), 1:147–190. For an argument that Urban was Welsh and more of an outsider at the royal court than most of his peers, see Denis L. Bethell, "English Black Monks and Episcopal Elections in the 1120s," *English Historical Review* 84 (1969): 673–698.

and notes) and with clear demarcations between the probable original material and the later accretions.[21]

Among the accretions of the final century before the book was gathered are all of what are called "narratives." These are the discursive accounts of events leading up to the particular donations that the charters record. Even if records of actual transactions have filtered through various compilations from earlier documents, the tales of disputes and how they were resolved all lack archaic elements and thus appear to be recent compositions.[22] All twenty-four of the cases with spiritual sanctions are extracted from such narratives, and thus of all the material in this vast collection, precisely what interests us most is from the part that is most suspect. None of the spiritual sanctions deployed in the *Book of Llandaff* has a known precedent in Wales. And since there is no evidence of such practices in England either, it appears that the compiler(s) of the book knew the standard usage of northern France. Even if the scenes described did not take place, in telling them the compiler showed how he wanted people to think of the way the bishops of Llandaff had handled troublemakers in the past and thus what they could expect the present bishop to do now and in the future. If the purpose was to issue a warning, he surely would not have made up something so fanciful that no one would have believed it.[23]

We should inquire in parallel fashion about lay violence—whether it was indigenous or imported. To be sure, there was violent conflict

21. Evans and Rhys, *Book of Llan Dav*, pp. vii–xxx; Davies, *Llandaff Charters*, pp. 1–2, 92–129.

22. Davies, *Llandaff Charters*, pp. 21–23. Davies's detailed analysis confirms the judgment of Evans (Evans and Rhys, *Book of Llan Dav*, p. xxiv): "The charters pure and simple are, on the face of them, genuine; while the Synodal accounts, though based on facts, are clothed in the words of the compiler, and decorated by certain touches calculated to impress rebellious subjects with a salutary fear of church discipline. Hence the interpolated passages about bells being inverted, about relics and crosses being removed from the altar and placed on the ground, at a time earlier by several centuries, than the commencement of such methods for enforcing obedience to the ecclesiastical power." Evans's accompanying note deals only with the use of interdict, citing the last and most liturgically complex of the cases mentioned in the text above.

23. The same reasoning is used by John W. James in "The Excommunications in the *Book of Llan Dâv*," *Journal of the Historical Society of the Church in Wales* 8 (1958): 5–14. James was troubled by the anachronistic use of interdiction, which led him to question the historical accuracy of such details as the stripping of the altar and the deposition of the crosses and relics. He did not know where to seek precedents for such practices, but the cursing he confidently traced to the druids. Without the benefit of Wendy Davies's research, he concluded that the bare outline of information in the charters was genuine but that the twelfth-century editor wrote them up in the terminology of his day.

in pre-Norman days. One leading Welsh historian has characterized the political life of the pre-Conquest period as a "litany of family and inter-dynastic conflicts, raids, kidnappings, and murders."[24] There were new types of conflict in the early twelfth century, though, conflict specific to the coming of the Normans. But it is not enough to say that the conquerors were greedy, for these same Norman lords were known for generous stewardship toward churches in their home territories. Recent investigation has focused on precisely this point, stressing the "massive transfer" of rights and income from Welsh churches to the Norman lords' own religious foundations in Normandy or in England. Tewkesbury Abbey in Gloucestershire, for example, grew rich on lands in Glamorgan. The Normans showed a great distaste for the Welsh church; they preferred to transfer wealth from it to churches that, in their view, really mattered.[25] To be sure, the Normans established and sponsored monastic communities in Wales; indeed, they introduced there the current liturgical spirituality of black monasticism, including that of Cluny. Yet they founded no abbey; they founded nineteen priories in South Wales, of which eighteen were dependent upon mother houses in England, Normandy, or other French principalities.[26]

The spiritual sanctions were swept in on this same colonial wave. The narratives of theatrical scoldings of powerful lay wrongdoers at Llandaff did not come out of the culture of Wales but rather sprang from that of Norman England or Normandy; they represented one more aspect of Normanization, along with the territorial diocese, the Benedictine monastery, the church dedication to Saint Peter, the synod, subjection to the church of Canterbury, and appeals to the court of Rome.

There is a postscript in the *Book of Llandaff* where a fifteenth-century scribe made reference to an excommunication formula that Saint Teilo supposedly received from a pope in the sixth century. In a blank space at the bottom of a page partway through the book, he reported the following:

> Be it known that the great sentence of excommunication of St. Teilo, which he obtained at the Roman Court against any who infringe the liberties or

24. Robert R. Davies, *Conquest, Coexistence and Change: Wales, 1063–1415* (Oxford, 1987), p. 24.
25. Ibid., pp. 180–181.
26. F. G. Cowley, *The Monastic Order in South Wales, 1066–1349* (Cardiff, 1977), pp. 9–17, 270.

privileges of the cathedral church of Llandaff, was read and promulgated in the usual way on the saint's day in 1410, and that within a few days seven persons who had thus transgressed went wildly insane, and remained that way for the rest of their lives.[27]

Although we lack the text of this formula, we can reasonably suppose that the Llandaff seven would not have reacted so strongly had a prelate merely announced that he was going to excommunicate some wrongdoers. In any case, the scribe inserted his report on the very page containing an all-encompassing "Privilege of Saint Teilo," which includes a provision that those who violate the terms of the privilege be cursed and excommunicated. The main body of this privilege, it so happens, was lifted directly from a bull issued by Pope Calixtus II in 1119.[28] Thus the formula used in 1410 did not date from the time of Saint Teilo, but rather, like all the rest of Llandaff's maledictory sanctions, was from the reign of Bishop Urban. That was a time when the Norman aristocracy, who lived under relatively tight control in Normandy and England, had virtually the free run of Wales. Such sanctions were perhaps never put into use in Wales (or anywhere else in the British Isles except once in Dublin, in 1197), but testimonies to their use in Normandy and elsewhere on the Continent are another matter.

Francia

The earliest recorded use of a liturgical clamor took place at Tours in 996. In that year Fulk Nerra, the count of Anjou, was besieging Tours; he and his men entered the cloister of Saint-Martin and severely damaged the house of one of the canons. A possible motive is that the house had fortifications of a sort that Fulk was trying to eliminate from the territory he controlled. The canons in any case rejected his authority and took offense at this "unheard-of atrocity." Their reaction was to place the bodies of the saints and the crucifix on the floor. They put thorns around these and also upon the tomb of Saint Martin. They kept the doors of the church closed day and night, letting in no local people, but only pilgrims. Not long after, Count Fulk came voluntarily to Saint-Martin to make amends. From the house of the master of the school he walked barefoot to the church and, with his retinue, entered humbly. He went to the tomb of Saint Martin and there, in the presence of

27. Evans and Rhys, *Book of Llan Dav*, pp. 118–121, 350. Cf. Walter de Gray Birch, *Memorials of the See and Cathedral of Llandaff* (Neath, Wales, 1912), p. 75.
28. Davies, *Llandaff Charters*, pp. 18–19.

the bishop of Angers, promised God and Saint Martin that he would not repeat such behavior. He also paid his respects before the relics and the crucifix. This peaceful resolution of the crisis apparently achieved precisely what the monks had set out to accomplish. It is the more remarkable because of the reputation of Fulk as an exceedingly aggressive and ruthless man.[29]

A few more examples are needed to demonstrate the general form and flavor of these cases, and then some peculiar variants will be examined. The historian Ordericus Vitalis describes a humiliation in telling of a rebellion against Norman authority that took place in 1090 in the county of Maine. The local lay notables organized this rebellion, secure in their control of the city of Le Mans and surrounding strongholds. Their plan was to bring back a descendant of the former count of Maine from pre-Norman times. They were opposed in this plan by the bishop, named Hoel, and not surprisingly, since he held his see by King William's gift. Hoel excommunicated the whole lot of the rebels, and in return they captured him and put him in prison. They said they intended to keep him there until their man arrived to take up the office and title of count, in defiance of the Normans. "Meanwhile," says Ordericus,

> the church of God shared in the affliction of its bishop. The holy images of the Lord on the crucifixes, and shrines containing the relics of saints, were taken down; the doors of the churches blocked up with thorns; the ringing of bells, the chanting of offices, and all the accustomed rites ceased, as the widowed church mourned and gave itself up to weeping.

The rebellion against the Normans did not crumble, but the bishop was soon released.[30]

The monks of Saint-Médard of Soissons employed a similar spiritual sanction in 1033 when engaged in a property dispute with Goscelin,

29. Louis Halphen, *Le comté d'Anjou au XIe siècle* (Paris, 1906), pp. 348–349; Olivier Guillot, *Le comte d'Anjou et son entourage au XIe siècle*, 2 vols. (Paris, 1972), 2:27. This case is discussed by Patrick Geary, "Humiliation of Saints," in *Saints and Their Cults: Studies in Religious Sociology, Folklore and History*, ed. Stephen Wilson (Cambridge, 1983), pp. 123–140. Again in 1155 the canons humiliated the relics, successfully forcing Hugh of Sainte-Maure to seek reconciliation. See MS, Paris, BN, Collection Touraine, vol. 5, no. 1774; this information and the reference were kindly brought to my attention by Sharon A. Farmer of the University of California, Santa Barbara. On Fulk, see Bernard S. Bachrach, "A Study in Feudal Politics: Relations between Fulk Nerra and William the Great, 995–1030," *Viator* 7 (1976): 111.

30. *Historia ecclesiastica*, 8:11, in *EHOV* 4:194–195.

duke of Lotharingia. King Henry I had given Goscelin a villa on the Moselle that the monks claimed had been granted to them centuries earlier by Charlemagne. Goscelin, in their view a shameless person "untouched by the fear of God," refused to give over the disputed land. The monks, "not knowing which way to turn," decided to appeal to God, "who has never abandoned those who trust in him." The account, told of course from the monks' point of view, then says that the abbot arranged for things to happen in such a way that the king would become terrified regarding his unjust donation. The abbot deprived his beloved church of divine offices; he laid out on the floor the bodies of the saints, specifying that when the mercy of God arrived to help, the relics would be restored to their proper place of honor.[31]

"Finally, after about a year," when the duke was resting in a monastery during a journey to the royal court, he had a vision that brought matters to a head. As Goscelin slept, he dreamed he witnessed a discussion about the disputed villa among the three patron saints of Saint-Médard: Saints Sebastian, Gregory, and Médard. In particular they talked of what they should do about the man who was holding property of their church from the king. Suddenly they turned on him and began to beat him "severely." Goscelin woke up bleeding profusely from the nose and mouth. He interpreted the cause of this apparition and attack to be the possession he had unjustly received from the king and was even more unjustly keeping. He returned the land and repented, blaming his own recklessness and speaking everywhere about the merits of the saints. The monks restored the relics to their place amid great honor and praise for God.

The pressure of the humiliation in this story does not appear to have acted upon the king, as the abbot had announced beforehand was his intention, or for that matter upon the duke. Instead it acted upon the saints. If the story is to hold together, we must assume that the saints turned violent in the vision out of their frustration at being kept in a state of humiliation for a full year. They in turn acted directly upon Goscelin, while the king, though not completely blameless in this affair, got off free.

Again there is an indication that kings were beyond the reach of these sanctions in the story told of a visit to Saint-Germain-des-Prés by the young Philip I in 1061. The abbey church was loaded with exqui-

31. *Annales OSB* 4:383.

site, extremely precious objects, most donated by royal patrons going back as far as Childebert in the seventh century. Philip and his entourage entered the church "irreverently" and, as if driven to demonstrate that he could dispose of the church's treasure at will, Philip seized the gold cross that stood behind the altar of Saint Vincent and several other objects made of gold and set with precious gems; these in turn, in the manner of one of his forebears just back from a victorious campaign, he distributed to his admiring companions.[32]

With the king and his retinue still present, the monks called upon Saints Germain and Vincent for help. They placed the chests containing the saints' remains down on the floor, and with trembling voices they called upon the mercy of God. Among the king's men was Stephen, prefect of the city of Paris, a most irreverent man according to the monks, who in particular had egged Philip on in his sacrilegious enterprise. As they all stood about, a cloud of mist arose from the saints. The king, now realizing that his actions had been wrong and growing terrified, moved back from the others. The cloud settled about Stephen, "and so that a clear example of unambiguous divine vengeance be given, Stephen's eyes were instantly deprived of their sight." The king ordered the immediate return of all the precious objects. The lament of the monks turned to praise. The cross was again elevated to its original position. And the Parisian people, who had in the meantime gathered and witnessed the event, rejoiced at this display of divine power. Once again a king got off free, though one of his men was made to pay dearly for his rash behavior. Also notable in this account is the immediacy with which the monks deposed the relics, and the immediacy with which the saints reacted.

The cases recounted thus far show humiliations set in motion by a community of canons (Tours), by a bishop (Le Mans), and by two communities of monks (Saint-Médard and Saint-Germain-des-Prés). These constitute the norm for those able to make a clamor. Yet there is a popular element in some cases, where individuals or groups of laypeople made their own clamor, or made a clamor jointly with some clerics, or in yet another combination, made a clamor parallel to but sharply differentiated from one made by clerics. Some peasants living on lands of the Abbey of Sainte-Foy of Conques, for example, handled by themselves the case of a knight named Aichard who often let his

32. *Vita S. Germani episcopi Parisiensis (miraculum factum anno 1061)* (*AASSOSB* 4:111).

animals feed on the monastery's land. After they repeatedly asked him to stop this practice, he relented and removed all the animals except his favorite steed. The presence of this one horse still greatly disturbed the peasants, who made repeated clamors to Saint Foy for her intervention. "Then one day (Oh, what a terrific scene! [*o mira res*]), while the animal was feeding in the fields, its abdomen split open and its entrails, like those of poor Arius, spilled out on the ground."[33]

On an early September day at Provins, with the crops abundant but still not harvested, a hailstorm arose with hailstones "as large as fists" and "as hard as rocks." This was no time for distinctions, either social or ecclesiastical. The monks and all the people of the town ran together (*concurrent*) to the church; they placed the body of the blessed martyr on the floor, and all called out (*clamantes omnes*) tearfully: "Saint Aigulf, why are you sleeping? Why do you allow us to perish? If you are a true martyr of God, help us now in this moment of great need." Saint Aigulf stopped the hailstorm and thus saved the crops. Here there was no malefactor to be pressured or punished, just a saint to be reminded of his responsibility.[34]

A case involving separate, parallel clamors occurs among those miracles of Saint Bavon of Ghent that were recorded in the eleventh century. It is the case of one Siger of Meerbeke, who pillaged the hamlet of Houtem. He and his men took away everything they could lay their hands on, including the work animals. Houtem belonged to the Abbey of Saint-Bavon, and when Siger heard that the peasants were complaining about his behavior, he added insult to injury by "vomiting up sarcastic comments" about the abbey's patron saint. The peasants went to the abbey church in Ghent to bring their complaint directly to the saint. They brought with them the straps with which the animals had been tied in their stalls. At the saint's tomb they were in tears when they started to exclaim (*exclamare*): "Bavon, soldier of God, where are you? Siger, this follower of the devil, has injured you and your servants." The women among them let out with a *vero femineo clamore*, as if to wake up Saint Bavon, who, they lamented, seemed to be asleep

33. Patrick Geary, "La coercition des saints dans la pratique religieuse médiévale," in *La culture populaire au Moyen Age*, ed. Pierre Boglioni (Montreal, 1979), pp. 146–161. For Sainte-Foy: *Liber miraculorum Sancte Fidis*, ch. 31, ed. A. Bouillet (Paris, 1897), pp. 229–230. See the case of a blind beggar clamoring at the tomb of Saint Robert at la Chaise Dieu; *AASS*, Aprilis 3:323–324, discussed by Geary, "La coercition des saints," p. 151.

34. *Miracula S. Aigulfi*, ch. 4 (*AASSOSB* 2:639). The people and the monks also made a joint clamor to put out a fire; *Miracula S. Aigulfi*, ch. 5 (ibid.).

during their time of tribulation. To this point, the story, related of course by a clerical author, is of terrible injury inflicted upon poor people and of their moving complaint to their landlord and protector. The peasants of Houtem were making a popular clamor; then the monks took over.[35]

The monks placed the bodies of the saints on the floor. Although they were saddened by the terrible happenings at Houtem, they were "much more saddened by the deposition of the saints." They warned Siger, then they excommunicated him. In the meantime they advised the aggrieved peasants to be patient in awaiting the divine response. Siger did not change his ways either soon or willingly, but in another of his raids he received a wound that brought him to his death. His dying wish was to be reconciled with the monks of Saint-Bavon. When that was granted, the saints were returned to their rightful place with solemn litanies. The account leaves little doubt that it was the formal and learned clamor of the monks, carried out in the calm and deliberate manner appropriate to the liturgy, rather than the chaotic commotion stirred up by the peasants, that obtained the desired result.

Even if the peasants' clamor was not the one that worked, the authorities at Saint-Bavon were probably wise to allow the peasants in to make it. Their clamor was directed to the saint, and had access to him been blocked, the complaint might have been turned against those barring the way. The issue does not come under discussion in the *Miracles of Saint Bavon*, but the related issue of the comportment of pilgrims does get aired in the *Miracles of Saint Foy*. The tradition at the Abbey of Sainte-Foy was that during the nights preceding feast days pilgrims were allowed into the church. While the monks recited the psalms and the night office, the lay visitors, with their torches and candles, kept the vigil in their own way, telling stories and singing popular songs. The monks' disapproval of the pilgrims' behavior brought forth such terms as "absurd," "detestable," "horrifying," "boorish," and "unworthy." So strongly and unanimously did they feel about this matter that they decided to put an end to it, closing the church tight on the eve of the next feast day. The people showed up just the same and made a great clamor before the door. When the monks, who had the only keys, arrived for the night office, they found that the doors had

35. Maurice Coens, "Translations et miracles de Saint Bavon au XIe siècle," *Analecta Bollandiana* 86 (1968): 49–50, 63–64; 87 (1969): 416.

been miraculously swung open, and a large crowd awaited them inside. They could only take this to signify divine approval of a lay presence at vigils. A monk from farther north, Bernard of Angers, comments on this story by saying that after mulling it over for a while he thinks he can tolerate these crowds, with their rustic but innocent ways. "And besides, if one were to forbid this practice, the pilgrimage [*frequentatio sanctuarii*] could as a result diminish."[36]

Occasionally *clamantes* told why they chose to make a clamor or what they expected from it as a result. In the 1070s Abbot Hugh and the whole congregation of monks of the Abbey of Saint-Cybard of Angoulême kept up their "frequent prayers and public clamors before the body of St. Cybard" so that God, they said, would bring their oppressors to justice. The monks of Saint-Médard seem to have petitioned God by default, for we saw that they did not know which way to turn. At the Abbey of the Holy Trinity at Vendôme, the monks in 1074 also appear to have made a clamor by default, but the account of the events of that year makes clear precisely where else they should have been able to turn but could not. They were being put upon by a knight named Odo of Blazon, who with his men simply took over the church of Cheviré, which the monks claimed was theirs. Odo was doing these things with the consent of Fulk Rechin, the count of Anjou. Fulk was young and inexperienced; he did not really approve of Odo's behavior, but he was surrounded by aggressive knights and submerged in constant warfare. These circumstances kept him from dealing properly with the "persecutors of holy church."[37]

In a similar situation in Carolingian times, the monks would have had grounds (defective justice) to appeal directly to the king. But in 1074 the monks of Holy Trinity had to face the double problem of seeing many of their vital crops carried off while knowing they had no hope of receiving help from any human source. And so, convinced there would be no help from "the very one who ought to acquire justice for them," they turned with contrite hearts to making a clamor and

---

36. *Liber miraculorum Sancte Fidis*, 2:12 (De miraculo valvarum internarumque januarum, que ultro peregrinis clamantibus patuerunt), ed. A. Bouillet (Paris, 1897), pp. 120–122.

37. MS, Angoulême, Archives de la Charente, H¹ 1, f. 45v. *Cartulaire de l'abbaye cardinale de la Trinité de Vendôme*, ed. Charles Metais, 5 vols. (Paris, 1893–1904), 1:386–390. Cf. Penelope D. Johnson, *Prayer, Patronage, and Power: The Abbey of la Trinité, Vendôme, 1032–1187* (New York, 1981), p. 72.

complaint to God. They also took down from its high place the image of the crucified Lord and placed it upon a bed of thorns on the church floor. This gesture was undertaken, the text explains, not out of disrespect or disdain for this symbol of the Lord, but so that the malefactors would be frightened and would thus cease their unlawful invasions and theft.

Every day the monks prostrated themselves in prayer there by the feet of the crucified figure and recited litanies of psalms and masses. And this went on until Fulk became involved in a war with the count of Poitiers and needed help wherever he could get it. He made a public promise that if he prevailed in battle he would cause to be returned to Holy Trinity all that he had unjustly allowed to be carried off. He won the battle and kept his promise, leading Odo of Blazon to the abbey church, where together before an immense crowd they made restitution and promised never again to disturb the belongings of Holy Trinity. The cross was then restored to its proper place amid a joyous outpouring of applause and tears.

This story makes no mention of saints' relics; the only object humiliated is a crucifix. It is also noteworthy for two other reasons. The first is that it refers pointedly to the count, who had been turning a blind eye to the malefactor, as the one who should secure justice for them. The second is that it explains so clearly that the humiliation was meant not to show disrespect for the crucifix but rather to frighten the malefactor(s).

At the Abbey of Marchiennes in Flanders, with its precious relics of Saint Richtrude, there also appeared the phrase "with no hope of justice from men" before the monks let out their clamors (*emiserunt clamores*) amid the sounding of bells and launching of anathemas. The object was a knight named Hilouin who, safe in his chateau surrounded by water, continually raided a possession of Saint-Richtrude's, the little villa of Gouy. The monks became involved when they learned of the complaint (*planctus*) of the "little people" to Saint Richtrude. The author of the *Miracles of Saint Richtrude* laced his telling of this story with rhetorical questions. He said that the monks could find neither mercy nor consolation nor clemency. "So what? The abbot was depressed; his congregation was depressed. But what should they do? Wait for vengeance? But from whom?" At the end of this series of questions, in which the malefactor has been called "tyrant" and "second pharaoh," the author asks: "What then? Did he go unpunished? No way [*nullo modo*]." Then the author tells of the clamor. It took that clamor a year to take effect, a year to the very day and hour when Hilouin died of a wound. The community took note of this great miracle, acclaimed God, and extolled the virtues of Saint Richtrude.[38]

The use of the clamor at Marchiennes became directly tied to the lack of available justice during the chaos that followed the assassination of Count Charles the Good in 1127.[39] In one instance there was a knight, unnamed throughout the story, who had been preying upon the monks' lands. They in turn "struck him and his whole family with a horrendous anathema." Furthermore, the abbot went to court to complain to the count about this knight. The next time the knight was at court, Count Charles reproached him severely for maltreating the monks. Thus humiliated, the knight became enraged, but there was nothing he could do until that fateful day when the murderous conspirators cut down the count as he prayed in his chapel. The knight went wild. He burned a mill that belonged to the monks, and he threatened to burn down their whole monastery as well. The excommunication was frequently renewed, and a priest repeated the daily clamor (*clamor quotidianus*), with the whole community prostrate and the bells ringing. One day the knight rode by the church, heard the bells, and learned what they signified. The next day he was dead.[40]

Also in 1127, faced with another of these strongmen who bullied a village but remained untouchable in his isolated chateau, the monks decided to take the relics to the village, Sailly-en-Ostrevent, that he was harassing. They fasted and offered prayers for peace before the Lord every day. "During that year in which the relics of the saints remained at Sailly, the adversaries, out of respect for God and Saint Richtrude, did not dare disturb any of the belongings of the church." With what may be the echo of a daily clamor back at the abbey, the relics took the place of a local representative of comital authority in that troubled village and thus maintained social order.[41]

The *Miracles of Saint Ursmer*, the patron of the Abbey of Lobbes in Hainaut, afford us an opportunity to see, in succession, how the pres-

38. *Miracula S. Rictrudis*, 2:4 (*AASS*, Maii 3:138–139). Cf. Henri Platelle, "Crime et châtiment à Marchiennes," *Sacris Erudiri* 24 (1980): 163, 191–192.

39. *The Murder of Charles the Good*, tr. James B. Ross (New York, 1960).

40. *Miracula S. Rictrudis*, pp. 104–105; Platelle, "Crime et châtiment," pp. 164, 193–194.

41. *Miracula S. Rictrudis*, pp. 125–126; Platelle, "Crime et châtiment," pp. 163, 194–195.

ence of a powerful lord prevented violence, how his subsequent absence permitted it, how a humiliation prevented further violence, and most unusual of all, how those who witnessed the humiliation reacted. In 1060 at Blaringhem in Flanders, near Saint-Omer, two knights insulted each other in a quarrel that threatened to get out of hand. Their lord, Hugh, intervened in time to prevent the bloodshed that seemed certain to take place and made the two perform a public reconciliation. The peace did not last long, though, for as soon as Hugh went away and the two knights met, one ran the other through with a lance. Upon his return Hugh vowed in turn to kill the murderer, but he had sought sanctuary in a church. On the morning of Ascension Day the scene was set for a dramatic showdown when a crowd assembled before that church and found a company of knights prepared to block entry into the church. They were confronted by Hugh and his men, with swords drawn, prepared to force their way in to get the murderer. Enter Saint Ursmer.[42]

The monks of Lobbes were on a lengthy tour of Flanders with the relics of their patron, promoting peace and raising funds for the reconstruction of their monastery, destroyed in a recent war. They entered the scene at Blaringhem on the side of the sinner, who was facing nearly certain death. With their unknown saint, they parted the crowd as they filed into the church. They found the penitent knight stretched out before the altar as if already dead. They celebrated a mass and on account of the dangerous situation tearfully implored divine clemency with "litanies and all means." They put on special vestments for the principal mass and then humbly called upon Hugh to halt the coming clash of arms, but he ignored their pleas. At this point the monks put the relics of Saint Ursmer on the church floor in the midst of the crowd. The people standing about were astonished and humbly lowered their eyes. They showed by their comportment that they understood who was in their midst, even those who did not know him. Tears flowed from everyone's eyes. Piety and anger vied in the hearts of the enemies. In the end piety won out in Hugh, and he let the poor fellow go, with life and limb intact and even with his pardon. Because of what hap-

---

42. *Miracula Sancti Ursmari in itinere per Flandriam facta*, ch. 6 (*MGH, SS* 15, pt. 2:839). Cited and commented upon by Geoffrey Koziol, "Monks, Feuds, and the Making of Peace in Eleventh-Century Flanders," in *The Peace of God: Social Violence and Religious Response in France around the Year 1000*, ed. Thomas Head and Richard Landes (Ithaca, N.Y., 1992), pp. 245–250.

pened, about a hundred feuds were resolved among the knights gathered there that day.[43]

The accounts of cases in which clamors of various sorts were used thus corroborate the existence and purpose of the liturgical formulas presented earlier. Indeed, a few such accounts include the texts of the formulas used on the occasions they describe. Near the beginning of the twelfth century, to cite an example from Laon, when the canons of the cathedral church of that city excommunicated and anathematized Enguerrand of Coucy, whom they qualified as *tyrannus*, their counterparts at the church of Reims sent them a letter expressing solidarity. The letter contains a description of what they were doing at Reims to help out, namely placing the bodies of the saints on a litter on the floor and surrounding them with thorns. Then, it goes on to say, the canons stretch out humbly on the floor every day in front of the relics and "proclaim" against the persecutors of the church of Laon. Another example is the detailed description of a combined excommunication, malediction, and humiliation from Chartres that was mentioned earlier, which comes from the narrative in a notice containing the terms of the resolution of a dispute. The story, whose details and outcome need not detain us here, begins with the events of a Sunday afternoon in October 1210. It is thus time-specific down to the part of the day, and supplies liturgical details as well. In ways somewhat analogous, an account of events at Liège in 1212 includes such descriptive details plus an actual formula. The source is a saint's life that chronicles among other things the struggles between the prince-bishops of Liège and the dukes of Brabant. At a delicate point in 1212 the bishop assembled a council at Huy to launch a solemn excommunication and to instruct all the clergy of the diocese in the proper measures to take. These included circling the image of the cross and the relics of the saints with thorns and placing them on the floor in every church of the diocese, where also every Sunday and feast day the sentence against the duke and his accomplices was to be repeated. There follows the text of the prayers that were to be said daily by all clerics "with many tearful sighs,"

43. At home, the monks of Lobbes were put to the test by Jean, the castellan of Beaumont, who showed up with a cohort of knights bent on pillaging the monastery. They appealed to these unwelcome visitors to desist, but without success. Then they appealed to their patrons, Saints Ursmer and Ermin, who represented their last hope of maintaining respect for their property. They engaged in intensive prayer for three days, at the end of which the castellan went mad and died miserably. *Miracula SS. Ursmari et Ermini*, ch. 18 (*MGH, SS* 15, pt. 2:833).

including familiar collects, selections from psalms, and maledictions. The last words pronounced were, "So be it, so be it," and the concluding comment was, "Such a clamor was repeated daily in the church of Liège."[44]

Together the formulaic and narrative sources make it clear that the clamor was a ceremony in which social disorder and concomitant suffering were acted out and accepted hierarchies were inverted. Despite the insistence on the virtue of humility in prescriptions for the religious life, the monks were not hesitant in referring to the function they served in society, that of those who pray (oratores), as the highest function. When their inferiors, those who fight (bellatores), oppressed them, the religious were brought low. Not only does the prayer say "in the spirit of humility," but the accounts confirm that the monks did prostrate themselves. In 1152 the monks of Saint-Amand not only humiliated their relics on the floor in front of the altar, they also "humiliated their own souls in the dust, as they poured out their prayers before the supreme majesty."[45]

Bishop Godefrid of Amiens made a similarly close identification between himself and the relics he ordered deposed during a dispute in 1105. The precipitating incident included a humiliation of sorts, for Godefrid was riding with Adam, the provost of Amiens, when enemies of Adam approached, insulted him, knocked him off his horse, and dragged him away in chains, despite the bishop's *reclamatione et sup-*

---

44. Laon, twelfth century: Letter from the canons of Reims to the dean of the chapter at Laon, in *Opera omnia Guiberti de Novigento*, ed. Luc d'Achery (Paris, 1651), p. 822. Chartres, 1210: *Cartulaire de Notre-Dame de Chartres*, ed. Eugène de Lépinois and Lucien Merlet, 3 vols. (Chartres, 1862–1865), 2:57–58; *Histoire de Chartres et du pays chartrain*, ed. André Chédeville (Toulouse, 1983), p. 83. Liège, 1212: MS, Rome, Biblioteca Vallicelliana, H.6, f. 189r–v; *Vitae Odiliae liber III: De triumpho S. Lamberti in Steppes*, ch. 6 (*MGH, SS* 25:178). The reverse combination is possible as well; that is, a formula can contain evidence of a particular case. In the manuscript of one of the formulas from Sens, the lines now scratched out are thought to have contained the names of those against whom the clamor was said. See MS, Saint Petersburg, Public Library, lat. 4° v.I.35, f. 102r. In the manuscript (twelfth century) of a formula from Fleury, in the margin opposite the mention of the *iniqui et superbi suisque viribus* who are disturbing the monastery are written in a later hand the names Beatrix, Hugo de Digone, and Gichardus de Digone. See MS, Orléans, BM, 123, p. 339, and *The Monastic Ritual of Fleury*, ed. Anselme Davril, Henry Bradshaw Society 105 (London, 1990), pp. 42, 156. My thanks for this reference go to Thomas Head of Yale University; for the use of the clamor at Fleury, see his *Hagiography and the Cult of Saints: The Diocese of Orléans, 800–1200* (New York, 1990), pp. 190–191.

45. *Thesaurus novus anecdotorum*, ed. Edmond Martène and Ursin Durand (Paris, 1717), 1:431.

plicatione: "There was nothing the man of God did not do to liberate his friend." He tried prayers, humiliation of relics, interdict, and anathema, but since all these measures failed, and since it was only right that the bishop suffer if "his" church and "his" patron saints were suffering, Godefrid humiliated himself. He put aside the symbols of his office, put on a simple monastic robe, and went on foot to throw himself at the feet of the one who was holding his man in prison. Eventually he gained the provost's release.[46]

In tracking the results of clamors, it is important to recall that the sources are exclusively clerical. They are not likely to report failures, and rarely do they give insight into the point of view of their adversaries. One narrative from Saint-Maur-lès-Fossés at Sceaux is rather more candid than most. It deals with the case of a certain Wlfuimus and says that every day the monks sang seven psalms and prayed for the mercy of God against (*contra*) him. And he, later on, as he began to recover from the sufferings inflicted upon him as a result of the clamor, said that "the monks had tried to kill him with their prayers, or rather, their maledictions."[47]

Rites of Reintegration

The death of the alleged malefactor was frequently asked for in ecclesiastical curses, and death did indeed bring some of these cases to a conclusion. Yet the peace achieved in such instances was fragile, for there was usually a relative ready to take up the cause of the deceased. More commonly, though, the conflicting parties arrived at some form of settlement, and when such a peace was really established between a church and its enemy, the occasion called for liturgical celebration.

From the time of Regino's collection in the first decade of the tenth century, there existed a formula for marking the reintegration of an excommunicated person into the community of the faithful. There did not exist, however, or at least there has not come to light, any equivalent ceremony specifically designated for a person against whom a clamor was said, a humiliation was carried out, or curses were pronounced. To be sure, such a person was probably also ex-

---

46. *Annales OSB* 5:451–452; "Ubi preces nihil obtinent, sacras beati Firmini martyris aliorumque reliquiae humi deponit . . . interdictio subjicit eumque anathemate plectit."

47. *Historia translationis corporis S. Mauri abbatis in Fossatense monasterium agri Parisiensis* (*AASSOSB* 6:188–189): "Quod illi eum suis orationibus, immo (ut testabatur) maledictionibus, occidere voluissent."

communicated. Given the confusion of terminology we have noted among the various forms of exclusion or separation, someone only clamored against might well, in another's view, at some moment have been considered excommunicated. Nonetheless, even though liturgical sources have a formula for reconciling excommunicates, which bears brief examination here, the same narrative or historical sources that tell us how clamors were used supply occasional glimpses of the ways persons clamored against were brought back into the fold.[48]

The most noteworthy aspect of the ceremony of reconciliation given by Regino is the way it essentially reverses the rite of excommunication. Perhaps gathered from an earlier source, this rite places the initiative upon the person expelled (referred to as the one "excommunicated or anathematized") who now wishes to be readmitted. The officiating cleric is to be the bishop who earlier pronounced the sentence of excommunication. As before, he is accompanied by twelve priests. They take their places before the church door, ready to encounter the repentant excommunicate. The bishop asks him if he wishes to do penance for the act(s) that brought about the excommunication. The sinner prostrates himself before the bishop and in that position confesses his guilt, asks forgiveness, and promises to do penance, whereupon he stands and the bishop leads him by the right hand literally into the church building, symbolically back into Christian communion and society. The bishop imposes the penance and then writes letters to those clerics previously informed of the excommunication reporting the excommunicate's return to the church.[49]

This ceremony was included in the *Romano-Germanic Pontifical*, but added to it is a formula of absolution consisting of psalms and prayers. Two entire psalms (Psalms 37 and 53) and parts of two others (50 and 102) are said, followed by "prayers" of the type seen in the Saint-Wandrille and Compiègne formulas that are made up of lines from the Psalms. Several prayers follow that can be traced to the Gelasian and Gregorian sacramentaries and that may also derive from earlier

48. Cf. Roger E. Reynolds, "Rites of Separation and Reconciliation in the Early Middle Ages," in *Segni e riti nella chiesa altomedievale occidentale*, Settimane di studio del Centro italiano di studi sull'Alto Medioevo 32 (Spoleto, 1987), pp. 427–428.

49. Regino of Prüm, *Libri duo de synodalibus causis et disciplinis ecclesiasticis*, ed. F. G. A. Wasserschleben (Leipzig, 1840), pp. 375–376.

rites for repentant sinners. Then comes a series of benedictions, each followed by a responsorial "amen." Holy water and incense complete the ritual cleansing, and the bishop's final words, "Christ shall illuminate you," reverse the effect of the dashed-out candles at the close of the excommunication ceremony.[50]

The lifting of a ban of excommunication at a church council held at Jonquières, near Montpellier, in 909 consisted largely of benedictions, and these were said to replace the maledictions previously imposed. The archbishop of Narbonne and ten bishops absolved and blessed Sinuarius, count of Roussillon, his wife, and his entourage: "May there come over you and take hold of you all the blessings of the New and the Old Testaments, and may all the maledictions that we once imposed upon you be carried away from you forever. May you be blessed in town and blessed in the fields." And thus begins a series of benedictions, ending with the wish that they arrive before the gates of paradise in the company of the Archangel Michael, a series that certainly has to be a precise restatement of the original excommunication, but with the maledictions now transformed into blessings.[51]

No such liturgical details have been found in narratives about the use of clamors. The account from Chartres in 1210 is fuller than most in this regard, for it does mention the ringing of bells throughout the town, the gathering of a crowd of laypeople, the singing at full voice of the response "Rejoice, Maria," and the return of the relics to the altar with joy, exultation, and singing. Sparser, and more typical, is the text from Saint-Médard saying that the relics were returned "with due veneration," or the one from Saint-Germain-des-Prés saying "with all reverence." Holy Trinity of Vendôme admits to "a joyous outpouring of applause and tears," while the monks at Marchiennes were said to "acclaim the praises of God." Still, it is difficult to extract properly liturgical indications from these texts. At Saint-Bavon, following the death of Siger of Meerbeke, "the saints" were brought back to their proper places "with litanies and solemn masses." And at Saint-John-the-Baptist of Angers, where the canons humiliated the relics of Saint Lézin in the course of a struggle, once the opposing parties made peace

50. *PRG* 1:318–321. In an act of 833 giving instructions for an order of penance, Agobard of Lyons prescribes "psalms and prayers"; see *MGH, Capit.* 2:57.

51. Mansi 18:261–264; I am grateful to Amy Remensnyder, who gave me this reference when she was a doctoral candidate at Berkeley.

the canons sang psalms and praised God (*psallentes et laudentes deum*) as they put the relics back.[52]

The mournful, penitential quality of clamors thus finds its counterpart in the joyous celebrations of reconciliation. For this reason the clamor should not be thought complete until right order has been restored. And just as the disruption of the community had been acted out in the clamor, so too did the reestablishment of peace have to be acted out. The proper mood became one of thanksgiving, praise, and joy. And if the relics had been deposed, they now had to be restored with all due reverence to their usual place of honor. We can be reasonably certain of the purpose and tone of such a conclusion to a clamor, even though we lack a precise text for it.

Geography of the Use of Clamors

Something akin to a clamor took place as far east as the Saxon city of Bremen, on the Weser, in the middle of the eleventh century. Archbishop Adalbert (1043–1072) presided over a church that, according to the chronicler Adam of Bremen, was "continually assailed by the ill will of the dukes of this land, [and] was now at length reduced to nothing." Adalbert's reaction was surely not a unique, personal invention: "This calamity of his times he mournfully deplored daily, and for this reason he had special psalms designated by which he might take vengeance upon the enemies of the church."[53]

Of the known cases in which some form of the clamor was used and identified as such, only two occurred below the main axis of the Charente valley, namely at Conques, and one well to the east of the Meuse valley, at Corvey, which like Bremen is in the valley of the Weser. Both cases at Conques involved only laypeople and had nothing more formal about them than that the accounts of them used the word "clamor" (against a knight's steed left to feed abusively in a field; before the locked doors of the abbey church on the eve of a feast day). Conques had countless ties with churches farther north by which to explain this

52. Chartres: *Cartulaire de Notre-Dame de Chartres*, p. 60. Saint-Médard: *Annales OSB* 4: 383. Saint-Germain: *AASSOSB* 4:111. Vendôme: *Cartulaire de Vendôme*, 1:389. Marchiennes: *Miracula S. Rictrudis*, p. 139. Saint-Bavon: Coens, "Translations et miracles de Saint Bavon," p. 64. Angers: Du Cange 7:112.

53. Adam of Bremen, *History of the Archbishops of Hamburg-Bremen*, tr. Francis J. Tschan (New York, 1959), p. 162. For a startling encounter where he had his clerics sing psalms in the presence of the duke of Saxony, whom he considered an oppressor of his church, see p. 178.

usage; to cite what may be the most relevant one in this connection, the author of the *Miracles of Saint Foy*, the principal historical source for the abbey, was Bernard of Angers, who had studied under Fulbert of Chartres.[54]

As for the lone case far to the east, there Abbot Wibald informed Emperor Frederick I in 1152 of the depredations of two powerful lords against the people and lands of Corvey, and informed him further that the monks had placed the relics of Saints Vitus and Justinus on the floor along with the image of the crucified Lord and henceforth suspended the ringing of bells and the celebration of the Divine Office. Corvey was a ninth-century offspring of the Abbey of Corbie, which itself had been established two centuries earlier in Picardy on the Corbie River, a tributary of the Somme, near Amiens. Besides the name, it maintained close ties with the mother house, which makes entirely plausible its having a copy of Corbie's Cluniac customs, with their instructions on how to make a clamor to God *pro tribulatione*. The clamor actually made at Corvey in any case had the desired effect of drawing the attention of the proper public authorities, who duly intervened. Related occurrences in Dublin and Llandaff can be explained, as we saw, as ancillary to the process of Norman expansion into the British Isles. All the other known cases are concentrated in the arc stretching north and east from the Charente valley to the Meuse (see Map 2).[55]

Obviously many more clamors went into action than have been subjected to study here, and undoubtedly many such additional cases could be documented. The accidental nature of the survival of evidence, however, plus the likelihood that more evidence will be found in the future, renders pointless any discussion of statistics in these matters. In the course of my searching for clamors, both formulas and cases, the geographical parameters became clear at an early point, and as new evidence emerged it did so only from within these parameters, thus confirming rather than reshaping them.[56]

54. *Dictionnaire de biographie française* (Paris, 1933–), 6:44.
55. *Monumenta Corbeiensia*, ed. Philip Jaffé (Berlin, 1864), no. 384, pp. 515–516.
56. On the basis of these diminishing returns from further research, I decided to suspend research and to publish. Instead of seeing publication as marking some "definitive" stage in research, though, my view is that it will lead other scholars to come forward with formulas and cases that they already know about or will help them recognize such texts in the future when they come upon them. Such, in any case, has already been my

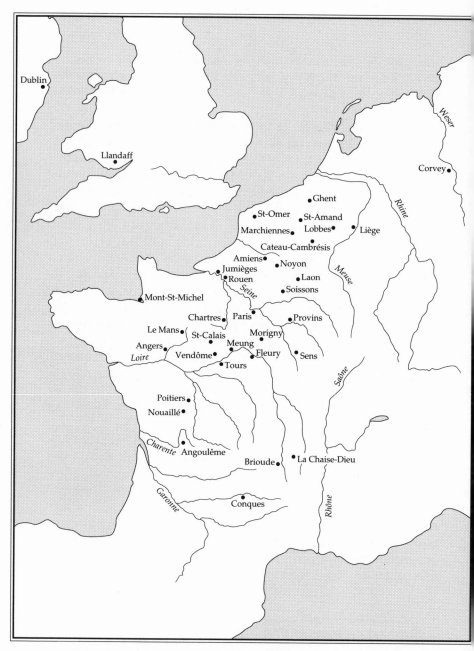

Map 2. Places where liturgical curses were used. Location of churches where there is evidence of the use of clamors or of some form of maledictory prayers. These churches are nearly all found in the arc between the Charente and the Meuse rivers.

If there is an extant formula but no known case from a particular church, then there is no proof that the formula was ever used. But if a clamor was used at a church and there happens not to be any surviving formula from that church, which we have seen is frequently the case, we can still confidently surmise that the religious of that church had a formula. Thus the map showing churches with formulas could be amended to include those places that are known to have been the scenes of clamors, even if no formulas are extant from them. The two maps of clamors, one of formulas and one of cases, strongly reinforce one another. Their essential shapes and densities are the same, a point rendered all the more significant by the fact that they are based upon two very different kinds of evidence.

The use of the clamor was effectively restricted to a period of two and a half centuries. That period began with the humiliation at Tours in 996 and concluded with a humiliation at Liège in 1255.[57] Clamors were regular occurrences in between, a time when the once powerful central authority of the Carolingians disintegrated and the traditional fissiparousness of the Frankish warlords, spurred by the emergence of the *milites*, was once again given free rein. Cases involving clamors were already thinning out in the first half of the thirteenth century, to become later on little more than curiosities or vestiges.

As a historical practice defined geographically as well as temporally, the liturgical clamor was not only concentrated in but effectively limited to the land of the Franks, for rarely did it spill out of the area between the Charente and the Meuse valleys. That same area, as we shall see, was one whose spiritual life had been invigorated at a critical period by Irish saints.

experience in the aftermath of publishing articles on this topic in 1975 and 1979. See appendix A.

57. Joannes Hocsem, *Chronicon*, 1:5, in *Gesta pontificum Leodiensium*, ed. Jean Chapeauville, 3 vols. (Liège, 1612–1616), 2:288.

5
Experts

TRADITIONS OF cursing flourished among all the peoples who together made up the European population. All their cultures included pronouncing, witnessing, receiving, fearing, fending off, and returning curses. To take an example from the time of the Roman occupation of Britain, a startling cultural encounter involving curses is reported by Tacitus in his *Annals*. In A.D. 60 the Roman army had been pursuing British tribesmen and at last had them trapped on the island of Anglesey, in the northwest corner of Wales. As the Romans arrived at the narrow and shallow strait that still separated them from their prey, they saw on the other side

> the opposing army with its dense array of armed warriors, while between the ranks dashed women, in black attire like the furies, with hair disheveled, waving brands. All around, the druids, lifting up their hands to heaven, and pouring forth dreadful imprecations, frightened our soldiers by the unfamiliar sight, so that, as if their limbs were paralyzed, they stood motionless, and exposed to wounds.

But spurred on by their officers and with "mutual encouragements not to quail before a troop of frenzied women," they moved across, broke the enemies' resistance, and "wrapped the enemies in the flames of their own fire-brands." Of particular note is the difference in the reactions of the troops and of the officers, a difference that is probably explained by disparate levels of cognitive development owing to social origin and that in any case permitted the temporary success of the women and the druids.[1]

The Greek and Roman conquerors and colonists of parts of Celtic Europe were well equipped with cursing traditions of their own. The

1. Tacitus, *Annals*, 14:30, in *Complete Works of Tacitus*, ed. Moses Hadas (New York, 1942), p. 337.

curse tablets, or *defixiones*, used by both Greeks and Romans were made of thin sheets of lead, about two inches square. Inscriptions were scratched on them, and then each was rolled up and pierced with a small iron nail. They were supposed to bring supernatural power to bear against other persons. The messages appeal to deities to perform such favors as causing a thief to suffer, spoiling some athlete's performance, or upsetting another's lawsuit, financial success, or love affair. About half of all the examples brought to light so far come from tombs and cemeteries; the other half come from such underground sources of water as wells, fountains, and baths.[2]

The Greek tombs near which (or sometimes in which) *defixiones* have been found are almost all, significantly, burial places of persons considered to have died young. Such persons were thought to have died with energy still unexpended; and since they could not have been resigned to their precocious deaths, the flow of their untapped energy was stimulated by resentful anger. Curse tablets placed close to these tombs were meant to tap the charismatic power emanating from the ungrateful dead. In later centuries, the attitude of Christian worshipers at the graves of martyrs was meant to tap similar kinds of energy.[3]

Underground water sources, the other common sites for finding *defixiones*, were special places of contact between this world and the other, places of ready access to supernatural beings who could help out in delicate personal situations. Roman baths were of course dedicated to recreation and good health; inscriptions found at or near them express thanks for cures gained and hopes for good health to continue or return. But the forces that could bestow could also withhold. At Lydney in Roman Britain, a tablet lists those suspected of taking a ring and asks that they not enjoy health until it is brought back.[4] At Bath,

2. David R. Jordan, "Defixiones from a Well Near the Southwest Corner of the Athenian Agora," *Hesperia* 54 (1985): 205–255, especially 206–207. Cf. *Curse Tablets and Binding Spells in the Ancient World*, ed. John Gager (New York, 1992).

3. Jordan, "Defixiones from a Well," pp. 205–255. Professor Jordan was most generous in writing to me, sending me material, and speaking to me about ancient Greek *defixiones*. My thanks to him, as also to Phyllis Williams Lehmann for putting me in contact with him and to Caroline R. Houser for arranging for his splendid lecture at Smith College. As for the connection with the graves of martyrs, Jordan's work calls to mind one of Peter Brown's most arresting images, where Brown compares the effect of Ambrose's having the remains of the martyrs buried within the church to the effect that one gets from having an electrician renovate an antiquated wiring system. See Peter Brown, *The Cult of the Saints: Its Rise and Function in Latin Christianity* (Chicago, 1980), p. 37.

4. R. G. Goodschild, "The Curse and the Ring," *Antiquity* 27 (1953): 100–102.

"May he who abducted Vilbia from me become as liquid as the water"; the magical power of each word inscribed was enhanced by its being written backward.[5]

The Germanic settlers brought their curses into the European arena. That a warrior among them who abandoned his men on the battlefield got cursed comes as no surprise.[6] More revealing of Germanic attitudes toward cursing was the reaction of an Anglo-Saxon king to cursing by native Britons. The story of this encounter, told by Bede in his *Ecclesiastical History*, offers an arresting parallel to the scene at Anglesey described by Tacitus. The major themes of Bede's *History* treat the coming, spread, and ultimate triumph of Roman Christianity in England. The leader of the mission was a Roman aristocrat named Augustine, an associate of Pope Gregory I. The principal object of the mission was to convert the pagan Anglo-Saxons to Christianity. A secondary object was to make contact with the small community of Christians among the Britons (descendants of those Christians of the final decades of Roman Britain), bring them into line with the Roman church, and enlist their help in the mission to the Anglo-Saxons.

Augustine established contact with the British Christians in 603. He urged them to abandon certain of their customs (those on which they differed with the Roman church) and to join in the project of evangelizing the heathen. Since the Britons were reluctant to do either, Augustine threatened them with a prediction—that if they refused to accept peace from their brothers, they would have war with their enemies; and that if they would not preach the true way of life to the Anglo-Saxons, they would suffer death at their hands. "Through the workings of divine judgment," says Bede, "this came to pass in every particular as Augustine had foretold." The sequel came when King Aethelfrith of Northumbria raised an army at Chester to fight an army of Christian Britons. Bede had earlier described Aethelfrith as "ignorant of true religion" and as having savaged the Britons more cruelly than all the other English leaders. Now this heathen king was about to do battle with Christians, called by Bede "faithless Britons." Bede, the Anglo-Saxon apologist for Roman Christianity, places himself clearly on the side of the Anglo-Saxon pagans against these Christians of the

---

5. Peter Salway, *Roman Britain* (Oxford, 1981), pp. 688–689.
6. The reference is to Godric in "The Battle of Maldon" in *Beowulf and Other Old English Poems*, tr. Constance B. Hieatt, 2d ed. (New York, 1983), p. 115.

"wrong" sort. As the two armies faced each other, the king looked across and saw a large assemblage of priests off to one side praying for the British fighters. They were monks from Bangor who had fasted three days to prepare for this moment. The king said: "If they are calling out to their God against us [*si adversum nos ad deum suum clamant*], then even if they do not bear arms they are fighting against us, assailing us as they do with prayers for our defeat." And so he ordered the first attack to be directed against these priests, and then he and his men "destroyed the rest of this wicked host, although not without suffering heavy losses. Of the monks who came to pray, about 1,200 perished and only fifty escaped." Although the Anglo-Saxon king in this episode showed much higher regard for Celtic prayers against enemies than did the Roman commanders in the story told by Tacitus, the result in the two cases was about the same.[7]

The rich cursing traditions of the Scandinavians include a curse of the gods upon a man who killed a god. It occurs in a story about the Danish king Hading, who unwittingly killed a god who was disguised as a sea monster ("a sky-dweller wrapped in another body"). The gods thereupon sent a woman to curse him for this sacrilege:

> Whether you tread the fields or set your canvas to the ocean, to you the gods will be hostile, and throughout the whole earth you shall find the elements of nature thwarting all your designs. Dashed down on land, tossed at sea, the perpetual companion of your wandering shall be the whirlwind; an inflexible stiffness will never desert your sails; . . . and your herd will perish with cold.

Indeed, strong winds toss his ship about, storms destroy his dwelling, and freezing temperatures kill his herd. Only by making sacrifices to the gods is Hading able to assuage their anger.[8] Close in spirit to the Greek and Roman *defixiones* is the bronze tablet dating from the eleventh century found at Lund; on a tool used in weaving ribbon, a runic inscription reads: "May all my misfortunes fall upon Sigvor's Ingemar."[9]

The few curses presented here, lone examples made to represent large repertories from the cultures of some of the major constituents of

7. *Bede's Ecclesiastical History of the English People*, 2:2, ed. Bertram Colgrave and R. A. B. Mynors (Oxford, 1969), pp. 134–143.
8. Saxo Grammaticus, *The History of the Danes*, tr. Peter Fisher, ed. H. R. Ellis Davidson, 2 vols. (Totowa, N.J., 1979), 1:29–30.
9. *I Vichinghi: Mostra archeologica a cura dei Musei di Malmö* (Florence, 1989), pp. 61–62.

Europe (the Greeks and Romans, the Celtic, Germanic, and Scandinavian peoples), did not lead directly into the Christian liturgical maledictions; the immediate sources for the latter have been located elsewhere. Even so, they attest to the presence of curses contemporaneous with and, so to speak, running parallel to the liturgical curses. And if they were not sources of liturgical curses in any literal sense of supplying particular words or phrases, they played a critical role in their development in a more general sense, by preparing and then exemplifying the mental structures that used, believed in, feared, and thus rendered efficacious maledictions of all sorts, including those monopolized by the clergy.

If the formal elements of liturgical maledictions can be traced to earlier, written sources, then we cannot explain these curses in their entirety as ancient pagan practices passing via oral tradition into Christian society. The fact is that there existed a widespread if not universal popular tradition of cursing, and that it provided a receptive mental framework for the use and efficacy of the more formal and learned religious cursing. Thus two types of malediction coexisted, one popular and informal, the other learned and formal; they probably also exerted occasional influence upon one another. In just one area of Europe, though, did an ancient, deeply rooted popular tradition of cursing merge with Christianity into a vigorous culture of religious cursing: Ireland.[10]

Irish Saints

The two most famous offspring of antiquity, the Roman Empire and the Christian religion, were born at roughly the same time, grew up together, and influenced one another indelibly. Each of them, once mature, would have been inexplicable—indeed unimaginable—without the other. Although the eastern provinces of the empire experienced Christianity earlier and more intensely than those in the West, none remained completely ignorant of its message and its ministry. Conversely, the small and radical Jewish sect established by Jesus and his followers expanded along Roman roads and within Roman commercial centers, gaining independence from its Palestinian origins and assum-

10. It was Mary M. McLaughlin who first suggested that I would find a crucial element in the argument of this book in the Irish saints' lives; her erudite and generously given advice was right on the mark. My deep gratitude goes to her and also to Lisa M. Bitel and Elizabeth Sloane Haugen for being my guides in reading Irish history.

ing along the way an institutional and intellectual structure based upon Roman models. A standard theme of the history of the first five centuries of the Christian Era is the Christianization of the Roman Empire. No less authoritative and significant a theme for the same period, however, is the Romanization of the Christian religion. These parallel developments and reciprocal influences occurred so organically that Roman Christian historians saw clearly within them a most audacious divine plan, the coincidence of universal religion with universal empire. God's intervention in time, the Incarnation, was seen as following upon and tied to the political unification of the world. In this connection, the peculiar interest of early Irish history is that Ireland was the first Christian country entirely outside the Roman political and cultural orbit. As a result, Irish Christianity was unique. In the analysis of the acculturation of *Romanitas* with *Christianitas*, Ireland serves as a scientific control.[11]

There was no sign of this uniqueness at the start. The first missionaries to Ireland, whether from Roman Britain or Roman Gaul, brought with them the church, the theology, the liturgy, and the spirituality that were current in the western Roman provinces in their time, the early fifth century. Patrick was just one, and perhaps not the first, of these missionaries; it was in the later collective memory that the stories of many individuals coalesced into that of a single heroic figure, the Patrick of legend. The historical Patrick, though, began his thirty-year apostolate in Ireland about 431.[12] His *Confession* portrays a humble, hardworking person, anxious not to offend but nonetheless suffering insult and persecution. It shows him deeply marked by the boyhood experience of being carried off and held as a slave in Ireland for six years,[13] which turned him toward a career of preaching Christianity to the Irish. His work was concentrated in the western and northern parts of the island. Where he was successful he set up bishops in territorial

11. For examples of many passages in Eusebius, see *Praeparatio evangelica* (PG 21:21–1408) and *Demonstratio evangelica* (PG 22:9–794, esp. 235–248). See Ernest Barker, *From Alexander to Constantine* (Oxford, 1956), pp. 472–477, and David S. Wallace-Hadrill, *Eusebius of Caesarea* (London, 1960), pp. 173–181, 193, 199.

12. Dorothy Africa, "Patrick," in *DMA* 9:462–466; R. P. C. Hanson, *Saint Patrick: His Origins and Career* (Oxford, 1968); Ludwig Bieler, "St. Patrick," in *NCE* 10:1099–1102.

13. *St. Patrick: His Writings and Muirchu's Life*, ed. A. B. E. Hood (London, 1978), pp. 23–34, 41–54. Cf. Kathleen Hughes, *Early Christian Ireland: Introduction to the Sources* (London, 1972), p. 246.

dioceses that were coterminous with petty kingdoms. Each bishop presided over a hierarchy of secular priests. In addition, Patrick transplanted to Ireland the newest forms of monasticism then current in Gaul, where the powerful impact of reports about the lives of monks and hermits in Egypt, Palestine, and Syria was then being felt. This was a monasticism noted for its rigorous asceticism and its determined separation from worldly affairs.[14]

The one other written work confidently ascribed to Patrick, in addition to his *Confession*, is a letter addressed to a British king named Coroticus. It is a letter of protest occasioned by a raid in which Coroticus and his men stormed a community of Irish Christians, slaughtering some and hauling the others off to prison with the probable intention of selling them into slavery. Patrick appeals for the release of the captives and warns those responsible for mistreating these Christians that they will face eternal punishment in hell in the company of Satan.[15] Such was Patrick's way of lodging a complaint against a powerful lay opponent. His manner of expression and behavior were in line with those of other literate Christians of the western Roman provinces in the fifth century.

Because of political and cultural upheaval in those provinces during the fifth and sixth centuries, however, the early missions to Ireland were not followed up. The Irish church, as established by Patrick and others, developed on its own, just as the Roman church evolved in its own way. For the two centuries after the death of Patrick there remains only scant historical evidence, although what there is indicates at first a continuation of Patrick's Roman-style church but then a growing tension between "Hibernian" and "Roman" factions. Once the Irish church came into view again in the later sixth century and in the course of the seventh, it was very different from the church of Patrick and company, both in structure and in spirituality.[16]

14. John Ryan, *Irish Monasticism* (Dublin, 1931); Clifford E. Lawrence, *Medieval Monasticism*, 2d ed. (London, 1989), p. 44.
15. *St. Patrick*, ed. Hood, pp. 35–38, 55–59.
16. Kathleen Hughes, "The Celtic Church: Is This a Valid Concept?" *Cambridge Medieval Celtic Studies* 1 (1981): 1–20; Giovanni Orlandi, "Dati e problemi sull'organizzazione della chiesa irlandese tra V e IX secolo," in *Cristianizzazione ed organizzazione ecclesiastica delle campagne nell'Alto Medioevo: Espansione e resistenze*, 2 vols., Settimane di studio del Centro italiano di studi sull'Alto Medioevo 28 (Spoleto, 1982), pp. 713–764; Richard Sharpe, "Some Problems concerning the Organization of the Church in Early Medieval Ireland," *Peritia* 3 (1984): 230–270.

The Irish church, left to itself, became essentially monastic, the most monastic church of Christendom. Every large clan had a monastery for men, and most had one for women as well.[17] The leading positions of abbot and abbess came directly under family control. Kindred and family indeed became the most important single factors in succession to ecclesiastical office. Only some of the monks became priests, and among them, within a given monastery, there was usually one who acted as bishop. The monastic oratories served as churches for the laity. Thus the Roman model of governance had been abandoned; there were no dioceses, and the office of bishop was considerably downgraded. Monasticism, which was still a fringe phenomenon elsewhere in the sixth century, had become the key structural element in the Irish church.[18]

The more eccentric forms of ascetic behavior engaged in by the Egyptians and other Eastern holy people were thought offensive by conventional Roman standards and were curbed in such Roman spiritual guides as Benedict's rule. But to Irish holy people they served for both inspiration and justification, as individuals among them strove to engage in the longest, most arduous, most humiliating of ascetic practices. Some gained reputations for near-starvation diets and excruciatingly long fasts, others for spending several hours of every night immersed in cold water reciting psalms, others for living in cells so small that they could never lie down, and so on.[19]

Closely tied to this ascetic ideal was a strikingly original view of penance. In the early church and still in the Roman church of late antiquity, confession took place before a public assembly; the publicly identified sinners underwent their prescribed penances and then in a solemn liturgical setting were granted absolution and readmitted into the community of Christians. The entire process was conducted under the aegis of a bishop and was available only once in the original believer's lifetime. The practice that developed in sixth-century Ireland involved a private exchange between sinner

---

17. Hughes, *Early Christian Ireland*, p. 235.
18. The leading work on Irish monasticism is Lisa M. Bitel's *Isle of the Saints: Monastic Settlement and Christian Community in Early Ireland* (Ithaca, N.Y., 1990), in which she accomplishes nothing less than the integration of early Ireland into the mainstream of modern historiography. See also Hughes, *Early Christian Ireland*, p. 235; and Donnchadh O Corrain, *Ireland before the Normans* (Dublin, 1972), p. 84.
19. Lawrence, *Medieval Monasticism*, pp. 45–46.

and confessor. The former confessed, and the latter prescribed an appropriate penance; the sinner accomplished the penance and received absolution from the confessor. Not only was it a private matter, but it was one that could be repeated indefinitely. Apparently developed as a form of discipline within the religious life, the monks expanded its use among the general population as they became confessors to laypeople. The penances the religious set for themselves were far more demanding than those they set for the laity.[20]

A characteristically Irish form of spiritual behavior, whether imposed as penance or chosen as ascetic exercise, was exile and aimless peregrination. Since comfort, joy, and security were all found within the bounds of home and family, exclusion from ritual observances as well as exile was an awful punishment to suffer in early Irish society, and for Christian ascetics voluntary exile meant renouncing all that was welcome and familiar. In the very period when Benedict was denouncing wandering holy men as fakes and prescribing stability of place as a monastic ideal, the Irish monks were experiencing and propagating an ideal of pilgrimage for the sake of bearing religious witness wherever their travels took them.[21]

It is not just the prodigious extent of the asceticism of the Irish monks that calls for comment, however, but also the use some made of it for coercing others. Asceticism initially is, and perhaps in most cases remains, a means of self-control.[22] Yet there is abundant evidence of ascetics' extending that control beyond themselves, projecting it in such a way as to constrain other people or move them toward some desired

20. Allen J. Frantzen, *The Literature of Penance in Anglo-Saxon England* (New Brunswick, N.J., 1983), ch. 1.
21. Nora Chadwick, *The Celts* (Harmondsworth, Eng., 1970), p. 149. *Rule for Monks*, ch. 1, in *RB*, pp. 170–171. Lawrence, *Medieval Monasticism*, p. 43. For caution about the extent to which the ideal of Irish peregrination represented actual practice, see Bitel, *Isle of the Saints*, pp. 222–234.
22. Indeed, a basic premise of Irish monasticism was that in order to keep the body in subjection, the stomach had to be kept empty. Fasting was as regular a part of the monastic routine as praying. See Columban, *Regula monachorum*, ch. 4, in *Sancti Columbani opera*, ed. G. S. M. Walker, Scriptores Latini Hiberniae 2 (Dublin, 1970), pp. 126–127; cf. Louis Gougaud, *Devotional and Ascetic Practices in the Middle Ages*, tr. G. C. Batemen (London, 1927), p. 147.

end.[23] The prayers of those 1,200 monks of Bangor against the Anglo-Saxon warriors, albeit not successful, did not just happen to follow a three-day fast; the monks fasted initially in order to fuel their prayers. In Ireland ascetics became especially adept at imposing control over others, in particular through fasting, and also through cursing.[24]

The monks of Clonard Abbey reacted to a theft, according to one account, by special fasting, so that God would permit the thief to be discovered.[25] Another monastic congregation fasted on behalf of its patron saint in order to obtain the legal rights due their monastery.[26] Laypeople imitated this behavior on occasion, as when a group from Leinster fasted so as to petition Saint Columba not to let them suffer defeat in battle.[27] These instances all involve fasting toward a specific end, always benevolent.

Stories from some of the saints' lives demonstrate instead the intentional use of fasting as a means of constraint. One tells of Saint Finnen, who with his friends arrived at the stronghold of a pagan warrior in Ulster and was denied admittance. They fasted against him (literally "at him" or "by him") until he granted them hospitality.[28] In the Irish version of Nennius's History, the saintly Germanus tried to get the British king Vortigern to give up an incestuous relationship with his daughter. At Vortigern's retreat in the mountains, Germanus, together with a group of priests, fasted for three days and three nights. At the end of that time Vortigern, with his entire entourage, was struck dead by a thunderbolt.[29]

23. Such projection of self-control onto other persons is treated in different contexts by Caroline W. Bynum, *Holy Feast and Holy Fast: The Significance of Food to Medieval Women* (Berkeley, Calif., 1987), pp. 189–218 ("Food as Control of Self") and 219–244 ("Food as Control of Circumstance"), where connections are made between fasting and spiritual authority. For a parallel argument on sexual continence and the power of prophecy, see Peter Brown, *The Body and Society: Men, Women and Sexual Renunciation in Early Christianity* (New York, 1988), pp. 66–69.

24. Thomas O Cathasaigh, "Curse and Satire," *Eigse* 21 (1986): 10–15; see also Tom Peete Cross, *Motif-Index of Early Irish Literature* (Bloomington, Ind., 1952), pp. 433–434 on fasting and pp. 401–404 on cursing.

25. *Vitae sanctorum Hiberniae*, ed. Charles Plummer, 2 vols. (Oxford, 1910), 1:270.

26. *Chronicon Scotorum: A Chronicle of Irish Affairs from the Earliest Times to A.D. 1135*, ed. W. M. Hennessy (London, 1866), pp. 310–313 (A.D. 1104).

27. Fred N. Robinson, "Notes on the Irish Practice of Fasting as a Means of Distraint," in *Putnam Anniversary Volume* (Cedar Rapids, Iowa, 1909), pp. 574–575.

28. Robinson, "Fasting as a Means of Distraint," p. 575.

29. Ferdinand Lot, *Nennius et l'Historia Brittonum: Etude critique suivie d'une édition des diverses versions de ce texte* (Paris, 1934), pp. 80–90, ch. 39 (p. 178), ch. 47 (p. 187).

The tradition of asking favors or boons, usually three boons, of God led in some instances to bargaining and to coercive fasting.[30] Saint Enda of Aran sought three favors from God. An angel appeared and granted him part of what he sought, then asked him to end his fast. Enda's stubborn reply was that he would continue his fast until he had been granted all three requests. The angel eventually backed down and said he would receive all he had requested from God.[31] Hostility appeared on both sides in the story of a monk who complained about his spiritual burdens. He had agreed with two other monks that they would recite a certain number of psalms, prayers, and hymns each day and that when one of them died the others would carry out his portion of the devotions. When the first one died his obligations were divided between the two survivors, according to their agreement. But when the second died, the third rebelled at carrying out the obligations of all three. To make his protest he fasted against God, and God in return informed him through an angel that he was angry about this behavior.[32]

The technique of fasting against someone to gain certain ends, however much it angered God in this tale of the three monks, originated long before the Christianization of Ireland. It was a traditional form of social communication and action by which a weaker or socially inferior person registered a complaint against a stronger, higher-ranking one. With the coming of written law codes, it appears particularly in connection with indebtedness. But whatever the issue, the plaintiff who fasts before the door of another party is assumed to be doing something both customary and acceptable. And the party who allows a plaintiff to die of hunger on his doorstep does so at great social and material cost.[33]

From fasting thus used as a means of coercion, it is not a long way to counterfasting and fasting contests. In one case, between a holy man and a layman, the contestants took to fasting all night while immersed

---

30. On saints bargaining with God, see Kathleen Hughes, *The Church in Early Irish Society* (Ithaca, N.Y., 1966), pp. 224–225.

31. *Vitae sanctorum Hiberniae*, 2:73–74.

32. Robinson, "Fasting as a Means of Distraint," pp. 579–580.

33. The Indo-European roots of this practice of fasting as a means of restraint, and comparisons between Indian and Irish custom, have been noted and discussed. See Robinson, "Fasting as a Means of Distraint," p. 569, n. 3, and Gougaud, *Devotional and Ascetic Practices*, pp. 153–154. Even if the connections are not all clearly established, it is surely more than casual coincidence that in the twentieth century the use of the hunger strike for political ends has reached its fullest development in India and Ireland.

in a river. The holy man won out only by tricking his opponent into thinking he was abandoning the contest. The layman in fact abandoned the fast first, and shortly afterward his wife gave birth to a child with only one eye. Such trickery by saints apparently did not violate the rules of the game.[34]

Adding hostile wishes onto the fast was also acceptable. Saint Fechin of Fobar and fellow monks fasted against King Raghallach of Connacht for being unfaithful to his wife. As they fasted they also prayed that he might die a vile death, and their prayer was answered.[35] Saints Patrick and Germanus are said to have taken such a dual approach to dealing with a community of heretics. It was Patrick who suggested that they fast for three days and three nights, with the provision that if the heretics still persisted they should be judged by God. On the third night, the earth opened and swallowed up the whole community.[36] It was Patrick who, in another story, negotiated at length with God through an angel. Early on, when the angel said that God was not giving Patrick everything he had asked for because the request was excessive, Patrick replied: "Is that his pleasure?" The angel affirmed that it was. "Then this is my pleasure," said Patrick; "I will not go from here until I am dead or until the requests are granted." In the end he got what he was asking for.[37] And it was Patrick, incensed by the cruel way a certain master named Trian treated his slaves, who both "fasted against Trian and cursed him and his heirs." Trian's horses dragged their master into a lake.[38]

Can this Patrick, who cursed his enemies to death, be the same Patrick who preached the gospel in Ireland between 431 and 461? The answer has to be both yes and no. The reports of these marvelous feats, found in the biographies, or lives, of the saint, surely mean to refer to the same person. But the Patrick of the lives—the earliest of which was written by Muirchu in the 690s, almost two and a half centuries after Patrick's death—is in fact utterly unlike that earlier "historical" Patrick. For the study of Patrick, there remain from his own time at least the

---

34. Robinson, "Fasting as a Means of Distraint," p. 582.

35. Ibid., p. 578.

36. *The Tripartite Life of Patrick, with Other Documents relating to That Saint*, ed. Whitley Stokes, 2 vols., RS 89 (London, 1887), 2:413–419.

37. *Tripartite Life*, ed. Stokes, 1:113–121. Note that one of the privileges Patrick, that one-time native of Britain, obtains is that no Saxons are to dwell in Ireland; ibid., pp. 116–117. Forget about snakes.

38. Ibid., pp. 218–221.

Confession and the *Letter to Coroticus* to supply some historical control. As an example, one can compare the *Letter to Coroticus* with a chapter of Muirchu's life telling about Coroticus's ill-treatment of Christians and about Patrick's letter. According to Muirchu, when Coroticus scoffed at Patrick's letter, Patrick prayed to the Lord to cast this traitor out of the present world. A short while later, as he sat upon his throne before all his friends and followers in court, Coroticus turned into a fox, slipped away, and was never seen again.[39] For most of the other great saints of the heroic period, such as Brigit (460–528), Ruadan (d. 568), Brendan (468–578), or Maedoc (d. 628), the earliest lives date from a few centuries later than their subjects' deaths, and these lives remain beyond reach of corroboration because of the lack of contemporaneous sources. Only two saints are known to us from biographies much closer to their own times, Columba (521–597), whose life was written by Adamnan between 688 and 704, and Columban (543–615), whose biographer, Jonas, wrote in about 640. At the other extreme, some of the details about these early saints are known to us only from lives included in compilations of much later date, such as the *Book of Lismore*, compiled in the fifteenth century. But compilations were, after all, gatherings of earlier texts, and further back in time than each of these hagiographical texts there possibly if not probably stands an oral tradition. Thus the most famous of the Irish saints lived in the fifth, sixth, and early seventh centuries; their biographies were written down starting only in the second half of the seventh century.[40]

Patrick, the Patrick of legend, looked for food as soon as he and his companions arrived from the Continent. They sailed into a bay and let down their fishing nets. Since they caught no fish, Patrick inflicted a curse on that bay, and they moved on.[41] In a similar situation later on, Patrick told some fishermen to cast their nets in a river. It was winter, and they explained to him that salmon were not usually found in the river at that season. Patrick insisted, so they cast their nets anyway, and caught a great many salmon; Patrick blessed the river.[42] This bal-

---

39. Muirchu, ch. 29, in *St. Patrick*, ed. Hood, pp. 77, 98.
40. Hughes, *Early Christian Ireland*, pp. 219–247, on hagiographical sources; Ludwig Bieler, "The Celtic Hagiographer," *Studia patristica* 5 (1962): 243–265; and Richard Sharpe, *Medieval Irish Saints' Lives: An Introduction to Vitae Sanctorum Hiberniae* (Oxford, 1991).
41. *Tripartite Life*, 1:34–37.
42. Ibid., pp. 142–143. Note what happened another time, when Patrick fell into a river. The opposite side he blessed, and it afterward had the best fishing in Ireland. The part he fell into, though, he cursed, and from then on "not much is caught there." Ibid.

anced delivery of blessings and curses marked the successes and failures of the mission. When Patrick first preached, Nathi, son of Garrchu, opposed him, and in return Patrick cursed him.[43] Sinell, son of Finchad, however, was the first who believed in God in Ireland through Patrick's preaching, wherefore Patrick bestowed a blessing upon him and his offspring.[44] And then there were the two brothers who reacted so differently to Patrick. One sent his servant to kill Patrick, and the other held the servant back. To the one who saved him Patrick promised descendants who would be priests and bishops, while he said of the one who wanted to kill him that his heirs would be few and accursed.[45] For a king who had long resisted him but then agreed to convert, Patrick did not transmute malediction entirely into benediction. Patrick had said to him, "Unless you believe now, you will soon die, for God's wrath will come down upon your head." When the king converted, Patrick said that because he had been such a stumbling block to the mission, even though his own reign was prolonged, none of his heirs would ever be king.[46]

Some of these stories were intended to reinforce property rights, as in the cursing to death of a horse sent to graze on the saint's land[47] or the cursing of a man who stole Patrick's horses.[48] Some stories reinforced religious discipline. When Columban learned that the monks of Luxeuil were ill, he went to them and ordered them to get up right away. Those who obeyed were cured. To those who did not get right up he promised a long continuance of their illness. "Wonderful revenge!" adds the author.[49] And there were stories with edifying moral lessons, such as the one about a woman who brought a basket of apples to Brigit of Kildare. A group of lepers approached Brigit at just that moment to beg for food, and Brigit told the woman to give them the apples. But the woman refused, insisting that she had brought the apples for Brigit and her sisters, not for some lepers. Brigit cursed the apples in the woman's barn (it had been full; they disappeared) and all the trees in her orchard (they were henceforth barren).[50] Patrick was

43. Ibid., pp. 32–33.
44. Ibid.; cf. pp. 52–53.
45. Ibid., pp. 110–111.
46. Muirchu, chs. 20–21, in *St. Patrick*, ed. Hood, pp. 72, 92–93.
47. Muirchu, ch. 25, in ibid., pp. 74–75, 95.
48. *Tripartite Life*, 1:108–109.
49. Jonas, *Vita Columbani*, ch. 12, "Mira ultio" (*MGH, SRM* 4:78).
50. *Lives of the Saints from the Book of Lismore*, ed. Whitley Stokes (Oxford, 1890), p. 190.

tireless in dispatching his enemies and foiling their plots; he transformed poisoned cheese that had been prepared for him into stones
and saw that fifty horsemen who pursued him plunged into a river
and drowned.[51] A royal enemy who drove Patrick and his companions
into a river succeeded only in eliciting from him a curse, that no one
of his line would ever again reign (and that no salmon would ever be
found in that river either).[52]

Certain of these saintly triumphs appear, at least in these greatly
compressed tellings, to have been too simple. Though the outcome of
any incident in a saint's life is not likely ever to be in doubt, there is
greater dramatic tension when the saint's powers are contested. Again
and again during the mission, Patrick was put to the test by pagan
priests (or wizards or druids) who served as spiritual advisers to the
kings Patrick was trying to convert. One, called a magician (*magus*) in
the text, challenged Patrick to "perform signs" before a large gathering
of spectators. The wizard "began his magical spells," and to the amaze-
ment of those present a waist-deep snowfall settled on the plain. Patrick challenged him to remove it, and when the magician admitted he
could not, Patrick made it disappear "quick as a flash." Then the wizard invoked demons and brought thick darkness over the land, but
again he could not remove the darkness, whereas the saint gave a
prayerful blessing and the sun shone brilliantly. The third test, a very
contrived contest about resistance to fire, ended in the death of the
magician and thus the complete vindication of the saint.[53] In a spectacular display of power, Patrick, having to contend with nine druids
who intended to kill him, raised his left hand to God in heaven—
instead of the right hand, which is used in blessing—and cursed the
leader among them. In an instant this chief druid fell down dead in
their midst. Since there happened to be several witnesses to this miracle, Patrick baptized many people that day.[54] Here in Ireland, then, as
elsewhere when missionaries made their initial contacts with an alien
culture, the missionary-saints had to compete with the indigenous holy
people.

Every chieftan approached by the missionaries had his own druids,

51. *Tripartite Life*, 1:182–185.
52. Ibid., pp. 68–71.
53. Muirchu, ch. 20, in *St. Patrick*, ed. Hood, pp. 70–71, 91–92.
54. *Tripartite Life*, 2:325–326. In a later version of the same story, fire from heaven kills
all nine wizards (ibid., pp. 132–135).

who were considered indispensable. The druids embodied the collective wisdom of society. In each tribal grouping they were the guardians of tradition, the historians, the storytellers, and the poets. Priests and medicine men with sacred powers as well, they gained and retained their positions of considerable influence in society through their skillful manipulation of words. Thus they took their places next to warriors as advisers. Some were undoubtedly more adept at certain of these functions than at others.[55]

The druids' power with words extended to incantations meant to gain supernatural ends. With their verses they could control and modify or redirect the forces of nature. "Satire," the conventional term for their rhymed curses, covers a broad range extending from the modern literary notion of satire to poems of abuse and slander, and still further to physically destructive spells. Druids could "rhyme to death" both man and beast.[56] Their skill at cursing was one of the principal indexes of their general worth and surely a motive for the respect they commanded. Stories abound of their competitions, of verse cappings that were tests of poetical skill and that included curses and countercurses marked by staggering escalation.[57]

The druids were of course not unique to Ireland, but their influence was more strongly felt there than elsewhere, a fact that can be attributed directly to the Romans. The much celebrated religious toleration of the Romans had its limits, and the druids usually found themselves beyond these limits. Perceived as enemies of Roman political order, the druids were seen as offering or leading or encouraging resistance to that order, and as a result they felt the full force of Roman military repression. The Roman soldiers we saw in Tacitus's account halted momentarily before crossing to Anglesey, but they soon regained their aggressive mood: "They bore the standards forward, cut down all resistance, and [as we saw above] wrapped the enemies in the flames of

---

55. *Vitae sanctorum Hiberniae*, 1:clx–clxii.

56. On the deadly powers of poets, see Kenneth Nicholls, *Gaelic and Gaelicized Ireland in the Middle Ages* (Dublin, 1972), p. 82. Note the case of a famous poet who was murdered in 1024. Within an hour his murderers were putrid. "This," says the recording annalist, "was a poet's miracle." See the *Annals of Ulster* for the year 1024, ed. W. M. Hennessy et al., 4 vols. (Dublin, 1887–1901), 1:552–555. See also Robert C. Elliott, *The Power of Satire: Magic, Ritual, Art* (Princeton, N.J., 1960), pp. 18–48.

57. Fred N. Robinson, "Satirists and Enchanters in Early Irish Literature," in *Studies in the History of Religions Presented to Crawford Howell Toy*, ed. David G. Lyon and George F. Moore (New York, 1912), pp. 95–130; on poetic competitions, see p. 117.

their own fire-brands. A force was next set over the conquered, and their groves, devoted to inhuman superstitions, were destroyed." Tacitus relates with evident disgust how the Britons deemed it a duty to cover their altars with the blood of captives and to consult their deities through human entrails.[58] Thus, even if the European part of the Roman Empire had an important Celtic cultural stratum, the influence and traditions of the druids had everywhere been reduced as a result of Roman policy. Meanwhile, on the Celtic fringe—that is, beyond the Roman *limes*—the druids, like the rest of Celtic culture, remained a vibrant force.[59]

By the fifth century A.D., with druidism obliterated or much reduced in all Roman territories, the missionaries who went beyond Rome's borders to Ireland found themselves face-to-face with druids. In the encounters related above, however—for example, when Patrick engaged in a series of contests with a druid—this was no longer a meeting of two alien cultures, for the Patrick involved was the mythical and not the historical one. On both sides the contestants were really druids. The acculturation of the Christian missionaries in fifth-century Ireland had been peaceful; none of them were martyred. Between the fifth and the eighth centuries, however, Patrick the provincial Roman Christian missionary had been absorbed into and transformed by traditional Celtic culture; he had become a superwizard who could outwit, outmaneuver, outrhyme, and outcurse any "merely" pagan druid. The virtues of the druids became saintly virtues. Cursing became a virtue of the saints.[60]

Cuimmín's poem on thirty-six of the leading saints of Ireland, although purporting to date from the seventh century, is a work put into writing in the eleventh. It is made up of quatrains, one per saint, that identify each one's most noteworthy virtues. Brigit was devoted to sheepherding and early rising, and Comgell of Ulster ate only on Sun-

58. *Complete Works of Tacitus*, ed. Hadas, p. 337.

59. The antidruid policy of the Romans began as early as the reign of Augustus. See Stuart Piggott, *The Druids* (New York, 1968), pp. 127–130.

60. *Vitae sanctorum Hiberniae*, 1:xciii; Hughes, *Early Christian Ireland*, p. 246. Note also the transformation of Brigit. Her cursing of the woman who did not want to turn over to the lepers the apples she had brought to Brigit does not happen in earlier versions of the saint's life. In the earliest version the incident of the woman bringing apples does not appear at all; when it does first appear, the woman gives the apples to the lepers, and Brigit blesses both the woman and her apple trees. See *Bethu Brigte*, ed. Donncha O hAodha (Dublin, 1978), pp. xiv, 29.

days. One male saint never looked at a woman in his whole life; more than one chose to live in a cell too small to lie down in. Senan loved lasting illness, and Cellach loved devotions that tortured his flesh. And then there was Saint Ruadan, "who loved malediction, which brought to an end the visiting of Tara."[61]

In the episode chosen by the poet to illustrate this saint's prowess, Ruadan cursed King Diarmait at Tara. Ruadan was seeking to liberate a kinsman whom Diarmait was holding captive. The king and the holy man exchanged curses, here paraphrased though kept in order:

> Your church shall fail; your rule shall collapse. A herd of swine shall occupy your monastery; Tara shall be deserted for many centuries before that happens. You shall have bad eyesight for the rest of your life; you shall be so dismembered at death that not all the pieces will be found for burial. A wild boar shall uproot your tomb; you shall dwell on a pile of sheep dung.

At this point Diarmait conceded the match abruptly and gave over his prisoner, acknowledging that Ruadan had greater favor with the Lord than he did. Such was the reputation of the saint whose holy specialty was cursing.[62]

Cuimmín did not include Saint Maedoc of Ferns (d. 626) in his poem, but if he had, Maedoc would have had a place as champion curser along with Ruadan. In one of the lives of Maedoc, the saint vaunts his own terrifying powers: "Woe to the man who trespasses on my sanctuary; woe to him who shall outrage my temple. He shall receive therefore in turn short life and hell." Or in another passage: "Five diseases the Son of God inflicts on those whom I excommunicate or who outrage me: consumption, cholera, paralysis, sudden death, and hell."[63] Thus Ruadan is joined by another cursing saint, whom his biographer shows bragging about his power to harm people with curses.

Both Ruadan and Maedoc went beyond spontaneous, occasional cursing; each clearly had some sense of ceremony in uttering a curse. When Ruadan went to Tara, he did more than exchange threats with Diarmait. As soon as his kinsman had been carried off, Ruadan, very angry, assembled his monks and went to ask the assistance of Brendan of Birr. The latter agreed to help; he assembled his monks, and together

---

61. Whitley Stokes, "Cuimmin's Poem on the Saints of Ireland," *Zeitschrift für celtische Philologie* 1 (1897): 59–73; for Ruadan, p. 67.

62. Charles Plummer, ed., *Lives of Irish Saints*, 2 vols. (Oxford, 1922), 2:315–316.

63. Plummer, *Lives of Irish Saints*, 2:276–278.

the two holy men went with their monks to Tara. Ruadan demanded the release of his kinsman, and the king flatly refused. The tale thereupon assumes an ominous tone: "The refusal was heard by Ruadan and Brendan and their monks. They proceeded to ring their bells, both large and small, against Diarmait so violently that they damaged the bells in ringing them. They also sang psalms of malediction and vengeance against him." There were twelve kings staying with Diarmait, each accompanied by one son. During the night, according to the story, all twelve of the boy visitors died. In the morning the kings went to Diarmait to protest, blaming the deaths on the psalm singing of the monks and of Saint Ruadan. The king could do nothing to help, but when the other kings went to Ruadan he prayed earnestly to God that the boys be brought back to life, and they were.[64]

The next night the king was frightened by a dreadful vision in which a great tree was felled by 150 woodsmen wielding broad-bladed axes. The king was awakened by the noise as the tree crashed to the ground. The sounds that then lingered in his mind were of the psalmody of Ruadan and his monks, and the ringing of their bells as they cursed him. At this point the king and the saint squared off for their definitive cursing match.[65]

The principal elements in this at least partially fictional ceremony at Tara are the assembly of monks, the ringing of bells, and the singing of "psalms of malediction and vengeance."[66] Whatever the size of Ruadan's entourage, he presumably enhanced its authority and appearance by having Brendan and his monks join them; having more participants surely enhanced each of the other elements of the ritual, since these involved sound. Such a large gathering of religious for the purpose of lodging a complaint had a counterpart in secular literature: poets sometimes joined in companies for pronouncing satires. Moreover, one of the Middle Irish treatises on versification contains directions for a complex ritual for use against a king who refuses the proper reward for a poem. It begins with fasting upon the king's land, then the poets gather on a hill. They

64. Ibid., pp. 314–315.
65. Ibid., p. 315.
66. Here I can do little more than follow, point by point, the analysis of Ruadan's cursing of Tara given by Patrick O'Neill in his excellent article, "A Middle Irish Poem on the Maledictory Psalms," *Journal of Celtic Studies* 3 (1981): 40–58; on Ruadan, pp. 40–42. Professor O'Neill was most kind to supply me with an offprint of this article.

stand back-to-back in a circle at the top of the hill—that is, facing outward in all directions—the leader among them facing the land of the king they wish to satirize. They recite their lines in a carefully prescribed way. If the poets are in the wrong, the earth of the hill will open and swallow them up; if they are justified, then the earth will swallow up the king and his wife and his son and his horse and his arms and his clothing and his hound.[67]

Portable bells, the second element, had special importance in the Irish church. They were essential attributes of important ecclesiastics, and some, like the bell of Saint Patrick, have survived as much revered relics. They had many uses, including cursing, as the qualification of certain bells as "ill omened" or "calamitous" indicates.[68] The bold claims of Saint Maedoc make frequent reference to the use of bells (and relics too, which sometimes function in a similar way) in cursing those who disturb or oppose him. "Woe to him who shall outrage my venerable church; woe to him against whom my bells utter voice; woe to him against whom my bells are rung every morning and every evening."[69] Or else, "Whoever they be against whom my bells are rung, they are destroyed and killed by them. The voice of my sanctuary and my relics places souls in hell."[70] According to the Life of Columba, when the monastic community at Iona was suffering from a springtime drought, the monks circled about the newly plowed fields carrying relics and calling upon their saint for help. The white tunic of Saint Columba they held aloft and shook, and books written in his own hand they opened on a hillside where once the holy man had been seen conferring with angels. Abundant rain soon fell, and a plentiful harvest followed in due course.[71] In the triad of bell, book, and candle traditionally associated with excommunication, the candle both illuminates the ceremony and symbolizes the expulsion of the excommunicate when it is snuffed out; the book represents the psalter; and the bell,

---

67. Robinson, "Satirists and Enchanters," pp. 108–109, 121–122. *Cath Maige Tuired: The Second Battle of Mag Tuired*, ed. and tr. Elizabeth A. Gray, Irish Texts Society 52 (London, 1982), pp. 50–55, and Whitley Stokes, "The Second Battle of Moytura," *Revue celtique* 12 (1891): 119–121.

68. O' Neill, "Poem on the Maledictory Psalms," p. 41. O'Neill calls attention to related speculation by Françoise Henry concerning some archaeological evidence.

69. Plummer, *Lives of Irish Saints*, 2:276.

70. Ibid., p. 277.

71. *Adomnan's Life of Columba*, ed. Alan O. Anderson and Marjorie O. Anderson (London, 1961), pp. 450–453.

from early Christian times in Ireland, is the broadcast medium for the curses.[72]

The chanting of maledictory psalms, the third key element of the cursing ritual, is based upon the belief, expressed in a ninth-century Irish commentary on the Psalms, that one of the prophecies of the Psalms is the malediction of sinners.[73] The ritual chanting of maledictory psalms is corroborated by a story in which Patrick sings them at some blackbirds that are annoying him,[74] and by two works that deal specifically with such psalms: the *Law of Adamnan*, and a Middle Irish poem. Adamnan (d. 704), abbot of Iona and biographer of Saint Columba, promulgated a law for improving the condition of women.[75] A part of the surviving text may date from his time, although the larger part of it dates from the ninth century.[76] This latter section includes a sanction clause promising blessings upon those who uphold its provisions and, for those who do not, a curse and an order for malediction. The curse on those who fail to uphold the law specifies short life with suffering and dishonor, as well as no salvation for their offspring. The order for malediction prescribes one psalm each day for twenty days and lists a saint with each text. In point of fact there are only nineteen psalms; the twentieth "maledictory psalm" is really a portion of Moses' parting curse and blessing in Deuteronomy 32. Of the nineteen psalms, eight are familiar from our earlier discussion of the psalms used in clamors, including number 108.[77]

In the Middle Irish poem on the maledictory psalms, a work that probably dates from the eleventh century, the lists of psalms and saints are nearly identical with those in Adamnan's law.[78] The first verse of

72. "Bell, Book, and Candle," in *Cyclopaedia of Biblical, Theological, and Ecclesiastical Literature*, ed. J. McClintock and J. Strong (New York, 1891), 1:736–737; for references to bells in Irish saints' lives, see *Vitae sanctorum Hiberniae*, 1:clxxvi–clxxvii.

73. *Hibernia Minora, Being a Fragment of an Old-Irish Treatise on the Psalter*, ed. Kuno Meyer, Anecdota Oxoniensia, 4:8 (Oxford, 1894), pp. 30–33.

74. *Tripartite Life*, 1:115.

75. *Cáin Adamnáin: An Old-Irish Treatise on the Law of Adamnan*, ed. and tr. Kuno Meyer (Oxford, 1905).

76. Adamnan, too, was transformed over time, as were Patrick and other holy people. See O'Neill, "Poem on the Maledictory Psalms," pp. 45–46.

77. *Cáin Adamnáin*, ed. Meyer, pp. 22–23. The psalms included here that do not occur in clamors are numbers 2, 5, 7, 13, 21, 35, 37, 38, 49, 52, and 68.

78. In the poem, Psalm 93 replaces Psalm 115; since in both works the order is that in which they appear in the psalter, in the poem the last psalm is number 108. See O'Neill, "Poem on the Maledictory Psalms," pp. 43, 46.

the poem explains the purpose of invoking these psalms, while the second shows how it should be done.

A selection from the psalms of the noble scholars—as Adamnan arranged them—measure without concealment—to curse every excommunicate from the church.

A band of holy men should be invoked—an achievement without reproach—together with chanting of psalms: a psalm for each day—a noble design—and a chief apostle or a venerable saint.[79]

The association of one saint with each of the psalms is called in another verse "a powerful achievement," but neither the purpose of such an association nor this characterization of it as "a powerful achievement" is explained.[80] Nonetheless, the account of Ruadan's visit to Tara gains further corroboration in these two different but related formulas for a cursing ceremony.

Further indications of Celtic saints' applying spiritual sanctions against powerful leaders come from Brittany and Wales. The relationship between those two areas was particularly close, for the main evacuation route taken by Britons fleeing Anglo-Saxon invaders in the fifth and sixth centuries went from Wales to Brittany. In about 550 an assembly of clerics and laypeople gathered at Le Mené-Bré in northern Brittany to condemn a murderous usurper and tyrant named Conomor. This Conomor was serving as regent for a nephew who was too young to take up the kingship he had inherited; the main grievance against him was his relentless campaign to have the boy killed. Those present in the assembly included Saint Hervé the blind poet and perhaps also Saint Samson of Dol, Saint Gildas, and Saint Teilo of Glamorgan. Against Conomor all those assembled launched an excommunication. Their gathering upon a hill to issue a joint excommunication suggests that they were following the ancient rite we saw earlier, in which the poets would assemble at the top of a hill, stand back-to-back look-

79. Ibid., p. 55.
80. Ibid., p. 56.

ing out in all directions, and utter a curse that was supposed to destroy the recipient.[81]

Although one can cite instances of cursing by holy people in the various Celtic lands, Ireland always remained preeminent in these matters. The only match for the Irish saints seems to be found in Wales, but the Welsh hagiographical tradition was late in forming (eleventh and twelfth centuries) and was probably subject to influences coming from Ireland.[82] And while various foreign observers took note of the cursing of the Irish saints, it is interesting that one such observer who was himself partially Welsh and who had a thorough knowledge of Wales, namely Gerald of Wales (c. 1147–1223), made much of Irish cursing. In his *History and Topography of Ireland*, Gerald reported several individual instances of cursing: of Saint Kevin against ravens, of Saint Nannan against fleas, and of Saint Yvor against rats (who were eating his books). He also noted that when Hugh Tyrrell carried off some clerics' cooking pot, "he was cursed with all the maledictions of the clergy," ending up burned in a terrible fire.[83] Besides these and other instances, Gerald devoted a short chapter to the subject, with a somewhat understated title: "That the Saints of This Country Seem to Be of a Vindictive Cast of Mind." Gerald's text says: "This seems to me to be a thing to be noticed, that just as the men of this country are during this mortal life more prone to anger and revenge than any other race, so in eternal death the saints of this land that have been elevated by their merits are more vindictive than the saints of any other region."[84] Modern research confirms these observations by Gerald of Wales. The next question to ask, though, is whether this vindictive cast of mind

81. *Vita Sancti Hervei*, ch. 27, ed. Arthur de La Borderie, "Saint Hervé, texte latin de la vie la plus ancienne de ce saint, publié avec notes et commentaire historique," *Mémoires de la Société d'émulation des Côtes du Nord* 29 (1892): 269, and for the ancient ceremony, Stokes, "Second Battle of Moytura," 90–93, 119–121. See also *Vita antiqua Sancti Samsonis dolensis episcopi*, chs. 3, 14, 17, ed. F. Plaine, *Analecta Bollandiana* 6 (1887): 122–123, 135, 139–140, and John W. James, "The Excommunications in the *Book of Llan Dâv*," *Journal of the Historical Society of the Church in Wales* 8 (1958): 11–12.

82. Wendy Davies, "Property Rights in Welsh *Vitae* of the Eleventh Century," in *Hagiographie, cultures, et sociétés, IVe–XIIe siècles* (Paris, 1981), pp. 515–533, especially pp. 515 and 518. A tale about Saint Columba that comes from eleventh-century Scotland has the saint cause the son of someone who refused him a favor to become ill. Referred to by Davies, p. 526.

83. Gerald of Wales, *The History and Topography of Ireland*, chs. 61, 64, 65, 79, tr. J.J. O'Meara (Harmondsworth, Eng., 1982), pp. 78, 80, 81, 89–90.

84. Ibid., ch. 83, p. 91.

accompanied the many Irish missionary-saints who traveled to the Continent.

Pilgrims on the Continent

The isolation of the Irish church lasted for nearly a century and a half after the time of Patrick's mission. It ended not with new missionaries coming to Ireland from the outside but with Irish pilgrims going out to meet the world. The most famous of these, Saint Columban (543–615), left Ireland for the Continent about 591 and never returned home. For over two decades he traveled and taught and founded monasteries in the lands of the Franks and, toward the end of his life, in northern Italy. The impact of Columban and his companions, and of their successors as well, should be seen against the backdrop of the pre-Columban church in Gaul.

In the South, in the more heavily Romanized parts of Gaul, the wealthy families of late imperial times gained and kept control of the Christian church. Men of senatorial rank moved effortlessly into the post of bishop, as if it were a natural thing to do, governing the region as bishops in about the way their forebears had done as Roman magistrates.[85] The families in these cases did not so much lose their sons to the church as establish through them dynastic control over episcopal sees. Such churchmen did not welcome charismatic holy people in their territories; they preferred to encourage (and control) the cults of dead holy people, that is, relics. Also, they were careful to write legislation that placed monasteries under their own episcopal control. The superiors and indeed most of the members of the monasteries of Provence and the Rhône valley came from the same Gallo-Roman aristocracy that supplied the bishops.[86]

Such dynastic control was found as far north as Tours, where in the 590s Bishop Gregory noted proudly that of his eighteen predecessors

85. K. F. Stroheker, *Der senatorische Adel im spätantiken Gallien* (Reutlingen, 1948); Martin Heinzelmann, *Bischofsherrschaft in Gallien: Zur Kontinuität römischer Führungsschichten vom 4. bis zum 7. Jahrhundert. Soziale, prosopographische und bildungsgeschichtliche Aspekte*, Beihefte der *Francia* 5 (Munich, 1976); and Georg Scheibelreiter, *Der Bischof in merowingischer Zeit* (Vienna, 1983).

86. Patrick J. Geary, *Before France and Germany: The Creation and Transformation of the Merovingian World* (New York, 1988), pp. 123–139. See also Edward James, "Ireland and Western Gaul in the Merovingian Period," in *Ireland in Early Medieval Europe*, ed. Dorothy Whitelock, Rosamond McKitterick, and David Dumville (New York, 1982), pp. 362–386.

all but five belonged to his family.[87] Even so, it was Tours that offered a different model of the religious life, because of that outsider and holy man Saint Martin, who to the horror of the episcopal establishment of his time became bishop of Tours in 385. Martin never completely gave up his life as a hermit while he served as bishop, and indeed the religious life of northern Gaul over the next few generations retained a disorganized and unstable quality.[88] The Frankish aristocrats followed Clovis's lead in converting to Christianity readily enough, but they were not particularly drawn to either the episcopacy or the monastic life. One Frank who did become a bishop resisted taking a position offered him in the South because he could not bear the thought of sharing the company of those sophisticated Gallo-Roman snobs (*senatores sophisticos ac iudices philosophicos*).[89] And the story of a holy man, the deacon Vulfolaic, is also instructive in this context; it shows how one who wished to imitate the eccentricities of a noted Syrian ascetic suffered at the hands of the clerical hierarchy of northern Gaul. Vulfolaic spent long periods, even in winter, standing barefoot on top of a column after the manner of Saint Simeon the Stylite. The local bishops ordered him to come down and then one day sent him on an errand and had workmen dismantle his column.[90] These are indications that neither the secular church nor the monastic offered the Germanic settlers any particular role in their newly adopted religion.

Then Columban along with twelve companions entered the scene. They landed in Brittany, passed through Dol, traversed Neustria, and went to the court of Childebert in Burgundy. The king welcomed them and gave them land at a place called Annegray in the Vosges Mountains.[91] All the while Columban was performing astounding miracles, and with each miracle his reputation spread. Besides those in need and the curious who flocked to see him, there were recruits. Soon there was need to establish another monastery, and Columban and his companions did so a few miles away at Luxeuil; again after a short while they set up still another one at Fountains. Luxeuil developed into the most eminent of all the Celtic foundations on the Continent. Most of the

87. Gregory of Tours, *Historia Francorum*, 5:49 (*MGH, SRM* 1:242).

88. Sulpicius Severus, *Vita Sancti Martini*, ch. 9, ed. C. Halm, Corpus scriptorum ecclesiasticorum Latinorum 1 (Vienna, 1866), 119. Lawrence, *Medieval Monasticism*, p. 43.

89. Gregory of Tours, *Historia Francorum*, 6:9 (*MGH, SRM* 1:254).

90. Ibid., 8:15 (*MGH, SRM* 1:333–335). Vulfolaic was a Lombard, but there is no reason to think the bishops would have reacted differently had he been a Frank.

91. Jonas, *Vita Columbani*, chs. 4–6 (*MGH, SRM* 4:70–72).

major Frankish families eventually had one member who entered Luxeuil or at least sojourned there.[92]

Columban was fearless in denouncing what he perceived as immoral
behavior, no matter who was involved. He intervened in this way in
the personal affairs of the Frankish monarchs and so ran afoul of the
formidable Queen Brunhilde. She had him expelled from Burgundy
and tried to have him expelled from all of Gaul. He traveled to Autun,
then to the Loire valley at Nevers, and from there downstream to
Nantes, from which he was to set sail. Only a combination of high
wind and waves, considered a miraculous sign, prevented his expulsion from Gaul. Pushed back to shore, Columban doubled back to Paris
and the Neustrian court at Soissons, where King Chlotar II (584–629)
welcomed him as a gift from heaven. He stopped at Meaux, where he
was the guest of a nobleman and royal adviser. Here and on several
other such visits, Columban formed close ties with the leading figures
in Frankish society, and in particular he made a lasting impression
upon their children, some of whom became noted promoters of the
monastic life. Farther to the east he traveled down the Moselle and
then up the Rhine. At Lake Constance he bade farewell to his close
companion Gallus, whose monastic foundation and eventual resting
place became the great Abbey of Saint Gall. Columban himself moved
on to northern Italy to the court of the Lombard king Agilulf, who
granted him a place to settle at Bobbio in the Apennines. Bobbio turned
out to be Columban's last foundation and his burial place.[93]

Luxeuil, Saint Gall, and Bobbio attracted waves of Irish monks over
the next few generations and spearheaded the foundation of dozens of
other monasteries made more or less in their image. For Luxeuil Columban composed a rule, which is the earliest Irish monastic rule extant.[94] Its extreme austerity is backed by severe discipline. Not long
after Columban's death, Luxeuil took up as well the more moderate
Rule of Saint Benedict and instituted a mixture of the two; it was this
mixed or combined rule that became the standard for the Continental
monasteries founded or reformed by Irish monks.[95]

The "Irofrankish" monasticism that emerged in northern Gaul in the
seventh century as a result of the Irish missions differed significantly

92. Jonas, *Vita Columbani*, chs. 7, 10 (*MGH, SRM* 4:74, 76).
93. Jonas, *Vita Columbani*, chs. 18–24, 26, 29 (*MGH, SRM* 4:86–88, 92–100, 106–107).
94. *Sancti Columbani opera*, ed. G. S. M. Walker (Dublin, 1970), pp. 122–181.
95. Lawrence, *Medieval Monasticism*, p. 49.

from that of pre-Columban times. It maintained close ties with royalty, right from Columban's initial visit to the court of Childebert. The new monasticism enjoyed the patronage of kings, queens, and nobles. The one serious royal obstacle to the mission, Queen Brunhilde, was eliminated by execution in 613, after which there followed a peaceful quarter century, under Dagobert I, when the new monasticism really took hold. From then on the establishing of monasteries went ahead without hindrance.[96]

Audoenus (or Ouen), son of a Frankish lord who had given hospitality to Columban, served at court, became secretary to King Dagobert, founded a monastery on his own lands east of Paris at Rebais, and peopled his new monastery with monks from Luxeuil.[97] Later, as bishop of Rouen, he fostered the new monasticism in the lower Seine valley. One of the first monks of Rebais, a nobleman named Philibert, served as abbot of that same house, went to visit both Luxeuil and Bobbio, and upon his return, went to the Seine valley where, in 654, with the help of Audoenus he established the monastery of Jumièges. Later still he founded Noirmoutier at the mouth of the Loire.[98] Wandregisel was another high official of the court of Dagobert who left to join the religious life. He traveled to Bobbio, and though he then wanted to go to Ireland, he settled for a decade at Romainmoutier in the Jura, an older monastic establishment that had recently been refounded by Austrasian nobles. From there he went to Rouen and with the assistance of Audoenus set up a monastery at Fontenelle known eventually by his name, the Abbey of Saint-Wandrille.[99] Another companion of Audoenus in the court of Dagobert was Eligius, or Eloi. It was not noble birth that brought him to court but his skill as a goldsmith. He achieved high rank and importance as head of the royal mint. In 632 he founded the Abbey of Solignac near Limoges, naming Remachus, a monk of Luxeuil, as first abbot. He founded a monastery for

96. The principal work on the influence of the Irish upon Merovingian monasticism is the book, first published in 1965, by Friedrich Prinz, *Frühes Mönchtum im Frankenreich: Kultur und Gesellschaft in Gallien, den Rheinlanden und Bayern am Beispiel der monastischen Entwicklung (4. bis 8. Jahrhundert)*, 2d ed. (Munich, 1988).

97. *AASS*, Aug. 4:805–807. See Prinz, *Frühes Mönchtum*, pp. 125–126.

98. *MGH, SRM* 5:568–606.

99. *Vita Sancti Wandregiseli (MGH, SRM* 5:13–24); for his desire to go to Ireland, ch. 9, p. 18.

women in Paris and still other monasteries, later on, when he was bishop of Noyon.[100]

The new monasteries were characteristically rural; the powerful aristocratic founding families endowed them with parcels of land from their own extensive holdings. In the countryside, often far from cities, these monasteries eluded episcopal control. If there was external control it was exerted by the founding families, who tended to take proprietary attitudes toward their own foundations. Many of the founding abbots and abbesses gained sainthood, and such honor, rather than separating them further from their families, instead reflected sanctity upon those families. In the new tradition of sanctity, the holy person's early history, high social status, experience at court, prowess with arms, and the like were not suppressed or downplayed but instead were emphasized in proportion as social status itself became a further indication of sanctity. The monastery became the spiritual center for the territory over which the family exerted political control; the monastic church became the family mausoleum, and the saintly relics within made it a storehouse of charismatic (and political) power.[101]

Many of the new monasteries were for women, and since these were often situated in remote places, the standard practice was to have some men in residence (though strictly segregated); these included field hands to work on the land and priests to perform liturgical functions. Such communities, even if called "double," were really made up principally of religious women and only secondarily of the men who assisted them; they remained under the direction of abbesses. One of the brothers of Audoenus, Ado, who had also been in the king's service at Paris, founded such a monastery at Jouarre, on his estates along the Marne. Its famous crypt, with its stunning collection of tombs, contains the remains of Ado, of his cousin Theodechild, the first abbess, and of several other of their relatives, all saints.[102]

The great royal patroness of the time was Queen Bathilde, wife and after 657 widow of Clovis II. She was instrumental in propagating the customs of Luxeuil, and she was the foundress of the Abbey of Corbie in Picardy. The first monks of Corbie were brought in from Luxeuil. At Chelles, not far from Paris, there was a monastery for women that,

---

100. *Vita Sancti Eligii*, 1:15, 17; 2:2, 5 (*MGH, SRM* 4:680–683, 695, 697).
101. Karl Bosl, "Il 'santo nobile,' " in *Agiografia altomedioevale*, ed. Sofia Boesch-Gajano (Bologna, 1976), pp. 161–163.
102. Edward James, *The Franks* (Oxford, 1988), pp. 132–135.

according to tradition, had been founded by Clotilda, the wife of the first Clovis. Bathilde in effect refounded it; she had it rebuilt and provided it with a landed endowment. Her attachment was such that she retired to it late in life to live out her days under the abbess whom, to be sure, she herself had appointed.[103]

Another of the double monasteries was at Nivelles, in Brabant. It was the first of the monastic foundations by the Arnulfung family of Austrasia (some of whose descendants ruled most of Europe and were known to posterity as the Carolingians). The widow of Pepin the Elder, Itta, had it built in the 640s, and she endowed it, naming her daughter Gertrude as the first abbess. Besides bringing in the mixed rule of Luxeuil, Gertrude sent to Ireland for monks to give instruction in the liturgy and in letters; for books she sent to Rome. At the end of her life she left a thriving institution, naming her niece to succeed her and remaining on call after death, as Saint Gertrude, to return whenever her beloved community needed her help.[104]

The effects of Irofrankish monasticism reached far beyond the monasteries themselves. By their location and the influence they exerted on their surroundings, the monasteries constituted an utterly new initiative toward evangelizing the countryside.[105] And though at first the monks encountered trouble with the Frankish bishops by refusing to submit to their control, they in time reformed the episcopacy itself. In the course of the seventh century alone, eleven monks of Luxeuil were named to Frankish episcopal sees. Some of the new-style bishops founded monasteries, and it can be said of all of them that they fostered the new monastic spirituality. They even brought some of the older, urban monasteries up to date by introducing the mixed rule of Luxeuil. Such was the case, for example, at Saint-Martin of Tours, Saint-Germain at Auxerre, Saint-Médard at Soissons, Saint-Aignan at Orléans, Saint-Pierre-le-Vif at Sens, and Saint-Denis outside Paris.[106]

The case of Riquier stands apart from these other saintly careers with

103. *DHGE* 12:604–605; Lawrence, *Medieval Monasticism*, p. 51.

104. *Bibliotheca sanctorum*, 13 vols. (Rome, 1961–1970), 6:288; J. J. Hoebaux, *L'abbaye de Nivelles, des origines au XIVe siècle*, Mémoires de l'Académie royale de Belgique 46 (Brussels, 1952), pp. 25–30, 45–70.

105. Paul Fouracre, "The Work of Audoenus of Rouen and Eligius of Noyon in Extending Episcopal Influence from the Town to the Country in Seventh-Century Neustria," in *The Church in Town and Countryside*, ed. Derek Baker, Studies in Church History 16 (Oxford, 1979), pp. 77–91.

106. Prinz, *Frühes Mönchtum*, p. 239.

their many intersections, social or political or religious. Neither a member of the royal court nor a monk of Luxeuil, Riquier lived in Picardy near the Channel coast, and there, early in the seventh century, he met two wandering missionaries from Ireland named Fichori and Chaidoc. He listened to their preaching, converted to the religious life, and in the Irish manner, made his (private) confession to them. His fame as a hermit spread widely; when it reached the court of Dagobert, the king sent him gifts. The monastery founded to honor his relics at the place he had lived became one of the great Carolingian religious houses.[107]

The unusual Celtic notion of penance plus the carefully coded penitential system of the Irish became the most widespread and lasting of Irish influences upon the Continent. Their two peculiar notions of penance were essentially that penance is private, and that it is endlessly repeatable. These notions, like other forms of Irish spirituality, derive from the druids' roles as spiritual counselors and correctors. From the druid the Christian holy man derived his role as "soul friend." Moreover, the public penance that prevailed in all other Christian countries flowed from the authority of the bishop. As the penance characteristic of the monastic life spread to the laity—that is, as monks began to administer penance to laypeople—lists of prescribed penances, the penitentials, were written down. The first of these were compiled in the sixth century by Saint Finnian and at the beginning of the seventh century in Italy by Saint Columban.[108]

Perhaps the best known, and surely the most studied, aspect of the Irish influence upon the Continent involved the transmission of ancient learning, the forms of handwriting, and the styles of manuscript illumination. The reputations of Luxeuil and Corbie are legendary in this regard.[109] Here, though, it is important to recall that the insular influence did not arrive in one installment only, in the time of Columban. It came in subsequent waves, as in the ninth-century visits of Irish

107. *AASS*, Apr. 3:445–466; Ludwig Bieler, *Ireland, Harbinger of the Middle Ages* (London, 1963), p. 95.

108. Frantzen, *Literature of Penance*, pp. 6, 32. Among other possible Irish contributions to Continental culture at this time are the Feast of All Saints (*NCE* 1:318–319) and royal anointment: Michael J. Enright, *Iona, Tara and Soissons: The Origin of the Royal Anointing Ritual*, Arbeiten zur Frühmittelalterforschung 17 (Berlin, 1985).

109. Leslie W. Jones, "The Scriptorium at Corbie: I. The Library," *Speculum* 22 (1947): 191–204; "II. The Script and the Problems," ibid., pp. 375–394. Pierre Riché, *Education et culture dans l'Occident barbare (VIe–VIIIe siècle)* (Paris, 1967), pp. 371–383; Max L. W. Laistner, *Thought and Letters in Western Europe, A.D. 500 to 900*, 2d ed. (Ithaca, N.Y., 1957), pp. 225–237.

pilgrims to the tomb of Saint Gall, which eventually made the abbey dedicated to Saint Gall a major Irish school and scriptorium.[110]

Péronne of the Scots (meaning "the Irish"), a monastery close to Corbie, was another post-Columban Irish colony on the Continent. It was set up to house the relics of an Irish monk-visionary named Fursa who, after several years in England, went to the court of Clovis II and then founded the monastery of Lagny just east of Paris. At his death in about 650, his body was entombed on a patrician domain at Péronne; a chapel was built there under the auspices of Eloi of Noyon, and soon the site was attracting many pilgrims, including holy people from Ireland. Two brothers of Fursa served as abbot of Péronne. Throughout the eighth century and until its destruction by the Northmen in 880, Peronna Scottorum kept its Irish character.[111]

Memories of the heroes of Irish religious life, the saints, were kept vivid by the texts recounting their deeds and the cults that honored them. At Péronne, for example, there were relics of Saint Patrick brought to France by Fursa. The monastery library contained copies of the writings of Patrick, the *Letter* and the *Confession*, plus a copy of one of the early lives.[112] Many of the manuscripts containing lives of the Irish saints were housed in, but also produced in, the religious houses of Francia. It is difficult to know who read or heard what was written in the saints' lives, but the later vernacular versions of these lives themselves indicate that the lives were to be read on, or at least were to supply homily material for, the apposite saints' days.[113] The extant liturgical calendars of Frankish Gaul, which kept order in the profusion of saintly cults, give evidence of active cults on the Continent of over forty of the Irish saints. The feast of Saint Brigit, for example, was celebrated at Re-

110. Bernhard Bischoff, "Il monachesimo irlandese nei suoi rapporti col continente," in *Il monachesimo nell'Alto Medioevo e la formazione della civiltà occidentale*, Settimane di studio del Centro italiano di studi sull'Alto Medioevo 4 (Spoleto, 1957), pp. 121–138; Bieler, *Ireland, Harbinger*, pp. 93–94.

111. Ludwig Traube, "Peronna Scottorum," in *Vorlesungen und Abhandlungen von Ludwig Traube*, ed. F. Boll, vol. 3 (Munich, 1920), pp. 95–119; Bieler, *Ireland, Harbinger*, pp. 97–99.

112. Prinz, *Frühes Mönchtum*, pp. 128–129; Bieler, *Ireland, Harbinger*, p. 99.

113. *Betha Adamnáin: The Irish Life of Adamnán*, ed. Maire Herbert and Padraig O Riain, Irish Texts Society 54 (London, 1988), p. 4; also Hughes, *Early Christian Ireland*, p. 235; James F. Kenney, *The Sources for the Early History of Ireland*, vol. 1 (New York, 1929), pp. 308–309.

bais, Meaux, Nivelles, Senlis, Corbie, Marchiennes, Saint-Amand, and among others, Saint-Vaast. After Brigit, the saint whose cult was most widely diffused on the Continent was Patrick.[114] For the nuns of Nivelles, the sanctity of their abbess Gertrude could only have been enhanced by her dying on 17 March, the feast of Saint Patrick.[115]

The Irofrankish monasteries were, for their time, elegant and beautiful places; by comparison with the rude huts that had previously housed the ascetics of northern Gaul, their living quarters were princely and their churches monumental.[116] Such a development can be explained by the high social standing of the founders and chief protagonists of this monasticism, and yet this development is not without irony, given the austerity of the Irish monastic life that inspired it. What could have been the appeal of Irish monasticism for the Franks? Clearly it was the role of the powerful families and the closely integrated nexus of families and monasteries, which was standard in Ireland, that made possible this striking cultural transfer. What the Franks and the Irish had in common was not some attraction to asceticism but rather the central social and political importance of monasticism. Put another way, up until then monasticism in both the Eastern and Western churches was a fringe, or marginal, institution. Monasticism began as—and for centuries continued to be—a lay protest movement, directed principally against the clergy. It was that way in Syria and Egypt at the start and was still so in Gaul and Italy in the sixth century. But monasticism, as we saw earlier, was first recovered from marginality by the Irish, who had no intervening (Roman) episcopal structure either to marginalize it or to give fervently spiritual people cause to rebel. This original cultural accomplishment the Irish then transferred, across the vast cultural gap separating them, to the Franks.[117]

---

114. Louis Gougaud, *Les saints irlandais hors d'Ireland* (Louvain, 1936), pp. 27, 142–158. For a ninth-century Bavarian litany that includes invocations to Columban, Fursey, Patrick, Columcille, Conigall, Adamnan, and Brigit, among many others, see Maurice Coens, "Les litanies bavaroises du *Libellus precum* dit de Fleury (Orléans MS. 184)," *Analecta Bollandiana* 77 (1959): 373–391.

115. This coincidence did not, of course, escape the attention of her Irish biographer, writing at Nivelles about 670. See *MGH, SRM* 2:453–464, especially 462–463. See also Hughes, *Church in Early Irish Society*, pp. 82, 93.

116. Geary, *Before France and Germany*, p. 173.

117. Clare E. Stancliffe, "Kings and Conversion: Some Comparisons between the Roman Mission to England and Patrick's to Ireland," *FS* 14 (1980): 59–94.

The Irish Sphere of Influence

The monastic movement headed by Luxeuil covered the map of Francia: Frankish Gaul north of the Loire and east to the Rhineland. The map of this Irish diaspora conforms closely to the map of the clamors.[118] The scriptoria, the style of the manuscripts, the saintly cults, the peculiar mix of the aristocratic and the ascetic: these are the crucial signs (see Map 3). The text of the clamor did not come from Ireland, but the passion that fueled it did. [119]

Continental saints did not curse the way the Irish saints did. Even the Irish saints on the Continent did not curse the way the Irish saints did at home: Continental culture clearly was not receptive to it. The cursing one finds in the life of Columban, which is certainly present, is nonetheless muted. It was muted by the Continental author of the life. The Irish practice of the individual holy person cursing did not take; it did not transfer. But Irish religious attitudes toward authority did carry over to the Continent. The religious and the powerful were, after all, on the same social level.

At the table of the bishop of Tours, Columban met Chrodowald, a Frankish lord who found himself on both sides of a dispute that divided the royal dynasty; he was tied by marriage to one of the main protagonists but was a loyal follower of the other, who was named Theuderich. Columban acknowledged this obligation of fidelity and asked only that Chrodowald take a message to his lord. "Announce thus to Theuderich that he and his children will die within three years, and his entire family will be exterminated by the Lord." The astonished man asked Columban why he predicted such things, and the latter's dry reply was, "I dare not conceal what the Lord has ordered me to reveal." All the inhabitants of Gaul, says Columban's biographer, subsequently saw this fulfilled. Such was Columban's manner in dealing with the powerful.[120]

With the saints, Columban seemed equally at ease. During his forced

---

118. *Columbanus and Merovingian Monasticism*, ed. H. B. Clarke and Mary Brennan, British Archeological Reports, International Series 113 (Oxford, 1981), p. 74; also James, *Franks*, p. 129, and Prinz, *Frühes Mönchtum*, maps V, VI, VIIA, VIIB.

119. See the concluding remarks of Maurice Coens to an article on invocations to Irish saints in a Bavarian manuscript, "Les litanies bavaroises," p. 391: "And finally, let us not fail to recall that the point of departure for the diffusion of certain types of prayer such as the *loricae*, as well as of the litanies of the saints, and of confessions, must be looked for across the sea, in Celtic territory."

120. Jonas, *Vita Columbani*, ch. 22 (*MGH, SRM* 4:95–96).

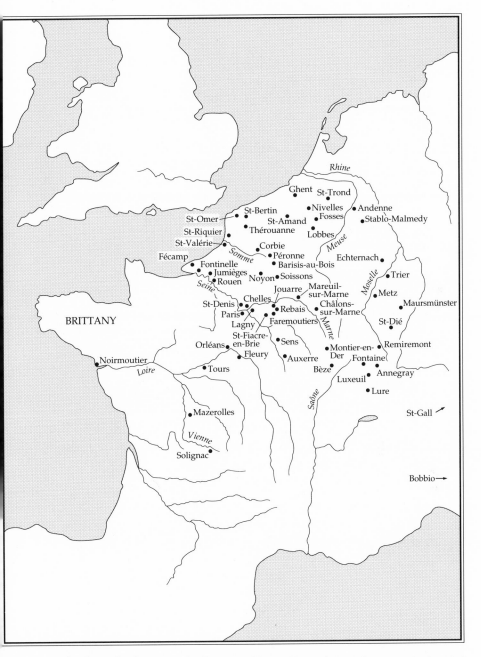

Map 3. Irish sphere of influence on the Continent. Monasteries and sites of monasteries founded or reformed by Irish pilgrims or by persons markedly influenced by Irish spirituality. Note that the heartland of the Frankish settlement stretches from the Loire River Valley north and east (but omitting Brittany) to the Rhine.

trip down the Loire, when he was being expelled from Gaul, Columban wanted to worship at the tomb of Saint Martin. The boatmen were under orders to prevent Columban from landing at any shrine, so they kept to a course in the center of the river. At Tours, Columban's prayers prevailed over the strength of the boatmen, and the boat turned miraculously in to shore. Columban spent the night in prayer before the tomb of Saint Martin and the next day returned to his companions and the boat. They informed him that while he was away all of their belongings, including some gold for distribution to the poor, had been stolen. "Having heard this, he returned to the grave of the holy confessor and complained that he had not watched by the relics of the saint only that the latter should allow him and his followers to suffer loss." Immediately the culprit began to be tormented, and he brought back all the stolen goods.[121]

It was Eloi of Noyon who, as we saw earlier, threatened the patron saint of his church when its belongings were stolen. The threat involved both ceasing all veneration of the saint and barricading the doors of her church with thorns.[122] The latter practice does not appear to be an Irish import, but the whole frame of mind (*mentalité*) and the mode of approaching the saint are unmistakably Irish. In a dispute over a forest that Eloi claimed for the church of Noyon, his unnamed opponent threatened to take the land by force; the excommunication warning Eloi issued was met by derision, and so he extended his right hand and cast the terrible sentence. As the bishop spoke, his contemptuous opponent collapsed on the floor, dead.[123] It was Audoenus who wrote the life of Eloi, the same who fostered the growth of Irish spirituality and the foundation of Irofrankish monasteries. The member of their circle who went furthest in his enthusiasm for things Irish was Wandregisel, who expressed a desire to go to Ireland and who himself wished to follow precisely the rigorously ascetic life of the Irish monks and tried to get his monks to do the same. It was Wandregisel who, on winter nights, recited psalms while immersed in a mountain stream amid chunks of ice (*in medio glaciarum*).[124]

The major area in which Irish spiritual influences made an impact

121. Ibid.

122. *Vita Sancti Eligii*, 1:30 (*MGH, SRM* 4:686–687); see above, conclusion to ch. 2.

123. *Vita Sancti Eligii*, 2:19 (*MGH, SRM* 4:710).

124. *Bibliotheca sanctorum*, 12:944–947; and *Vita Sancti Wandregiseli*, ch. 8 (*MGH, SRM* 5:17).

on the Continent coincided with the area of Frankish settlement. There the mixing of cultures produced a unique kind of monasticism. The primary characteristic of this monasticism was its integration into the fabric of aristocratic family life. A secondary characteristic, derivative of the first, was the bold use of spiritual sanctions, including curses, in particular when dealing with antagonists of their own high social standing. Although our search for textual sources of the maledictions led principally to the ancient Hebrews, the corresponding search for precedents in the practice of religious cursing has led to the Irish monks. Their contributions to the religious life of the Franks helped shape the contexts in which the culture of clamors flourished.

6
Contexts

FROM THE tenth century to the thirteenth, the heartland of ecclesiastical cursing lay between the valleys of the Charente and the Rhine. Essential to understanding the workings of clamors and curses in that region is the shared religious culture of the age, in particular the mirror-image relationship of maledictions and benedictions. Similarly important for establishing the juridical context of the clamor is the inverse relation between the remnants of the Carolingian system of justice and the remnants of the saints. And since the issue in the great majority of cases where clamors were used was property—usually land that had been granted to religious institutions by lay benefactors—attention will be given to relationships between donors and predators and in the end will come to focus upon the curious figure of the donor as predator.

Religion

The religious expression of Carolingian Europe was, as we observed earlier, fundamentally liturgical. With political legitimacy itself established by liturgy, the making of political agreements and judicial decisions also assumed a liturgical character. In addition to the considerably lengthened monastic liturgical cycle, in some monasteries of the tenth and eleventh centuries even the most banal parts of daily routine, apart from the recitation of the Divine Office, acquired an obsessively ritualized quality. A second and related element in defining the character of this liturgical religion is the dominant presence of the vocabulary, imagery, and thought patterns of the Old Testament. God the judge was distant and stern; divine judgments, never timid about displaying vengeance, were uncompromising.[1]

1. Barbara H. Rosenwein, "Feudal War and Monastic Peace: Cluniac Liturgy as Ritual Aggression," *Viator* 2 (1971): 132; Giles Constable, "The Ceremonies and Symbolism of Entering Religious Life and Taking the Monastic Habit, from the Fourth to the Twelfth

In this early Europe, with its Old Testament atmosphere, where the forces of nature remained an utter mystery to the small, poor, and widely scattered populace, a saint was an exceptional person thought to have a special immunity; the saint was a person blessed. Holy people could resist the devil and cope with situations that defeated most others. The great majority of people, the "others," needed continually to be blessed. At baptism the individual candidate, as we saw, was cleansed within by exorcism, bathed in the water of that ancient initiation rite, and blessed. The permanent condition of being baptized conferred by the ceremony of baptism lacked a counterpart in the rituals of blessing, however, despite their use of such phrases as "for ever and ever." The desire for blessings was insatiable. In the early centuries of Christianity, there remained notable ambiguities on the matter of post-baptismal sin and penance, but with the eventual triumph of the Irish view of repeatable confession and penance throughout the Latin West, the need for frequent, repeated blessings merely intensified.

The continuing obligation of bishops and priests to pronounce blessings drew its authority from God's commission to Aaron and his sons as transmitted by Moses (Num. 6:22–27). The only notable limitation was that no cleric was supposed to pronounce a blessing in the presence of another cleric of higher rank. There were blessings for people, blessings for things, blessings for places, blessings for occasions, and blessings to suit particular needs; many were in effect preventive blessings, intended to guard against unpleasant eventualities. Various divine and saintly, as well as ecclesiastical, agents were called upon to give their blessings.[2]

Formulas for benediction, hundreds of them, are found in sacramentaries of the seventh to the eleventh century. In the latter century there appeared a separate subcategory of the liturgical genre, the benedictional. This kind of book contained the forms to be used in the episcopal benediction, which is spoken during the mass. The formulas are arranged according to the liturgical calendar, with headings referring to particular days. The deacon prepares the congregation by saying, "Make yourselves humble for receiving the benediction" (*Humilitate vos*

Century," in *Segni e riti nella chiesa altomedioevale occidentale*, Settimane di studio del Centro italiano di studi sull'Alto Medioevo 32 (Spoleto, 1987), pp. 775–776.

    2. *DACL* 2, pt. 1:670–727, s.v. "Bénédiction."

ad benedictionem). The proper moment for such a benediction came after the *Pater Noster* and the *Libera nos Domine* (the embolism), and before the *Pax Domini.* That very time was of course also the appropriate moment for introducing a clamor into the mass—the appropriate time, that is, for either a benediction or a malediction.[3]

Among the ancient Jews, benedictions were given either by the laying on of hands or by raising both hands. In the Latin West, the gesture that eventually gained authoritative status was the familiar one of raising the right hand, palm toward the recipient, with only the index and middle fingers extended. It is found in Christian iconography as early as the third century, and it became the characteristic gesture of figures giving benedictions in Romanesque iconography, a usage confirmed by an exceptional raising of the left hand, as we saw above, to accompany a curse.[4]

The divine protection provided by benediction was regarded by some as a literal shield, invisible in some cases, capable in others of even rendering the blessed person invisible. Columban, at the height of his troubles with Queen Brunhilde, was under an order of expulsion from the kingdom. Soldiers came to get him at the monastery where he was staying. When they arrived he was seated in the vestibule of the church reading a book. They searched everywhere but could not find him. Several times they passed close by him. Their clothes brushed against his; a few soldiers tripped over him. To his delight, Columban perceived that though he could see them, to them he was invisible.[5]

Also Patrick was invisible to enemies who lay in wait to ambush him; they saw only wild deer passing. The prayer he composed to protect body and soul against devils and vices was thus called the "Deer's Cry."[6] In Ireland there also appeared the popular "breastplate" poems, or *loricae.* The "Breastplate of Patrick" summons virtues to stand between the speaker and all evils: "against every cruel, merciless power that may come against my body and soul, against incantations of false prophets, against false laws of heretics, against spells of wiz-

---

3. *Corpus benedictionum pontificalium,* ed. Edmond Moeller, 4 vols., Corpus Christianorum, series Latina 162–162C (Turnhout, 1971–1979), 1:vii–xiv.

4. *DACL* 2, pt. 2:746–758, s.v. "Bénir (Manière de)." On the right hand as a sign of power and an expression of benevolent divine will, see *ER* 2:247–253, especially p. 249, s.v. "Blessing." For the use of the left hand in cursing, see chapter 5, under "Irish Saints."

5. Jonas, *Vita Columbani,* ch. 20 (*MGH, SRM* 4:90).

6. *The Tripartite Life of Patrick, with Other Documents relating to That Saint,* ed. Whitley Stokes, 2 vols., RS 89 (London, 1887), 2:381.

ards, against every knowledge that has defiled man's body and soul."
Christ becomes a protective screen:

> Christ to protect me today against every poison, against burning, against
> drowning, against deathwound, so that I may have a multitude of rewards.
> Christ be with me, Christ before me, Christ behind me, Christ in me, Christ
> below me, Christ above me, Christ at my right, Christ at my left, Christ in
> breadth, Christ in length, Christ in height, Christ in the heart of everyone
> who thinks of me, Christ in the mouth of everyone who speaks to me, Christ
> in the eye of everyone who sees me, Christ in the ear of everyone who hears
> me.[7]

The *loricae* thus were prayers for protection against every sort of danger; some of them enumerated parts of the body and asked that each part be protected against the weakness toward which it naturally inclined.[8]

As Liebert, the bishop of Cambrai, lay on his deathbed in 1076, his companions read the Gospels so that the demons would be chased away by the breath of their reading. In Rogation Day processions, according to James of Voragine in the thirteenth century, brandishing the cross and ringing bells put demons to flight. Saint Francis, according to some of his closest companions, was saved from demons by the shield of his preferred form of blessedness, that is, joy. He taught his followers that though their bodies might be afflicted their faces should be joyful. He often said to them that if God's servants were both inwardly and outwardly joyful, demons could in no way harm them. The demons would grudgingly admit, "Since the servant of God has joy in both adversity and prosperity, we are unable to get at him to bring him harm."[9]

In an exemplum, or story for use in sermons (on the importance of directing one's confession to a priest), written down in the thirteenth century, a man who is out on the road late at night is accosted

7. *Tripartite Life,* 1:49–53.

8. Allen J. Frantzen, *The Literature of Penance in Anglo-Saxon England* (New Brunswick, N. J., 1983), pp. 85–86; for the influence of these prayers in England, see Thomas D. Hill, "Invocation of the Trinity and the Tradition of the *Lorica* in Old English Poetry," *Speculum* 56 (1981): 259–267. I learned much from conversations with both of these scholars.

9. Henri Platelle, "La mort précieuse: La mort des moines d'après quelques sources des Pays Bas du Sud," *Revue Mabillon* 60 (1982): 151–174. *The Golden Legend of Jacobus de Voragine,* tr. Granger Ryan and Helmut Ripperger, 2 vols. (New York, 1941), 1:279–280. *The Writings of Leo, Rufino, and Angelo,* ch. 97, in *Scripta Leonis, Rufini et Angeli, Sociorum S. Francisci,* ed. Rosalind B. Brooke (Oxford, 1970), pp. 260–261.

by a monster. He realizes right away that this is happening to him because of his sins. There being no priest around to whom he can confess, he confesses on the spot directly to God. The man remains awake in anguish all night long because ghastly creatures assault him unceasingly, but they never touch him. He is protected by an invisible shield that allows for him to be terrified but also lets him escape unharmed.[10]

These stories about shields record exceptional cases, but blessings were ordinarily only metaphorical layers or barriers of protection. The *Life of Saint Anthony* is precise on this point, saying that the saint, in his continuing battles with the devil, fortified his body with faith, fasting, and prayer. Without this protection he would have been easy prey. The exaggerated tales in which such defenses became literal shields dramatize the dangers of being outside a condition of blessedness and of dying without it. They thus reveal one of the keys to the functioning of curses. Excommunication, by asking that an individual be separated from the congregation of Christians, have the company of the devil, and above all be cursed (*maledictus*), was in effect stripping a person of the protection of benediction. In the view of one twelfth-century biblical commentator, when a just excommunication takes place, the affected party is thereby thrust "into the hands of the devil to do with as he wishes." An important component of the fear of malediction was this defenseless exposure to the forces of evil.[11]

Between the states of blessedness and of being cursed, there was no middle ground except high-risk vulnerability. The reality of curses is further attested by a prayer for protection against their effects that, in the end, urges that they be turned back upon those who launched them. Such views presuppose a dualistic religious outlook, not necessarily as represented in the church's most profound, licensed thinkers, but as accepted and lived, without (much) reflection, by the vast majority of its followers. Such, precisely, was the dominant outlook in the Carolingian and post-Carolingian world. Just as there was no middle way between heaven and hell, there was no way to be neutral about

10. *Liber exemplorum ad usum praedicantium,* ed. Andrew G. Little, British Society of Franciscan Studies 1 (Manchester, 1908), pp. 51–53. The lesson of the exemplum, by the way, is that although a confession made directly to God in an emergency may be valid, of far greater value is one made to a priest according to the regulations laid down by the church.

11. Athanasius, *Vita Sancti Antonii,* ch. 5 (PG 16:358). The anonymous twelfth-century commentator is cited in Elisabeth Vodola, *Excommunication in the Middle Ages* (Berkeley, Calif., 1986), p. 46.

the ever-present dangers that menace human beings. Demons were real and were just waiting for a chance to penetrate, wherever possible, the shield of blessedness.[12]

Among monks a widely held belief was that the whole matter of salvation would be settled in a struggle between angels and devils at the time of death. One of the letters of Saint Boniface, written about 717 to Eadburga, abbess of Saint Mildred of Thanet, recounts the astonishing scenes observed by a monk who had died and then returned to life to tell what he had seen. The first thing the monk reported was that everywhere angels and devils were engaged in battles over souls. He witnessed part of a debate about his own soul, with accusations from one side about his sinful behavior and praise from the other for the virtues he had practiced. Without revealing the outcome of that debate, the text moves on to a description of sinners suffering in hell, among whom was Ceolred, the king of Mercia who had recently died. Boniface thought that Ceolred had been a terrible king, and in another letter to Ceolred's royal successor he set out a lengthy catalog of Ceolred's misdeeds, clearly meant as a warning. The vision of the monk who returned from hell was probably retold for the same motive.[13]

The monk said that Ceolred was protected by an angelic screen against the assault of demons. It looked like a huge open book suspended over his head. As the demons swirled around him they demanded that the angels who were protecting the king withdraw their protection. The demons brought up a long list of damning charges against the former king and threatened to shut him in the deepest dungeon of hell and to torment him forever, as he deserved. Against this plea the angels had to admit that they could not build a strong case, that on account of his own demerits they could no longer help him. "So they withdrew the shelter of the protecting screen, and the demons with triumphant rejoicing gathered together from every part of the universe . . . and tormented the king with indescribable cruelties."[14]

---

12. *Capitularia regum Francorum*, ed. Etienne Baluze, 2d ed. (Venice, 1773), 2:460. The lack of a middle way is one of the central arguments in Jacques Le Goff, *The Birth of Purgatory*, tr. Arthur Goldhammer (Chicago, 1984).

13. Jacques Paul, "Le démoniaque et l'imaginaire dans le *De vita sua* de Guibert de Nogent," in *Le diable au Moyen Age* (*doctrine, problèmes moraux, représentations*), Sénéfiance 6 (Aix-en-Provence, 1979), pp. 371–399; MGH, *Epist.* 3:252–257, 339–345.

14. MGH, *Epist.* 3:252–257; tr. Ephraim Emerton, *The Letters of Saint Boniface* (New York, 1940), pp. 25–32.

In line with this immediate, symbiotic relationship between angels and demons, between good and evil, cursing was the obverse of blessing. The pattern of treating benedictions and maledictions as similar in form and opposite in meaning was already set, at least for later Western religious thought, by the time Deuteronomy (chs. 27 and 28) was composed. Moreover, the carefully balanced mechanism of benedictions and maledictions left no room even for imagining other alternatives. In the prayerbook of the Rhenish nun Hildegard of Bingen, eight illustrated scenes representing the beatitudes of the Sermon on the Mount are paired with eight corresponding scenes of maledictions (e.g., Blessed are the peacemakers; cursed be the discordant) (see Fig. 8).[15] In countless sanction clauses the same limited pair of alternatives is repeated: "If they keep this covenant, may they be blessed; if not, may they be cursed."[16]

The spiritual authority to bless, like all spiritual power, was in part acquired through the voluntary assumption of the condition of poverty. Along with fleeing from the world, embracing poverty was a cliché of the religious life with a lengthy tradition. But while the vocabulary of the religious life held to tradition, the social situations in which it was played out changed considerably through time. The economy of Carolingian and post-Carolingian Europe—that is, before the commercial revival of the eleventh and twelfth centuries—was precariously weak, with most of the population living barely at subsistence level. Among the few who were better off were those devoted to the religious life. Here, surely, is a paradox. How can it be that by embracing poverty one gains a place among the minuscule elite of the comfortably well off? The resolution of this paradox lies in a nexus of related facts. First, as mentioned in chapter 1, the nature of the society was such that the very notion of poverty referred principally to a condition of powerlessness. Second, most of the religious of the precommercial age of Europe came from the directing or controlling classes of society. And so, in the third place, what they renounced when they joined the religious life was their

---

15. Jean-Claude Schmitt, *La raison des gestes dans l'Occident médiéval* (Paris, 1990), pp. 154–172.

16. For this pattern in Celtic charters, see Wendy Davies, "The Latin Charter-Tradition in Western Britain, Brittany and Ireland in the Early Medieval Period," in *Ireland in Early Medieval Europe*, ed. Dorothy Whitelock, Rosamond McKitterick, and David Dumville (New York, 1982), pp. 263–266.

Figure 8. Beatitudes and curses were paired by Hildegard of Bingen (1098–1178) in her prayerbook and these pairings were illustrated in at least two versions of the prayerbook produced within a few decades of her death. In this example, "Blessed are the merciful" (*Beati misericordes*) is matched with "Cursed be the ferocious" (*Maledicti feroces*). In the upper register a merciful person dispenses food to the hungry and clothes to the naked. In the scene below two wildly violent men kill an unarmed person, one holding him pinned down while the other runs him through with a sword. MS, Vienna, Österreichische Nationalbibliothek, cod. 2739, f. 24v; reproduced by permission.

power: the horses and weapons and other instruments and symbols of earthly power.[17]

Meanwhile, the relative wealth of churches and ecclesiastical institutions found justification in the prime function of all churches—the worship of God—which in this age was done mainly through liturgy. The best society could afford was not too good for the sanctuaries in which the saints were honored and God was worshiped. Western monasticism from the seventh century to the twelfth took great pride in the splendor and riches of its churches. Wealth was not opposed to religious devotion but rather was an index of its intensity and validity. The churches at York and Hexham were tiny treasure-houses in the bleak and poor landscape of seventh-century Northumbria.[18] When Benedict of Aniane's new monastery was built at Inden in the century following, "he took great care to acquire precious ecclesiastical vestments, silver chalices, and whatever else he deemed necessary for the *opera Dei*."[19] John of Salerno commented that Saint-Martin of Tours in the tenth century was "a place full of virtue, remarkable for miracles, overflowing with riches, excelling all in the practice of religion."[20] The massive churches of the great age of black monasticism (late tenth century to early twelfth) were built on a larger scale than these forerunners but on the same principle.[21] Even as a new spirituality took shape in the twelfth century and leveled stinging attacks upon the old ("What is all this gold doing in the sanctuary of the Lord?" asked Saint Bernard), Abbot Suger gave voice to the old view with undiminished vigor as he formulated an aesthetic theology to justify the stupendous new abbey church at Saint-Denis. The religion of the age was thus presided over by a caste of specialists who professed poverty, spurned power, and in the

---

17. On the aristocratic origins of monks and nuns, see Clifford E. Lawrence, *Medieval Monasticism: Forms of Religious Life in Western Europe in the Middle Ages*, 2d ed. (New York, 1989), pp. 71–72; and Georges Duby, *The Three Orders: Feudal Society Imagined*, tr. Arthur Goldhammer (Chicago, 1980), p. 190. See also Barbara H. Rosenwein and Lester K. Little, "Social Meaning in the Monastic and Mendicant Spiritualities," *Past and Present*, no. 63 (1974): 10–11.

18. Eddius Stephanus, *Life of Wilfrid*, chs. 16, 22, in *The Age of Bede*, tr. J. F. Webb (Harmondsworth, Eng., 1983), pp. 122, 128.

19. Ardo, *Vita Benedicti Anianensis*, chs. 17–18 (*MGH, SS* 15, pt. 1:206–207).

20. *Vita Sancti Odonis*, 1:16 (*PL* 133:51).

21. Wolfgang Braunfels, *Monasteries of Western Europe: the Architecture of the Orders*, tr. Alastair Laing (Princeton, N.J., 1980), pp. 47–66.

midst of an economy of utter misery, indulged in a spirituality founded upon conspicuous consumption.[22]

The monopoly this caste held on spiritual power, itself parallel to the monopoly on military power held by the warrior class, gave it the only access to divine authority and the only means of communication between the living and the dead. The religious blessed the dying and the dead, they buried the dead, and they prayed thereafter for the salvation of the dead. The living, in their desire to help the departed, had to rely upon the intervention of the religious. The living provided material support for the religious, who in turn assisted the dead in their quest for salvation. This transaction is fundamental for understanding how religion was then related to society, the economy, and politics.[23]

The names of those the religious undertook to pray for were inscribed in registers called by such terms as "books of life" (libri vitae) or "memorial books" (libri memoriales). The earliest of these now extant dates from the year 784. The practice at first was to list living persons as well as deceased, but from the eleventh century on they listed only the dead. Also at first the practice was to list simply the members of one's own monastery, whereas by the eleventh century these no longer constituted a majority of the names entered. To begin with, religious communities contracted to pray for each other's members; moreover, they were constrained to pray for certain ecclesiastical and secular authorities; and to be sure they made a special effort to pray for their benefactors. Ever larger numbers of lay people sought some form of confraternal tie with monasteries that afforded them the spiritual benefits attained exclusively through monastic prayer. In some instances it is apparent that the names were entered in blocks, perhaps of entire monastic communities or of extended families. Benefactors, for example, usually made donations not just on their own behalf or only on behalf of their closest kin, but for the salvation of many if not all their relatives, those deceased as well as the living; thus many names might be brought along with a lone lay sponsor. The necrology of the Cluniac

22. Bernard, Apologia ad Guillelmum, in Sancti Bernardi opera, ed. Jean Leclercq, Henri Rochais, and Charles Talbot, 8 vols. (Rome, 1957–1977), 3:104. Abbot Suger on the Abbey Church at Saint-Denis, ed. and tr. Erwin Panofsky, 2d ed. by Gerda Panofsky-Soergel (Princeton, N.J., 1974), pp. 15–29, 82–121. Georges Duby, The Early Growth of the European Economy: Warriors and Peasants from the Seventh to the Twelfth Century, tr. Howard B. Clarke (Ithaca, N.Y., 1978), pp. 216–217.

23. Duby, Three Orders, pp. 175–176.

nuns at Marcigny-sur-Loire lists ten thousand names, while the *liber memorialis* of Reichenau Abbey contains four times as many. The persons named were to be recommended during the Eucharist. There was no way all the names could be read out at each mass; instead, the book was placed on the altar during the mass, and the monks prayed for all who were listed there. Along these lines, over thirty sacramentaries, which when put to use were placed on altars, have been found to have names of people to pray for written in the margins. And in order to tap the spiritual power contained in the altar more directly still, at Reichenau the monks had hundreds of names of people to be prayed for etched or written on the stone surface of the altar.[24]

The phrase "book of life" occurs frequently in the Bible, always figuratively; in the Book of Revelation, it is said that they are not destined for salvation "whose names have not been written in the book of life" (17:8), and that anyone whose name is not written in the book of life shall be cast into the lake of fire (20:15). But in the Romanesque religious world such registers existed as material objects, and the frequent use of biblical phrases about names being inscribed in or excised from books conjured up not imaginary registers floating on clouds but real ledgers kept among the regularly used liturgical paraphernalia of churches and, during the mass, placed in view on (and, as it were, plugged into) the altar.[25]

The manipulation of this power to list and pray for someone—or not to, as the case may be—is apparent in a letter sent in 1022 by the canons of Saint Mary's of Chartres (the cathedral) to Herbert, bishop of Lisieux. Saint Mary's had a number of dependent churches in the diocese of

---

24. Nicholas Huyghebaert, *Les documents nécrologiques,* Typologie des sources du Moyen Age occidental 4, rev. ed. by Jean-Loup Lemaître (Turnhout, 1985); Karl Schmid and Joachim Wollasch, "Die Gemeinschaft der Lebenden und Verstorbenen in Zeugnissen des Mittelalters," *FS* 1 (1967): 365–405; Joachim Wollasch, "Ein cluniacensisches Totenbuch aus der Zeit Abt Hugos von Cluny," *FS* 1 (1967): 406–443; *Das Verbrüderungsbuch der Abtei Reichenau,* ed. Johanne Autenrieth, Dieter Geuenich, and Karl Schmid, in *MGH, Libri memoriales et necrologia,* n.s., 1 (Hannover, 1979), and supplement (1983): *Die Altarplatte von Reichenau-Niederzell.* Jean-Loup Lemaître, *Mourir à Saint-Martial: La commémoration des morts et les obituaires à Saint-Martial de Limoges du XIe au XIIIe siècle* (Paris, 1989), pp. 33–34.

25. Auguste Molinier, *Les obituaires français au Moyen Age* (Paris, 1890), lists 650 documents; Jean-Loup Lemaître, *Répertoire des documents nécrologiques français,* 3 vols., Recueil des historiens de la France, Obituaires 7 (Paris, 1980–1987), lists more than 3,000 of them. On the political significance of names, see Andrew W. Lewis, *Royal Succession in Capetian France: Studies on Familial Order and the State,* Harvard Historical Studies 100 (Cambridge, Mass., 1981), pp. 9–11, 47–50, 57–58.

Lisieux, and Herbert must have asked the mother church to pay for each of them a tax called "visitation dues." The reply of the canons points out that this exaction was contrary to custom: "The bishops of holy memory in whose dioceses we have churches have always shown their loving and reverent devotion to our most holy lady by not exacting from us, her unworthy servants, the payment that you demand." Next the canons caution the bishop against bringing upon himself the blame for causing them to suffer, since, they assure him, they are inspired by concern for his welfare. Moreover, "We hope to see you listed in the list of benefactors of our blessed community, so that as we continually offer sacrifice to the Lord for them, and thus also for you, and recount in his presence your good works, we may declare that you, too, are worthy of being included in the book of heavenly life."[26]

In the case of a dispute that had a harmonious ending, the monks of Marmoutier came to an agreement with Geoffrey of Saint-Amand, who, according to them, had been plundering lands at Sentier that they both claimed. We do not know what measures they took against him, but when he gave up his claims the monks, as was usual in such instances, forgave him and henceforth included him in their prayers, thus becoming advocates in the cause of his salvation.[27]

The intermediaries in this process of helping to save benefactors and relatives were the saints. The cult of saints had become focused upon relics, but no matter in what form or quantity the remains of a saint were present, the whole, live saint was there in them. The saint was an active participant in the life of the community, someone to talk with, someone to seek advice from, above all someone to call upon in times of need. The saint who delivered the desired help was to be thanked with praise, tears, and gifts (including, in some cases, new clothing and new housing). The monks of Marmoutier frequently called on Saint Martin to alleviate their crises; once during a drought they went in procession to his tomb and promised to dress him in gold if he would help them out.[28]

The religious encouraged the cult of the saints among the laity; they

---

26. *The Letters and Poems of Fulbert of Chartres*, ed. and tr. Frederick O. Behrends (Oxford, 1976), pp. 112–115. The *liber vitae* for the church is lost, but much of it was copied into the necrology that replaced it in 1027. Behrends reports that it includes no entry for Bishop Herbert.

27. *Cartulaire de Marmoutier pour le Vendômois*, ed. A. de Trémault (Vendôme, 1893), no. 42.

28. *De beato Bartholomaeo abbate*, ch. 13 (*AASSOSB* 9:402).

gave instruction in the legends and miracles of the saints, and thereby they gained support for the cult center and its guardians (themselves) but also raised the expectations of the faithful. At certain festivals statues were dressed up in special ways and the relics were put on special display. For fund-raising drives the relics were sometimes taken out for a trip called a *circumvectio*, as at Lobbes or when Saint-Amand burned down in 1066 and the body of the saint was carried about Gaul to solicit help in building a new church; in difficult times relics were taken out to the walls to forestall an enemy or out to the fields to seek relief from flood or drought.[29] And then there were statues and images that took initiatives of their own. Critical in the conversion experience of Francis of Assisi was the figure of Jesus on a painted crucifix that spoke words of encouragement to him. We know from an exemplum about a woman who spoke rudely to a statue of the Virgin and in turn was punished by Mary with "perpetual misery."[30]

Thus could the faithful come to have great expectations and accordingly, on occasion, suffer great disappointments. Some saints had of course to be awakened from their slothful indifference and, if need be, beaten upon. Some simply had to be awakened from their sleep. The repose of Saint Benedict at Fleury was more than once interrupted by the protests of exasperated inhabitants of his lands, like the elderly woman who folded back the altar cloth and beat on the altar with her fists while excoriating the saint for his sloth. And at Saint-Calais-sur-Anille (between Vendôme and Le Mans) a group of agitated peasants arrived at the monastery after dark, were allowed in by the caretaker, and with similar care for the altar cloth, took to beating upon the tomb/altar with sticks and shouting at the hitherto unresponsive saint inside. Jesus too was sleeping when the canons of Saint-Martin at Etampes-

---

29. *Annales OSB* 4:623. Radbod, *Libellus de miraculo S. Martini*, ch. 6 (*MGH, SS* 15, pt. 2:1243). *Miracula S. Bercharii*, ch. 30 (*AASSOSB* 2:825). Pierre Héliot and M.-L. Chastang, "Quêtes et voyages de reliques au profit des églises françaises au Moyen Age," *Revue d'histoire ecclésiastique* 59 (1964): 789–822 and 60 (1965): 5–32; also Pierre-André Sigal, "Les voyages de reliques aux XIe et XIIe siècles," *Voyage, quête, pèlerinage dans la littérature et la civilisation médiévale*, Sénéfiance 2 (Aix-en-Provence, 1976), pp. 73–104.

30. Thomas of Celano, *Vita secunda S. Francisci*, ch. 10, in *Analecta Franciscana*, vol. 10 (Quaracchi, 1926), p. 137. Caesarius of Heisterbach, *Dialogus miraculorum*, ed. Joseph Strange, 2 vols. (Cologne, 1851), 2:62. The compiler's comment is as revealing as the tale itself: "If those who despise sacred images incur such great punishment, I think that those who venerate them merit considerable (divine) grace" (ibid., p. 63). For this and other references to talking statues, see Ilene H. Forsyth, *The Throne of Wisdom: Wood Sculptures of the Madonna in Romanesque France* (Princeton, N.J., 1972), p. 3.

les-Vieilles stirred up a mob against the monks of Morigny who had come to claim the Church of Saint-Martin, which had recently been given to them. The crowd surged toward the monks' quarters, armed with sticks and stones and shouting (*cum maximis clamoribus*). The monks also had to shout out their appeals to God, and they were saved only when Jesus awoke from his sleep and, by calling in the local militia, came to the rescue.[31]

Such familiarity with sacred figures and such human reactions upon their part make one wonder how a clamor looked to those who were clamored to. That saints reacted to clamors, we deduce from the circumstantial evidence of the results obtained (as in the punishment of oppressors); but how did they perceive clamors, either formal or of the rough, spontaneous sort? We are permitted a glimpse from the other side of the altar in a vision reported in 1147 by a monk from Liège named John. As he lay in bed suffering from a high fever, he was approached by Saint Maurice, who complained that John frequently went to stay on an estate where there was a little church dedicated to Saint Maurice, but that John practically never said mass there or even sang the Divine Office. The encounter seems to be about a straightforward matter of guilt until the moment when John asked the saint why, since he took such an interest in this tiny, out-of-the-way oratory, he did not bother to protect the poor tenants of the estate. The saint decided to teach John a lesson. All of a sudden, reports the monk, he found himself standing by the altar in that oratory next to Saint Maurice, who was holding him close to his side. In the midst of the church they saw a group of poor men and women with their hands stretched out before them, who appeared to be praying. One of them came forward to the altar, banged on it with his hands, then looked up and said:

> "O Saint Maurice, great martyr, why don't you help me? Why don't you save me from the robbers who take everything I have and who seek to take me, defenseless, and kill me?" The saint jostled John as if to make sure he was paying attention and then answered: "You yourself are the worst robber you can be and a companion of thieves, never failing to do evil whenever you can. Woe to you who plunder others, for you shall be plundered." The

31. Thomas Head, *Hagiography and the Cult of Saints: The Diocese of Orléans, 800–1200* (New York, 1990), p. 190; *Miracula S. Carilesi ad ipsius sepulchrum facta*, ch. 1 (*AASSOSB* 1: 629); *La chronique de Morigny (1095–1152)*, 2:12 ("Christus a sonno surrexit"), ed. Léon Mirot (Paris, 1909; 2d ed. 1912), pp. 44–46.

man persisted: "Why do you sleep? Why do you close your ears to our prayers? Why, great saint, do you not take notice of our troubles? Look, I am ruined by evil men." The blessed martyr replied: "You deserve to suffer these things; the wonder is that the earth doesn't open and swallow you up, you who have never been faithful to the cause of God, to whom you belong and from whom you live, for you commit sacrilege in holding back tithes, in cheating on monastic dues, in evading all servile obligations and thus exposing yourself to many enemies such that every saint disdains to help you."[32]

In this singular clerical imagining of a saint's view of a clamor and his angry reply, the monk's shortcomings are insignificant compared with the gross improprieties of the layman.

The religious world of the clamor was therefore a world made up of benedictions, poverty, dazzling sanctuaries, ceremony, litanies, curses, visions, and divine vengeance, as well as of saints who cured the sick, raised the dead, slept, talked (back), owned property, and on occasion fought to protect it.

Justice

The transfer of legal complaints from courts to sanctuaries and the shift from law to liturgy as a means for dealing with them raise questions about how Carolingian justice was supposed to operate and what happened to it. In theory, justice was supposed to begin and end with the king, for he was both the fount of justice—the one who delegated judicial authority to subordinates—and the final court of appeal. In keeping with his Germanic heritage, he was the chief warlord of his people, and as such led the powerful among them into battle; he also exercised the ban (Latin *bannum*), which refers to his jurisdiction over crimes of violence and his power to summon all free men to arms. At the same time, the more recently acquired heritage of Christianity and the king's anointment with holy oil at the hands of bishops also made him the chief protector of God's church and the champion of the weak or poor (meaning essentially the unarmed). No less a warlord or leader of fighters, within his society the king had to restrain the powerful from

32. John of Liège, *Visio status animarum post mortem* (PL 180:183–184); I am grateful to Victoria Morse, who brought this text to my attention in a graduate seminar at Berkeley. On visions see Michel Aubrun, "Caractères et portée religieuse et sociale des 'Visiones' en Occident du VIe au XIe siècle," *Cahiers de civilisation médiévale* 23 (1980): 109–130; and Peter Dinzelbacher, *Vision und Visionsliteratur im Mittelalter*, Monographien zur Geschichte des Mittelalters 23 (Stuttgart, 1981).

harming the weak. His person was sacred, and sacred was the duty he promised to carry out at the time of his anointment—to be the guardian of peace and justice.[33]

From remote times, in performing his duties the king had the assistance of his companions the *comites* or counts. In the systematic organization of a territorial administrative structure by the Carolingians in the eighth century, the key figure was the count and the key geopolitical unit the county, which in many cases overlay the old Roman unit of the city and its surrounding countryside, respectively the *civitas* and the *pagus*. In the Frankish kingdom there were over five hundred counts and counties. The counts were appointed and sent out—and could be recalled—by the king. The count was assisted by a viscount and, in subdivisions of the county called vicariates, by vicars, whom the count had the authority to name and recall. Within the pagus or county, the count exercised the ban and other royal prerogatives. He was above all responsible for administering justice to maintain social order and peace. The *mallus*, or county court, met in two or three sessions a year but had no fixed location. Wherever it met, the count called upon local notables of good reputation—*boni homines*, usually lesser landholders—to assist him in questioning litigants and witnesses.[34]

Communication between the king and the counts was maintained in various ways. The king summoned counts to assemblies, where he made his will known to them directly. Besides sending royal messages to individual counts, the court issued documents, such as the capitularies that promulgated legislation, that went to all counts and held equally throughout the kingdom. The king also used the option of sending out inspectors or messengers, the *missi dominici* (often a team made up of a bishop and a count), who went on their missions bearing considerable royal authority.[35]

33. Rosamond McKitterick, *The Frankish Kingdoms under the Carolingians, 751–987* (London, 1983), p. 77. Robert-Henri Bautier, "L'exercice de la justice publique dans l'empire carolingien," in *Positions des thèses, Ecole nationale des Chartes* (Nogent-le-Rotrou, 1943), pp. 9–18.

34. Karl-Ferdinand Werner, "*Missus-Marchio-Comes*: Entre l'administration centrale et l'administration locale de l'empire carolingien," in *Histoire comparée de l'administration (IVe–XVIIIe siècles)*, ed. Werner Paravicini and K. F. Werner, Beihefte der *Francia* 9 (Munich, 1980), pp. 191–239; McKitterick, *Frankish Kingdoms*, pp. 87–92; Jean-François Lemarignier, *La France médiévale: Institutions et sociétés* (Paris, 1970), pp. 46, 73; Edmond Perroy, "Carolingian Administration," in *Early Medieval Society*, ed. Sylvia Thrupp (New York, 1967), pp. 129–146.

35. Werner, "*Missus-Marchio-Comes*," pp. 195–196; Lemarignier, *La France*, p. 73.

Such are the outlines of the Carolingian administrative structure (apart from the royal court itself) that existed in the latter part of the eighth century. The accumulated modifications of this structure, some radical, others barely perceptible, led over the course of two centuries to a fundamentally different structure altogether. To begin with, a trend toward long tenures for counts—indeed, what were in effect life terms—appeared early. Moreover, the original notion of the count as a close associate of the king and hence as someone from the same geographical area and cultural circle, who then went out to represent royal authority in an outlying territory, also rather soon gave way to the practice of naming a local magnate of the county in question to serve as count. This development opened the way to the countship's becoming the preserve of a few powerful local families, or just one family, and hence to its becoming hereditary. Indeed, during the reign of Louis the Pious the comital office did in many areas become hereditary in practice, although not yet so in principle. And since counts did not receive salaries but lived off the royal lands that went with the title, the more that title was considered hereditary the less those lands were truly at the disposal of the king, becoming instead possessions of the comital dynasty.[36]

The great events of the reign of Louis the Pious had much to do with this transformation of the comital office, in particular the Viking incursions and the rebellions of the king's sons. The military superiority of the Franks, which lay behind their political domination of much of western Europe, was almost useless before the unpredictable hit-and-run tactics of the Vikings. Smaller local forces provided better defense than a larger but more central one, which could not move quickly enough to counterattack the Vikings or cut off their escape. And in the family quarrels and civil wars among the heirs of Louis the Pious, counts were among the powerful men inevitably drawn into the conflict and hence frequently placed in opposition to the monarch. In some of the most troubled years of the 840s no *missi dominici* are known to have gone on missions; by then even they were being chosen from among local magnates rather than from among notables of the royal court; shortly beyond the middle of the ninth century the office itself appears to have fallen into disuse.[37]

36. McKitterick, *Frankish Kingdoms*, pp. 87–88.
37. Werner, "*Missus-Marchio-Comes*," pp. 197–198; Lemarignier, *La France*, pp. 92–93.

In response to the need for a stronger unit larger than the too-small county but smaller than the unwieldy, unresponsive kingdom, first Louis the Pious and then Charles the Bald established regional commands, sometimes with the title duke (*dux*), in which groups of counties were entrusted to powerful individuals. A notable example of such a person is Robert the Strong (d. 866), ancestor of the Capetians, who at one time was count of Angers, Autun, Auxerre, Blois, Nevers, and Tours. This reduction in the number of persons directly subordinate to the king had the apparent intention of making royal control more efficient, but one of its effects was to provide the nuclei, some evident by the end of the ninth century, of large territorial principalities such as Burgundy and Flanders.[38]

Certain events of the year 877 reveal changes in attitudes toward the countship. King Charles the Bald agreed to go to Italy that year to assist the pope, whose territory was under attack by Saracens. In preparation for his departure, the king summoned his counts to an assembly at Quierzy-sur-Oise. In exchange for their continuing support, he granted that he would henceforth not govern without their counsel. Then the king decreed that in the case where a count died during this royal expedition to Italy, the late count's eldest son was to take over his father's duties until the king returned and appointed a new count. The final phrase of this decree indicates that the king still reserved the right to dispose of countships, whereas the first part of it seems to acknowledge the current expectation that countships were hereditary.[39]

The king departed and the magnates rebelled, but then it was the king who died in transit. His son Louis the Stammerer had to bargain to get his inheritance. The old system of election of the king by the magnates of the realm, an empty formality under the earlier Carolingians, was brought back to life. The monarchy was in the hands of the magnates. Four weak reigns followed in rapid succession. At the death of Charles the Fat in 888 without a legitimate heir the magnates elected one of their own, the count of Paris, Odo, son of Robert the Strong, who reigned as king of the west Franks for eleven years.

It is more than coincidence that this major step from hereditary to

38. Jan Dhondt, *Etude sur la naissance des principautés territoriales (IXe–Xe siècles)* (Bruges, 1948); *Institutions seigneuriales*, vol. 1 of *Histoire des institutions françaises au Moyen-Age*, ed. Ferdinand Lot and Robert Fawtier (Paris, 1957); McKitterick, *Frankish Kingdoms*, pp. 228–257.

39. Lemarignier, *La France*, p. 94.

elective kingship occurred in the same years when the heredity of the countship was replacing the king's free selection of counts. Since hereditary office in this period generally implied greater stability, this simultaneous transformation indicates a passing of relative stability from the level of the kingdom to that of the county. The breakup of the royal monopoly on minting and its devolution to counts in this same period is one more sign of such splintering of royal authority in the west Frankish kingdom. Another is seen in the history of documents emanating from the royal chancery: from 751 to 884, the Carolingian kings issued 275 capitularies. These were legislative acts, valid for the entire kingdom; their like was not to be seen again for over three centuries. What followed them were only ad hoc acts called diplomas, or what when issued by sources below the royal level are called charters.[40]

Although the election of a Robertian in 888 did not bring the Carolingian line to an end, it interrupted it for the first time since the accession of Charlemagne's father in 751 and thereby demonstrated that an alternative line existed. The Carolingians were restored in 898 and remained an active presence and force in the west Frankish kingdom for nearly a century more. But the electors turned to a Robertian in 922 and still another the following year. The dominant figure in the Robertian family and in the kingdom in the middle of the tenth century was Hugh the Great, who, though never king, took the title *dux Francorum*. When in another succession crisis in 987 the magnates turned to Hugh the Great's nephew, also named Hugh (and known to posterity as Hugh Capet), there was nothing startling or revolutionary about their choice. What did take place in the century between the election of Odo in 888 and that of Hugh Capet in 987 was the continued drain of royal prerogatives away from the monarchy and toward the counts and the territorial magnates and princes. There was a similar drain on royal wealth through the continued parceling out of land and the issuing of grants of immunity from taxes to ecclesiastical institutions.[41]

In the meantime attacks from the outside continued. The Saracen base established in Provence in 890 rendered much of the Rhône valley

40. Ibid., pp. 95–106.

41. Jean Dunbabin, *France in the Making, 843–1180* (Oxford, 1985), pp. 68, 133–140; Edward James, *The Origins of France: From Clovis to the Capetians, 500–1000* (London, 1982), pp. 183–187.

unstable. The Magyar raids on Laon in 919 and on Berry in 937 showed the heartland of Frankish power to be vulnerable as well. And the Viking menace remained along the coasts and in all the major river valleys of Francia.[42] In the presence of such real, but utterly unpredictable, threats and in the absence of an adequate royal system of defense, the royal monopoly on military fortification also slipped down the political chain of command. Of course the Crown itself ordered defensive fortifications built and authorized counts and viscounts and bishops to do the same. But castle building did not wait for royal initiative or approval in the tenth century, when an astonishing array of fortifications, many of them illegal, spread over the landscape. The powerful not only built fortifications but came henceforth to live in them. Castles in the tenth and early eleventh centuries were of the motte and bailey type, essentially wooden stockades, placed where possible on high ground, with a strong tower within and a moat and fence outside. Stone came into use for such constructions only later in the eleventh century. However constructed, castles were islands of security under the command of a castellan, where people and animals and precious belongings could be rushed to safe refuge in case of attack.[43]

The Carolingian military obligations under the ban permitted counts to call upon all free men to serve, either directly by bearing arms or indirectly by providing material or financial support. The large presence of foot soldiers in the Carolingian armies became outmoded, however, as improvements in armor weakened the effects of blows struck or weapons thrown by men on foot. Increasingly the kind of fighter believed almost exclusively useful was the mounted warrior, identified in tenth-century texts as a knight (*miles*). Many *milites* were originally recruited from modest social levels and supplied with horses and weapons. With such power they soon had occasion to accumulate wealth and, as a social group, to form a military aristocracy. Where once there had been a relatively small noble class of mounted warriors who in times of battle commanded

42. There were prayers *pro tribulatione* occasioned by all three groups of attackers; the anti-Viking version asked for deliverance "from the savage nation of the Northmen, which is devastating our realm." See Marc Bloch, *Feudal Society*, tr. L. A. Manyon (Chicago, 1968), p. 41.

43. Gabriel Fournier, *Le château dans la France médiévale: Essai de sociologie monumentale* (Paris, 1978), pp. 53–90.

large groups of free men summoned to perform their duty, there now began to form a larger nobility, based entirely on the function of fighting, over which they held a virtual monopoly. The patrimonies they passed along to their heirs included the instruments and symbols of their military might. In most of the Continental vernacular languages the term for *miles* acknowledged the horse (*cavallus*) as the defining characteristic of the new kind of fighter: *cavalarius*, *cavaliere*, *caballero*, *chevalier*, and so on. The corresponding German term *Ritter* refers indirectly to the horse by calling the knight a "rider," whereas the English word "knight" derives from a term for attendant or servant and thus evokes instead the social origins of this category. In the new political order of the late tenth century, the key unit of defense was the fortified place headed by a castellan with his garrison of *milites*, or knights.[44]

Through all the vicissitudes of the tenth century, it is astonishing that the fundamental unit of Carolingian justice, the *mallus* of the count, lasted as long as it did. But the centrifugal forces at work on the kingdom struck the county as well, and sooner or later during the half century around the year 1000, in several of the regions of Frankish territory county government collapsed. The process and timing differed from place to place, but eventually all the chipping away of regal authority—and of that comital authority that in theory and for long in practice was regal in origin—brought the Carolingian structure of the *pagus* to the breaking point. The count could not maintain order in his entire county. He could not compel every castellan to respect his authority or submit to the jurisdiction of his court. The effective unit of government (although "power" would be a more accurate term than "government") was the castle and the land surrounding it that the castellan and his knights could control. The ban was exercised by this lord of the castle over all those he could make subject to him; banal lordship was based solely on power. Some counts became little more than castellans themselves, and those who had control over a number of castles derived their power not from the comital title but, in each particular unit of land, from the control of the nearest castle. The territorial principalities that resisted these tendencies most successfully were Flanders and

44. P. Van Luyn, "Les *milites* dans la France au XIe siècle," *Le Moyen Age* 77 (1971): 5–51, 193–238.

Normandy, but their presence even in those areas confirms their general nature.[45]

The collapse of comital authority had grave consequences for social order. The strong, fortified place, originally conceived as a place of refuge for the defenseless under attack by outsiders, became instead a base of operations for a group of powerful local men who felt free to prey upon the people who lived on the lands outside it. This devolution of power to the castellany carried no trace of the notion of public authority associated with the rules of king and count (perhaps already largely dissipated over several generations of hereditary countship); similarly lacking in banal lordship was any vestige of the holy responsibility to maintain peace and justice conferred upon the king by anointment and delegated by him to his counts. Without such restraints as either public or sacred trust, the regime of the castellans often became little more than organized pillage, rule by the local gang leader and his henchmen. Political control, stripped of myth, theory, or abstract loyalties, was reduced to the immediate, physical presence of military power.[46]

Ecclesiastical institutions were especially sensitive to the social and political transformations taking place at the end of the tenth century. With the dissipation of so much royal authority, in particular the royal grants of immunity and privilege, churches lost their most important protector. And with the disabling of comital courts, an abbot confronted by troublemakers could no longer rely on the count to bring them to justice. The worldly interests of monasteries were sometimes entrusted to lay agents, called "advocates" in much of northern and east-central France, and in times of trouble an abbot should have been able to call upon his advocate for help. But the absence of reliable justice meant that a monastery lacked even ordinary recourse for disciplining a corrupt advocate, as for example at Fleury, where the monks complained that the ravages inflicted by their own advocate brought greater harm than the depredations of

45. Georges Duby, "The Evolution of Judicial Institutions: Burgundy in the Tenth and Eleventh Centuries," in his *The Chivalrous Society*, tr. Cynthia Postan (Berkeley, Calif., 1980), pp. 15–58; Jean-Pierre Poly and Eric Bournazel, *La mutation féodale, Xe–XIe siècles,* Nouvelle Clio 16 (Paris, 1980), pp. 81–103; Dunbabin, *France in the Making*, pp. 143–150.

46. Duby, *Early Growth of the European Economy*, p. 176, calls banal lordship "really a kind of legitimized and organized pillage"; James, *Origins of France*, p. 192, says that "castles were now centers not of government but of protection rackets"; and Dunbabin, *France in the Making*, pp. 146–147, refers in this context to protection rackets and extortion.

outsiders. In 1046 a lord named Gerard usurped the advocacy of some of the possessions of Saint-Eloi of Noyon. Since he remained indifferent to separate excommunications by two bishops, Abbot Remi and his monks opened all the reliquaries in their church and placed the bodies of the saints on the floor, "as if to make part of the injury done to the abbey fall upon them." The prayers said by the monks before these bodies were enough to make Gerard change his mind.[47] In one region after another, then, even though churchmen controlled the largest quantity of land, since they lacked the proper means to protect their lands, these lay exposed as easy prey. The potential for promiscuous pillaging of ecclesiastical properties was not lost on greedy, unrestrained knights.[48]

Even in such unpromising circumstances there were still courts that functioned. Landlords ran courts to which their semifree and bound dependents were required to respond. These landlords, who included new-style castellans as well as old-style Carolingian aristocrats, and bishops and abbots as well as secular lords, imposed an arbitrary justice, free of any higher court of appeals and tempered only by what the collective memory identified as custom. They used these private courts not as forums of equity but as sources of support for their habits of wasteful display. Moreover, the stakes in tightening control over dependents were on the increase as circumstances permitted landlords to organize agricultural production on their lands less exclusively for subsistence and more for the market.[49]

Meanwhile the courts run by counts and other magnates that did not collapse altogether evolved into voluntary tribunals of arbitration. Lords could not compel parties to attend them. Occasionally their deliberations led to judgments (*judicia*), but more often to compromise

47. Dunbabin, *France in the Making*, pp. 118–119; Lot and Fawtier, *Histoire des institutions françaises*, 1:15, 22, 365, 372–373. Fleury: *Recueil des chartes de l'abbaye de Saint-Benôit*, ed. Maurice Prou and Alexandre Vidier, 2 vols. (Paris, 1900–1932), 1:182–185. Noyon: *Annales OSB* 4:466–467 and, for a fuller account, MS, Paris, BN, lat. 12669, f. 72r–v.

48. Duby, *Three Orders*, pp. 151–152. Daniel F. Callahan, "William the Great and the Monasteries of Aquitaine," *Studia Monastica* 19 (1977): 326–327, observes that one-third of the developed land of Aquitaine was in ecclesiastical hands and remarks that "such ready prey" was "irresistible." For stimulating observations on the sacking of ecclesiastical property in a later historical context, see Carlo Ginzburg, "Saccheggi rituali: Premesse a una ricerca in corso," *Quarderni storici* 65 (August 1987): 615–636.

49. Duby, *Three Orders*, p. 152; Duby, *Early Growth of the European Economy*, pp. 168–180; Ronald G. Witt, "The Landlord and the Economic Revival of the Middle Ages in Northern Europe, 1000–1250," *American Historical Review* 76 (1971): 965–988.

settlements (*concordiae* or *conventiae*).[50] Still, Carolingian ideals of lordship persisted and were sporadically present in those lords who felt obliged to listen to the supplications of their inferiors and to respond to them with mercy (and to their persecutors with vengeance). This kind of justice, based not upon an impersonal body of law but rather upon a very personal model of lordship, had deeper roots and for that reason flourished more readily in the homeland of the Franks, north of the Loire. Farther south, where vestiges of Roman law were more common, relationships among the powerful were seen instead as horizontal agreements based upon a Roman contract between equals.[51]

From the late nineteenth century to the middle of the twentieth, historians of law—in reality mostly historians of legal institutions—saw only a void in France after the collapse of Carolingian public justice. The lack of what they considered to be proper judicial institutions and practices gave them a vision of eleventh- and twelfth-century French society as lawless and chaotic. "Feudal anarchy" was a standard phrase in their vocabulary. In more recent decades, historians of law have approached the same period not by looking for familiar institutions but by inquiring in the manner of ethnographers about how people in that society settled their disputes. Free from prejudgments about lawless societies, they have painstakingly gathered evidence and submitted it to analysis. Their findings fit patterns familiar to the field of legal anthropology, which has uncovered a large variety of options for settling disputes in traditional societies that lack strong states.[52]

Pioneering studies of the settlement of disputes in France between A.D. 1000 and 1200 have found that feuds and disputes over property were settled mainly by arbitration and compromise. The arbitrators were not judges and usually made no pretense of constituting a court, but they were friends or relatives—in any case close enough associates of the disputants to pressure them to be conciliatory and eventually to

---

50. Duby, "Evolution of Judicial Institutions," p. 23.

51. Elizabeth Magnou-Nortier, *La société laïque et l'église dans la province ecclésiastique de Narbonne (zone cispyrénéenne) de la fin du VIIIe à la fin du XIe siècle* (Toulouse, 1974), pp. 298–302; and Paul Ourliac, "La *convenientia*," in *Etudes d'histoire du droit privé offertes à P. Petot* (Paris, 1959), pp. 3–12.

52. For the historiographical development and also pertinent bibliography in legal anthropology, see Patrick Geary, "Vivre en conflit dans une France sans état: Typologie des méchanisms de règlemente des conflits (1050–1200)," *Annales, ESC* 41 (1986): 1107–1133. For examples in European history, see John Bossy, ed., *Disputes and Settlements: Law and Human Relations in the West* (New York, 1983), and Wendy Davies and Paul Fouracre, eds., *The Settlement of Disputes in Early Medieval Europe* (New York, 1986).

settle for a compromise. The gathering in which they met, sometimes called a *placitum*, which could mean something as informal as "discussion," had no set procedures. The arbitrators were in no position to test particular cases against generally accepted laws. Their purpose was nothing so abstract (or so grand) as to render justice, but was simply to find a way both parties could exit from the dispute with their honor intact and with part of the disputed object (the land or whatever).[53]

Communities were small, and opponents in a feud—like different parties who could plausibly lay claim to the same property—were not apt to be strangers to one another. In any property dispute, much more was at stake than the land, to mention only the honor, name, or community standing of the litigants. In such a setting, a judicial system that awarded everything to one party and left the other with nothing would have created a greater problem than it resolved. Besides the fact that there was no adequate police power for enforcing such a resolution, the very notion of a court's leaving a powerful local figure humiliated and empty-handed would have posed a threat to community stability. Hence, as matters usually did work out, an angry, perhaps indignant or insulted litigant would come under pressure from relatives, friends, or acquaintances to be calm and to be willing to treat. What these arbitrators were able to hold out as a likely result was not "victory" but undiminished status. In the early twelfth century, an Anglo-Norman writer on the law observed that judgments separate litigants, whereas agreements bring them together. He could have added that they have the same effect on whole communities. Moreover, according to the same author, an agreement supersedes the law, and amicable settlement a court judgment.[54]

Not only was a compromise settlement better than an all-or-nothing verdict, but even no settlement at all was better than such a verdict.

53. Fredric L. Cheyette, "*Suum cuique tribuere*," *French Historical Studies* 6 (1969–1970): 287–299; Stephen D. White, "*Pactum . . . Legem Vincit et Amor Judicium*: The Settlement of Disputes by Compromise in Eleventh-Century Western France," *American Journal of Legal History* 22 (1978): 281–308; on the prevalence of agreements over judgments, p. 292. On the meaning of *placitum*, see idem, "Inheritances and Legal Arguments in Western France, 1050–1150," *Traditio* 43 (1987): 55–103, at p. 68: "In fact our only reason for using the term 'court' at all in referring to the forum in which a dispute was settled is often based, not on evidence about the procedure used or the outcome reached, but simply on the fact that it is the term used by monastic scribes—even in cases where terms such as 'assembly' or 'gathering' seem to us more apt and where the term *placitum*, if the scribe used it, could best be glossed as 'discussion.' "
54. White, "*Pactum . . . Legem Vincit*," p. 308.

Some disputes dragged on for years and years, being passed along from one generation to the next as part of the patrimony. In many communities the norm was not peace occasionally disturbed by conflict, but conflict now and then heated up, now and then cooled down. The tension generated by conflict was not exclusively disruptive of community; in some instances it served as an element of cohesion.[55]

Ecclesiastics were fully involved in the affairs of their world, including this arbitration process that developed for resolving disputes. Bishoprics and monasteries were themselves landowners, and bishops and abbots covered the range from powerful magnates to petty castellans. Given these roles and the sizable endowments entrusted to them, their ways of acting in these capacities were not much different from those of their secular contemporaries. But their reactions to the rampaging of the *milites* did go beyond what most other landlords did. One of their most inventive (and best known) initiatives was to gather large assemblies of people and make them promise to uphold the peace. The precise techniques varied from one assembly to another, but the essential elements consisted of an initiative taken by bishops and abbots; a strong monastic presence; a very large, socially diverse popular presence; a massing of saints' relics; preaching about the crisis at hand, with an attempt to focus mass public disapproval upon the perpetrators of the crisis; the taking of oaths by those assembled to maintain the peace; and the launching of spiritual sanctions against transgressors of the peace.[56]

One of the first such gatherings took place at Charroux, about halfway between Poitiers and Limoges, in 989. A monk named Letald from the monastery of Saint-Mesmin, at Micy, near Orléans, wrote an account of the carrying of the body of Saint Junien from his monastery to this assembly. He explains that a group of bishops and abbots decided to gather together the bodies of many saints because of the cur-

---

55. Geary, "Vivre en conflit," pp. 1113–1118. See the example of Chorges in Provence (pp. 1110–1113), where conflict was endemic through the entire second half of the eleventh century and no settlement lasted long. Hardly fit for the tight organization of a thriller, this was the endless stuff of soap opera or saga.

56. Dieter Hägermann, "Der Abt als Grundherr: Kloster und Wirtschaft im frühen Mittelalter," in *Herrschaft und Kirche: Beiträge zur Entstehung und Wirkungsweise episkopaler und monastischer Organisationsformen*, ed. Friedrich Prinz (Stuttgart, 1988), pp. 345–385. Frederick S. Paxton, "History, Historians, and the Peace of God," in *The Peace of God: Social Violence and Religious Response in France around the Year 1000*, ed. Thomas Head and Richard A. Landes (Ithaca, N.Y., 1992), pp. 21–40.

rent intolerable devastation of the Lord's vineyard by sinful oppressors. He does not fail to mention that people were also present, but they were surely secondary to the saints. Indeed, as he put it, streams of people accompanying relics converged upon Charroux; they came from Poitiers, Limoges, and other places in the surrounding area.[57] The official text that remains from this council reports that three formal decrees were passed, all in the form of *si quis* clauses: if anyone breaks into a church or carries off anything from it by force, may he be anathema; if anyone plunders the sheep, oxen, donkeys, cows, goats, or pigs of agricultural laborers or other poor people, may he be anathema; and if anyone attacks a priest or deacon or any cleric who is unarmed, may he be anathema and be kept away from the threshold of the holy church of God. These decrees were repeated at a council (very different in composition, for both the popular element and the relics were missing) at Poitiers about 999.[58]

In the decade between Charroux and Poitiers, a gathering similar to that of Charroux took place at Limoges in 994. This gathering was called jointly by the bishop of Limoges and the abbot of Saint-Martial, and the immediate issue was an epidemic of Saint Anthony's fire (ergot poisoning) rather than war or peace; the latter issue was, however, not absent. A three-day fast was declared, during which relics were brought to Limoges from churches throughout the region. Waves of delegations arrived, their identities announced by the relics they accompanied into the city. The star performer was Saint Martial. Taken from his crypt and out of his church, the patron of Limoges was borne in procession to a hill outside the walls, a place henceforth known as the Mount of Rejoicing because of the joyous thrill felt by the crowds assembled there. Numerous miraculous cures marked the occasion. The epidemic subsided, and the duke of Aquitaine and a number of other princes swore to uphold a pact of peace and justice.[59]

This account of the gathering at Limoges matches in some particulars what Letald wrote about Charroux. As the work of Adémar of Chabannes, a monk of Saint-Martial, however, it was written more than

57. Letaldus Monachus, *Delatio corporis S. Juniani in synodum Karrofensem* (PL 137:823–826).
58. Charroux: Mansi 19:89–90; see appendix C, text 5, and *Peace of God*, ed. Head and Landes, pp. 327–328. Poitiers: Mansi 19:265–268.
59. *Chroniques de Saint-Martial de Limoges*, ed. Henri Duplès-Agier (Paris, 1874), p. 6; Léopold Delisle, "Notices sur les manuscrits originaux d'Adémar de Chabannes," *Notices et extraits des manuscrits de la Bibliothèque Nationale* 35 (1896): 290.

three decades after the event. Adémar lived between approximately 989 and 1034; despite his family's strong ties with Saint-Martial, his monastic career had started at Saint-Cybard in Angoulême, but he eventually came to associate himself totally with the Abbey of Saint-Martial. He was both a prolific historian and a capable liturgist, and he placed these skills entirely at the service of his adopted monastery. He became obsessed with the idea that Saint Martial had been one of the apostles, to the point where his writings were saturated with an intense partisanship in the cause of establishing the saint's apostolicity; thus his writings, though always interesting for the insights they give into his mind and world, cannot be relied on for the accuracy of what they report. What Adémar says took place at the Council of Limoges in 994 is that the prelates called upon everyone to observe peace and justice and then promised that once violent plundering and the oppression of the poor had been suppressed, enduring peace would settle in Aquitaine. And Adémar says that the prelates equated those who persisted in upsetting the peace with traitors and urged that they be driven away from the company of faithful Christians.[60] Adémar propagated a recently composed life of Saint Martial, perhaps even adding a few touches of his own—a life that made Martial into a younger contemporary of Jesus, sent personally by Peter on his apostolic mission to Gaul. And in his sermons, where Martial becomes a heavenly patron of peace itself, Adémar urged that the saint's life be read to congregations.[61]

The bishop who cosponsored the Council of Limoges in 994, Alduin (994–1014), was also one of the earliest prelates to institute the practice of interdict, a kind of liturgical strike intended initially to annoy the faithful but ultimately to channel that annoyance into community hostility toward those who were disturbing the peace. Adémar calls it a "new practice" (*novam observantiam*) and identifies precisely the root causes and new modalities: "In order to punish the rapine of the *milites* and the devastation of the poor, he had all monasteries and churches cease from the divine cult."[62]

60. Richard A. Landes, "Between Aristocracy and Heresy: Popular Participation in the Limousin Peace of God, 994–1033," in *Peace of God*, ed. Head and Landes, pp. 184–190.

61. Ibid., pp. 191–194; Daniel F. Callahan, "The Sermons of Adémar of Chabannes and the Cult of St. Martial of Limoges," *Revue Bénéndictine* 86 (1976): 251–295; and idem, "Adémar de Chabannes et la paix de Dieu," *Annales du Midi* 89 (1977): 21–43.

62. Landes, "Between Aristocracy and Heresy," in *Peace of God*, ed. Head and Landes, p. 196.

Another council at Limoges, in 1031, was the occasion of a long report by Adémar that included his claim that those in attendance favored his thesis that Martial had been an apostle. In this instance the time of his writing was very close to the events described. The text includes a full discussion of the problems posed by the peacebreakers and what should be done about them. Again there was discussion of the use of interdict, with the abbot of Limoges giving advice about the specific forms to follow: the entire land of Limoges was to be bound by public excommunication, in such a way that no one could be buried there or carried to another diocese for burial. "At about the third hour let the bells ring out in all churches, and with all lying prone face down, let them say prayers on account of troubles and for peace . . . then let the altars in all the churches be stripped clean." The crosses and ornaments were to be put away, as a sign to all of mourning and sadness.[63] The council went right to the heart of the matter of the revolution of the *milites*, by cursing first them (*excommunicamus illos milites . . . maledicti ipsi*) and then their weapons and horses (*maledicta arma eorum et caballi eorum*), at once the symbols and the instruments of their oppressive power.[64]

From these beginnings in Aquitaine the idea of holding peace assemblies spread to Burgundy and Flanders and other regions of Francia, picking up the strong endorsement of the leaders of some of the territorial principalities. In Flanders the impetus for propagating this practice came from Count Baldwin IV. The first declaration concerning peace was made at Douai by Bishop Gerard of Cambrai in 1024. Gerard was not an enthusiastic supporter of the peace assemblies, because of the danger he saw in amassing laypeople in such a way, yet he was apparently responding to pressure from the count.[65]

It is thus in the same half century (between approximately 980 and 1030), the one that historians identify as marking the ultimate devolution of political authority, that prelates and then princes took the initiative to foster social cohesion with religious enthusiasm and to punish with spiritual sanctions those who persisted in violating the

63. Mansi 19:541–542; see appendix C, text 10.

64. Ibid., col. 530. On the council held in 1031 at Bourges as well as the one at Limoges, see Guy Devailly, *Le Berry du Xe siècle au milieu du XIIIe* (Paris, 1973), pp. 142–146.

65. Geoffrey Koziol, "Monks, Feuds, and the Making of Peace in Eleventh-Century Flanders," in *Peace of God*, ed. Head and Landes, p. 239. Also in 990 the bishops assembled in council at Anse confirmed to the monks of Cluny the privilege of imposing excommunication and anathema; Mansi 19:99–100.

social order. Moreover, the earliest known texts of the liturgical clamor as well as the earliest known uses of it fall within precisely the same period. The clamors and the peace gatherings have in common the following key elements: the presence of a large gathering of laypeople; the building of a sense of community among these people centered on the cult of the patron saint; preaching that stressed both the positive aspects of this relic-centered community and the obviously negative aspects of the violent attacks against it; and then the dramatic gestures that acted out the troubled history of the community, including the expulsion and utter exclusion from further contact of those who were considered its enemies.[66]

Peace assemblies were thus cut from the same cloth as the clamors. Their uses were different: a clamor was put into use in a particular church at the time of a particular provocation, whereas a peace assembly was intended to deal with the general problem affecting a whole region over an extended period. But this distinction should not be made brittle by an overly legalistic definition, for there is a most significant middle ground between the two. At councils held in Flanders at Lillebonne, Douai, Thérouanne, and Laon, the assembled bishops ordered the following: that on Sundays and feast days all the priests in those respective dioceses bless in their prayers those who uphold the peace and curse those who violate it.[67] In many different regions, ceremonies and explanatory sermons as well were used to make frequent and regular reaffirmations of the commitments to peace undertaken in the greater assemblies.[68]

In any given instance where the peace was menaced or violated, what happened subsequently depended mainly on the presence and disposition of some higher authority. As we saw earlier, the monks of Holy Trinity at Vendôme, when in trouble in 1074, did not spurn re-

---

66. Some of the most potent of maledictory formulas followed the peace assemblies on a southern trajectory. In about 1040 Abbot Odilo of Cluny, along with the bishops of Arles, Nice, and Avignon, sent a letter about the Truce of God, including formulas, to northern Italian clerics; these in turn published a similar document not long afterward. The texts are found in *MGH, Const.* 1:596–598; see appendix C, text 11. For a version from still farther south, see Roger E. Reynolds, "Odilo and the *Treuga Dei* in Southern Italy: A Beneventan Manuscript Fragment," *Mediaeval Studies* 46 (1984): 450–462.

67. Koziol, "Monks, Feuds, and the Making of Peace," p. 257: "Presbiteris autem precipimus ut in festivitatibus ac diebus dominicis qui hanc pacem observaverint pro illis preces agendo benedicant. Illos vero qui infregerint aut qui infractoribus concesserint maledicant."

68. Ibid., pp. 255–257.

course to the law but made a clamor against the count of Anjou because he was "the very one," in their view, "who ought to acquire justice for them."[69] And the monks of the Abbey of Marchiennes, when threatened by a knight in the 1120s, used both a "horrendous anathema" against the knight and a complaint about him to Count Charles the Good. The count held the knight in check, and although the monks still felt threatened, they were safe. But when the count was assassinated in 1127, chaos (in the person of that knight among many others) was let loose upon the land, and the monks were left to rely upon their daily clamor to Saint Richtrude.[70] On a more modest social level, the story of the relics of Saint Ursmer being humiliated to keep a lord from capturing and punishing a murderer began with a simple quarrel between two knights. Push came to shove, and their lord, Hugh, intervened to avoid bloodshed and stage a public reconciliation. But just as soon as Hugh went away, one of the knights murdered the other.[71] The immediate presence of superior power was the law the *milites* understood best.

Another test would be to see what happened when a lord returned home after a lengthy absence. In the early decades of the twelfth century, the monks of Morigny (near Etampes, in the diocese of Sens) seem to have had their fill of troubles with predators. Of all their enemies the worst, according to the *Chronicle of Morigny*, was a knight named Bovard, a man said to be without spiritual values. He and his men invaded some of the monastery's possessions, burning down buildings and killing the farm animals. Bovard lived on land held by Guy, the lord of Rochefort, but because Guy was away in the Holy Land, there was no hope, lamented the *Chronicle*, of bringing Bovard to justice. Bovard became ever more insane in his behavior and threats until the day when, quite unexpectedly, word came that Guy was about to arrive back from Jerusalem. The abbot hastened to meet him on the way, greet him with the customary kiss, and persuade him to be his guest. The lord and his retinue plus all those from his castles who had rushed to greet him were received with great honor and care. The abbot discreetly refrained from mentioning the problem that weighed on his mind.

69. *Cartulaire de l'abbaye de la Trinité de Vendôme*, ed. Charles Metais, 5 vols. (Paris, 1893–1904), 1:386–390.
70. *Miracula Sanctae Rictrudis* (*AASS*, Maii 3:104–105).
71. *Miracula Sancti Ursmari in itinere per Flandriam facta*, ch. 6 (*MGH, SS* 15, pt. 2:839).

But the next day, which was a Sunday, they went in procession to-gether to the Church of Saint-Arnoult at Iveline. After the church serv-ice, Guy held an audience for the several people who had come to see him with problems, and there and then the abbot made a clamor to him concerning Bovard (*abbas de Bovardo clamorem fecit*). The very next day, at Rochefort, Bovard was brought to justice before the lord; also present was the lord's brother-in-law, also named Guy, who was the viscount of Etampes. The abbot gained full satisfaction, for Bovard and his people ceased their lawless behavior and undertook not to disturb the monastery again. The turning point in this account is obviously the reappearance of the local lord after a long absence and the abbot's making a clamor to Guy and not to the monastery's patron saint. Not least noteworthy is that Guy's justice was remarkably swift.[72]

The availability or lack of justice thus had everything to do with the deployment of the liturgical clamor. To understand why and how and to what effect prayers of tribulation or liturgical maledictions or relic humiliations were put into play in particular situations, we must look closely at the immediate circumstances of place and time. The presence or absence of even one key figure could explain everything. While on a general level it was the collapse of the system of Carolingian public justice that spurred the resort to liturgy as an instrument of social or-der, clamors were used in areas that were not altogether lacking in responsible lords or mechanisms for resolving disputes. In fact, in those areas where the clamor did appear—almost exclusively north of the Loire—it was not necessarily used in isolation but often occurred be-fore, or after, or instead of, or even simultaneously with similarly structured clamors to earthly authorities. And since in these same areas there was also, we need to recall, a strong tradition of lordly justice, their inhabitants had expectations of efficacious replies (combining the right mixture of mercy and vengeance) to their supplications. It was not a total lack of any kind of authority, and certainly not the anarchy seen by several generations of historians, but the temporary failure of responsible authorities (including saints) to reply, for whatever rea-son—and we have noted such motives as complicity in the wrongdo-

---

72. *La chronique de Morigny*, 2:11 (ed. Mirot, pp. 40–41). There remains a disturbing discordance between the hostile rhetoric used in the initial description of Bovard and the utterly tame language of the settlement arranged at the climactic gathering of the two parties in the presence of authorities. This discordance will reclaim our attention in the following section.

ing, absence on pilgrimage, sleep, and assassination—that brought out the clamor.[73]

The collapse of public justice and its replacement by the combination of this quite personal justice of the seigneurs with the practice of arbitration were unique to the western and north-central parts of the old Carolingian empire. The internal conflicts within the dynasty plus the devastating impact of the Moslem, Magyar, but especially Viking incursions had so dispersed central authority and so militarized the landscape that only sporadically could the *milites* be restrained from plundering the unarmed, undefended *pauperes*. No such devolution of authority took place in the British Isles, in German territories, or in either the Italian or the Iberian Peninsula. And neither did liturgies of tribulation such as the clamor or large public peace assemblies come into use in those lands. The social and political transformation of Francia between 980 and 1030 was accompanied in ecclesiastical communities by the organized and frequent application of spiritual sanctions against oppressors.

Property

That ecclesiastical institutions faced obstacles in bringing their adversaries to justice does not mean that those adversaries were always guilty, or even as malicious as the sources make them out to be. The available sources, it is important to keep in mind, are almost exclusively ecclesiastical, yet they occasionally contain information that supports the monks' adversaries. Even Goscelin, the duke whom the monks of Saint-Médard considered "untouched by the fear of God"— the one we earlier saw beaten up by three saints in a dream—had after all received from the king the property that was at the basis of the dispute.

Readers will detect a familiar ring in the story told by the monks of Cluny about the strongman Walter of Berzé, whose castle allowed him to dominate the road between Cluny and Mâcon. Denounced as a fearless and reckless instigator of evil schemes, this castellan was said to lay waste ferociously the lands and vineyards of Saint Peter—meaning of course Cluny, situated at Berzé—causing extensive damage and destruction. The monks warned him, but whether they put their spiritual

73. Cf. Barbara H. Rosenwein, Thomas Head, and Sharon Farmer, "Monks and Their Enemies: A Comparative Approach," *Speculum* 66 (1991): 764–796.

weapons to work against him, the sources do not say. It appears altogether likely that they did, but in any event he came forward in 1050
to renounce all claims to the lands he had disturbed. The ceremony
marking this quitclaim dramatized the reversal of Walter's attitude, for
the once proud warrior now knelt humbly before the relics of Saint
Peter and the abbot of Cluny. He swore an oath of loyalty to the saint
and commended his two young sons to the abbot, promising that they
would one day take the same oath.[74]

The mechanism by which this dispute between the monastery and
the castellan was settled is not spelled out, but Walter's quitclaim includes his acknowledgment that the land in question had already been
held peacefully by the Abbey of Cluny in his father's time. The categories of right and wrong or victim and oppressor thus seem clearly
defined, and yet one concluding detail obscures this clarity: the monks
awarded Walter three hundred solidi (fifteen pounds). Why did they
do this? The sources offer no direct answer, leaving little to go on
except the obvious disjuncture between, on the one hand, Walter's violent behavior and the monks' uncompromising Old Testament rhetoric of condemnation and, on the other, this rather matter-of-fact
monetary settlement between the two parties. The intervening change
of attitude suggests at least partial acknowledgment by the monks that
there was something to Walter's claim.

To pursue this matter further, we need to reopen and supply more
information about the case of Bovard, the notorious oppressor of the
Abbey of Morigny, and Guy, the lord of Rochefort, whose return from
the Holy Land brought an abrupt end to Bovard's depredations, followed by his peaceful reconciliation with the monks. It turns out that
Bovard was the son-in-law of the founder and chief patron of the monastery, a lord named Ansell. The founder's son Garsadon, when preparing to go to the Holy Land, made a conditional donation to Morigny
of a place called Guemarvilla, the condition being that if he were to
die while on his pilgrimage (the text says "while on God's road"), the
monks would simply redeem the villa from the persons holding it in
trust. Garsadon did die in the East and the monks got the villa, but
members of his family—his mother Adelaide to begin with—raised
objections and then obstacles to the monks' keeping it.

---

74. *Recueil des chartes de l'abbaye de Cluny,* ed. Auguste Bernard and Alexandre Bruel,
6 vols. (Paris, 1876–1903), 4:417–418.

Adelaide was the wife of the founder and was once considered a leading benefactress of the monastery; now as an opponent she suffered a miraculous foot injury that made walking difficult for the rest of her life. The next family member to intervene was Stephen, the husband of a granddaughter of Adelaide, whom the *Chronicle of Morigny* calls a most powerful man with a great talent for evil. This man swore he would never permit the monks to make the villa their own. There seemed no way to appease him, according to the monks, but then he was struck dead by divine justice before many witnesses; the account does not say whether anyone had solicited either Adelaide's foot injury or Stephen's ultimate "justice." But then came forward Bovard, whom the monks considered the worst of the lot (only now do we understand that the lot of which he was the worst was the founder's family). There follows in the chronicle the account of Bovard's depredations during the absence of Guy of Rochefort and of the rapid settlement that took place upon Guy's return.

When that showdown was held in the presence of the two Guys, Bovard, accompanied by his wife (a daughter of the founder) and sons, promised to put an end to the lawbreaking he had engaged in, and he conceded all those things that Garsadon and his father had given to the monks. It still took considerable effort by the monks, including a payment of over seventy pounds to Bovard, to quash all other claims to the villa and gain unimpeded possession.[75]

Once again a monastery is seen to have made a money payment to the very person whom a short while before the monks had been calling their worst enemy. Moreover, as with Walter of Berzé, there turns out to have been a long-standing personal connection between the family of the "malefactor" and the monastery, a connection that was likely to continue in the future, since at the gathering held to work out and agree upon a settlement, again in each case, the strongman's sons were present and were committed to upholding that settlement.

Close investigation of large numbers of charters shows other apparent anomalies besides money payments to former "predators"—practices that, whether anomalous or not, could not emerge from studies of individual charters only. Seen in the aggregate, however, and over the long haul, the more than five thousand extant charters of the Abbey of Cluny have revealed to one scholar the fate of particular properties,

75. *La chronique de Morigny*, 2:11 (ed. Mirot, pp. 40–41).

allowing her to note how, for example, certain of them appear to have been donated several times over. In addition, some pieces of property appear to have moved back and forth between "donors" and monasteries. The apparently repeated donations were mostly reconfirmations by heirs of original donors, but in some cases they were restitutions that followed hostile seizures; the apparent transfers of property from monasteries to "donors" were part of a complex web of social relations in which gifts and favors were constantly in circulation.[76]

Further evidence of such practices and of their nature emerges from the systematic examination of that part of a charter called *laudatio parentum*, which means "approval of relatives." A majority of donation charters issued between A.D. 1000 and 1200 included such approval, by which potential heirs and other interested relatives gave their consent to the declared intention of a donor to transfer a certain property to a religious institution. There is no indication that donors had to secure such consent, but doing so was apparently the norm.[77]

Participating relatives did more than just sign a document, because a transfer of considerable size and value called for some kind of ceremony to mark the occasion. Carolingian law specified that the donor sign the charter containing terms of the donation and then place it on the altar of the receiving church.[78] A meal or reception usually followed in either the monastery or the donor's house—in any case a ceremony at which the consenting relatives were present. Donations also sometimes needed to be confirmed, basically whenever the original circumstances changed substantially, as when a donor died and the principal heir gave assurance that he did not intend to contest or otherwise disturb his father's donation. Confirmation called for another document and another ceremony. In any group of charters all referring to the same donated property, the list of consenting relatives is never the same twice. The variations are bewildering, and we generally lack suf-

76. Barbara H. Rosenwein, *To Be the Neighbor of Saint Peter: The Social Meaning of Cluny's Property, 909–1049* (Ithaca, N.Y., 1989), pp. 59–74, 122–125.

77. Stephen D. White, *Custom, Kinship, and Gifts to Saints: The "Laudatio Parentum" in Western France, 1050–1150* (Chapel Hill, N.C., 1988); on p. 12, White says this practice was "generally similar throughout France and in other parts of Europe." For Picardy, see Robert Fossier, *La terre et les hommes en Picardie jusqu'à la fin du XIIIe siècle*, 2 vols. (Paris, 1968), 1:262–266. For Burgundy, see Constance B. Bouchard, *Cistercians, Knights, and Economic Exchange in Twelfth-Century Burgundy* (Ithaca, N.Y., 1991), pp. 79–87.

78. *MGH, LNG* 5:64. For an example of a donation charter that refers to this act, see White, "Feuding and Peace-Making in the Touraine around the Year 1100," *Traditio* 42 (1986): 242.

ficient information on donors' families to untangle them. One pattern that does emerge and carry conviction stems from the observation that a male donor's brothers and sons virtually never appear in the same list of consenting relatives; in this case it seems that an unmarried male donor got his brothers to sign, whereas the same donor, at a later stage of his life, got his sons to sign.[79]

In keeping with behavior characteristic of a gift-exchange economy, a donation usually led to a gift in response. To be sure, the most valued commodity that monks had was prayer (another was the right to a monastic burial), and the basic transaction involving these donations was indeed an exchange of land for prayers. Stephen the cleric left a manse and half of a church along with revenues to the monastery of Vierzon, the agreement being that if he wished to become a monk the monks would accept him, and that in any case when he died they would bury him and pray for him.[80] The Lady Ansgarde, being ill in 998, also donated land to the monks of Saint-Peter of Vierzon. They in turn granted that her husband Hatton and their daughter Ada could enjoy the income from that land while they lived. And these two undertook to make an annual payment of three shillings to the monastery on 29 June, the feast of Saints Peter and Paul.[81] Cluny's records show that about 978 the monastery transferred temporary control of thirteen villas to Leutbald, a well-connected cleric (and future bishop of Mâcon), a transfer that seems really to be a reverse donation. But the properties in question had been given to Cluny in the first place by Leutbald's father, uncle, and another relative. Now the monastery was giving them to Leutbald as a life estate, meaning that when he died they would revert to the monastery.[82] When Eldinus gave a vineyard to Cluny in 989, he received a somewhat smaller vineyard in return. The transaction was principally a consolidation of holdings to the mutual benefit of two proprietors, who were also neighbors.[83] The ceremony marking a donation was also the occasion for the recipient to make an immediate material countergift, such as a book or a knife or some coins. Thus, on a ceremonial level as well, the monastery ac-

---

79. White, *Custom, Kinship, and Gifts to Saints*, p. 107.
80. *Cartulaire de l'abbaye de Saint-Pierre de Vierzon*, ed. Guy Devailly (Paris, 1963), p. 183.
81. Ibid., pp. 128–130.
82. Rosenwein, *To Be the Neighbor of Saint Peter*, pp. 117, 120.
83. Ibid., pp. 80–81.

knowledged its debt to its benefactors with suggestive if not commensurate gifts.[84]

In thousands upon thousands of instances, with their many variations, individuals and kin groups, in making donations to religious communities, established or reinforced social ties with those communities. Giving was not alienation; it was neither definitive nor, as we have just seen, one-way; it did not provide closure. On the contrary, giving was an eminently social gesture; it was opening, forward-looking, and constructive. Property transactions worked as a sort of social adhesive, and as such they called for repair from time to time and complete renovation at longer intervals.[85] A donor would give some land to a monastery but retain some use or income from part of it while he lived. The monastery might grant him confraternal status in return, meaning that he would receive all the spiritual benefits normally accorded the monks of that community. The family name would be regularly recalled in the monks' special prayers for their benefactors. When the donor died, he would be buried by the monks, and his eldest son would reconfirm the donation. The monastery might give a portion of the original donation as a life estate to a surviving family member. A younger son might meanwhile be received into the religious community as a novice, by which act two families would be joined: that of the donor together with the monastic *familia*. And so it could go through several generations. It is not difficult to see how such a family could feel possessive about that monastery, much as some modern patrons regard the universities, museums, opera companies, or orchestras they support.

But family disagreements are notorious, particularly where property is concerned. Over a third of all donation charters lack an endorsement by relatives, and since lists of assenting relatives include on average only three names, they virtually all excluded some potentially dissenting relative. And then those who did sign could claim that they were coerced or did not fully understand what they were agreeing to, or that the recipients had not kept the terms of the agreement.[86] But overshadowing all such immediate pretexts was a more general, long-term prob-

84. White, *Custom, Kinship, and Gifts to Saints*, pp. 166–167.

85. Eric John, "*Secularium Prioratus* and the Rule of St. Benedict," *Revue Bénédictine* 75 (1965): 212–239; Rosenwein, *To Be the Neighbor of Saint Peter*, p. 202, uses the term "social glue."

86. White, *Custom, Kinship, and Gifts to Saints*, p. 51.

lem. The generosity of landlords to religious foundations, which reached its high point in the years around 1000, together with the enduring Germanic custom of dividing the patrimony of a deceased lord among all his offspring, ran counter to the efforts of landlords bent on enlarging their holdings and rendering them more productive.[87] The ways they confronted these issues led eventually to changes that far transcended the immediate problems, to mention only the development of primogeniture and the sacralization of marriage. But on a less grandiose level, landlords exploited their ties of kinship and whatever influence they could muster to obtain compensatory grants out of ecclesiastical property from the heads of religious houses. And consistent with their own interests, the latter were willing to bestow on their kinsmen and friends the use of some of the land that had been offered to the patron saints of their churches. Right through the twelfth century landlords of course continued to make pious benefactions, but one could reasonably ask whether what some of these gave to religious foundations was as much as they in turn received from those foundations.[88]

More basic still were problems arising from the very nature of property and of donations, an area where it would be particularly misleading to project modern notions. In the absence of a strong state, and with the moribund condition of Roman property law, the norms governing land were basically those of the late Roman and early Germanic periods. The relevant consequences of this included the lack of any absolute dominion and hence the impossibility of transmitting dominion with a gift of land. Besides, a donor could not impose his will through time upon his kin and heirs.[89] In addition, it was standard practice for there to be overlapping claims on a terrain. Often the *lau-*

---

87. See the lament of Guibert of Nogent: "Those gifts that their parents . . . made to the holy places, the sons now withdraw entirely or continually demand payment for their renewal, having utterly degenerated from the good will of their sires," in *Self and Society in Medieval France: The Memoirs of Abbot Guibert of Nogent (1064?–c. 1125)*, ed. and tr. John F. Benton (New York, 1970), p. 63, cited by White, *Custom, Kinship, and Gifts to Saints*, p. 52.

88. Duby, *Early Growth of the European Economy*, pp. 169–171; "Cartularies of religious houses leave an impression that members of the aristocracy in the twelfth century sometimes gave away less than they reclaimed doggedly from the benefactions of their ancestors."

89. Ernst Levy, *West Roman Vulgar Law: The Law of Property*, Memoirs of the American Philosophical Society 29 (Philadelphia, 1929), pp. 167–168; White, *Custom, Kinship, and Gifts to Saints*, pp. 53, 174.

datio in a charter included the landlord from whom the donor held the land he was seeking to alienate. Here again we must stress that in giving a gift of land, the donor did not so much release a possession to another party as create or strengthen a tie with that party. The economic aspect of the transaction is not to be denied, but importance must be attached to its social and symbolic significance as well.[90]

For the various motives suggested here, in addition to the tempting attractiveness of extensive and unprotected properties of ecclesiastical institutions, challenges (*calumniae*) were born. That is, if no friendly deal was worked out at the start, a claimant could launch a challenge in various ways, such as (at some places and times) going to court, arranging a battle or an ordeal, or calling on influential friends to intervene on his behalf. But we have seen how unreliable courts were. And though trials by battle and ordeal were much talked about, they were very infrequently arranged and usually had long delays built into them. Moreover, of those arranged only very few were carried out, and when one actually did take place, the significance of its outcome was open to dispute.[91] The knights we have seen—the likes of Walter of Berzé, Bovard, and Stephen—all began by invading and taking possession of what they wanted. Instead of trying to achieve their goal by several different ways and, once these were exhausted, resorting at last to violence, these *milites*, as one would expect of people who lived by the sword, acted first and talked later. Violence was their preferred first step, which legal tradition qualified as *vindicatio*, meaning the extrajudicial seizure of property by self-help.[92] The compensation given challengers in compromise settlements sometimes explicitly includes forgiveness of debts they owed the monastery for damages they inflicted at the outset in pressing their claims.[93] If this initial violent action

90. Rosenwein, *To Be the Neighbor of Saint Peter*, p. xii, and Aron Gurevich, "Représentations et attitudes à l'égard de la propriété pendant le Haut Moyen Age," *Annales ESC* 27 (1972): 523–547. See also Chris Wickham, "Vendite di terra e mercato della terra in Toscana nel secolo XI," *Quaderni storici*, no. 65 (1987): 355–377; the author cautions against construing a land market where (in eleventh-century Italy and thirteenth-century England) one finds the earliest evidence of land sales, which, he says: "always formed part of a wider set of social strategies, their purpose less simple personal enrichment than the construction of social relationships, clienteles, and factions, as often outside the village as inside."

91. White, "Inheritances and Legal Arguments," p. 97, and the same author's *Custom, Kinship, and Gifts to Saints*, pp. 51, 72.

92. Levy, *West Roman Vulgar Law*, pp. 209–219.

93. White, "Pactum . . . Legem Vincit," p. 296.

developed into an enduring military engagement, just as in cases of disputes between secular lords the term used was *guerra*, meaning private war, as distinguished from the more general term for war, *bellum*. *Guerrae*, like self-help, had very limited aims; they were intended mainly as acts of restrained if not ritual aggression for the purpose of forcing the adversary to make a deal.[94] Thus the standard pattern that emerges from studies of *calumniae* undertaken in several regions was that self-help came first, to be followed by the intervention of some friendly and perhaps interested parties in search of a compromise settlement.[95]

Given all that has been said about ties between kin groups and religious foundations lasting through multiple generations, the notion of self-help as a "first step" should be understood as the first step in a particular episode, perhaps preceded by many other episodes involving give and take. It is the same with the compromise settlement, which was most likely not a "final step," settling for all time the connections between a family and a monastery, but rather the act that closed an episode. There were no long-range guarantees about the disposition of property and, again, no legally sure ways for a donor to bind his heirs to respect his will in the future.[96]

Where, then, do clamors fit into the pattern of *calumniae*? The standard monastic complaint is that certain evil men are attacking the monks' lands, laying them waste and robbing them of what they need to serve the saint and care for the poor. Having pleaded in vain with the attackers to cease their belligerence, and there being no sign of an imminent peacemaking initiative, the monks then proceed to the denunciation and liturgical cursing of their adversaries. The clamor was the monastic response to the warrior's self-help.

The contrast between the extreme rhetoric of malediction and the matter-of-fact tone of the settlement can thus be understood as the monastic parallel to a similarly sharp contrast, that between the knight's violent self-help and his ready acceptance of the settlement. These contrasts should not be thought of as a kind of political or diplomatic negotiation where calculation of self-interest, cynicism, and sometimes ideology govern alliances and changes in alliances. Of

94. John W. Baldwin, *The Government of Philip Augustus: Foundations of French Royal Power in the Middle Ages*, pp. 214–215; and Geary, "Vivre en conflit," p. 1118.

95. White, "Pactum . . . Legem Vincit," p. 293.

96. White, *Custom, Kinship, and Gifts to Saints*, pp. 196–200.

course we cannot analyze the inner workings of each party involved in a dispute in the eleventh century, but we do have clear indications that interpersonal relations—in particular within the warrior class, which supplied monks as well as fighters—were heavily invested with affect and thus highly volatile. From the history of Gregory of Tours in the sixth century to the epic poem of Raoul of Cambrai in the twelfth, there are chilling scenes in which convivial banquets are transformed by a single unfriendly word into horrendous displays of verbal and physical violence. Lifelong friends suddenly become bitter foes, while in other settings mortal enemies just as suddenly become companions in arms.Warrior societies in general—and this particular one is no exception—do not regard temperate, considerate behavior as virtuous or see comprehension of and tolerance for others' points of view as praiseworthy.[97]

What these warriors cared about was honor. Their monastic brothers and cousins engaged in lifelong struggles to supplant pride with humility, but for warriors there were no such restraints.[98] When they violated honor or regarded theirs as violated, there was trouble. When dishonored they felt shame, a standard catalyst of violence. But there was no shame in invading a monastery, no shame in killing an adversary, no shame in switching sides. There had to be reasons for any such actions, but these were easy to find, especially in the good counsel of trusted companions. There was shame instead in being put down by peers or in the view of peers.[99]

Accepting a compromise settlement at the conclusion of a dispute was a particularly honorable act. There had to be something for everyone, and no loss of face for anyone. To achieve such settlements was the task of the arbitrators, whose principal qualification was not knowledge of some body of abstract law but personal acquaintance with the parties to the dispute. Just as when the warrior's attack disrupted the

97. On the murderous and then warm and friendly and once again murderous relationship between the Frankish warriors Sichar and Chramnesind: Gregory of Tours, *Historia Francorum*, 9:19 (*MGH, SRM* 1:501–502); on the enmity and then alliance between two knights, Gautier and Bernier: *Histoire de Raoul de Cambrai et de Bernier, le bon chevalier*, chs. 231–241, tr. R. Berger and F. Suard, Trésors littéraires médiévaux du nord de la France 2 (Troesnes, 1986), pp. 148–156; George F. Jones, *The Ethos of the Song of Roland* (Baltimore, 1963), pp. 36–42.

98. Lester K. Little, "Pride Goes before Avarice: Social Change and the Vices in Latin Christendom," *American Historical Review* 76 (1971): 16–49.

99. Cheyette, "*Suum cuique tribuere*," pp. 294–295.

peace of the community (the monastery, its benefactors, and its neighbors) in the first place and the liturgical response of the religious ab-
stracted and acted out that disruption, so now when an agreement was
reached and peace restored, there was again a liturgical celebration of
the community's reintegration. Joy and friendship immediately took
the place of hostility. The document or some object symbolic of the
agreement was placed on the altar; psalms of rejoicing were sung; and
the reunited parties kissed and shared a meal.[100]

In light of the fragile structure of this community, we need to return
one more time to the sanction clauses of charters, which spell out the
punishment for those who, in the future, might violate the agreement
recorded in those documents. As I noted earlier, such clauses almost
invariably begin with the phrase *si quis* ("if anyone"). Most charters
do not bother to identify potential violators more specifically than that,
but the ones that do are most revealing. In 974 Adèle, countess of
Anjou, made a bequest to Saint-Aubin of Angers; the sanction clause
of the charter drawn up for the occasion begins, "If anyone from
among my relatives or friends . . . if my son or my daughter is tempted
to go against this donation."[101] In the Lady Ansgarde's donation to
Vierzon in 998, the sanction clause says, "If anyone rises up at the
instigation of the devil, a relative or a son or grandson, or a neighbor,"
and so on.[102] "A relative or brother or nephew or neighbor" is the
combination in another charter of Vierzon.[103] Particularly frequent is
the phrase "if any of my heirs." These examples call attention to a
widespread awareness on the part of donors and recipients alike that
future challenges could reasonably be expected from heirs, other relatives, friends, or neighbors of the donor. And finally, one last potential
troublemaker is occasionally identified, as in the charter prepared by
the monks of Saint-Aubin for the count of Anjou to sign in 966: "If
anyone . . . *if I myself*, or any of my progeny or any of my heirs."[104] The
formula used by the monks of Vierzon did the same with a donor
named Berengarius about 1000 when they included this phrase: "If

---

100. Examples of the symbols of gifts being placed on the altar are in Ordericus Vitalis,
Historia ecclesiastica, 5:19, in *EHOV* 3:186–193; White, "*Pactum . . . Legem Vincit*," p. 297.
101. *Cartulaire de l'abbaye de Saint-Aubin d'Angers*, ed. A. Bertrand de Broussillon, 3
vols. (Angers, 1903), 1:9.
102. *Cartulaire de Vierzon*, pp. 129–130.
103. Ibid., p. 148.
104. *Cartulaire de Saint-Aubin*, 1:6 (emphasis added).

anyone, *either I myself* or any heir or any other person."[105] For the written record, the word "anyone" should have been sufficient; but for the ceremony marking the occasion of a donation, by the same logic that it served the interests of the beneficiaries to describe in detail the punishment that awaited violators, it was also wise to specify potential violators, since at least some of these were present.

And so the donor himself or herself was made to pledge not to go back on the agreement being spelled out at that moment, not to take back the donation or any part of it, nor in the future to contest the monks' possession of the property being transferred. This was not such a far-fetched precaution (on the part, remember, of the beneficiaries' scribes), as one can see from the instances of donors and donors' heirs who became predators.[106] These same instances also confirm that clamors and curses were not directed against nameless, faceless enemies, against outside agitators, or against outlaws, pagans, heretics, and the like. Instead, clamors and curses—integral parts of a shared legal culture as well as of a system of shared religious beliefs—were employed as a tactic in trying to bring about an accommodation in an ongoing dispute with a local notable, well known to the religious community, which responded to his violently aggressive behavior with similarly aggressive rhetoric. Thus the very malefactors who rode over the saint's lands, wreaking havoc and making life miserable for God's poor, were in other moments monastic benefactors, worthy of a payoff and a meal as well as of the monks' unending prayers and blessings.

105. *Cartulaire de Vierzon*, pp. 160–161 (emphasis added). For Norman charters, see Emily Z. Tabuteau, *Transfers of Property in Eleventh-Century Norman Law* (Chapel Hill, N.C., 1988), p. 206.

106. The cartulary of Saint-Julien of Brioude records a donation by the brothers Bertrand and William of Vieille-Brioude, and the same two men are soundly cursed in an excommunication formula pronounced against them by the canons of Saint-Julien. See *Cartulaire de Brioude [Liber de honoribus sancto Juliano collatis]*, ed. Henry Doniol (Clermont-Ferrand, 1863), pp. 80–81, and *Spicilegium Brivatense: Recueil de documents historiques relatifs au Brivadois et à l'Auvergne*, ed. Augustin Chassaing (Paris, 1886), pp. 24–25.

Conclusion:
New Contexts

ALL OF the prevailing circumstances that fostered the formulation and subsequent use of clamors and curses changed significantly in the course of the twelfth and thirteenth centuries. The problem posed by the lack of any reliable assurance that a donor's wishes would be followed after death did not disappear but diminished notably. On the other hand, the justification of the clamor in terms of the lack of any alternative form of justice did effectively vanish. In the religious sphere, meanwhile, the preeminence of the Old Testament gave way to that of the New.

The revival of Roman law in Italy in the twelfth century and the subsequent spread of its influence north of the Alps did much to clarify notions involving property—in particular ownership, inheritance, and alienability. At about the same time, some bodies of customary law in the North were being reduced to writing, with similar effects of clarification and standardization. Inseparable from these changes was the development in a university setting of the bookish study of the law and the growth of a professional corps of legal experts. Together the newly authoritative law codes and the lawyers had a tidying-up effect upon juridical confusion arising from complex, multiple claims and overlapping jurisdictions. One sign of greater certainty about ownership in thirteenth-century France is that gifts came to constitute a decreasing proportion of property alienations, whereas the proportion of sales was rising. This change was due in part to tenants' gaining rights of alienation (which often, though, required payment of a fine in recognition of the greater claim, *domaine éminent*, of the lord), but it also signals the advance of a market economy into a sector previously governed almost entirely by the norms of gift exchange.[1]

The disappearance after about 1200 of the clauses containing the approval of relatives signals the shift to clearer rules of inheritance, culminating in the triumph of primogeniture. In a transitional phase, there appeared just the signatures of heirs or potential heirs, identified as such, but then they dropped out as well. The freedom of potential donors came in one sense to be limited; a portion of the patrimony (*réserve lignagère*) was reserved to the rightful heirs. At the same time, however, the portion that was not under this kind of familial restraint was the more clearly available for alienation.[2]

A major development affecting donors and makers of wills in this time was the strengthening of assurances about the future of donations. Donors, that is, were increasingly able to stipulate that not only they themselves but also their heirs would guarantee and refrain from upsetting the particular donation being recorded. Ecclesiastical leaders, from their side, were pressing the point that gifts to churches were irrevocable. Heirs were thus being legally obligated to support their forebears' alienations into an indeterminate future. This development is found in northern French donation charters from about 1230 on.[3]

The charters themselves had a different look. Whereas most donation charters had once been crafted by scribes of the ecclesiastical beneficiaries, now they were the work of notaries and lawyers. And whereas those charters used to contain biblical citations or allusions and long witness lists, as well as sometimes elaborate narratives and sanction clauses of the sort studied in this book, the newer ones consisted mainly of conventionalized legal formulas.[4] Thus when conflicts over property did arise the fundamental shift in ideas and practices surrounding land tenure had so changed that recourse to the liturgical

1. Stephen D. White, *Custom, Kinship, and Gifts to Saints: The "Laudatio Parentum" in Western France, 1050–1150* (Chapel Hill, N.C., 1988), pp. 191–192. Richard C. Hoffmann, "Tenure of Land," in *DMA* 11:678.

2. White, *Custom, Kinship, and Gifts to Saints*, pp. 192–193; Georges Duby, "Lineage, Nobility, and Knighthood: The Mâconnais in the Twelfth Century, a Revision," in his *The Chivalrous Society*, tr. Cynthia Postan (Berkeley, Calif., 1980), pp. 59–80.

3. Dominique Barthélemy, *Les deux âges de la seigneurie banale: Pouvoir et société dans la terre des sires de Coucy (milieu XIe–milieu XIIIe siècle)* (Paris, 1984), p. 98. White, *Custom, Kinship, and Gifts to Saints*, p. 194.

4. White, *Custom, Kinship, and Gifts to Saints*, pp. 193–194.

clamors and curses was no longer appropriate. Still, changes in the law, in legal theory, and in legal practice would ultimately have had little effect were it not for simultaneous transformations in the institutions of justice.

The rise of strong principalities, including the rise of the royal principality to a position of preeminence, is the central drama of French political and institutional history of the twelfth and thirteenth centuries. Within each principality, with variations in detail, the key areas of power were military, fiscal, and judicial. In all three areas fundamental transformations occurred, such that the institutions in place by the middle of the thirteenth century bore little resemblance to their counterparts of a hundred years earlier.

The first change of note in the area of justice is the appearance of trained professionals. Documents of the 1170s record the presence of men called *jurisperti* or *viri prudentes*, who had professional legal training and were serving as judges. A second change is seen in the results of cases, wherein the compromise arrangements (*concordiae*) so characteristic of the eleventh century gave way to judgments (*judicia*), and in this connection a third change is the keeping of more and fuller written records of the proceedings. A fourth change is registered in the new tendency for court sessions to be held at regular intervals.[5]

In 1190 the government of Philip II issued a special ordinance in preparation for the king's departure on a crusade to the Holy Land; the ordinance was in fact regarded also as the king's testament. Here the new system of royal justice is fully spelled out. Throughout the king's domain the system was in the hands of paid professional officials, the baillis, who were to conduct monthly assizes. At these assizes the baillis were to provide swift justice, to defend royal rights, to hear appeals (*clamores*), and to make a written record of fines due the royal treasury. The ordinance also gave attention to regularizing the schedule and procedures of the royal court in Paris. Here the *clamores* could include complaints against the king's baillis themselves, as well as appeals from seigneurial courts on grounds of "defect of justice." Overall, then, by the thirteenth century—earlier in some places than in others—disputes were being taken over and ar-

5. John W. Baldwin, *The Government of Philip Augustus: Foundations of French Royal Power in the Middle Ages* (Berkeley, Calif., 1986), p. 38.

gued in legal terms by professional experts before duly appointed judges in regularly functioning courts. Meanwhile the judicial culture of the *concordiae* atrophied.[6]

These major institutional developments are confirmed by a shift in the comportment of aggrieved ecclesiastical corporations starting about the middle of the twelfth century. Henceforth abbots and other prelates whose churches faced serious difficulties opted to make their clamors, if the alternative was open to them, before competent judicial officers. By being brought into courts, the clamor was thus returning home after its lengthy sojourn in sanctuaries. In a parallel development, spiritual sanction clauses were phased out and replaced by the material or physical punishments that governments were confident of being able to impose upon the guilty.[7]

Important as were these changes in notions of property and its transferability and in the administration of justice, the decline of liturgical clamors and curses must especially be seen against the backdrop of changes in religious sensibility. A leading historian of theology has called the essential religious phenomenon of this age "the evangelical awakening."[8] Indeed, the most striking but also most important aspect of the transformation of spirituality in the twelfth century was the fading of its Old Testament character and replacement by an emphasis upon the New Testament. It is evident at the start of the twelfth century in Saint Anselm's "Prayer for Enemies," where he says: "If what I ask for my enemies at any time is outside the rule of charity, whether through weakness, ignorance, or malice, good Lord, do not give it to them." It is evident in the advance of ethical reasoning, favored by the new levels of cognitive achievement reached in the schools, for example in the reflections of Master Anselm of Laon on the consequences of the different purposes for which excommunications are launched. It is also evident

6. Ibid., pp. 101–102, 137–138, 144; Fredric L. Cheyette, "*Suum cuique tribuere*," *French Historical Studies* 6 (1969–1970): 289, 295–297.

7. For clamors involving the Abbey of Saint-Denis in the twelfth century, see Martial-Alphonse Chazaud, ed., *Fragments du cartulaire de la Chapelle-Aude* (Moulins, 1860), pp. 108–109, 120, 121. For a clamor to a papal legate: in 1174 the abbess of Notre-Dame of Saintes, Agnes of Barbezieux, addressed a clamor against William Helias, who was holding on to land previously granted to the abbey, to the papal legate John of Poitiers; see Théodore Grasilier, ed., *Cartulaires inédits de la Saintonge*, 2 vols. (Niort, 1871), 2:73–75.

8. Marie-Dominque Chenu, "The Evangelical Awakening," in *Nature, Man, and Society in the Twelfth Century: Essays on New Theological Perspectives in the Latin West*, ed. and tr. Jerome Taylor and Lester K. Little (Chicago, 1968), pp. 239–269.

early in the thirteenth century in the lives of the early Francisians, lived in self-conscious imitation of Jesus and the apostles.[9]

In precisely the same period when the prevailing spirituality of conspicuous consumption, lavish liturgy, vicarious prayer, ritual charity, gift exchange, and vengeance arrived at its most splendid heights, the makings of a radically different spirituality were being assembled. Most of the leading critics of the established religious order spoke from direct personal experience with black monasticism: Romuald of Ravenna at Sant'Apollinare, Peter Damian at Pomposa, John Gualbert at San Miniato, Bernard of Tiron at Saint-Cyprian, Norbert of Xanten at Siegburg, and Robert of Molesme in three monasteries, of which one was Molesme. For their many differences, these all sought to reform the religious life, and the model they had in mind was more the company of Jesus and his followers than the powerful monastic corporations they had belonged to and rejected. In the view of Peter Damian, who inspired so many religious to become hermits or to join the greatly simplified monastic life at Camaldoli or Fonte Avellana, knowledge of the Gospel and of the deeds and sayings of the Desert Fathers was sufficient, whereas the prolonged chanting, sounding of bells, and dazzling garments and ornaments of the monks he regarded as superfluous. Both Bernard of Tiron and Robert of Arbrissel, the founder of Fontevrault, preached the gospel in western France and perceived their choice of poverty lived in imitation of the apostles as legitimation of their preaching. Robert of Molesme, the founder of Cîteaux, favored a strict adherence to the Rule of Saint Benedict, for "we observe many practices that cannot be found in it while at the same time we neglect many of its provisions."[10] Meanwhile, the founder of Grandmont, Stephen of Muret, rejected the Rule of Saint Benedict and provided no new rule for his monastic community because, as he taught his followers, the Gospel is the only appropriate rule for governing the religious

9. *Opera omnia Anselmi*, ed. Francis S. Schmitt, 6 vols. (Edinburgh, 1946–1961), 3:73–75; tr. Benedicta Ward, *The Prayers and Meditations of St. Anselm* (Harmondsworth, Eng., 1973), pp. 216–219. Charles M. Radding, *A World Made by Men: Cognition and Society, 400–1200* (Chapel Hill, N.C., 1985), pp. 200–254; Alexander Murray, *Excommunication and Conscience in the Middle Ages*, The John Coffin Memorial Lecture (London, 1991), p. 16, and some of the works he cites in n. 11: Odon Lottin, *Psychologie et morale aux XIIe et XIIIe siècles*, 6 vols. (Gembloux, 1948–1960), 5:97; Ludwig Hödl, *Die Geschichte der scholastischen Literatur und der Theologie der Schlüsselgewalt* (Münster, 1960), p. 14. Giovanni Miccoli, *Francesco d'Assisi: Realtà e memoria di un'esperienza Cristiana* (Turin, 1991), pp. 148–189.

10. Ordericus Vitalis, *Historia ecclesiastica*, 8:26, in *EHOV* 4:312–313.

life. And one of those followers extended the idea by inversion: "All Christians who hold consistently to the faith," he wrote, "can be called monks."[11]

The criticisms of the monastic order formulated by the religious reformers provide glimpses into the life of the cloister. Sometimes this criticism was frontal, as in Bernard of Clairvaux's famous diatribe against the size and splendor of monastic churches. But other times it was indirect, as in the ideals and kinds of life that reformers set up and attracted recruits to, which by their very nature were implied criticisms of the old order. The Carthusians, who did without tapestries and rugs and precious metals in their churches, made no distinctions of status in celebrating the office of the dead. Moreover, they stated that how they furnished their churches and how they conducted services in them were matters of choice; clearly such practices were intended to distinguish the Carthusians from their mainstream contemporaries. All the reform movements involved simplifying to some extent the liturgy, the architecture, the vessels and vestments, the meals, and the rest of the daily routine; this was done in the name of the Gospel and the model of the apostolic life.

Criticism of the current monastic establishment extended to the ways religious communities dealt with adversaries. Norbert of Xanten, for example, who later founded the Premonstratensians, when offered the position of provost of the collegiate church of Saint-Martin of Laon, did not turn it down, but he stated his terms. He said that in carrying out his mission to preach the word of God he had a resolve that he was determined not to violate for fear of endangering his soul.

And this is our resolve: not to seek what belongs to others, not to claim restitution through legal pleadings or secular judges or complaints of anything taken from us, and not to bind anyone by the fetters of anathema on account of injuries or damages inflicted upon us. Instead, to sum it all up briefly, I have, in keeping with a wiser understanding, chosen to live a fully evangelical and apostolic life. Thus I do not refuse the charge, provided that the canons who occupy that church are willing to abide by such a way of living.

11. *Liber de doctrina*, ch.1, in *Scriptores ordinis Grandimontensis*, ed. Jean Becquet, Corpus Christianorum, continuatio mediaevalis 8 (Turnhout, 1968), pp. 5–6. For all of these religious reformers, see Lester K. Little, *Religious Poverty and the Profit Economy in Medieval Europe* (Ithaca, N.Y., 1978), pp. 70–96.

The canons were terrified by these words and replied: "We do not want this man over us, for neither our customs nor those of our predecessors would recognize such a master. May we be allowed to live as we do now; God wishes to castigate, not to mortify" (*Liceat nos vivere sic; castigare deus vult, non mortificare*).[12]

Stephen of Muret zeroed in directly on the monastic clamor and specifically related maledictions to it; he also provided a theological explanation for his opposition to this aspect of prevailing spiritual practice.

> When someone does harm to a community of religious and these make a clamor to God, reading maledictions against their malefactors, it is almost as if they were preventing the Lord from henceforth exercising justice. Yet God, who opposes vindictiveness, replies to them: "I now intervene, because you did not trust in me, while by cursing you brought punishment upon yourselves."

From this denunciation Stephen turns to his view of the proper way for monks to react in such a situation.

> First of all the malefactor ought to be summoned to explain why he acted as he did. And if he were to reply that he did so out of need, then the religious should help him. If, on the other hand, he acted out of pride, let the entire assembly of the cloister pray to God with all their heart that He forgive him; and may God either convert him or else bring him to justice without delay.[13]

In a wholly different context and using different means, the assembled hierarchy of the Western church took action against the liturgy of humiliation during the second half of the thirteenth century. In 1274 the Second Council of Lyons forbade the practice of humiliating the cross as well as either images or statues of the Virgin or of other saints.[14] This prohibition formed part of a more general section of the council's proceedings on various types of suspension of worship. No mention was made of relics or clamors or maledictions. Although the extant evidence indicates that for several decades the use of humiliation had been on the decline, the practice must have still had considerable vigor in 1274 to merit the attention of such a council. The same holds true, on a more local level, for the council assembled over eighty

---

12. *Vita Norberti archiepiscopi Magdeburgensis*, ch. 9 (*MGH, SS* 12:678–679).
13. *Liber de doctrina*, ch. 59 (ed. Becquet, p. 35).
14. Mansi 24:92.

years later at Castres, near Saint-Quentin in Picardy, where an almost identical prohibition was enacted.[15] The Lyons version of the text was incorporated into canon law in 1313.[16] Both versions characterize humiliation as a "detestable abuse," done by persons of "unspeakable impiety" who aggravate the interruption of worship by placing these sacred objects on the floor amid brambles and thorns.

One conciliar decree, even repeated once or a few times, was not sufficient to root out a liturgical practice in use for three centuries. Besides, the liturgy remained vibrant, capable of producing new variants. A case in point is the antiphon *Media vita*, known throughout Latin Christendom, which functioned as a liturgical curse in the territory stretching from the Meuse valley, particularly in and around Liège, eastward through the Rhineland and beyond to the Weser. Its modest, penitential message has nothing of a curse about it:

> In the midst of life we are already in death,
> From whom can we seek help except you, Lord,
> Who on account of our sins is rightly angered?
> Holy God, holy strong, holy and merciful Savior,
> Deliver us not to bitter death.

> [*Media vita in morte sumus,*
> *Quem quaerimus adiutorem nisi te, Domine,*
> *Qui pro peccatis nostris iuste irasceris?*
> *Sancte Deus, sancte fortis, sancte et misericors Salvator,*
> *Amarae morti ne tradas nos.*][17]

Still, there are links between the second line and that part of *In spiritu humilitatis* that says, "There is no one who can console it [this, your church] or liberate it except you, our God," while the third line echoes part of the invocation of the clamor. We should also recall that a variant of the fourth line was sung, as reported by James of Voragine, in Rogation Day processions. Similar textual affinities exist between and the antiphon *Salve Regina* and *In spiritu humilitatis*.[18]

Though their purposes may have varied widely, these antiphons

---

15. Du Cange 7:114.

16. *Liber Sextus*, lib. 1, tit. 16, "De officio ordinarii," cap. 2 (*CIC* 2:986).

17. Otto Hellinghaus, *Lateinische Hymnen des christlichen Altertums und Mittelalters*, 2d ed. (Münster, 1927), p. 42; Francis J. Mone, *Hymni Latini medii aevi*, 2 vols. (Freiburg im Breisgau, 1853), 1:397–399.

18. José-Maria Canal, "De *clamoribus liturgicis* et de antiphona *Salve Regina*," *Ephemerides liturgicae* 72 (1958): 199–212.

came somehow to be regarded, perhaps because of the shared phrases, as prayers of divine supplication in times of trouble and of vengeance against enemies. The connection is made in two manuscripts (of the fourteenth and fifteenth centuries) from farther west than the Meuse—Cambrai, to be precise. The earlier includes a clamor under the title "Proclamation against Malefactors" (*Proclamatio contra malefactores*), with directions that the chorus sing the antiphon *Media vita* and then that the priest say the collect *In spiritu humilitatis.*[19] In the later one, the clamor is headed "Against Those Who Harm the Church" (*Contra malefactores ecclesiae*); again the *Media vita* precedes the clamor, although another prayer for times of tribulation intervenes.[20] Thus, as liturgical formulas go, the *Media vita* is definitively linked with the clamor, both in its wording and in the prescriptions for its use.

In terms of linkage in the way the *Media vita* and the clamor were actually used, seven known instances occurred during the thirteenth century at Liège, Trier, and Bremen. In one case it was combined with a humiliation. In another a community of nuns sang the *Media vita* and the *Salve Regina* sadly each day against an opponent, while in yet another monks "made a clamor to God" against their opponent and "sang tearfully the antiphon *Media vita* while lying prostrate and saying the customary, appropriate prayers." The practice was probably even more widespread, given that in a synod held at Cologne in 1310 the bishops of Cologne, Liège, Maastricht, Minden, and Osnabrück ruled "that imprecations not be made nor the *Media vita* sung against persons" (*quod non fiant imprecationes nec cantetur Media vita contra aliquas personas*).[21]

Once again a conciliar prohibition did not suffice to eliminate a liturgical usage, for this one was still vigorous in 1455 when the nuns of Mariensee sang the *Media vita* and threw lighted candles and stones at the earnest reformer who had come to improve their lives. In the same period, however, this prayer was becoming domesticated as it was translated into the vernacular in German territories and the Lowlands, expanded upon, and set to music. It came to rest in a hymn

---

19. MS, Cambrai, BM, 29, f. 286r.
20. MS, Cambrai, BM, 55, f. 175v.
21. Cologne, 1310: Mansi 25:242. For specific references and more discussion, see Lester K. Little, "*Media Vita* between Maas and Weser," in *Pauvres et riches. Société et culture du Moyen-Age aux temps modernes: Mélanges offerts à Bronislaw Geremek à l'occasion de son soixantième anniversaire*, ed. Stanislaw Bylina et al. (Warsaw, 1992), pp. 223–229.

composed by Martin Luther in 1524 and, still in its original version, in the service of burial in the *Book of Common Prayer* as well as on memorial plaques in Dutch churches.[22]

Seen in the light of these transformations, textual and contextual, the clamor was but a vestige of its former self. One could say the same of the curses pronounced by the bishop of Barcelona against the thieves who stole the silver plate from his church in 1634. Although his action is an undoubted indication of long-term historical continuity—of what Fernand Braudel called "the long haul" (*la longue durée*)—such evidence is sporadic, and this instance by itself is more a vestige than evidence of a vital practice. Even such occasional vestiges, though, serve as reminders of the lasting truth of a curse ascribed to that champion curser among Irish saints, Maedoc of Ferns. It is a curse that itself contains the last word on religious cursing: "Woe to that person," warned Saint Maedoc, "whose neighbor is an angry saint."[23]

22. A. H. Hoffmann von Fallersleben, *Geschichte des deutschen Kirchenliedes bis auf Luthers Zeit* (Hannover, 1861), pp. 325–326. *Liedboek voor de Kerken* (The Hague, 1973), pp. 412–415. John E. Booty, *The Book of Common Prayer, 1559* (Charlottesville, Va., 1976), p. 309. My thanks to Henk van Os for a visit to Spijk and for this reference: H. G. de Olde, "Twee gedachtenisborden in de kerk van Spijk," *Groninger Kerken* 5 (March 1988): 13–15.

23. John H. Elliott, *The Revolt of the Catalans* (Cambridge, 1963), p. 33. Fernand Braudel, *On History*, tr. Sarah Matthews (Chicago, 1980), pp. 25–54. *Lives of Irish Saints*, ed. Charles Plummer, 2 vols. (Oxford, 1922), 2:278.

appendixes

This yf we doe [i.e., repent], Christe wil deliver us from the curse of the law, and from the extreme malediccion whiche shall lyght upon them that shalbee set on the left hand; and he wyl set us on his right hand and geve us the blessed benediccion of hys father, commaundyng us to take possession of hys glorious kyngdome, unto the whiche he vouchafe to bryng us al, for hys infinite mercye. Amen.

Service for the first day of Lent,
The First Prayer Book of Edward VJ, 1549

Appendix A

Gathering Clamors

NOT INFREQUENTLY, medieval history begins in the seventeenth century; that is to say, investigations into the "Middle Ages" usually must proceed through works of the learned scholars, mostly Benedictines, who in the seventeenth and eighteenth centuries first studied that earlier period systematically and sympathetically. These works continue to be indispensable, from the *Glossarium* of Charles Du Cange, which remains the principal dictionary of medieval Latin, and the treatise of Jean Mabillon that established the discipline of reading and analyzing manuscripts, to the multivolume editions of texts assembled by Luc d'Achery (1609–85), by Etienne Baluze (1630–1718), and by Edmond Martène (1654–1739). Starting in the 1690s, Martène undertook the publication of liturgical texts, based on extensive travel and his own transcriptions of hundreds of manuscripts, many of them no longer extant.[1]

Martène's compendium includes two clamor manuscripts from Tours in a chapter titled *De clamore pro tribulatione,* which he placed right before the chapter on excommunication. In the enlarged edition of 1736 he included part of the malediction from Saint-Wandrille. Martène's references to manuscripts tend to be casual: "ancient codex from the Abbey of Jumièges" would be a typical entry. As a reference this is charming but quite useless. Fortunately, a modern expert on liturgical manuscripts, Aimé-Georges Martimort, has rendered Martène's tomes far more useful by listing the current location, whenever he was

---

1. Charles Du Cange, *Glossarium ad scriptores mediae et infimae Latinitatis,* 3 vols. (Paris, 1678); Jean Mabillon, *De re diplomatica* (Paris, 1681); Luc d'Achery, *Spicilegium sive Collectio veterum aliquot scriptorum,* 13 vols. (Paris, 1655–1677); Etienne Baluze, *Capitularia regum Francorum,* 2 vols. (Paris, 1677); Edmond Martène, *De antiquis ecclesiae ritibus,* 3 vols. (Rouen, 1700–1702); 2d ed., 4 vols. (Antwerp, 1736–1738); 3d ed., 4 vols. (Venice, 1763–1765).

able to track it down, of each manuscript Martène consulted, plus the relevant bibliography.[2] Throughout Du Cange's *Glossarium* also, reference is made to manuscripts in the entries, for example, under *clamor ad Deum* and under *reliquiae* (where he sets out extensive evidence of relic humiliation), but Du Cange has not been favored by a project even resembling that of Martimort. In another way, though, Du Cange has been being modernized by scholars for many years—in fact, by an international commission formed in 1929 to provide a new dictionary of medieval Latin. A national section of the commission in each European country is responsible for combing the Latin sources produced in that country during the Middle Ages for material to be included in such a dictionary. The progress registered to date varies considerably from one country to another, but no matter whether many or few results have been published, scholars are usually able to consult materials gathered by the various national commissions (some on file cards, some on computer printouts, etc.). My work benefited greatly from my being able to consult the files of the national Du Cange commissions in Munich, Oxford, Paris, and Rome, looking up such key terms as *anathema*, *clamor, excommunicatio, maledictio,* and the like.[3]

Other, more specialized products of Counter-Reformation erudition gave copious information as well as assurance that the "other Middle Age," the long one, continued to flourish in the seventeenth century.[4] Particularly noteworthy for my purposes were a tract on benedictions and maledictions by a German Jesuit named Jacob Gretser and a tract on excommunication by Jacques Eveillon, a canon of the cathedral of Angers.[5]

2. Aimé-Georges Martimort, *La documentation liturgique de Dom Edmond Martène,* Studi e testi 279 (Vatican City, 1978).

3. Du Cange 2:351–352 (*clamor ad Deum*) and 7:112–114 (*reliquiae*). Anne-Marie Bautier, "La lexicographie du Latin médiéval: Bilan international des travaux," in *La lexicographie du Latin médiéval et ses rapports avec les recherches actuelles sur la civilisation du Moyen Age,* Colloques internationaux CNRS 589 (Paris, 1981), pp. 433–453. Mme Bautier was most helpful in orienting me in the use of the files in Paris and in encouraging me to consult the files in other countries. For annual reports titled "Dictionnaires du Latin médiéval" (the authors vary), see this publication of the Académie royale de Belgique: *Bulletin de la classe des lettres et des sciences morales et politiques.*

4. Jacques Le Goff, *Pour un autre Moyen Age: Temps, travail et culture en Occident: 18 essais* (Paris, 1977), p. 11; English translation by Arthur Goldhammer: *Time, Work, and Culture in the Middle Ages* (Chicago, 1980), p. xi.

5. Jacob Gretser, *Libri duo de benedictionibus et tertius de maledictionibus* (Ingolstadt, 1615); and Jacques Eveillon, *Traité des excommunications et monitoires avec la manière de publier, exécuter et fulminer toutes sortes de monitoires et excommunications* (Angers, 1651).

The inventories of liturgical manuscripts in French public libraries drawn up by Victor Leroquais, in particular his catalogs of sacramentaries and pontificals, turned out to be the most useful tools of research in this investigation. The special virtue of his inventories is that he listed in them all the contents of the manuscripts he examined, including much material that did not fit into any of the established liturgical categories—certainly the case with the objects of my research. In addition, he provided thorough indexes for each of his multivolume inventories. Thus I found relevant manuscript references under such terms as *clamor, maledictio,* and *In spiritu humilitatis.*[6]

Early on in my research it was not difficult to see that the material I was finding was almost exclusively French; the few manuscripts located outside France seemed obviously to be of French provenance in one of two ways: the customal of Farfa exemplifies a non-French work copied from a French model, while the Saint Petersburg pontifical from Sens is found in that city because a Russian collector brought it there from France and sold it to the imperial government in 1805.[7] The question that thus arose quite insistently was whether this nearly complete domination by French material gave an accurate reflection of the actual historical situation or whether instead this was a skewed image stemming from various modern historical interferences with the sources: (1) the French Revolution with the resulting concentration of manuscript material in French public libraries, which in turn had imposed upon them from Paris a uniform cataloguing system along with archivists and manuscript librarians all trained in one way; and (2) Leroquais's thorough volumes, which among inventories of liturgical manuscripts are in a class by themselves. Having failed on my own to locate any evidence of formulas for a clamor or use of a clamor in either Iberia or the British Isles (except for obvious imports), I undertook to consult experts on the history of those areas, including specialists in liturgy. Although the individuals who replied demonstrated considerable interest and gave generous assistance, they confirmed that nothing of the sort was known to them in their territories. For information on Iberia

6. Victor Leroquais, *Les sacramentaires et les missels manuscrits des bibliothèques publiques de France,* 4 vols. (Paris, 1924); idem, *Les pontificaux manuscrits des bibliothèques publiques de France,* 4 vols. (Paris, 1937); idem, *Les psautiers manuscrits des bibliothèques publiques de France,* 3 vols. (Mâcon, 1940–1941).

7. Michel François, "Pierre Dubrowsky et les manuscrits de Saint-Germain-des-Prés à Lénigrad," *Revue d'histoire de l'église de France* 43 (1957): 333–341.

I gratefully acknowledge the assistance of Charles J. Bishko (Virginia), Robert I. Burns (Los Angeles), Antonio Garcia y Garcia (Salamanca), J. N. Hillgarth (Toronto), José Janini (Valencia), Antonio Linage (Madrid), José Mattoso (Lisbon), Anscario Mundo (Barcelona), and Alexandre Olivar (Montserrat). For consultation on Anglo-Saxon liturgy, I am grateful to Christopher E. Hohler, formerly of the Courtauld Institute, and Michael Lapidge of Cambridge.

In 1949 a German scholar published a brief article calling attention to the existence of the clamor and listing ten examples of it; he also devoted a few pages of the same article to the *Salve Regina*.[8] A decade later a Spanish scholar wrote on these same two devotions, putting more emphasis on the connections between them.[9] In the meantime, scholars working on the history and significance of saints' relics, starting with an article by Heinrich Fichtenau in 1952, were calling attention to the humiliation of relics.[10] Of the various entries in dictionaries and encyclopedias I consulted, the most substantial by far is the article on curses in pagan antiquity and the early Christian centuries published by Wolfgang Speyer in 1969.[11] The most suggestive model for dealing with religious cursing in the context of an anthropological history is the influential work of Keith Thomas on religion and magic published in 1971.[12]

In an article in 1932 the hagiographer Baudouin de Gaiffier showed the important role of saints in protecting and reclaiming property.[13] Many useful leads came from histories of particular religious houses and of the disputes they became involved in with some of their neighbors, or from histories of political conflict in particular regions, notable

8. Romuald Bauerreis, "De 'Clamor,' eine verschollene mittelalterliche Gebetsform und das Salve Regina," *Studien und Mitteilungen zur Geschichte des Benediktiner-Ordens und seiner Zweige* 62 (1949–1950): 26–33.

9. José Maria Canal, "De 'Clamoribus liturgicis' et de antiphona 'Salve Regina,' " *Ephemerides liturgicae* 72 (1958): 199–212; idem, *Salve Regina Misericordia: Historia y leyendas en torno a esta antífona* (Rome, 1963).

10. Heinrich Fichtenau, "Zum Reliquienwesen im früheren Mittelalter," *Mitteilungen des Instituts für österreichische Geschichtsforschung* 60 (1952): 60–89; Nicole Herrmann-Mascard, *Les reliques des saints: Formation coutumière d'un droit* (Paris, 1975), pp. 226–228; and Patrick J. Geary, "Humiliation of Saints," in *Saints and Their Cults: Studies in Religious Sociology*, ed. Stephen Wilson (Cambridge, 1983), pp. 123–140.

11. Wolfgang Speyer, "Fluch," in *Reallexikon für Antike und Christentum* 7:1160–1288.

12. Keith Thomas, *Religion and the Decline of Magic: Studies in Popular Beliefs in Sixteenth- and Seventeenth-Century England* (New York, 1971), especially pp. 502–512 on cursing.

13. Baudouin de Gaiffier, "Les revendications de biens dans quelques documents hagiographiques du XIe siècle," *Analecta Bollandiana* 50 (1932): 123–138.

examples of both types being works by Henri Platelle on the Abbey of Marchiennes and on the county of Flanders.[14] In addition, studies of saintly cults, including occasional expressions of hostility toward saints by worshipers, have opened important perspectives on the demands that the faithful made upon saints.[15]

But it was not just from the writings of other scholars that I gathered information on clamors. By publishing articles on the clamor in 1975 and 1979, and by lecturing frequently on the topic in the same period, I called that liturgical practice to the attention of various scholars who in turn directed me to examples they had come across in their own work. Among these was Michael McCormick of Harvard, then a doctoral candidate at Louvain, who alerted me to the marginal malediction in the Sens sacramentary in the Vatican, and the late Mary Mansfield, then a doctoral candidate at Berkeley, who sent me references to three clamors I did not know about that she had come across in French libraries. Since lecturing and publishing articles turned out to be a productive way to uncover more examples of clamors, I expect this book to do its part as well. The likelihood that more formulas will come to light renders premature at this point—even counterproductive—the making of a stemma. Far from being what our teachers used to call "definitive," this book takes its place in the process of learning more about religious sensibilities of the European past, presenting what we now know in the full expectation that it will stimulate searches for and reports on yet more manifestations.

14. Henri Platelle, "La violence et ses remèdes en Flandre au XIe siècle," *Sacris erudiri* 15 (1971): 101–173; idem, "Crime et châtiment à Marchiennes: Etude sur la conception et le fonctionnement de la justice d'après les Miracles de Sainte Rictrude (XIIe s.)," *Sacris erudiri* 24 (1980): 155–202.

15. Miklós Boskovits, "Immagine e preghiera nel tardo medioevo: Osservazioni preliminari," *Arte Cristiana* 76 (1988): 93–104, especially fig. 2.

Appendix B

Elusive Evidence

THERE HAVE been obstacles along the way, some accidental to be sure, but others put in place by people who would not
have wanted this investigation to be made. In addition to the problems of neglect, fire, flood, theft, and the like, which have had a
role in the survival of all types of manuscripts, it is important to
remember that the voices of the evangelical awakening called out
against cursing by the religious and that the humiliation of relics
was specifically outlawed by the Second Council of Lyons; thus one
can reasonably expect that not all the formulas for these services
continued to be copied into new liturgical books. Just as musicians
before the first decades of the nineteenth century showed little interest in music composed more than a generation or two before
their own time, so that little care went to preserving either antiquated musical scores or musical manuscripts, there was no com-
pelling reason for a master of liturgical ceremonies to keep a
defunct ceremony on the books.[1]

Mutilated manuscripts, however, tell a different story. In manuscripts that include representations of the devil, it is not unusual to
find that the devil's face has been erased (usually by scraping) or in
some other manner canceled.[2] When in 1770 the papacy ceased to
promulgate an annual bull of excommunication, a practice that had
drawn much criticism, one of the critics, Emperor Joseph II, issued
edicts ordering that the offensive text be removed from books, or at

1. Joseph Kerman, *Contemplating Music: Challenges to Musicology* (Cambridge, Mass.,
1985), pp. 33, 64. My thanks for the reference (and the book) to Andrea Dell'Antonio.
Such desuetude would explain why some seventeenth-century copies of Bernard of Cluny's customal omit his chapter on the clamor, e.g. MSS, Paris, BN, lat. 13877 and BN,
Bourgogne, XI, ff. 39r–139r.
2. This point was kindly brought to my attention by Paolo Tomea of the Università
Cattolica del Sacro Cuore of Milan.

least papered over.[3] In a similar vein there are cases where pages with curses have been cut out of liturgical books, but only a peculiar set of circumstances lets us know that this has happened and what was on the missing pages. In a twelfth-century lectionary from the Abbey of Saint-Corneille in Compiègne, there is a cursing formula under the title "Malediction upon the Unjust" (*Maledictio super iniustos*). The formula takes up part of both the front and back of folio 74. Both sides have thirty lines of writing, the cursing formula beginning on the eleventh line of the front side, going down to the bottom of that side and then continuing on the top fourteen lines of the reverse side. Someone apparently tried to get rid of the curse, and only the curse, but was foiled in the attempt. The culprit simply cut away the bottom two-thirds of the page, making a slice right under the tenth line of writing on the front side, that is, just above where the malediction begins, and then down the left side of the page close to the binding. One wonders how long the satisfaction of this textual surgeon lasted, for sooner or later it occurred to someone that the back of the piece that remained bound in the book contained ten lines of curses and that all but four lines of the back of the piece that was cut away contained material unrelated to curses. How was this embarrassing dilemma resolved? The amputated piece was sewn back into the book, and the sewing job suggests that this operation took place as far back as the seventeenth century (see Fig. 9).[4]

In another instance of cutting and reattaching, a similar motive might have been involved, although the comical miscalculation is missing. The codex in question is a pontifical made for the bishop of Cologne in the thirteenth century; on the folios from 103 to 113 it contains the standard formulas for excommunication and absolution. The formula with curses, the *excommunicatio terribilior*, is on 103, front and back, with its final sentence, about the dashing out of candles, going over onto the first few lines of folio 104. All of 103 was at some point cut out and then sewn back in.[5]

3. *Dictionnaire de droit canonique*, 2:1136; for the bull in question, *In coena Domini*, see appendix E.

4. MS, Paris, BN, lat. 17304, f. 74r–v. The repair was surely done before the most recent rebinding, which was during the reign of Louis Philippe (1830–1848). Opinion varies on how much earlier to date the repair. My thanks to the Conservateur en chef of the Department of Manuscripts at the BN, Marie-Pierre Laffitte, for responding to my inquiry about this.

5. MS, Vat., Ottoboniani lat. 167, ff. 103r–104r.

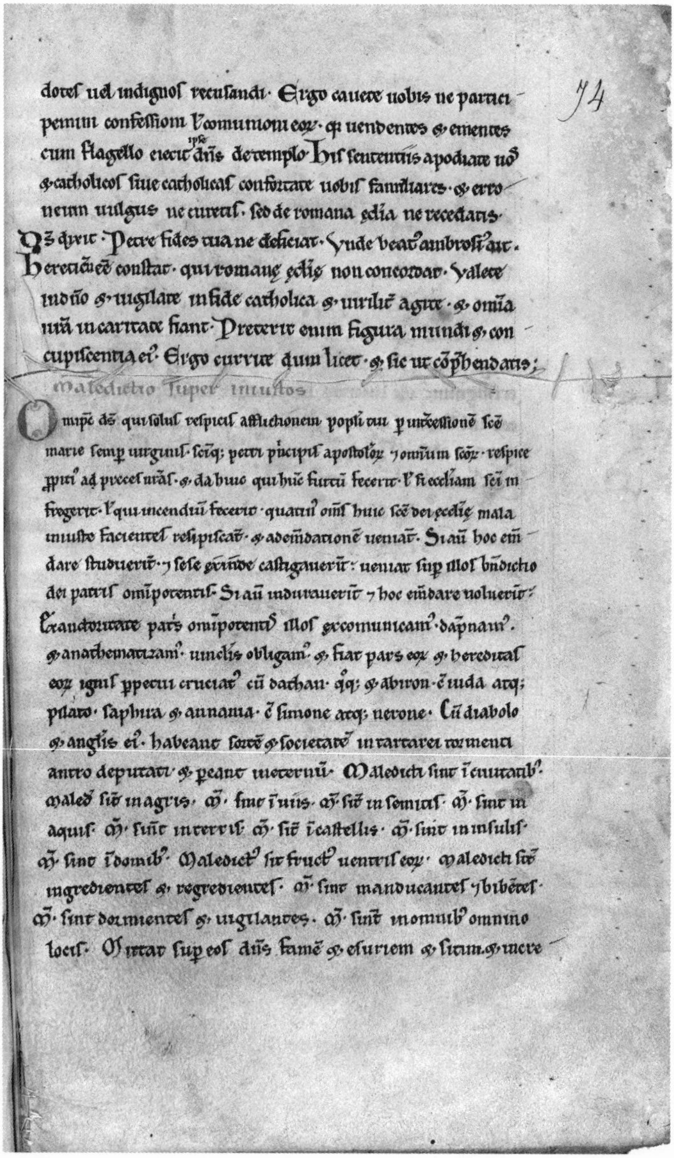

Figure 9. An attempt to suppress evidence of a malediction is apparent in this thirteenth-century missal from the Abbey of Saint-Corneille of Compiègne. Where the formula under the title "Curse against the unjust" (*Maledictio super iniustos*) begins one-third of the way down the page, a cut was made across the page just above the title and down the left side; then the piece was sewn back. MS, Paris, BN, lat. 17304, f. 74r; by permission of the Bibliothèque Nationale.

These two instances together reflect purposeful attempts to eliminate evidence of curses from liturgical books, but these attempts were undone, for whatever reasons, and we are left with proof of the intended mutilation. Is there any reason to think that where mutilation was fully carried out maledictory texts were involved? "Yes, in some instances," would be an appropriate response. The main reason is that many clamors and cursing formulas were placed near the very beginning or the very end of the codices in which they were written.[6] Note that the third column of the chart "Clamors and Cursing Formulas" (appendix F), headed "Folios/Marginal?" gives first the folios or page numbers and then a judgment, expressed as yes or no, on whether the formula text can be considered marginal because of its placement in that particular manuscript volume. Of the sixty-two formulas listed on that chart, I judge thirty-five to be marginally placed in their respective codices. It is frequently the case that the initial or final pages of a codex are missing, precisely the pages on which are found so many of the curse formulas that have survived. But since the pages are missing, no one can say for sure what was written on them.

A simple alternative to excising evidence is to ignore it. One example concerns the malediction from the Abbey of Saint-Martial written into one of the famous Bibles produced at that monastery. In a study of the decoration of the manuscripts of Saint-Martial, Danielle Gaborit-Chopin refers to the practice of copying important documents into the various blank spaces of the "first" Bible of Saint-Martial. Her notes then have an inventory of the contents of the Bible, including every text inserted into those blanks except the malediction, which is on folio 220, front and back. The end of the malediction on 220 verso is followed by a copy of a papal letter, which she does allude to in her reference to "an important act concerning Saint-Martial" on 220v, but there is no mention of the malediction. Even so, the formula was no secret, for it is duly mentioned in the Bibliothèque Nationale manuscript catalog entry for lat.5^{II}.[7]

6. For an instance where pages were cut from the body of a book but suspicion of removing a curse is still called for, note a Carthusian liturgical collection with 214 folios that has three folios cut out between ff. 168 and 169. Where the text resumes on f. 169 (of which the bottom half has been cut away), the prayer *pro serenitate* shares several words of a clamor: "Ad te domine clamantes exaudi . . . pro peccatis nostris juste affligimur." See MS, Grenoble, BM, 338, ff. 168v–169r.

7. Danielle Gaborit-Chopin, *La décoration des manuscrits à Saint-Martial de Limoges et en*

Another example of such oversight, difficult to consider unintentional, occurs in an edition of the Sens sacramentary in the Vatican Library. This edition is the work of a modern expert on the history of the liturgy, and it is, as one would expect, compulsively thorough. When the editor got to the Credo page of the manuscript, he moved right along with a faithful transcription of the Creed (an example of scholarly activity of doubtful utility) but then failed to mention, even in a footnote, the existence of the very prominent curse that fills the margins around the Creed on folios 48v and 49r and v. Léopold Delisle, however, had seen it and made no attempt to keep it a secret in his study of sacramentaries.[8]

In one last case I wish to cite, no willful suppression is involved; instead the problem arises from nothing less banal than an overzealous application of editing guidelines. Peter Dinter's edition of the customs of the Abbey of Farfa, called the *Liber tramitis*, is based principally upon the eleventh-century Vatican manuscript from Farfa (Vat. lat. 6808). For the first of the control manuscripts he used a copy of the same, which was made, also in the eleventh century, for Saint Paul's Outside the Walls in Rome (San Paolo f.l.m., Archivio, 92). The resulting edition is as thorough and scientific an edition as one could expect or even desire. Yet there is a problem, and it arises from one of the simplest rules for making an edition based on more than one manuscript—namely, that the main text of the edition should follow the best or most authoritative manuscript, while the notes ought to show the variants that occur in the other manuscript(s). This rule is useful for indicating words or phrases that have been added or left out, spelled differently, put in a different case or tense, and so on.

As it happens, the first of the two chapters on the clamor in the San Paolo manuscript starts a third of the way down page 167, which contrary to standard pagination is on the left-hand side of the book.

Limousin du IXe au XIIe siècle (Paris, 1969), pp. 43, 176–177; *Bibliothèque Nationale: Catalogue général des manuscrits latins*, vol. 1, ed. P. Lauer (Paris, 1939), pp. 4–5.

8. The edition is contained within an article by Adrien Nocent, "Un fragment de sacramentaire de Sens au Xème siècle: La liturgie baptismale de la province ecclésiastique de Sens dans les manuscrits du IXème au XVIème siècle," in *Miscellanea liturgica in onore di Sua Eminenza il cardinale Giacomo Lercaro*, vol. 2 (Rome, 1967), pp. 649–794; pp. 734–737 include the text from ff. 48v–49v without any mention of the marginalia. Cf. Léopold Delisle, "Mémoire sur d'anciens sacramentaires," *Mémoires de l'Académie des Inscriptions et Belles-Lettres* 32 (Paris, 1886): 166.

The pagination was added in the eighteenth century. Page 168 strikes the reader as odd from the first glance because, in violation of the usual method of constructing a codex with smooth sides of vellum facing smooth sides and rough sides facing rough, page 167 on the left is smooth and yet 168 on the right is rough. Next one sees that the text at the top of 168 is not a continuation from the bottom of 167. The reason for all this is simply that an intervening page of the original manuscript is missing—and missing from before the present pagination was put in. Dinter faithfully follows the rules on variants by indicating in a note that in the San Paolo manuscript the words between word X and word Y are lacking. What he says is true, but word X is the very last word on one page (167) of the manuscript and word Y is the very first word on the following page, and what he has missed seeing (or at least saying) is that the intervening words are missing because the entire page they were on is missing—indeed, the sliver of it still bound in between pages 167 and 168 shows that it had been cut out. As for the contents of the missing page, they include the call to use the curses of both the Old and New Testaments against the "persecutors."[9]

Thus, although the conclusion to appendix A above is optimistic about finding more formulas, a note of caution must be added, for some of the evidence has been eliminated, and even where it remains we cannot be sure that even the best-trained experts will report accurately and fully on what they have seen.

9. *Liber tramitis aevi Odilonis abbatis*, ed. Peter Dinter, Corpus consuetudinum monasticarum 10 (Siegburg, 1980), p. 247. In his description of the San Paolo manuscript, pp. XXX–XXXI, he mentions that pages are missing at the beginning and at the end of the codex.

A Miscellany of Curse Formulas

1. *Pontifical, Sens, Late Ninth Century*

O M N I P O T E N S   D E U S qui solus respicis afflictionem omnium ad te clamantium, qui lacrimas pupillorum ac viduarum ad aures
tuas misericorditer pervenire concedis, respice super nos famulos tuos
beate dei genetricis marie sanctique Stefani protomartiris Christi et
sancti petri principis apostolorum adque omnium sanctorum [erasure]
qui nos sua voluntate impie affligit. Tu enim nosti omnium actiones
antequam celum et terram fieret. Et ideo per intercessionem beate
marie sanctique protomartiris Christi Stefani piisimique domini [rest
of page cut away] pasci et vestri debemus a nobis auferunt et suis
usibus deputant quatinus resipicant et recordentur quia non benefa-
ciunt qui illos quos tuo proprio sanguine redemisti tam graviter dam-
nant et affligunt devastando et depredando et auferendo et tollendo
villas et res nostras [the writing on the next four lines is scraped out].
Veniant super illos omnes maledictiones quibus deus omnipotens illos
maledixit qui dixerunt domino deo recede a nobis scienciam viarum
tuarum nolumus et qui dixerunt ereditate possideamus sanctuarium
dei. Fiat pars eorum et hereditas ignis perpetui cruciatus cum dathan
quoque et habbiron iuda atque pilato simone et nerone [unclear] vocis
meritis suis iustissime exigentibus sentenciam percipiant. Cum quibus
cruciatu pepetuo sine fine torqueantur ita ut nec cum christo et sanctis
eius in celesti quiete societatem abeant sed abeant societatem cum diabolo et sociis eius in inferni tormentis deputati et pereant in aeternum.
Maledictis sint in civitatibus, Maledictis sint in agris, Maledictis sint in
viis, Maledictis sint in semitis, Maledictis sint in aquis; maledictis sint
in terra, Maledictis sint in castellis, Maledictus fructus ventris illorum,
Maledictis sint in domibus et egredientes, Maledictis sint ingredientes,
Maledictis sint, Maledictis sint manducando, Maledictis sint bibendo,

Maledictis sint stando, Maledictis sint sedendo, Maledictis sint ambu-
lando, Maledictis sint [unclear]ando, Maledictis sint vigilando, Male-
dictis sint dormiendo, Maledictis sint in omnibus omnino locis. Mittat
dominus super eos famem et esuriem et increpationem et in omnia
opera illorum que faciunt donec conterat eos et perdet velociter de
terram. Per unam viam gradiantur contra hostes suos et per septem
fugiant donec dispergaritur omnia regna terre. Percuciat eos dominus
amentia et cecitate ac furore mentis et palpent in meridie sicut palpare
solet cecus in tenebris et nesciant dirigere vias suas. Omni tempore
calumniam substineant et opprimantur violentia nec abeat qui liberet
eos. Uxores eorum fiant vidue et desolate gementes pro angutiis. Filii
et filie eorum tradantur alteri popolo in captivitatem in dentibus oculis
eorum et non sit fortitudo in manibus eorum ut liberent eos. Constitue
domine super eos peccatores et diabolus stet a dextris eorum. Omnes
iste maledicciones et omnes maledicciones que sunt in euntis libris
veniant et descendant super eos et persequentes adpreendant eos donec intereant. Amen.[1]

2. *Excommunication Formula, about 900*

Ex auctoritate Dei omnipotentis Patris et Filii et Spiritus sancti, et sanctorum canonum, sanctaeque et intemeratae virginis Dei genitricis Ma-
riae, atque omnium caelestium virtutum, angelorum, archangelorum,
thronorum, dominationum, potestatum, Cherubin ac Seraphin, et sanctorum Patriarcharum, Prophetarum, et omnium Apostolorum et Evan-
gelistarum, et sanctorum innocentium, qui in conspectu agni soli digni
inventi sunt canticum cantare novum, et sanctorum martyrum, et sanctorum confessorum, et sanctarum virginum, atque omnium simul sanctorum et electorum Dei, excommunicamus et anathematizamus hunc
furem, vel hunc malefactorem, et a liminibus sanctae Dei Ecclesiae se-
questramus, ut aeternis supplicis cruciandus mancipetur cum Dathan
et Abiron, et cum his qui dixerunt Domino Deo: Recede a nobis, scien-
tiam viarum tuarum nolumus. Et sicut aqua ignis extinguitur, sic extinguatur lucerna ejus in secula seculorum, nisi resipuerit et ad

1. MS, Saint Petersburg, Public Library, lat. 4°v.I.35, ff. 101v–103v; on this manuscript
see Antonio Staerk, *Les manuscrits latins du Ve au XIIIe siècle conservés à la Bibliothèque
Impériale de Saint-Pétersbourg* (Saint Petersburg, 1910), pp. 151–173, and the thesis of Neils
Krogh Rasmussen at the Institut Catholique de Paris, "Les pontificaux du haut moyen
âge: Genèse du livre de l'évêque" (1977). The spelling, capitalization, punctuation, and
word endings in this and other Latin documents reproduced in this appendix are frequently irregular and inconsistent; I have not tried to regularize them.

satisfactionem venerit. Amen. Maledicat illum Deus Pater, qui homi-
nem creavit. Maledicat illum Dei Filius, qui pro homine passus est.
Maledicat illum Spiritus sanctus, qui in baptismo effusus est. Maledicat
illum sancta crux, quam Christus pro nostra salute hostem triumphans
ascendit. Maledicat illum sancta Dei genetrix et perpetua virgo Maria.
Maledicat illum sanctus Michael, animarum susceptor sacrarum. Maledicant illum omnes angeli et archangeli, principatus et potestates,
omnisque militia caelestis exercitus. Maledicat illum Patriarcharum et
Prophetarum laudabilis numerus. Maledicat illum sanctus Iohannes
praecursor et baptista Christi praecipuus. Maledicat illum sanctus Petrus et sanctus Paulus atque sanctus Andreas, omnesque Christi Apostoli, simul et ceteri discipuli, quattuor quoque Evangelistae, qui sua
praedicatione mundum universum converterunt. Maledicat illum cu-
neus martyrum et confessorum mirificus, qui Deo bonis operibus pla-
citus inventus est. Maledicant illum sacrarum virginum chori, quae
mundi vana causa honoris Christi respuenda contempserunt. Maledicant illum omnes sancti qui ab initio mundi usque in finem seculi Deo
dilecti inveniuntur. Maledicant illum caeli et terra et omnia sancta in
eis manentia. Maledictus sit ubicunque fuerit, sive in domo, sive in
agro, sive in via, sive in semita, sive in silva, sive in aqua, sive in
Ecclesia. Maledictus sit vivendo, moriendo, manducando, bibendo,
esuriendo, sitiendo, jejunando, dormitando, dormiendo, vigilando, am-
bulando, stando, sedendo, jacendo, operando, quiescendo, mingendo,
cacando, flebotomando. Maledictus sit in totis viribus corporis. Maledictus sit intus et exterius. Maledictus sit in capillis, maledictus sit in
cerebro. Maledictus sit in vertice, in temporibus, in fronte, in auriculis,
in superciliis, in oculis, in genis, in maxillis, in naribus, in dentibus
mordacibus, in labris, sive molibus, in labiis, in gutture, in humeris, in
armis, in brachiis, in manibus, in digitis, in pectore, in corde, et in
omnibus interioribus stomacho tenus, in renibus, in inguinibus, in fe-
more, in genitalibus, in coxis, in genibus, in cruribus, in pedibus, in
articulis, et in unguibus. Maledictus sit in totis compagnibus membro-
rum; a vertice capitis usque ad plantam pedis non sit in eo sanitas.
Maledicat illum Christus filius Dei vivi toto suae majestatis imperio, et
insurgat adversus eum caelum cum omnibus virtutibus quae in eo
moventur, ad damnandum eum, nisi poenituerit et ad satisfactionem
venerit. Amen. Fiat, fiat. Amen.[2]

2. *Capitularia regum Francorum ab anno 742 ad annum 922*, ed. Etienne Baluze, 2 vols.
(Venice, 1772–1773), 2:469–470.

3. "More Terrible" (Terribilior) Excommunication Formula, Early Tenth Century

Canonica instituta et sanctorum patrum exempla sequentes, ecclesiarum dei violatores et possessionis earum invasores, vastatores, vel raptores atque depraedatores aut homicidias N. in nomine patris et filii et virtute spiritus sancti necnon auctoritate episcopis per Petrum principem apostolorum divinitus collata, a sanctae matris ecclesiae gremio segregamus ac perpetuae maledictionis anathemate condemnamus. Sintque maledicti in civitate, maledicti in agro, maledictum horreum eorum et maledictae reliquiae illorum, maledictus fructus ventris eorum et fructus terrae illorum. Maledicti sint ingredientes et maledicti egredientes. Sintque in domo maledicti, in agro profugi; veniantque super eos omnes illae maledictiones quae dominus per Moysen in populum divinae legis praevaricatorem se esse missurum intentavit. Sintque anathema maranatha, id est pereant in secundo adventu domini. Nullus eis christianus Ave dicat. Nullus presbyter missam cum eis celebrare praesumat vel sanctam communionem dare. Sepultura asini sepeliantur et in sterquilinium sint super faciem terrae. Et sicut hae lucernae de manibus nostris proiectae hodie extinguuntur, sic eorum lucerna in aeternum extinguatur nisi forte resipuerint et ecclesiae dei quam leserunt per emendationem et condignam penitentiam satisfecerint.[3]

4. "Pope Leo" Excommunication Formula, 937

Leo episcopus servus servorum Dei. Dilectissimis fratribus et filiis archiepiscopis atque suffraganeis eorum, abbatibus et monachorum congregationibus in Francia commanentibus, salutem perpetuam. Indicatum est nobis, filii carissimi, quod in vestris regionibus malignorum hominum perversitas creverit, ita ut res vestras in suis pravis usibus redigere cupiant. Quapropter ex auctoritate Dei patris omnipotentis et filii eius domini nostri Iesu Christi et spiritus sancti paracliti, atque eximie beati Petri apostoli necnon et beate Marie matris domini et per beatos angelos, apostolos, martires, confessores ac virgines, excommunicamus eos atque maledicimus qui possessiones servorum sancti Martini et quicquid ad illos pertinent, tollunt et perperam invadunt. Sit pars eorum cum Dathan et Abiron quos terra pro sua su-

3. PL 140:859–860.

perbia vivos absorbuit et cum Juda proditore qui dominum pretio vendidit. Amen. Fiant filii eorum orphani et uxores eorum viduae. Nutantes transferantur filii eorum et mendicent. Eiciantur de habitationibus suis. Scrutetur fenerator omnem substanciam eorum et diripiant alieni labores eorum. Et iterum. Omnes qui dixerunt: Hereditatem possideamus sanctuarium Dei; Deus meus, pone illos ut rotam et sicut stipulam ante faciem venti. Amen. Sicut ignis qui comburit silvam et sicut flamma comburens montes, ita persequeris illos in tempestate tua, et imples facies eorum ignominia, ita ut erubescant et confundantur et pereant. Amen. Sintque maledictiones ille quas dominus super filios Israel per Moysen promulgavit super illos qui bona et villis sancti Martini depredantur, sintque maledicti in civitate, maledicti in agro et in omni loco. Amen. Maledicta cellaria eorum; maledictus fructus ventris eorum, maledicta omnia quae illorum sunt et maledicti egredientes et regredientes. Amen. Disperdat eos dominus de terra velociter, percuciat eos dominus fame et siti egestate frigore et febri donec pereant. Amen. Tradat illos dominus corruentes ante hostes eorum; sintque cadavera eorum in escam cunctis volatilibus celi et bestiis agri, percuciat eos dominus ulcere pessimo scabie quoque et prurigine amentia et cecitate. Amen. Palpentque in meridie sicut palpare solet cecus in tenebris. Amen. Et sicut dominus beato Petro apostolo eiusque successoribus cuius vicem tenemus quamvis indigni potestatem dedit ut quodcumque ligarent super terram ligatum esset et in celis et quodcumque solverent super terram solutum esset et in celis ita illis si emendare noluerint celum claudimus et terram ad sepeliendum negamus et dimergantur in inferno inferiori solvantque quod gesserunt sine fine. Amen. Si autem ad penitentiam et emendationem venerint et secundum modum culpe fructus dignos penitentie fecerint, omnia mala ista avertat Deus ab illis et nos parati sumus ad recipiendum et orandum pro illis. Si autem ad emendationem noluerint venire, perpetuo anathemate feriantur, ita ut ecclesias Dei non intrent; pacem cum christianis non habeant nec ullam participationem faciant. Corpus et sanguinem domini nec in die mortis percipiant sed eterne oblivioni traditi tanquam pulvis ante faciem venti fiant et cum diabolo et angelis eius perpetuis ignibus tradantur. Et sicut lucerna ista extinguitur, sic extinguantur anime eorum in fetore inferni. Amen.[4]

4. *Papsturkunden in Frankreich*, ed. Johannes Ramackers, 6 vols. (Göttingen, 1932), 5: 344–345.

5. Canons of the Council of Charroux, 989

I. Anathema infractoribus ecclesiarum: Si quis ecclesiam sanctam infregerit, aut aliquid exinde per vim abstraxerit, nisi ad satis confugerit factum, anathema sit.

II. Anathema res pauperum diripientibus: Si quis agricolarum, ceterorumve pauperum, praedaverit ovem, aut bovem, aut asinum, aut vaccam, aut capram, aut hircum, aut porcos, nisi per propriam culpam, si emendare per omnia neglexerit, anathema sit.

III. Anathema clericorum percussoribus: Si quis sacerdotem aut diaconum vel ullum quemlibet ex clero arma non ferentem, quod est scutum, gladium, loricam, galeam, sed simpliciter ambulantem, aut in domo manentem invaserit, vel ceperit vel percusserit, nisi post exinationem proprii episcopi sui, si in aliquo delicto lapsus fuerit, sacrilegus ille, si ad satisfactionem non venerit, a liminibus sanctae dei ecclesiae habeatur extraneus.[5]

6. Archbishop Arnulf of Reims, Warning and Anathema for Predators upon the Church of Reims, 990

Quid tibi vis praedonum Remensium scelerata manus? Nihilne te movent pupilli et viduae lacrymae nec advocatus eorum? Velis nolis, dominus tuus ipse testis et judex et gravis ultor cujus judicium non effugies. Vide quid ante oculos ipsius egeris. Sanctam pudicitiam virginum non erubuisti: matronas etiam barbaris verendas nudas reliquisti: orphanum et pupillum non respexisti. Parvum tibi hoc. Accessisti ad templum matris dei cunctis mortalibus reverendum, ejus atrium perfregisti polluisti violasti. Quod oculi ibi viderunt concupivisti: quod manus attrectare potuerunt, rapuisti. Et nos quidem contra divinum ac humanum jus, misericordia abutentes, quod cibi et potus abstulisti, non indulgemus, sed propter impia tempora non exigimus. Exigimus autem reliqua omnia, quae pollutis manibus pervasisti ac retines. Redde ergo aut sententiam damnationis in pervasores rerum ecclesiasticarum a sacris canonibus promulgatam eam in te latam multotiesque ferendam excipe.

Anathema in praedones.

Auctoritate omnipotentis dei, patris et filii et spiritus sancti, interveniente et adjuvante beata Maria semper virgine, auctoritate quoque et potestate apostolis tradita nobisque relicta, excommunicamus ana-

5. Mansi 19:89–90.

thematizamus maledicimus damnamus et a liminibus sanctae matris
ecclesiae separamus vos, Remensium praedonum auctores factores
cooperatores fautores et a propriis dominis rerum suarum sub nomine
emptionis abalienatores.

Obtenebrescant oculi vestri qui concupiverunt; arescant manus quae
rapuerunt; debilitentur omnia membra, quae adjuverunt. Semper la-
boretis, nec requiem inveniatis, fructuque laboris vestri privemini. For-
midetis ac paveatis a facie persequentis, et non persequentis hostis, ut
tabescendo deficiatis. Sit portio vestra cum Juda traditore Domini in
terra mortis et tenebrarum donec corda vestra ad plenam satisfactionem convertantur. Hic autem sit modus plenae satisfactionis ut omnia
injuste ablata praeter cibum et potum propriis dominis ex integro res-
tituatis coramque Remensi ecclesia poenitendo humiliemini qui sanctam Remensem ecclesiam reveriti non estis. Ne cessent a vobis hae
maledictiones scelerum vestrorum persecutrices quamdiu permanebitis
in peccato pervasionis. Amen, fiat, fiat.[6]

7. Abbey of Saint-Martial, Late Tenth Century

Notum vobis facimus fratres de malis hominibus qui devastant terram
domini nostri marcialis et invadunt et predantur et diripiunt eam et
pauperes nostros flagellant et tollunt eis paupertatem suam de qua
debent servire sanctum marciali et domino abbati et monacis. Hoc scilicet illi qui dixerunt haereditate possideamus sanctuarium dei. Igitur
illi qui terram sancti marcialis tenent et pervadunt et tenentes non ser-
viunt domino abbati et fratribus. Sint maledicti et excommunicati et
anathematizati a consorcio omnium fidelium christianorum dei. Veniant super [eos] maalediccio omnium sanctorum dei. Maledicant illos
angeli et archangeli dei. Maledicant illos patriarche et prophaete. Maledicant illos omnes apostoli et omnes martires et omnes confessores
et omnes virgines et maxime sanctus marcialis cui malefaciant. Con-
fundat et destruat et disperdat a facie terre. Veniant super eos omnes
maledicciones iste et adprehendat eos. Maledicti sint in civitate. Maledicti in campis. Maledicti sint in mansiones et foras mansiones. Maledicti sint stantes et sedentes. Maledicti sint iacentes et ambulantes.
Maledicti sint dormientes et vigilantes. Maledicti manducantes et bi-
bentes. Maledicti sint in castellis et in villis. Maledicti in silvis et in
aquis. Maledicte sint uxores eorum et infantes eorum et omnes qui eis

6. Mansi 19:95–96.

consentiunt. Maledicti sint cellaria eorum annone eorum et omnia vasa illorum in quibus bibunt et in quibus manducant. Maledicte sint vinee eorum et messes eorum et silve eorum. Maledicti sint servi eorum si eis consenciunt. Maledicta sint omnia iumenta et animalia eorum in stabulis et foras stabulis. Mittat dominus super eos famem et sitim, pestilenciam et mortalitatem donec consumentur de terra. Percuciat eos dominus calore et frigore. Sit celum quod super eos est eneum et terra quam calcant ferrea. Tradat dominus corpora eorum in escas volatilibus caeli et bestiis terre. Percuciat eos dominus a planta pedis usque ad caput. Fiat habitacio eorum deserta et non sit qui inabitet. Perdant quod habent et eo quod non abent non adquirant. Foras devastet gladius et intus pauor. Si sementes in terra iecerint parum colligant, vineam si plantaverint non bibant vinum de illa. Mittat dominus super eos plagas magnas infirmitates pessimas et perseverantes nisi emendaverint. Si autem emendare noluerint deo et sancto marciali accipiant damnacionem cum diabolo et angelis ejus in infernum et cum datan et abiran jeene ignibus cumburantur. Amen amen. Sic extingatur memoria eorum in secula seculorum.[7]

8. *Clamor That Comes before They Say the Pax Domini,*
   Composed by Lord Fulbert concerning Enemies of the
   Church, Besançon, Eleventh Century

In spiritu humilitatis et in animo contrito ante sacrum altare tuum et sacratissimum corpus et sanguinem tuum, domine ihesu, redemptor mundi, accedimus, et de peccatis nostris pro quibus iuste affligimur culpabiles coram te nos reddimus. Ad te, domine ihesu, venimus, ad te prostrati clamamus quia iniqui et superbi suisque viribus confisi undique super nos insurgunt. Terras sancti Joannis et sancti Stephani invadunt depraedantur et vastant. Pauperes tuos cultores earum in dolore et famem atque nuditate vivere faciunt. *Tormentis etiam et gladiis occidunt, nostras etiam res unde vivere debemus in tuo sancto servitio et quas beate animae huic loco pro salute sua reliquerunt diripiunt nobis etiam violenter auferunt. Ecclesia tua haec domine, quam pricis temporibus fundasti et in honore sanctorum Joannis apostoli et Stephani protomartyris*

---

7. MS, Paris, BN, lat. 5[ll], f. 220r–v; ed. Lester K. Little in *Revue Mabillon* 58 (1975): 386–387. The final word of the text is written in Greek. For comment on the vogue of inserting an occasional Greek word or name into texts written in central France in the decades around A.D. 1000, see Jane Martindale, "Conventum inter Guillelmum Aquitanorum comes et Hugonem Chiliarchum," *English Historical Review* 84 (1969): 528, n. 3.

tui sublimasti, sedet in tristitia, nec est qui consoletur eam et liberet, nisi tu Deus noster. Exsurge domine Jesu in adjutorium nostrum, conforta nos et auxiliare nobis. Expugna impugnantes nos. Frange etiam superbiam illorum qui hunc locum et nos affligunt, et affligere cupiunt. Tu scis domine qui sunt illi, et nomina eorum, corpora et corda antequam nascerentur tibi sunt cognita. Quapropter eos domine sicut scis justifica in virtute tua; fac eos recognoscere prout tibi placet sua malefacta et libera nos in misericordia tua. Ne dispicias nos domine clamantes ad te, sed propter gloriam nominis tui et misericordiam, visita nos in pace et erue nos a presenti angustia.[8]

9. Customs of Farfa, about 1030

Pro adversa preces faciendam. Hac ratione faciendus est aecclesiastici ordinis clamor ad deum. Ad missam principalem iam dicta oratione dominica ministri ecclesiae cooperiant pavimentum ante altare cilicio et desuper ponant crucifixum et textum evangeliorum, et corpora sanctorum, et omnis clerus in pavimento iaceat prostratus canendo psalmum, Ut quid deus reppulisti in finem sub silentio. Interim duo signa percutiantur ab ecclesiae custodibus. Solusque sacerdos stet ante dominicum corpus et sanguinem noviter consecratum, et ante praedictas reliquias sanctorum et alta voce incipiat hunc clamorem dicere: In spiritu humilitatis et animo contrito . . . visita nos in pace et erue nos a praesenti angustia. Amen. Quo clamore facto reportentur reliquiae suis locis, et dicat sacerdos sub silentio collecta Libera nos quaesumus Domine.
Item. De eadem in alia definitione. Cum surrexerint e capitulo die dominico sonet custos signum, agant orationem. Dein exeat sacerdos cum infantibus et praeparant se ad missam. Tunc sonet signum denuo, quod maius est, duas vices pro adunatione principali. Ad expletionem evangelii dicatur Credo in unum Deum. Quo expleto ascendat armarius in pulpitum et nuntiet plebi malitiam persecutorum. Dein procedat alius frater et legat anathemata, vel maledicta tam novi, quam veteri testamenti secundum utilitatem ac jussionem a sede apostolica acceptam, et a vicinis episcopis probationem datam maledictionem non emen-

---

8. F. I. Dunod, *Histoire de l'église, ville et diocèse de Besançon,* 2 vols. (Besançon, 1750), vol. 1, *Preuves,* pp. viii–ix. The Chartres version of 1020 is similar but considerably shorter. Instead of naming the patron saint(s), it says: "Terras sanctuarii tui nobis commissi invadunt." And then it does not contain the part of the Besançon formula that is italicized here. René Merlet and J.-A. Clerval, *Un manuscrit chartrain du XIe siècle* (Chartres, 1893), pp. 237–238.

dantibus, benedictionem eis qui se praeparant ad emendationes. Qua lecta extinguantur candelas, pulsentur omnia signa. Dimissas prosternant se omnes in terra et hos psalmos decantent, Domine quid multiplicati sunt. Deus noster. Deus in adiutorium, vel istos duos adiungentes ad deum nostrum, Benedixisti, Fundamenta, vel quales habuerint constituti ex aliis. Capitula, Ostende nobis. Esto nobis domine. Exsurge domine. Orationes, Concede nos famulos tuos, quaesumus, domine perpetua mentis et corporis. Omnipotens sempiterne deus mestorum, vel sicut diximus decretas habuerint. Surgentes cantent offerendam et perficiant missam. Aliis diebus cotidianis agant ita: Mox ut surrexerint e capitulo, veniant et dicant in primis quinque psamlis pro defunctis, et tunc sonentur signa, et hejiciant se in humo et dicant sicut supra.[9]

10. Interdict and Clamor, Council of Limoges, 1031

Odolricus interea venerabilis pater familiae beati Martialis, sedens in cathedra iuxta primatem Lemovicensem, sacris ut erat indutus ornamentis, dare coepit consilium episcopis dicens: Hic vos, carissimi, decernere oportet medicinam, quam contra generalem morbum adhibeatis. Si enim de pace tenenda, sicut est vestra voluntas, principes militiae Lemovicensis vobis obstiterint, quid contra ista sit agendum? Dixerunt episcopi: Hac in re petimus, carissime, ipse date consultum. Quibus ille: Nisi de pace acquieverint, ligate omnem terram Lemovicensem publica excommunicatione; eo videlicet modo, ut nemo nisi clericus aut pauper mendicans aut peregrinus adveniens aut infans a bimatu et infra in toto Lemovicino sepeliatur, nec in alium episcopatum ad sepeliendum portetur. Divinum officium per omnes ecclesias latenter agatur et baptismus latentibus tribuatur. Circa horam tertiam signa sonent in ecclesiis omnibus et omnes proni in faciem preces pro tribulatione et pace fundant. Poenitentia et viaticum in exitu mortis tribuatur. Altaria per omnes ecclesias, sicut in parasceue, nudentur, et cruces et ornamenta abscondantur, quia signum luctus et tristitiae omnibus est. Ad missas tantum, quas unusquisque sacerdotum ianuis ecclesiarum obseratis fecerit, altaria induantur et iterum post missas nudentur. Nemo in ipsa excommunicatione uxorem ducat. Nemo alteri osculum det, nemo clericorum aut laicorum, vel habitantium vel trans-

---

9. *Consuetudines Farfenses,* ed. Bruno Albers, Consuetudines monasticae 1 (Stuttgart and Vienna, 1900), pp. 172–174.

euntium, in toto Lemovicino carnem comedat, neque alios cibos quam illos, quibus in quadragesima vesci licitum est. Nemo clericorum aut laicorum tondeatur neque radatur, quosque districti principes, capita populorum, per omnia sancto obediant concilio.[10]

11. Truce of God in the Archdiocese of Arles, about 1037–1041: Sanction Clause

Qui vero treuvam promissam habuerint et se scientibus infringere voluerint, sint excommunicati a Deo patre omnipotente et filio eius Iesu Christo et Spiritu sancto et de omnibus sanctis Dei sint excommunicati, maledicti et detestati hic et in perpetuum, et sint damnati sicut Dathan et Abiron et sicut Iudas qui tradidit Dominum, et sint dimersi in profundum inferni sicut Pharao in medio maris, si ad emendationem non venerint sicut constitutum est.[11]

12. Cluniac Customs Gathered by Bernard of Cluny, 1070s: Part 1, Chapter 40

Quomodo fiat clamor pro tribulatione ad populum sive ad deum. Quotiens autem ad missam minorem in diebus privatis signa minime pulsantur, unus tantum conversus obsequitur; incensum non offertur, neque diaconus vel subdiaconus casulis utuntur, neque cappa in choro habetur, neque a pueris sed a toto conventu responsorium cantatur, neque tres ante altare cerei accenduntur; subdiaconus ad offerendam et post communionem quod de puero dictum est totum perficit; caetera omnia uno eodemque modo aguntur, nisi si vivorum missa est, ut in diebus festis a priore tantum offertur et ab eodem pax a diacono accipitur popularibus danda et diaconus communicat; quod si pro qualibet necessitate in privatis diebus minor missa matutinalis fuerit, omnes ad offerendam vadunt unus a diacono pacem accipit et ipse diaconus communionem sacram percipit. Et sciendum, quod ad matutinalem missam, credo in unum deum non cantatur, nisi populus ad audiendum convocetur, quod hoc modo solet fieri: cum aliquo predone vastante res ecclesiae volunt inde ad populum querimoniam facere precipitur ut omnes populares die domenica ad majorem ecclesiam conveniant et tunc cantatur missa matutina ad crucifixum; finito evangelio incipit sacerdos credo in unum deum post cujus finem, dicta of-

10. Carl Mirbt, *Quellen zur Geschichte des Papsttums und des römischen Katholizismus*, 3d ed. (Tübingen, 1911), p. 105.
11. *MGH, Const.* 1:597.

feranda, quidam frater ascendit pulpitum et de preceptis divinis aliquantis per primum loquens tandem manifestat eis tribulationem, suggerens eis ut faciant elemosynas atque rogent deum quatinus illum malefactorem pacatum eis reddat, et commutet de malo ad bonum; adjungit quoque quadam homilia persuasoria dicens: scitis quia si aufertur nobis nostra substantia, non possumus vivere. Rogate ergo fratres deum et nos faciemus ad eum proclamationem. His dictis incipitur in choro responsorium Aspice domine vel Congregati sunt inimici nostri, et omnia signa tunc interim parumper pulsantur. Finito autem responsorio signisque dimissis dicit conventus hos tres psalmos Domine quid multiplicati, Deus noster, Ad te levavi, quibus addunt haec capitula: Post partum, Esto nobis, Memor esto, Dominus vobiscum, Concede nos famulos, de S. Maria, et alia de tribulatione.[12]

13. Short and Long Clamors, Tours, Thirteenth Century

De utroque clamore et de officio basso. Quando de aliquo malefactore non potest ecclesia habere emendam, ad Missam, post Pater noster, antequam dicatur Pax Domini, dicit diaconus clamorem parvum, scilicet Omnipotens sempiterne Deus qui solus respicis afflictiones hominum et cetera. Et, quando dicitur, stant omnes ad terreiam, et etiam presbiter, genu flexo ante altare, tenens in manibus Corpus Domini. Qua dicta, dicunt psalmum Ad te levavi, et sonant clericuli campanas chori, et post dicit presbiter capitula cum collecta, scilicet Hostium nostrorum. Qua dicta, dicunt omnes Amen alta voce.

De magno clamore et reliquiis ad terram positis. Ad agravandam manum ecclesie, quandoque deserit officium altum, et fit submissum officium, quod debet fieri in hunc modum: omnes clerici descendunt de stallis ad terram, et in ordine dicitur totum submissa voce; nec finiuntur antiphone cum neuma, nec incensatur. Septimanarii accendunt duplum tantummodo, et extingunt, et sonant in capa chori, nec offerunt duplum clerico, nec accenduntur cerei in rastro, et ebdomadarius dicit Benedicamus et versiculos, et fit Missa sine ordine, et debent esse clerici in presbiterio, et juvenes circa altare, et clericuli in choro sedere, sed diaconus et subdiaconus dicunt Epistolam et Evangelium in superliciis, et alia omnia cantantur insimul, et sic fit in omnibus Missis privatis; et sonatur tantummodo ad Horas omnes campana chori que vocatur Ira-

---

12. *Ritus et consuetudines Cluniacenses,* ch. 40, in *Vetus disciplina monastica,* ed. Marquard Herrgott (Paris, 1726), pp. 230–231.

ta. Et, si oporteat quod corpora sanctorum sint humi reposita, fit in hunc modum: post Primam, classico sonante campanarum, veniunt omnes in chorum, et incipiunt septem psalmos cum letania, et tunc vadunt majores persone cum ministris ecclesie, et ponunt ad terram, ante formam subdecani, Crucifixum argenteum, et omnes capsas ubi Sancti requiescunt, et spinas desuper, capsa beati Martini in loco suo cooperta et spinis circundata; et in medio navis ecclesie, ponunt crucifixum ligneum, spinis undique coopertum, omnibus portis ecclesie fortiter obseratis, parvo ostio ibi relicto. Lucescente die, debent sonare Matutine, et post dicuntur insimul Prima, Tercia, Missa et Sexta. Ad Missam, post Pater noster, antequam dicatur Pax Domini, dicit diaconus clamorem magnum In spiritu humilitatis, et sunt omnes ad terreiam in choro, et presbyter ante altare tenens manibus Corpus Domini. Qua dicta, dicunt Quid gloriaris, et sonant clericuli campanas chori, et juvenes omnia magna signa. Post dicitur capitula cum collecta, et ad omnia respondet chorus alta voce. Sero dicuntur Hore similiter insimul.[13]

14. Pontifical of Henri de Ville-sur-Illon, Bishop of Toul, 1420

Malediction en fransois contre les malfactours de laglise. Devant la face de la maieste divine du pere du fil et du saint esprit. Nous dolans et gemissans des griefs oppressions dampmaiges et vilonnies fais a nous a notre eglise a nos ministres prestes. clers. religious. hommes femmes et subges de nostre evechie. la quelle est opprimee et grevee en biens rentes revenues franchises iuridiction et droitures en meubles et non meubles tant a la mort comme a la vie. par gens qui doubtent par dieu et sainte eglise et ses commendements les quels ont petite memoire de lour saulvement. Ainsois font ou font faire ou sueffrent a faire malicieusement les dis dampmaiges et empechements par eulx et par aultres secretement et en hault. Or est ainsi qu'ils sont obstines en lour malices et pechies. Et non que volons ensuire les ancyens peires du vielz et novel testament. si comme il est proprement contenus en la sainte escripture dont sainte eglise est enluminee et toute chretientey. Et ainsi comme nos predecessours lont acoustumey pour le temps quil vivoient. amonnestons generament et especialment les malfatours des-

13. Rituel de Saint-Martin de Tours (XIIIe siècle), ed. A. Fleuret (Paris, 1899–1901), pp. 147–148.

susdis qui ont fait ou fai faire par eulx ou par aultres font ou feront ou ont pourchassie secretement ou en hault les dampmages dessusdis. et qui empechent la iuridition de notre eglise. et qui donnent ont donney ou donront confort favour et aidde aus dis mafatours. que dedens. xxx. iours ils aient satisfais des dompmaigres griefs oppressions iniures et empachements fais et perpetres a nous et notre eglise. Et si non que de la bouche dieu soient ils maldis. de la malediction dont dieu par la bouche des sains prophetes maldisoient ceulx qui faisoient contre les commendements. et dont nos predecessours en lours vivant maldisoient les malfatours de lour eglise en disant: De lauctorite de dieu le trespuissant la vierge marie de saint piere et saint poul et dou benoit saint. N. et de toute la court de paradix et de la notre maldis soient tous generament et especialment li malfatours qui ont fait pourchassie affaire ou fait faire par eulx ou par aultres ou feront scienment soit en hault ou en secret. et quil ont donney confort ou donront favour aidde par eulx ne par aultres aux dis malfatours. amen. Maldis soient ils en villes et en citey. amen. Maldis soient ils aux champs et defuers. amen. Maldis soient lour maisons et lour granges. amen. Maldis soient ly biens et ly fruis de lour terres. Amen. Maldis soient lours enfans et lours femmes. amen. Maldis soient ils en alant en venant en veillant et en dormant. amen. Maldis soient lour grosses bestes et menues. amen. Si maldis soient ils quils soient ades en fam et en famine par toute lour vie. amen. Si maldis soient ils quil soient ades en pestillence et en mechies de cuer et de corps. amen. Sy maldis soient ils que dieu envoye sur lour biens et sur leur terres feu et flemme en lieu de pluye. et de rouzee. amen. Si maldis soient ils que leurs femmes et leurs enfans soient dechas par tous pays et quil soient nus en la mains de leurs ennemis. amen. Sy maldis soient ils que quant il morront ils soient gettes aux champs et devores des bestes savayges. amen. Maldis excommenies entredis anathematysies soient ils. amen. Sy maldis soient ils comme fuit dathan abyron quils pour leurs meffais furent transglutis de la terre tous vis. amen. Si maldis soient ils comme fuit cayin qui tua son frere. amen. Et tout ensi comme ceste chandaille gettee in terre est estinte ainsi soient ils estains et privers de lamour de dieu et de toute la court de paradix. iusque a tant quils averont satisfait plainnement a nostre ditte eglise. Amen.[14]

14. MS, Paris, BN, lat. 12079, ff. 265v–267v. Carol Bresnahan Menning, a specialist in Italian Renaissance history at the University of Toledo, transcribed and analyzed this text when she was an undergraduate at Smith College.

Fulbert of Chartres as Author of *In spiritu humilitatis*

FULBERT, BISHOP of Chartres from 1006 to 1028, frequently had to contend with powerful military lords who raided at will the possessions of his diocese. As we have seen, he made appeals for help to the constituted authorities, but when this help was not forthcoming he resorted both to cursing malefactors and to suspending worship.[1] As to his possible authorship of the prayer beginning *In spiritu humilitatis*, this matter is perhaps best approached in reverse chronological order, beginning with J. P. Migne in the nineteenth century and working back to the eleventh century. In Migne's collection, in the volume containing the works of Fulbert of Chartres, there is a text titled "Clamor that comes before they say the Pax Domini, composed by Lord Fulbert concerning enemies of the church" (*Proclamatio antequam dicant Pax Domini, Composita a domino Fulberto pro adversariis Ecclesiae*). After that title comes the familiar text, beginning *In spiritu humilitatis* and ending *erue nos de presente angustia*.[2] Migne apparently accepted the attribution of this prayer to Fulbert of Chartres. He gave as his source Dunod, *Histoire de Besançon*, vol. 1, *Preuves*, p. viii.

F. I. Dunod's history of Besançon, published in 1750, includes among the documents presented as evidence the text reprinted by Migne, title and all, from the word *Proclamatio* to the word *angustia*. The patron saints referred to in the prayer are Stephen and John the Baptist, who were indeed the patron saints of the cathedral of Besançon. Dunod just mixed this text indiscriminately with other documents, with no more

---

1. Jean Leclercq, "L'interdit et l'excommunication d'après les lettres de Fulbert de Chartres," *Revue historique de droit français et étranger*, 4th ser., 22 (1944): 67–77.
2. *PL* 141:353–354.

specific reference to a source than the phrase "very old manuscript." His only comment was printed in the margin opposite the mention of *domino Fulberto*: "I think this refers to Fulbert of Chartres."[3] The manuscript read by Dunod has not come to light, so we are left to wonder whether this marginal comment about Fulbert of Chartres is original with Dunod and also whether the title *Proclamatio . . . Fulberto* appeared on the manuscript before him exactly as he transcribed it. In 1965 a search for the Besançon manuscript with a clamor produced no positive result.[4]

Although the manuscript read by Dunod has so far not been found, another one that sheds light on the problem has turned up. Written in central Italy in the late eleventh century, it contains a collection of canonical texts that support a pro-papal line. At the end of this collection and written in the same hand as the collection stands the prayer *In spiritu humilitatis*; it bears essentially the same title as the one transcribed by Dunod: "Clamor to be said in front of the altar before the Pax Domini, composed by Lord Fulbert concerning enemies of the church" (*Proclamatio ante altare antequam dicatur pax domini composita a domno fulberto pro adversariis ecclesiae*); the body of the prayer is also the same as in the transcription by Dunod, except for the patron saints.[5] Thus despite the similarities in the prayers the Italian manuscript cannot be the Besançon manuscript that Dunod saw; its clamor refers to a church dedicated not to Stephen and John the Baptist but to the Virgin Mary. The author of this canonical collection, Bernold, came from Constance, in Switzerland, where he was a canon of the cathedral church, and its patron was the Virgin Mary. We are allowed to think that Bernold's acquaintance with the clamor came from this church and that its copy of the clamor is closely related to the Besançon copy. In the

---

3. F. I. Dunod, *Histoire de l'église, ville et diocèse de Besançon*, 2 vols. (Besançon, 1750), vol. 1, *Preuves*, viii–ix.

4. J.-M. Canal, "En torno a S. Fulberto de Chartres (+ 1028)," *Ephemerides liturgicae* 80 (1966): 211 ff.

5. MS, Vat. lat. 3832, f. 195r. I am very grateful to Katherine Christiansen and Stephanie Tibbets of the Institute of Canon Law at the University of California, Berkeley, for bringing this text to my attention. For the collection of canonical texts that the clamor immediately follows, see J. J. Ryan, "Bernold of Constance and an Anonymous *Libellus de Lite: De Romani Pontificis Potestate Universis Ecclesias Ordinandi*," *Archivum historiae pontificiae* 4 (1966): 9–24. Note the heading on the version from Saint Mary's of the Irish, Vienna: *Oracio Volperti episcopi pro tribulacione*, and see above, ch. 1, n. 85.

year 811 Besançon became the seat of an ecclesiastical province, and one of the dioceses contained in this province was Constance.[6]

Thus a plausible connection can be made between a now lost manuscript that was seen at Besançon in the middle of the eighteenth century and an eleventh-century Italian manuscript now in the Vatican. At least the attribution to "Lord Fulbert" goes back to the eleventh century. A remaining problem is that the Besançon formula does not conform precisely to any of those from Chartres. Instead, it is the same as the one copied from a set of Cluniac customs (now lost) for the Abbey of Montepuli and subsequently for Farfa. Still, Fulbert knew and corresponded with Abbot Odilo of Cluny, and a direct influence of some of Fulbert's spiritual writings (concerning the nativity of the Virgin) upon those customs has been established. Moreover, a letter from Fulbert to Odilo telling of atrocities being committed by knights on his lands says that he has already excommunicated them, that he will now seek the assistance of the count of Chartres, the duke of Normandy, and the king of France, and that if all these fail to help he will have no option left except to do these things he has sent to Odilo. What "these things" are is not spelled out, and there is not even agreement that the reading I have suggested is correct; but the implication of such a reading is that Fulbert was sending Odilo a clamor formula.[7]

6. Rosamond McKitterick, *The Frankish Kingdoms under the Carolingians, 751–987* (London, 1983), pp. 372–373.

7. *Liber tramitis aevi Odilonis abbatis*, ed. Peter Dinter, Corpus consuetudinum monasticarum 10 (Siegburg, 1980), pp. 162–164, 245–247. *The Letters and Poems of Fulbert of Chartres*, ed. and tr. Frederick Behrends (Oxford, 1976), pp. 178–179; René Merlet and J.-A. Clerval, *Un manuscrit chartrain du XIe siècle* (Chartres, 1893), p. 236.

Appendix E

Vestiges in the Age of Reformation and Counter-Reformation

A S T H E history of the antiphon *Media vita* shows, formal liturgical cursing continued well beyond the heyday of the clamor. Occasional glimpses of cursing or of attitudes toward cursing by religious persons suggest another, less formal kind of vestige. One such person is the Dominican at Bologna who in 1445 wrote into a book of devotions the first six verses of Psalm 34 under the title "Verses to be said against enemies."[1] Another is Mary Rowlandson of Lancaster, Massachusetts, who was taken captive by Wampanoag and Narragansett warriors in 1676 and later was given a Bible that one of her captors found in his share of booty.

> So I took the Bible, and in that melancholy time, it came into my mind to read first the 28. Chap. of Deut., which I did, and when I had read it, my dark heart wrought on this manner, That there was no mercy for me . . . but the Lord helped me still to go on reading till I came to Chap. 30 the seven first verses, where I found, There was mercy promised again, if we would return to him by repentence; and though we were scatered from one end of the Earth to the other, yet the Lord would gather us together, and turn all those curses upon our Enemies.[2]

Still further removed from the liturgy are those instances of religious persons, employing curses that have no textual connection with the religious tradition. The status of the speaker rather than the choice of words gave force to the remarks of Parson Samuel Dunbar when he

---

1. MS, Bergamo, Biblioteca Civica, MMB 629, f. 20r–v; this text was kindly brought to my attention by Francesco Lomonaco.
2. *Held Captive by Indians: Selected Narratives, 1642–1836*, ed. Richard Van Der Beets (Knoxville, Tenn., 1973), p. 51.

stood before the First Suffolk County Congress, held on 16 August 1774 at Doty Tavern in Stoughton, Massachusetts, and prayed that God would send a strong northeast gale to dash the British fleet to pieces on Cohasset Rock.[3] The variations on this theme are many, but the following paragraphs will deal only with a few of the major liturgical vestiges.

The Service of Commination in the Book of Common Prayer

Following the Churching of Women among the occasional services in the *Book of Common Prayer* comes a penitential service called "Commination." First introduced in the earliest version of the prayer book, that of 1549, but under the title "The first day of Lent, commonly called Ash Wednesday," and then in 1552 called "A Commination against sinners with certain prayers to be used divers times in the year," it found its present, full title in 1661: "A Commination, or Denouncing of God's anger and judgments against sinners, with certain prayers to be used the first day of Lent, and at other times, as the Ordinary shall appoint."[4]

Before Communion on the appointed day, the priest mounts the pulpit to tell the congregation that in the early church there existed a discipline of public penance for notorious sinners to be carried out at the beginning of Lent. He explains that its dual purpose was to save those sinners and to deter others from following their bad example.

> In the steede whereof until the saide disciplyne maye bee restored agayne (whiche thynge is muche to bee wished), it is thoughte good that at thys tyme (in your presence) shoulde bee read the general sentences of goddes cursyng agaynste impenitente sinners, gathered out of the xxvii. Chapter of Deuteronomie, and other places of scripture. And that ye should aunswere to every sentnece, Amen.

The priest then reads out ten curses, after each of which the people answer by saying, "Amen."

3. Daniel T. V. Huntoon, *History of the Town of Canton, Norfolk County, Massachusetts* (Cambridge, Mass., 1893), p. 196; my thanks for the reference to Robert Keighton of Curry College.
4. Joseph H. Maude, *The History of the Book of Common Prayer* (New York, 1899), p. 110. The *American Prayer Book*, first published in 1786, omitted the Commination; see Francis Procter, *A New History of the Book of Common Prayer, with a Rationale of Its Offices*, rev. ed. (London, 1910), p. 239. I am grateful to Bernard Hamilton of the University of Nottingham for suggesting that I look into the service of Commination.

Cursed is the man that maketh any carved or molton image, an abominacion to the Lorde, the woorke of the handes of the craftes manne, and putteth it in a secrete place to wurship it.
And the people shal aunswere, and saye:
Amen.
Minister: Cursed is he that curseth his father, and mother.
Answere: Amen.

After the final curse, there comes an exhortation to repent, followed by Psalm 51, the Lord's Prayer, and two collects.[5]

The change in the appointed time for the Commination from Ash Wednesday to "divers times in the year" between the 1549 and 1552 editions of the prayer book has been attributed to Martin Bucer, the German reformer who arrived from Strasbourg in 1549 and who completed a criticism of the prayer book in 1551.[6] Without intending to cast doubt upon Bucer's influence or upon that of the other reformers who commented on the first edition, one should note that the regular reading of curses at various times of the year was a long-standing tradition in the English church. The statutes of a synod held at York in 1195 provided as follows:

> That the dishonesty of calumniators, and the wickedness of rash swearers may be checked, through fear of the Divine judgment, we do order that, for the future, every priest, three times in the year, with candles lighted and bells ringing, shall solemnly excommunicate those who, in recognizances and other matters of testimony, shall have knowingly and wilfully been guilty of perjury, and those who shall wickedly cause others to be guilty of perjury, and shall on every Lord's day denounce them as excommunicated; to the end that the frequent repetition of the malediction may withdraw those from their iniquity, whom the accusation of their own conscience does not deter therefrom.[7]

Statutes from other dioceses and subsequent synods specify the number of times per year variously, but the usual number is three or four, and some specify use of the vernacular. A York manual dated 1403 refers to this rite as "the grete cursinge that our holy faders, popes, and archebisshops hathe ordeyned, for to be published at the leste iii. in the yere, in eury parysshe chirche: that is to saye, the first Sonday of Lente or the seconde; and also some Sonday after Mawdlen tyde, or

5. *The First Prayer Book of King Edward VJ*, ed. Vernon Staley, Library of Liturgiology and Ecclesiology for English Readers, 2 (London, 1903), pp. 361–368.
6. Procter, *New History of the Book of Common Prayer*, p. 76.
7. *The Annals of Roger of Hoveden*, ed. Henry T. Riley, 2 vols. (London, 1853), 2:365.

ellis before, as it may best fall; and also some Sonday in the Advente before Christmas, and thus holy Chirche useth throughout all the places in Cristendome."[8]

There is evidence elsewhere of regular, repeated excommunications and cursings, though with considerable variety in both texts and timing. Perhaps the earliest instances were the repeated sanctions promoted by the peace assemblies. In any case, to turn to an example from the fourteenth century, a Bavarian monastic sermon book of that time lists classes of sinners who ought to be excommunicated three times a year, specifying Palm Sunday, Maundy Thursday, and Ascension Day (*in palmis, in cena domini, in assumptione*).[9] In the Welsh example noted earlier, when the "great sentence of excommunication of Saint Teilo" was read in the cathedral of Llandaff in 1410, and thereby produced immediate results in the madness of the seven wrongdoers who were present, that reading was said to take place "in the usual way on the saint's day" of that year.[10] And as if to demonstrate the discretion permitted prelates in this matter, one English bishop had Deuteronomy 28 substituted for the Great Excommunication in the quarterly reading of curses in 1538.[11]

Thus while the desire to restore a practice of the primitive church in 1549 undoubtedly stemmed from a Protestant reforming initiative, the ritual reciting of curses upon an annual cycle had already been going on for some 350 years. To say that the irregular or occasional recitation of specific curses, which was so common between the tenth and twelfth centuries, declined and practically vanished altogether is true; but is not the whole truth, for a real extension of it in time can be found—transformed to be sure—in the guise of regular recitations of generic curses and excommunications all through the early modern period.

Papal Excommunications at the Lord's Supper

The papacy was an avid promoter of regularly pronounced but generic excommunications. Popes resorted to occasional and specific ex-

8. *Manuale et processionale ad usum insignis ecclesiae Eboracensis*, ed. William G. Henderson, Surtees Society 63 (Durham, 1875), p. 122.

9. MS, Munich, Bayerische Staatsbibliothek, CLM 19118, f. 111v.

10. John G. Evans and John Rhys, eds., *The Text of the Book of Llan Dav* (Oxford, 1893; photo reprint Aberystwyth, 1979), pp. 118–121, 350.

11. Procter, *New History of the Book of Common Prayer*, p. 641, n. 3.

communications as well, to be sure, witness the case of Pius II canonizing to hell Sigismondo Malatesta in 1461,[12] but by the thirteenth century at the latest popes were also issuing annual generic excommunications.[13] The day chosen was Maundy Thursday, and the name given the annual bull was "At [the feast of] the Lord's Supper" (In coena Domini). A mixing of the two types perhaps prepared—or even suggested—the transition from one type to the other. In at least two instances, excommunications of particular, very noteworthy persons were carried out by popes on this particular feast day (Maundy Thursday): Emperor Henry IV by Pascal II in 1102, and Emperor Frederick II by Gregory IX in 1227.[14] For excommunications of whatever type, the choice of Maundy Thursday carried a weighty message, for that day had long been regarded in traditional spirituality as a special moment in the liturgical year for the reconciliation of penitent sinners. The choice only emphasized that the accursed were utterly impenitent.[15]

The mature form of the bull In coena Domini, after a lengthy period of development, was reached in 1511 in the reign of Julius II. The preamble states that the intention of the bull is preservation of the purity of the faith and of the unity of the church. Most editions of the bull list about twenty categories of delinquents who are to be excommunicated and anathematized, including heretics, those who appeal papal decisions to future church councils, pirates in the Mediterranean, those who counterfeit papal documents, those who kill, wound, or detain persons traveling to or from the Holy See, and so on.[16]

The great period of this bull spanned the sixteenth and seventeenth centuries, when Luther, Calvin, Zwingli, and company swelled the ranks of the "heretics." For the year 1610 it began:

Excommunicamus et anathematizamus ex parte Dei omnipotentis, Patris et Filii et Spiritus Sancti, auctoritate quoque beatorum Apostolorum Petri et

---

12. *The Commentaries of Pius II*, book 5, tr. Florence A. Gragg, ed. Leona C. Gabel, Smith College Studies in History 30 (Northampton, Mass., 1947), pp. 374–376. My thanks to Frederick J. McGinness of Mount Holyoke College for bringing this text to my attention.

13. *Dictionnaire de droit canonique*, 2:1132–1136.

14. *The New Schaff-Herzog Encyclopedia of Religious Knowledge*, 5:471–472.

15. *Dictionnaire de droit canonique*, 2:1132.

16. *Bullarium diplomatum et privilegiorum sanctorum Romanorum pontificum*, 25 vols. (Turin, 1857–1872); examples: 5:490–493 (Julius II, 1511); 6:218–224 (Paul III, 1536); 11:617–624 (Paul V, 1610).

Pauli, ac nostra, quoscumque Hussitas, Wikleffistas, Luteranos, Zuinglianos, Calvinistas, Ugonottos, Anabaptistas, Trinitarios, et a Christiana Fide apostas, ac omnes et singulos alios haereticos.[17]

Critics as far back as Peter Damian had castigated the popes for making excessive use of anathemas.[18] The Protestant reformers successfully portrayed the popes as frequent and frightening launchers of curses, a point that followed from one of their basic theological principles, namely that people can in no way influence what God chooses to do.[19] An example of this portrayal that also calls attention to the annual proclamation of *In coena Domini* occurs in the writings of Pietro Martire Vermigli, an Italian Protestant who went into exile in Switzerland and Germany and then, like Bucer, arrived in England in 1549. The occasion was a curse in the book of Judges (17: 1–4), on which Vermigli wrote a commentary. The biblical passage tells of a man who said to his mother: "You remember the eleven hundred pieces of silver that were taken from you, and how you called down a curse on the thief in my hearing? I have the money; I took it and now I will give it back to you." She asks for a blessing upon her son and has him dedicate the money to preparing an idol for worship.

Vermigli first takes up the problem of idol worship and then turns to the cursing:

> The mother curseth the theefe whosoever he were . . . and she curseth, as men in a manner use to do, in adversities. Yea and God himself also used curses in the old testament, in the assembly to the mount Hebal and Garizim. The priest also cursedly prayed for barennes, diseases, losse of children, and other thinges of like sorte. And in our time, the Pope, by what wicked zeale I know not, in the day of the supper of the Lord sendeth forth curses upon all those which have alienated themselves from his institution and sect.[20]

The papal practice of issuing *In coena Domini* just before Easter each year continued nonetheless. That and the publicity about it generated by detractors together make it plausible that Protestant polemicists stirred up anxiety and opposition during crises in 1681 and again in 1745 by pa-

17. Ibid., 11:618.
18. *PL* 144:214.
19. *The Works of John Knox*, ed. David Laing, 6 vols. (Edinburgh, 1895), 1:37–39, 259, 308; 3:58.
20. Pietro Martire Vermigli, *Most Fruitful and Learned Commentaries of Doctor Peter Martir Vermil* (London, 1564), f. 237v. This text was kindly brought to my attention by Giulio Orazio Bravi, and I received assistance in reading it from Ruth Mortimer, curator of rare books in the Smith College Library.

rading a twelfth-century maledictory formula from the cathedral of Rochester under the title "The Pope's Dreadful Curse" and claiming that if there were a Catholic restoration such curses would fall upon the Protestant faithful.[21] Finally, however, telling criticisms from Catholic rulers added to those of Protestant opponents brought Clement XIV to abolish *In coena Domini* in 1770, a fitting conclusion to the decade in which the nine volumes of *Tristram Shandy* had appeared.[22]

The Excommunication of Baruch Spinoza

On 27 July 1656 in the Portuguese synagogue of Amsterdam, the governing council of the congregation enacted the solemn excommunication of Baruch Spinoza, then in his twenty-fourth year. The young man, whose grandfather had emigrated from Portugal, practiced faithfully the religion in which he was brought up until his father's death in 1654. Thereafter he became openly critical, provoking a series of warnings that culminated in the governors' writ of excommunication:

> The gentlemen of the governing council make known to you that, having been aware for some time of the wrong opinions and comportment of Baruch de Espinoza, they have tried by various means and promises to dissuade him from his evil ways. Unable to bring about any improvement, but on the contrary obtaining more information every day of the horrible heresies that he practiced and taught, and of the monstrous actions that he performed, and as they had many trustworthy witnesses who in the presence of the same Espinoza reported and testified against him, which convinced them; and all this having been examined in the presence of the rabbis, they decided with the latters' consent that the same Espinoza should be excommunicated and separated from the people of Israel, as they now banish him with the following excommunication [*herem*]:
> By the sentence of the angels and the word of the saints, we excommunicate, expel, curse, and damn Baruch de Espinoza with the consent of the Blessed God and with the consent of this holy congregation in front of the holy scrolls with the 613 precepts that are written therein, with the excommunication by which Joshua cursed Jericho, with the malediction by which Elisha cursed the youths, and with all the curses that are written in the Law. May he be cursed by day and cursed by night; may he be cursed when he lies down and cursed when he arises; may he be cursed when he goes out and cursed when he comes in [*malditto seja de dia e malditto seja de noute,*

21. Evidence of tension within the Anglican church on this matter in 1689 is seen in a proposal for altering the service of Commination, namely, to replace the curses from Deuteronomy with the Beatitudes; the proposal did not pass. See Procter, *New History of the Book of Common Prayer*, p. 219.

22. *Dictionnaire de droit canonique*, 2:1136.

malditto seja em seu deytar, e malditto seja em seu levantar, malditto elle em seu sayr, e malditto elle em seu entrar]. May the Lord not pardon him; may the anger and wrath of the Lord rage against this man, and bring upon him all the curses that are written in the Book of Law, and may the Lord destroy his name from under the heavens, and separate him to his injury from all the tribes of Israel with all the maledictions of the firmament, which are written in the Book of Law. But you who cleave unto the Lord your God are all alive this day.

After that word of assurance for those who remain faithful, the authorities issued this warning to anyone showing sympathy either to Spinoza himself or to his ideas: "We warn that nobody should communicate with him orally or in writing, or show him any favor, or stay with him under the same roof, or within four ells of him, or read any paper composed or written by him."[23]

Among the possible origins of this formula in Iberian sources is the "edict of faith" issued by inquisitors. One such edict, promulgated by Andres de Palacio at Valencia in 1519, enumerates offenses against the holy Catholic faith, which mainly came down to standard Jewish and Moslem observances, and then delivers a series of blistering curses against those who engage in them (offenses or observances, as the case may be). The offenders are excommunicated, anathematized, cursed, segregated, and separated. They are to share the fate of Pharaoh, the people of Sodom and Gomorrah, and Dathan and Abiron; they are cursed with the curses of Deuteronomy and the Psalms.[24]

Another possible source, from further back in time, would be in the oaths administered to Jewish witnesses in court cases involving Christians, particularly when they are going to testify against Christians. The witness, in this Catalonian example from the thirteenth century, is made to swear by the one who said: "I am the Lord your God, who brought you out of the land of Egypt, and out of the house of bondage" (and twenty other oaths that follow this same form), as well as swear by the twenty-four books of the law and by the twelve tribes of Israel. To each statement put to the witness in this way, the witness must reply "Amen." The court officer then says to the witness: "If you know the truth but you prefer to lie under oath, may there come over you

23. For the Portuguese text, see Israel S. Revah, *Spinoza et le Dr. Juan de Prado*, Etudes juives 1 (Paris, 1959), pp. 57–58.
24. Cecil Roth, *The Spanish Inquisition* (New York, 1964), pp. 76–85. Maria Cervantes, a Smith College senior in 1980, kindly alerted me to this text.

all these maledictions and seize you." Reply: "Amen." "May you be cursed in town, and cursed in the field. May your granary be cursed and may your remains be cursed." Reply: "Amen." Ten paragraphs later, the final oath returns to the main point: "If you know the truth yet testify falsely, may your soul go to that place where dogs deposit their feces." Reply: "Amen."[25] Such oaths imposed on members of subgroups within a mixed society by the dominant group have a long history, some of which was played out in the Iberian peninsula.[26]

25. Fernando Valls Taberner, *Los usatges de Barcelona: Estudios, comentarios y edicion bilingue del texto* (Barcelona, 1984), pp. 126–130.

26. See various "Jews' oaths" employed in Islamic countries in Norman A. Stillman, *The Jews of Arab Lands: A History and Source Book* (Philadelphia, 1979), pp. 165–166, 267–268. Howard Adelman of the Jewish Studies Program at Smith College kindly discussed these matters with me.

Clamors and Cursing Formulas

T H E C H A R T below gives basic infomation on fifty-six manuscripts that contain sixty-two clamors or curse formulas. In column
one, the provenance of each manuscript is indicated by a place name,
the name of the church (i.e., its patron), and, if the church was a monastery, an asterisk. Multiple manuscripts from the same place are indicated by superscript letters. The second column lists the present
location of the manuscript, giving the place, the repository, and the call
number, as well as the date or century of its production and its genre.
Abbreviations used only here are: pontif = pontifical; Bib Ste Gen =
Paris, Bibliothèque Sainte-Geneviève; sacrament = sacramentary; B Fac
Med = Bibliothèque de la Faculté de Médecine; mis = missal; psal =
psalter; hymn = hymnal; hours = book of hours; cart-hist = cartulary/
history; Vall = Biblioteca Vallicelliana; confrat = confraternity; KCA =
Kent County Archives; St. Pet'bg = Saint Petersburg; Schottenkl = Vienna, Schottenkloster. The third column gives the folio or page numbers of the formulas and a yes-or-no answer to the question whether
the placement of the formula in the manuscript can be considered marginal. The fourth column gives the title or first words of each formula,
and the fifth column indicates the mention within that formula of, respectively: Clamor (Cl), In spiritu humilitatis (In), Humiliation (Hu),
Malediction (Ma), Excommunication (Ex), or Anathema (An). Editions
of any of the formulas that have been edited are listed in footnotes.

Provenance Place/patron * = monastery	Manuscript/ location/date/ type	Folios/ marginal?	Title, or beginning of text	Contents
Admont Blaise*	Admont Stiftsbib 86/15 c/pontif	72v–74 no	*Hic est ordo qualiter fiat clamor in tribulacione*	ClIn¹
Arras Mary	Bib Ste Gen 126 12 c/sacrament	211v yes	*In spiritu humilitatis*	ClIn
Autunª Symphorien	BN lat 12824 18 c/cartulary	p. 41 no	*Oratio canonicorum s. Symph. in afflictione*	In
Autunᵇ Symphorien	BN lat 18354 1721/cartulary	35–36 no	*Oratio canonicorum s. Symph. in afflictione*	In
Besançon Stephen	[lost]	—	*Proclamatio antequam dicant pax domini*	ClIn²
Caen Stephen*	Montpel. B Fac Med 314/11 c/ mis	93–94v no	*Invocatio ad deum pro malefactoribus*	ClIn
Cambraiª Mary	Cambrai BM 29 14 c/psal/hymn	286r–v yes	*Proclamatio contra malefactores*	ClIn
Cambraiᵇ Mary	Cambrai BM 55 15 c/psal/hours	175v–176v yes	*Contra malefactores ecclesiae*	ClIn
Chartresª St. Père*	[Chartres BM 577] 11 c/sacrament	1 yes	*Contemplatio*	In
Chartresᵇ Mary	Chartres BM n.a. 4/1020/obituary	134v–135v yes	*Hic est ordo qualiter fit clamor*	ClIn³
Chartresᶜ Mary	[Chartres BM 1058] 1204–39 ordinary	p. 330 ca yes	*Hic est ordo qualiter fit clamor*	ClIn⁴
Chartresᵈ Mary ·	[Chartres BM 509] 14 c/mis	77r–v yes	*Hic est ordo qualiter fit clamor*	ClIn
Chartresᵉ Mary	[Chartres BM 502] 14 c/mis	430r–v yes	*Clamor ad deum prosequentibus ecclesiam dei*	ClIn

Provenance Place/patron * = monastery	Manuscript/ location/date/ type	Folios/ marginal?	Title, or beginning of text	Contents
Chartres[f] Mary	BN lat 17310 14 c/mis	309r–v yes	*Clamor ad deum pro persequentibus ecclesiae dei*	ClIn
Cluny Peter*	BN lat 13875 1067–8/customal	83–84 no	*Quomodo fiat clamor pro tribula. ad populum sive ad deum*	Cl[5]
Compiègne[a] Corneille*	BN lat 17304 12 c/lectionary	74r–v no/cut	*Maledictio super iniustos*	MaExAn
Compiègne[b] Corneille*	BN lat 17319 13 c/mis	216r–v yes	*Pro tribulatione ecclesiae preces*	In
Compiègne[c] Corneille*	BN n.a.l. 2358 13 c/prayer bk	36v–37v no	*Pro tribulatione ecclesiae preces*	InEx
Constance Mary	Vat lat 3832 11 c/canon law	195 yes	*Proclamatio ante altare antequam dicatur pax domini*	ClIn
Corbie Peter*	BN lat 13874 12 c/customal	83r–v no	*Quomodo fiat clamor pro tribulatione ad deum*	Cl
Dijon Benigne*	Dijon BM 122 11 c/pontif	3v yes	*In spiritu humilitatis*	In
Farfa Mary*	Vat lat 6808 12 c/customal	96r–v no	*Pro adversa preces faciendam/Item de eadem in alia diffin.*	ClInHu MaAn[6]
Fleury Benedict*	Orléans BM 123 12 c/ritual bk	pp. 339–340 no	*Clamor [pro] malefactoribus*	ClIn[7]
Fontinelle Wandrille*	Rouen BM Y 208 16 c/cart-hist	148–151v no	*S. Wandregisilus . . . ex stirpe francorum regia procreatus*	Ma[8]
Jumièges Mary*	Rouen BM A 293 12 c/gospel bk	148v–150v yes	*Maledictio*	InMa ExAn[9]
Liège St. Lambert	Rome Vall H.6 17 c/saint's life	189r–v no	*Qualis erat super his eccl. lamentatio. [Proclamatio]*	ClHu MaEx[10]

Provenance Place/patron * = monastery	Manuscript/ location/date/ type	Folios/ marginal?	Title, or beginning of text	Contents
Limoges Martial*	BN lat 5^{II} 10 c/Bible	220r–v yes	*Notum vobis facimus fratres de malis hominibus qui devastant*	MaExAn[11]
Marcigny-sL Trinity*	BN n.a.l. 348 12 c/necrology	7v–8 yes	*In spiritu humilitatis*	In[12]
Oño Holy Savior*	BL Add 30044 1116/confrat rule	66v–72 no	*In nomine sanctae et individuae Trinitatis*	ClMa ExAn
Poitiers Peter	[lost] 1170s/charter	— no	*Ante sacratissimum corpus et sanguinem tuum*	ClEx[13]
Reims Mary	Reims BM 350 13 c/necrology	6 yes	*In spiritu humilitatis*	InEx[14]
Remiremont[a] Peter*	BN lat 823 12 c/mis	344v yes	*Invocatio pro tribulatione ad missam antequam agnus dei dicatur*	In
Remiremont[b] Peter*	BN lat 14283 15 c/mis	81v no	*Hec oratio dicenda est a sac. antequam dicatur agnus dei*	In
Rochester Andrew	Maidstone KCA DRc/R1/12 c cart	98–100 no	*Excommunicatio*	MaExAn[15]
Rome[a]/Trinity of the Irish*	Vat Chigi C.VI. 173/11 c/prayer bk	27–28 no	*Incipit ordo pro adversariis qualit. contra eos proclametur*	ClIn[16]
Rome[b] Paul*	Rome S Paolo flm 92/12 c/customal	p. 167 no/cut	*Pro adversa preces facienda/Item de eadem in alia diffin.*	ClInHu [Ma][An][17]
St.-Amand[a] Amand*	Valenciennes BM 121/12 c/mis	89r–v no	*Quomodo fit clamor pro tribulatione*	Cl
St.-Amand[b] Amand*	Valenciennes BM 107/12 c/prayer bk	83v yes	*Canonica instituta*	MaExAn
St.-Denis[a] Denis*	Montpel B Fac Med 314/13 c mis	92v yes	*Excommunicatio contra malefactoribus*	ExAn

Provenance Place/patron * = monastery	Manuscript/ location/date/ type	Folios/ marginal?	Title, or beginning of text	Contents
St.-Denis[b] Denis*	Montpel B Fac Med 314/13 c mis	93 yes	*In spiritu humilitatis*	In
St.-Germans German*	Rouen BM A 27 11 c/pontif	183–184 yes	*Sic maledicendi sunt omnes resistentes dei voluntati*	MaExAn[18]
Ste-Barbe-en-Auge/Barbara*	Bib Ste Gen 96 12 c/sacrament	220–221v yes	*Missa contra raptores ecclesiae*	ClIn
Senlis[a] Frambourg	Bib Ste Gen 1190 11 c/gospel bk	5v yes	*Auctoritate dei omnipotentis*	MaEx
Senlis[b] Frambourg	Bib Ste Gen 1190 11 c/gospel bk	13v–14 yes	*In spiritu humilitatis*	In
Sens[a] Stephen	Vat Reg lat 567 10 c/sacrament	48v–49v yes	*Maledictio adversus ecclesiae dei persequtores*	MaEx
Sens[b] Stephen	St. Pet'bg Lib 4° v.I.35/late 9 c pontif	101v–104 no	*Omnipotens deus qui solus respicis afflicitione*	Ma
Sens[c] Stephen	St. Pet'bg Lib 4° v.I.35/late 9 c pontif	105v–107 no	*Immensus dolor nos urget*	MaEx[19]
Sens[d] Rémi*	Sens BM 20 14 c/ritual bk	pp. 226–227 yes	*In spiritu humilitatis*	In
Toul[a] Stephen	BN lat 12079 1420/pontif	265v–267v no	*Malediction en fransois contre les malfactours de l'aglise*	MaExAn
Toul[b] Stephen	BN lat 12079 1420/pontif	267v–272 no	*Alia maledictio contra malfactores ecclesiae*	InMa ExAn
Tours[a] Maurice	BN n.a.l. 1589 11 c/sacrament	1v–2 yes	*Antequam agnus dei dicatur*	In[20]
Tours[b] Martin*	Tours BM 196 11 c/sacrament	289v–290 yes	*Canonica instituta et sanctorum patrum exempla*	MaExAn

Provenance Place/patron * = monastery	Manuscript/ location/date/ type	Folios/ marginal?	Title, or beginning of text	Contents
Tours[c] Maurice	BN lat 10504 13 c/mis	261–263v yes	*Oratio cum persecutio est in sancta matre ecclesia*	InMa
Tours[d] Martin	[Tours BM 1508] 13 c/customal	no	*Clamor parvus*	Cl[21]
Tours[e] Martin	[Tours BM 1508] 13 c/customal	no	*Clamor magnus*	ClInHu[22]
Trier[a] Maximin*	[lost] 12 c/gospel bk	end yes	*Clamor adversus persecutores*	ClIn[23]
Trier[b] Maximin*	[lost] 11 c/Bible	7 yes	*In spiritu humilitatis*	InMa ExAn[24]
Verdun[a] Airy*	Verdun BM 103 12 c/gospel bk	1 yes	*In spiritu humilitatis*	In[25]
Verdun[b] Vannes*	Verdun BM 141 12 c/ritual/psal	26 no	*In spiritu humilitatis*	In
Verdun[c] Mary	BN lat 966 14 c/pontif	207–210 yes	*Maledictio malefactorum in episcopatu virdunensis*	InMa
Vienna/Mary of the Irish*	Schottenkl 189 12 c/prayer bk	77v yes	*Oracio Volperti episcopi pro tribulacione*	In
Winchester Mary*	BL Royal 2.B.V 11 c/psal	1r–v yes	*Dominator omnium quaesumas qui omnem diligis iustitiam*	Ma[26]

1. Adolph Franz, *Die Messe im deutschen Mittelalter* (Freiburg-im-Breisgau, 1902), pp. 206–207.

2. François I. Dunod, *Histoire de l'église, ville et diocèse de Besançon*, 2 vols. (Besançon, 1750) 1, preuves: viii–ix.

3. René Merlet and J.-A. Clerval, *Un manuscrit chartrain du XIe siècle* (Chartres, 1893), pp. 237–238.

4. Yves Delaporte, *L'Ordinaire chartrain du XIIIe siècle* (Chartres 1953), pp. 196–197.

5. Marquard Herrgott, *Vetus disciplina monastica* (Paris, 1726), pp. 230–232.

6. Peter Dinter, *Liber tramitis aevi Odilonis abbatis*, Corpus consuetudinem monasticarum, 10 (Siegburg, 1980), pp. 244–248.

7. Anselme Davril, *The Monastic Ritual of Fleury*, Henry Bradshaw Society 105 (London, 1990), pp. 156–157.

8. Lester K. Little, "Formules monastiques de malédiction aux IXe et Xe siècle," *Revue Mabillon* 58 (1975): 390–399.

9. Edmond Martène, *De antiquis ecclesie ritibus*, 2d ed. (Antwerp, 1736–38), 2:905–906.

10. *MGH, SS*, 15:178.

11. Little, "Formules monastiques," pp. 386–387.

12. Gustav Schnürer, *Das Necrologium des Cluniacenser-Priorates Münchenwiler (Villars-les-Moines)*, Collectanea Friburgensia, n.s. 10 (Freiburg, 1909), p. 109.

13. Du Cange 7:113.

14. Pierre Varin, *Archives administratives de la ville de Reims*, Collection des documents médiévaux sur l'histoire de France (Paris, 1839), 1, part 2:502–503.

15. Felix Liebermann, *Die Gesetze der Angelsachsen*, 3 vols. (Halle, 1903–1916), 1:439–440.

16. José-Maria Canal, *Salve Regina Misericordia: Historia y leyendas en torno a esta antifona* (Rome, 1963), pp. 301–302.

17. Dinter, *Liber tramitis*, pp. 244–248.

18. Gilbert H. Doble, *Pontificale Lanaletense: A Pontifical formerly in use at St. Germans, Cornwall (Bibliothèque de la Ville de Rouen A.27 CAT. 368)*, Henry Bradshaw Society 74 (London, 1937), pp. 130–131.

19. Luc D'Achery, *Spicilegium sive Collectio veterum aliquot scriptorum*, 13 vols. (Paris, 1655–1677), 10:635–636.

20. Martène, *De antiquis ritibus*, 2:320–321.

21. A. Fleuret, *Rituel de Saint-Martin de Tours (XIIIe siècle)* (Paris, 1899–1901), p. 147.

22. Ibid., pp. 147–148.

23. Edmond Martène and Ursin durand, *Voyage littéraire de deux bénédictins de la congrégation de S. Maur*, 2 vols. (Paris, 1717–1724), 2:291–292.

24. Karl Hampe, "Reise nach England vom Juli 1895 bis Februar 1896," *Neues Archiv* 22:410–413.

25. Jean Leclercq, "Une prière des moines de Saint-Airy," *Revue Bénédictine* 57 (1974): 224–226.

26. Canal, *Salve Regina Misericordia*, pp. 165–166.

Index of Manuscripts

General Index

Library of Congress Cataloging-in-Publication Data

Little, Lester K., 1935-
    Benedictine maledictions: liturgical cursing in Romanesque France
/ Lester K. Little.
        p. cm.
    Includes bibliographical references and index.
    ISBN 0-8014-2876-9
        1. Blessing and cursing—History—Middle Ages, 600–1500.
    2. Catholic church—Liturgy—History.   3. Monasticism and religious
orders—France—History—Middle Ages, 600–1500.   4.   France—Church
history—To 987.   5. France—Church history—Middle Ages, 987–1515.
    I. Title.
    BX2045.C87L58 1993
    271′ . 1044′09021—dc20   93-25079